MARTIN BUBER
AND THE
HUMAN SCIENCES

MARTIN BUBER
AND THE
HUMAN SCIENCES

Editor-in-Chief
Maurice Friedman

Executive Editor
Pat Boni

Associate Editors
Lawrence Baron,
Seymour Cain,
Virginia Shabatay,
and John Stewart

STATE UNIVERSITY OF NEW YORK PRESS

Published by
State University of New York Press, Albany

For information, address State University of New York Press,
State University Plaza, Albany, N.Y., 12246

Production by Cathleen Collins
Marketing by Theresa Abad Swierzowski

Library of Congress Cataloging in Publication Data

Martin Buber and the human sciences / edited by Maurice Friedman.
    p.   cm.
    ISBN 0-7914-2875-3 (alk. paper). — ISBN 0-7914-2876-1 (pbk. :
alk. paper)
    1. Buber, Martin, 1878–1965—Contributions in humanities—
Congresses.   2. Buber, Martin, 1878–1965—Contributions in social
sciences—Congresses.   3. Humanities—History—20th century—
Congresses.   4. Social sciences—History—20th century—Congresses.
I. Friedman, Maurice S.
B3213.B84M423   1996
181'.06—dc20   95-19176
                                                         CIP

10 9 8 7 6 5 4 3 2 1

Contents

v

             Commitment to Our Common Future
             IVAN BOSZORMENYI-NAGY   371

Chapter 27   Ethical Imagination: Repairing the Breach
             BARBARA R. KRASNER AND AUSTIN J. JOYCE   383

             List of Contributors   399

             Index   403

Preface

Martin Buber (1878–1965) was one of the truly universal figures of the twentieth century. He was a great philosopher, a consummate writer, a world-famous scholar and translator of the Hebrew Bible (the "Old Testament") into German, and interpreter and literary recreator of Hasidism—the popular Jewish mysticism that he almost single-hand-edly made part of the heritage of the Western world. He was one of the most learned men of his time, a universal scholar with an amazing command of languages and disciplines of knowledge. He was a genius with an inexhaustible store of creativity that produced a treasury of books, essays, poems, stories, a novel, and a play. His poetical philosophical classic *I and Thou* is universally recognized as one of the most influential books of the twentieth century. His biblical interpretation includes *The Kingship of God; Moses; The Prophetic Faith;* and *Two Types of Faith* (Jesus and Paul). His interpretations of Hasidism include his Hasidic chronicle-novel *For the Sake of Heaven; Tales of the Hasidim* (*Early Masters* and *Later Masters*); *Hasidism and Modern Man;* and *The Origin and Meaning of Hasidism.* His philosophical anthropology is expounded in *Between Man and Man; The Knowledge of Man;* and *Good and Evil.* But above all he was, as Hermann Hesse wrote of him in nominating him for a Nobel Prize in Literature, one of the few truly wise men alive in the world in his day. His famous philosophy of dialogue, or the "I-Thou relationship," has had a revolutionary impact on Jewish and Christian theology and religious thought in our time, and it has an ever-growing influence on the fields of aesthetics, psychology and psychotherapy, education, speech communication, sociology, and social thought. Martin Buber was a pioneer in the religious and communal socialism that underlay many of the kibbutzim in Israel (*Paths in*

Utopia), and he was the best-known spokesman for Jewish-Arab rap-prochement both before and after the creation of the state of Israel (*A Land of Two Peoples*).

Martin Buber and the Human Sciences grows out of an International Interdisciplinary Conference on Martin Buber's impact on the Human Sciences that was held at San Diego State University, 21–23 October 1991. With myself as director and a distinguished international sponsoring committee and a local working committee made up of myself and Professor Lawrence Baron, Dr. Seymour Cain, and Laurel Mannen, this conference was four years in the making. Despite very sparse funding indeed, the conference was a signal event, with papers given by scholars from seven countries and from many fields.

The specific focus of this conference was "dialogue" as the foundation of and integrating factor in "the human sciences." We are using dialogue in the special sense which Buber made famous in his philosophy of dialogue: mutuality, presentness, openness, meeting the other in his or her uniqueness and not just as a content of my experience or of my thought categories, and knowledge as deriving in the first instance from dialogical knowing—mutual contact—rather than the knowledge of a subject about an object. By the "human sciences" we mean not a specific content or field, such as the humanities, but material that can be meaningfully approached in the phenomenological and dialogical way that has come to be associated with the term, hence, the humanities, education, psychology, speech communication, anthropology, history, sociology, and even, in some cases, economics.

Martin Buber and the Human Sciences is, with three exceptions, a selection from the wealth of papers presented at this conference. It was not possible to use the papers in their fullness. For the most part they had to be cut down to a maximum of twenty manuscript pages. Nor was it in any way possible to include in this volume all of the papers presented at this conference. Instead, our editorial committee spent two years going over all the papers, in some cases excluding papers because of their quality, in some asking that they be rewritten, in many cases asking for cuts, and in a number of happy instances, accepting the papers just as they were in content, style, and length. In a few cases, those who were asked to revise and/or cut their papers did not reply, as a result of which we could not include them.

We feel that this selection, like the conference itself, presents a broad spectrum of Buber's impact on the human sciences, which we have defined broadly to include not only the traditional humanities but also much that is traditionally classified as psychology and the social sciences. It demonstrates that more than a quarter of a century after

Martin Buber's death in 1965, his influence is still a powerful one in a great many countries and in a great many fields. Although Buber did not leave us a systematic philosophy, his philosophy of dialogue and his philosophical anthropology have proved seminal for any number of thinkers and fields, from philosophy to hermeneutics and from economics to literary theory and aesthetics.

A special word needs to be said about the three papers that we have included that were not presented at our conference on Buber's impact on the human sciences. The first half of my introductory essay "Martin Buber's 'Narrow Ridge' and the Human Sciences" was delivered at the conference in the form of a public lecture. But the second half formed part of a paper that I delivered as the keynote speech at the Sixth Annual Conference on Methodology in the Human Sciences in Ottawa, Canada, in 1987. Its original title was "Dialogue and Philosophical Anthropology as Keys to the Integration of the Human Sciences." The second addition is Jerry Lawritson's "Martin Buber and the Shoah," written by him in response to two papers delivered at the conference which contained critiques of Buber's response to the Holocaust. And finally, Rose Graf-Taylor's application of Buber's philosophy of dialogue to feminist psychology was felt to be important to make up for the two papers on feminism given at the conference but not selected by the editorial committee.

When I searched through the literature, I was surprised to find how many new books on Buber had appeared in various languages since I compiled a bibliography of writings about Buber for the 1976 Phoenix paperback edition of my book *Martin Buber: The Life of Dialogue*, published by the University of Chicago Press. I have not attempted to compile a bibliography of Buber's works or of books about Buber for this volume, since that sort of Buber scholarship goes beyond the scope and purpose of *Martin Buber and the Human Sciences*. If Buber's influence on theology is not so great as it was in the era when Karl Barth, Emil Brunner, Reinhold Niebuhr, H. Richard Niebuhr, and Paul Tillich flourished, it has spread and deepened in other fields—so much so that I myself can no longer keep track of it.

We wish to acknowledge a grant from the Lucius N. Littauer Foundation, which was of substantial help in getting the manuscript of this book ready to send to the press.

Maurice Friedman, Editor-in-Chief
September 1994

Executive Editor's Note on Abbreviations

Inasmuch as almost all of the essays in this book cite specific works of Martin Buber and Maurice Friedman, we have used the initials of their particular titles for brevity and, insofar as possible, consistency. We have not repeated in the individual references at the end of each chapter the publishers of the works cited, merely the book's title or initials thereof.

The following titles refer to only those works of Buber and Friedman which are cited in the essays in *Martin Buber and the Human Sciences*. The initials in parentheses are generally found within the text and denote the reference. In some cases, Buber's or Friedman's name and date is cited by the author of the essay in the body of the text, and the reader should refer to the author's reference at the end of the essay to identify the source.

Buber, Martin

ABH	*A Believing Humanism: Gleanings by Martin Buber.* (1969). Trans. with an introduction and explanatory comments by Maurice Friedman. New York: Simon and Schuster.
ABH (1990)	*A Believing Humanism: My Testament 1902–1965.* (1990). Trans. with explanatory comments by Maurice Friedman. Atlantic Highlands, NJ: Humanities Press.
BMM	*Between Man and Man.* (1965). Introduction and afterword by Maurice Friedman, trans. by R. G. Smith. New York: Macmillan.
DJ	*Der Jude und sein Judentum.* Cologne: Joseph Melzer.

Daniel
: *Daniel: Dialogues of Realization.* (1964). Trans. with an introductory essay by Maurice Friedman. New York: Holt Rinehart Winston. New York: McGraw-Hill, 1965, paperback.

EC
: *Ecstatic Confessions.* (1985). Ed. by Paul Mendes-Flohr, trans. by Esther Cameron. San Francisco, CA: Harper and Row.

EG
: *Eclipse of God: Studies in the Relation between Religion and Philosophy.* (1988). Trans. by Maurice Friedman and others, with an introduction by Robert Seltzer. Atlantic Highlands, NJ: Humanities Press.

FTSH
: *For The Sake of Heaven: A Hasidic Chronicle-Novel.* (1969). Trans. by Ludwig Lewisohn. NY: Atheneum (Macmillan).

G&E
: *Good and Evil: Two Interpretations.* (1980). New York: Scribner's (Macmillan).

HMM
: *Hasidism and Modern Man.* (1958). Ed. and trans. Maurice Friedman. New York: Harper & Row. New York: Horizon Press, 1958 (paperback).

HMM, (1988)
: *Hasidism and Modern Man.* (1988). Ed. and trans. with an introduction by Maurice Friedman. Atlantic Highlands, NJ: Humanities Press.

I and Thou
: *I and Thou.* (1958). 2nd. rev. ed., with postscript by author added. Trans. by Ronald G. Smith. [Denoted as *I and Thou* (Smith).]

I and Thou
: *I and Thou.* (1970). Trans. by W. Kaufmann. New York: Charles Scribner's Sons. [Denoted as *I and Thou* (Kaufmann).]

Ich und Du
: *Ich und Du* (1983 [1923]). Heidelberg: Lambert Schneider.

IW
: *Israel and the World: Essays in a Time of Crisis.* (1948). New York: Schocken.

KG
: *The Kingship of God.* (1990). Trans. by Richard Scheimann. Atlantic Highlands, NJ: Humanities Press.

KM
: *The Knowledge of Man.* (1965). Ed. with an introductory essay (ch. 1) by Maurice Friedman, trans. by Maurice Friedman and Ronald Gregor Smith. New York: Harper and Row.

KM, 1988
: *The Knowledge of Man: A Philosophy of the Inter-human.* (1988). Ed. with an introductory essay (ch. 1) by Maurice Friedman, trans. by Maurice Friedman and Ronald Gregor Smith. Atlantic Highlands, NJ: Humanities Press.

LTP	*A Land of Two Peoples: Martin Buber on Jews and Arabs.* (1983). Ed. with commentary by Paul R. Mendes-Flohr. New York: Oxford University Press.
LBS	*The Legend of the Baal Shem.* (1969). Trans. by Maurice Friedman. New York: Schocken.
LMB	*The Letters of Martin Buber.* (1991). Ed. by Nahum N. Glatzer. New York: Schocken.
Meetings	*Meetings.* (1973). Ed. and trans. with an introduction and bibliography by Maurice Friedman. LaSalle, IL: Open Court.
Moses	*Moses: The Revelation and the Covenant.* (1958). New York: Harper Torchbooks. Reprinted 1988, Atlantic Highlands, NJ: Humanities Press.
OB	*On The Bible.* (1982). Ed. by Nahum N. Glatzer, with an introduction by Harold Bloom. New York: Schocken.
OJ	*On Judaism.* (1967). Ed. by Nahum N. Glatzer. New York: Schocken.
OZ	*On Zion.* (1986). New York: Schocken.
OMH	*The Origin and Meaning of Hasidism.* (1960). Ed. and trans. with an introduction by Maurice Friedman. New York: Horizon. New York: Harper Torchbooks, 1960, paperback. Reprinted 1988, Atlantic Highlands, NJ: Humanities Press.
PU	*Paths in Utopia.* 5th ed. (1949). Trans. by R. F. C. Hull. Boston: Beacon. Reprinted 1988, New York: Macmillan.
PW	*Pointing the Way: Collected Essays.* (1957). Ed. and trans. with an introduction by Maurice Friedman. New York: Harper and Bros. Reprinted 1990, Atlantic Highlands NJ: Humanities Press.
PF	*The Prophetic Faith.* (1949). Trans. from the Hebrew by Carlyle Witton-Davies. New York: Macmillan.
Replies	"Replies to My Critics." (1967). Trans. by Maurice Friedman in Paul Arthur Schilpp and Maurice Friedman, *PMB* [see below]. LaSalle, IL: Open Court.
TH:Early	*Tales of the Hasidim: Early Masters.* (1948). Trans. by Olga Marx. New York: Schocken. Reprinted in 1991 in one volume as *Tales of the Hasidim: Early and Later Masters*, New York: Schocken.
TH:Later	*Tales of the Hasidim: Later Masters.* (1948). Trans. by Olga Marx. New York: Schocken. Reprinted in 1991 in one volume as *Tales of the Hasidim: Early and Later Masters*, New York: Schocken.

TTF   *Two Types of Faith.* (1961). Trans. by Norman P. Goldhawk. New York: Harper Torchbooks (The Cloister Library). Reprinted 1986, New York: Macmillan.

WoM   *The Way of Man According to the Teachings of Hasidism.* (1959). Foreword by Maurice Friedman. Wallingford, PA: Pendle Hill.

Friedman, Maurice

AJH&EW   *Abraham Joshua Heschel and Elie Wiesel: "You Are My Witnesses."* (1987). New York: Farrar, Strauss, Giroux.

CO   *The Confirmation of Otherness: In Family, Community, and Society.* (1983). New York: Pilgrim Press.

CP:ROH   *Contemporary Psychology: Revealing and Obscuring the Human.* (1984). Pittsburgh: Duquesne University Press.

DHI   *Dialogue and the Human Image: Beyond Humanistic Psychology.* (1992). Newbury Park, CA: Sage.

ENR   *Encounter on The Narrow Ridge: A Life of Martin Buber.* (1991). New York: Paragon House.

HDP   *The Healing Dialogue in Psychotherapy.* (1985). New York: Jason Aronson.

HHI   *The Hidden Human Image.* (1974). New York: Dell.

LoD   *Martin Buber: The Life of Dialogue.* (1960). 1st paperback ed. New York: Harper Torchbooks.

LoD, 1976   *Martin Buber: The Life of Dialogue.* (1976). 3rd ed. with new preface and bibliography added. Chicago: University of Chicago Press.

MBE   *Martin Buber and The Eternal.* (1986). New York: Human Sciences Press.

MBLW:Early   *Martin Buber's Life and Work: The Early Years 1878–1923.* (1981). New York: E. P. Dutton. Detroit: Wayne State University Press, 1988 (paperback).

MBLW:Middle   *Martin Buber's Life and Work: The Middle Years 1923–1945.* (1983). New York: E. P. Dutton. Detroit: Wayne State University Press, 1988 (paperback).

MBLW:Later   *Martin Buber's Life and Work: The Later Years 1945–1965.* (1984). New York: E. P. Dutton. Detroit: Wayne State University Press, 1988 (paperback).

TR   *Touchstones of Reality: Existential Trust and the Community of Peace.* (1972). New York: E. P. Dutton.

TWE   *The Worlds of Existentialism: A Critical Reader.* (1964).
               New York: Random House. Reprinted 1973, Chicago:
               University of Chicago Press (paperback). Reprinted with
               full-scale updating preface, 1991, Atlantic Highlands,
               NJ: Humanities Press (paperback).
Interrogation "Interrogation of Martin Buber." (1964). In Sydney
               Rome and Beatrice Rome, eds., *Philosophical Inter-*
               rogations, 13-117. Buber section conducted, edited, and
               Buber's responses trans. by Maurice Friedman. New
               York: Rinehart and Winston.

               Rome, Sydney, and Rome, Beatrice, eds.

PI   *Philosophical Interrogations.* (1970). New York: Harper
               and Row.

               Schilpp, Paul Arthur, and Friedman, Maurice

PMB   *The Philosophy of Martin Buber.* (1967). LaSalle, IL:
               Open Court. Cambridge: Cambridge University Press.

PART I

INTRODUCTION

CHAPTER 1

MARTIN BUBER'S "NARROW RIDGE" AND THE HUMAN SCIENCES

MAURICE FRIEDMAN

THE NARROW RIDGE

Buber wrote a story in 1907 for his second book, *The Legend of the Baal Shem*, called "The New Year Sermon," in which he first used the term "the narrow ridge." A year is like a circle; you go around a narrow ridge with abysses on either side. Later, Buber used the term to denote the narrow ridge between various forms of abstractions, such as freedom vs. discipline, individualism vs. collectivism, or nationalism vs. universalism. It was a way of adhering to the concrete. While Buber was a great scholar, he was also the most concrete person that I have ever known, and he insisted on concreteness in those he talked with. In writing my book *Encounter on the Narrow Ridge*, I wanted to say that the narrow ridge was not just a way of thinking, though it did permeate Buber's thinking too. So here I want to share with you just a few little bits of autobiographical fragments and touch on how they affected his thought and how that way of life and that thought relates to the human sciences.

BUBER'S ENCOUNTER ON THE NARROW RIDGE

Born in Vienna, Buber lived with his parents in a house under which flowed the Danube canal, the sight of which he would enjoy with a certainty that nothing could happen to him. Then, in his fourth year of life, his mother suddenly disappeared. No one knew where she went, and young Martin was sent to live with his paternal grandparents, the great Midrash scholar Solomon Buber and his wife, on their estate in Galicia. They never mentioned his mother to him at all, probably because, since they were noble people, they didn't talk to each other about it any more than was necessary. He assumed that she would come back, until one day when he was with a child a few years older than himself, a neighbor child taking care of him. "I can hear to this day her answer: 'No, she will never come back,'" Buber later recounted. "I cherished no doubt the truth of her words; they cleaved to my heart, and every year they cleaved deeper and deeper. After ten years I came to understand it as concerning not only me but all persons and after another ten years I coined the term 'Vergegnung'—'mismeeting,'" said Buber. When Buber grew up he discovered that his mother had run away to Russia with an army officer, where she lived and had two daughters. Buber's father had remarried with the permission of the rabbi. When Buber was thirty-four his mother came to see him and his wife Paula and the two children, Rafael and Eva. "When I looked into her still astonishingly beautiful eyes," he said, "I heard from somewhere as a word addressed to me 'Vergegnung'"—'mismeeting.'"

Yet Buber's conclusion to this story is not about mismeeting at all. Rather, he learned from that hour on the balcony about genuine meeting. What always struck me about this story was that Buber did not cling for a lifetime to his mother as Marcel Proust to his mother and Franz Kafka to his father. The heart of what Buber called the "eternal Thou" is existential trust—the readiness to go out again and meet with your whole being, and he did this with remarkable fullness. As Ivan Boszormenyi-Nagy points out, when they didn't talk about his mother, young Martin must have felt shamed because to have a mother who is too shameful to talk about is hard for a young child. Often children feel that they have to choose between one parent or the other, and that destroys "the triadic basis of justice" that Barbara Krasner talks about. Buber really held on to both his father who was present and his mother who was absent, and that may be the root of the I and the Thou—the refusal to choose one or the other. He held the tension between the two parents. Buber said that the mystery at the heart of dialogue is the unity of the contraries—the *coincidentia oppositorum*, or coincidence of opposites. They do not just blend into one happy harmony. You hold the tension, and nonetheless you do not simply split apart. He opposed with all his force the polarization as well as the politicization of reality that is so common in our day.

Here is already a deep key to Buber's whole life and to what became his thought. He seemed to think in dyads, not only I-Thou and I-It but also person and individual, *gnosis* vs. *devotio*, *emunah* vs. *pistis*, being vs. seeming. Yet to turn that into a kind of Manichean dualism, as Walter Kaufmann said in 1978, is to miss entirely what he was doing, namely, holding the tension. Buber was a disciple of Wilhelm Dilthey, the phenomenologist. Buber really meant these dyads as ideal types; he did not mean for us to choose one or the other. That is why it has always been a complete misunderstanding of the I-Thou relationship to imagine that Buber thought it was possible or desirable to have only the I-Thou, or that he saw the I-It as evil in any way. He saw as evil only the refusal to return to the Thou but not the "It" itself—"Without It we cannot live." That's a clue to Buber's whole life; it is a clue to his thought and certainly a clue to the human sciences.

It was Buber's teacher Wilhelm Dilthey who coined the famous distinction between the *Naturwissenschaften* and the *Geisteswissenschaften*, commonly translated as the "natural sciences" and the "human studies," or the "human sciences." Actually, the word *geistes* doesn't mean human; it doesn't mean "spiritual" either. In German it is somewhere between the spiritual, the cultural, and the intellectual. People have rightly complained about Dilthey's terminology as an oversimple dichotomy. I myself have long insisted that psychology ought to be considered not only a *Naturwissenschaft* but also a *Geisteswissenschaft*. Buber believed that science itself was based upon the Thou—actual intuitions of Thou, but the elaboration had to do with the It. Buber's contribution is precisely that to him science is not It or Thou but rather, like his philosophy, it is the alternation between the two—the going back and forth.

Buber was kept at home by his grandmother, who believed that the royal road to education was languages. So she had him taught languages, and Buber didn't have to go to school at all until he was ten years old. When he received an honorary doctorate from the Sorbonne he told of a French teacher who taught him salon French, which he disliked so intensely that one day when they were walking by a lake the young child pushed the salon teacher into the lake! Buber went to what can be called a one-room schoolhouse, a gymnasium with a majority of Catholic students and a minority of Jewish students (the Ruthenians had schools of their own). He tells of how the Jewish students had to stand in the midst of a sacral ritual in which no dram of their being could take part while the Christian students and the master said the Trinity.

In the same school, a couple years after he came there—he was about twelve—there was a fall utterly spoiled by rain. When the weather was nice they used the recess to stroll around and talk and play games in the courtyard. During this particular fall they had to sit quietly at their desks for a whole recess. Two boys undertook to entertain the others with clownlike games, with clownlike agility. They tried to keep their faces straight so the Master would not discover what they were doing. The boys did not speak to each other about this. After a couple of weeks their games took on an unmistakably sexual character, and the faces of the two boys looked like the faces of the souls tormented in hell, which young Buber's Catholic schoolmates had told him about with the tone of experts.

After that had gone on for a while, the Master called young Martin into his study and said, in the kind considerate voice they knew as invariable, "Tell me what you know about these two boys." "I know nothing!" he screamed. Then in the same kind and considerate voice the Master said, "We know you well; you are a good boy. You will help us." "I wanted to shout, 'Help? Help whom?'" Buber recollected. "Instead of which I was led away weeping as never before in my life and almost unconscious. When I got home the look I remembered on the Master's face was no longer a kind and gentle one but a frightened one. I was kept at home for two weeks; when I returned the bench where the two boys sat was empty and remained empty for the rest of the school year."

With this convulsion of his childhood, says Buber, "I began the long series of experiences that taught me the problematic relation between maxim and situation and the true norm that demands not our obedience but ourselves." By maxim Buber meant the third-person statement, such as, "Early to bed, early to rise, makes a man healthy, wealthy, and wise" or "Honesty is the best policy." Maxims mean everyone and no one, but they do not mean *you*. Situation on the other hand, as Buber discovered then, is something unique. It demands a unique response; it is unique itself; it is a unique relationship between you and it. Perhaps for the first time in Buber's life he discovered that he was not just being called upon to be a "good boy." There *was* a maxim here: "A good boy is one that helps us, the masters." And there was a contract, too: "We will reward you for your help by confirming you as a good boy." The masters knew what was happening or they would not have called him in. They just wanted to separate the sheep from the goats. They wanted confirmation by young Martin, which he found he could not give them. He was asked to do something else, and he fell into a stalemate, which is why he went home almost unconscious.

The other thing Buber learned (he *knew* it only much later obviously) was that true norms demand not our obedience but ourselves. What he would call the untrue norm is the one that splits us into an immediate part and a rebellious part. This is connected with what I call the "contract"—the confirmation that comes only conditionally, with strings attached; we confirm you insofar as you are a good boy/girl, churchgoer, citizen, soldier, whatever. Such a norm, of course, is from the above down, and the rebellious part is still there, repressed into unawareness, protest, resentment. Even if you are confirmed, somewhere in your being, perhaps not consciously, you know it is not *you* that is being confirmed—it is the "good boy." Like the prodigal son's brother who stayed home and was upset when the father killed the fatted calf for the prodigal son, the "good boy" never allowed the evil urge to take him away and come back. He had just stayed there—the good son. Even if you grew up and went to one or another psychologist or psychoanalyst and they removed your guilt, you still would feel unlovable because of this contract. The true norm is not above us; it faces us as a question—the question of the situation addressed to us to which we respond. God gives the question but nothing of the answer. The answer is human; it can be mistaken. It is a thing of fear and trembling, said Buber in "The Question to the Single One."

This true norm does not imply ethical anarchism. "No responsible person is a stranger to norms," wrote Buber. "But the norm does not exist in the person as a maxim or a habit but only in some layer of your being of which you are perhaps unaware, coming out in unexpected ways in the face of the unique, the unforeseen situation." Buber did not reject command; what he rejected was command as a universal. Franz Rosenzweig, in his famous essay "The Builders," says, "*Gesetz*, the universal law, must be translated into *Gebot*, the personal command." Rosenzweig tells us that we get from Gesetz to Gebot, from the universal law to personal command, by deciding what we can do—*das Tubare*, as he called it. That is not what Buber meant by command at all. To Buber I have to be really the one who is asked—that is *mitzvot*, that is command. He could not accept anything which turned it into a universal, yet he does not mean we can live without law, but the true law is Torah—teaching. It can never be divorced entirely from God's speaking voice. So again we have "the narrow ridge"—something that affected his whole approach. Buber spent a lifetime of work in retelling Hasidic tales and Hasidic teachings; he spent a lifetime translating and interpreting the Hebrew Bible; he read voluminously; he worked extremely hard; yet he refused ever to turn the teaching of the Torah or the life of the Hasidim into fixed rules and universal laws.

Just before World War I, a young man came to see Buber after Buber had had a morning of mystic ecstasy. Buber was friendly and attentive; he answered the questions the young man put. But he failed to guess the question the young man did not put. After such a morning of mystic ecstasy, which was customary for him in those days, he was not really present in spirit. Later he learned this was a question of life and death—not that the young man had committed suicide, as some imagine. He was killed at the front, as Buber told me himself, out of despair that did not oppose its own death.

Buber took this as a judgment not just of that moment but of that whole way of life which split the exalted hours from the everyday hours. "What after all does a person who is in despair but comes to see one hope for but a presence which says in spite of all there is meaning," said Buber. Not reality, not philosophy, not wise words, but a presence. That was the judgment on a way of life in which he was not fully present. The result was that Buber gave up a mysticism that was natural for him. In one of the last poems Buber wrote before he died, the voice said, "Come to the other side over this big void," but then another voice said, "No, it's right here where you are." If you contrast Buber's early interpretation of Hasidism in his justly famous "The Life of the Hasidim" (*The Legend of the Baal Shem*), the whole first section is *hitlahavut*, the burning ardor of ecstasy. But ecstasy dropped out of Buber's later interpretation of Hasidism in favor of hallowing the everyday—here where one stands.

What Buber was rejecting, for the rest of his life, was a dualism in which we have a beautiful sphere up there and something else here. That's why he said that we don't have the holy in the world, we have the spirit, by which I think he meant culture, ideas, and ideals. We take it with grim seriousness, but that's all we do. We will not allow it to have any binding claim on our lives. "No amount of hypocritical piety has ever reached this concentrated degree of inauthenticity."

Hasidism teaches that the wretchedness of our lives comes when we are not open to the holy, wrote Buber. "A life that is not open to the holy is not only unworthy of the spirit, it is unworthy of life." Buber does not mean by openness to the holy that we should be saints or superhuman, but, as the Kotzker Rebbe said, "humanly holy"—in the measure of the human, of our own personal, unique responses. Buber is talking about the life of dialogue where everything can be a sign that addresses us; everything can be a messenger of God, as Nachman of Bratzlav put it, that brings you back to your connection with reality outside of yourself and to some possibility of genuine dialogue.

A month before the young man came to see him, Buber was visited by the old Reverend William Hechler, who was one of the first supporters of Zionism. This man he had met on a train in the late 1890s—Buber had shown him what he called pathetic verses he had written on his people's awakening, and Reverend Hechler carried these off with him to the Grand Duke of Baden, the uncle of the Kaiser. Later, without Buber's knowledge, Hechler published them in Herzl's famous journal *Die Welt* after supplying it with even more pathetic subtitles, Buber said. Hechler was one of the last people that Herzl saw before he died in 1904, but Buber had lost touch with him. In 1914 Reverend Hechler showed up in Buber's home in Zehlendorf, a suburb of Berlin, and he unfolded a large map, what we would call a histomap. On the basis of his studies of *The Book of Daniel*, he came to tell Buber there would be a "world war." "I never heard the phrase before," Buber said. "I knew it must be something utterly unlike any previous war that would consume history and with it mankind." Reverend Hechler, who was an Anglican priest, was also a tutor in the royal courts of Europe.

Hechler stayed with the Bubers for a while, then Buber walked his guest to the train. When they came to the corner where the black path met the railroad tracks, Reverend Hechler stopped, put his hand on Buber's shoulder and said, "Dear friend! We live in a great time. Tell me: Do you believe in God?" Buber reassured him and put him on the train. But when he got back to that spot, he asked himself, "Did I tell the truth? Do I really believe in the God whom Hechler meant?" He resolved not to leave the spot until an answer came. Then the words came as of themselves: "If to believe in God means to be able to talk *about* him in the third person, then I do *not* believe in God. But if to believe in him means to be able to talk *to* him, then I do believe in God." Then again, "The God who could give Daniel such exact information about the world war is not my God, is not our God. But the God to whom Daniel prayed in his suffering is my God and the God of all" (*PMB*, 3–39; *Meetings*, 17–61).

Does that mean a rejection of rational thought? No. But it is what prevented him from being a theologian. God to Buber was not an "it" of any sort, even with a capital "I," not even an "it" of the nature of person. God cannot be expressed but only addressed. Many people speak *to* God who do not know how to speak about God; many people speak about God but do not speak to God. That is something Buber remained true to for the rest of his life. He firmly refused ever to subsume God under Aristotle's law of noncontradiction.

My old teacher and great philosopher, Charles Hartshorne, used to say to me as he was advising me on my doctoral dissertation, "Buber is no metaphysician." But when he wrote the essay on Buber's metaphysics for *The Library of Living Philosophers* volume that I edited, he began with the sentences, "Buber is no metaphysician. Buber is one of the greatest metaphysicians." Then he proceeded to remake Buber into the image of Whitehead, as he said himself. When Buber responded he said, "I read your essay several times; I'm afraid I can only agree with the first of your two statements," namely that he was no metaphysician (*PMB*, 717). Following Whitehead, who goes back to Plato, Hartshorne said you have to choose: either God is absolute and nonrelational or God is relational and not absolute. Buber, in contrast, spoke of God as the Absolute Person who *is* not person but *becomes* one, so to speak, in order to know and be known, to love and be loved by us. He meant this as a paradox, and a paradox does not fit Aristotle's law of noncontradiction. But then Buber never thought that A or not-A sums up our relation with God. He never even thought it summed up our relationship with one another. Nor do I think so, because if we were really identical to each other we would not need to speak, and we were entirely other we could not speak. It is not just that we have something in common, as the marriage counselor thinks. There must be something else, and it is the arrows coming together and the arrows coming apart.

BUBER'S PHILOSOPHY OF DIALOGUE

Buber was a true philosopher. He was not a systematic one, but he was a coherent one. I have studied him carefully over the years, and I do not find any major emphasis on any major contradictions in his thought. "I don't speak *ex cathedra*," Buber said, "If there is a problem I am willing to go into it." But Buber held that the unique could not be subsumed under rational categories (Rome and Rome, 51–53). Nathan Rotenstreich, a philosopher at the Hebrew University in Israel, concluded that when Buber says that in the life of faith the dictionary is put down, he implied that for him dialogue is empty of content. "No, I'm very much concerned with content," Buber replied, "but the content is not a general content." It is again and again a unique content, a situational content (*PMB*, 697). Buber did not reject any sort of morality as a rule of thumb, but anything that gets in between us and the address of the situation. A morality like that he would see as nondialogical. The same is true of any theology that gets between us and our relation to God. Buber took very seriously the actual hearing of the life of and in dialogue. Every symbol of God, whether subtle or crude, is equally untrue because it turns God into an "it," but God allows us to come to him through these symbols, so we may surmise, until, as happens ever again, they swell up and obstruct the road to God by claiming themselves to be the Absolute. As the Zen Buddhists say, "They take the finger pointing at the moon for the moon itself." At that point you absolutize something that is relative. That is idolatry. Then comes round the hour of the philosopher who destroys the images that no longer do justice to God in order that the religious person can set out across the darkness to a new meeting with the nameless Meeter (*EG*, 45ff.).

I sent Martin Buber a baccalaureate speech I gave at the University of Vermont in 1961, where I referred to Albert Camus as an atheist. He wrote back and said, "Don't call him an atheist. He is one of those people I speak of in religion and philosophy who destroy the images that no longer do justice to God." In that sense he was a religious person, even though he called himself an atheist. Actually, Albert Camus said to R. W. B. Lewis, "I do not mind being called 'religious' in Buber's sense of the term, an I-Thou relationship." When Camus wrote *Resistance, Rebellion, and Death*, I. F. Stone, who edited *Dissent*, wrote a long article entitled "Albert Camus—the Life of Dialogue," taking the subtitle from my first book on Buber. Stone concluded his article by saying, "Albert Camus lived the only life worth living, the life of dialogue."

When Buber accepted the Peace Prize of the German Book Trade in 1953 he was bitterly criticized in Israel and in the Yiddish press in America. For years Buber had refused to speak publically in Germany, saying, "The Germans have become faceless to me." Finally, as the result of German persistence and what he read by Romano Guardini concerning German guilt, he was able to go to Germany. At his lecture in Bonn, attended by the president of the West German government, Theodore Heuss, and many other notables, Buber spoke as no one had yet spoken. He began by telling all those assembled that he could not express his thanks to the German Book Trade for the honor conferred on him without at the same time stating the sense in which he accepted it.

> About a decade ago a considerable number of Germans . . . under the indirect command of the German government and the direct command of its representatives, killed millions of my people in a systematically prepared and executed procedure whose organized cruelty cannot be compared with any previous historical event. I . . . have only in a formal sense a common humanity with those who took part in this action. They have so radically removed themselves from the human sphere, so transposed themselves into a sphere of monstrous inhumanity inaccessible to my conception, that not even hatred, much less an overcoming of hatred, was able to arise in me. And what am I that I could here presume to "forgive"! (*PW*, 232)

But then Buber went on to talk about others who suspected but were afraid to investigate and still others who become martyrs, committed suicide, or allowed themselves to be killed rather than take part in what happened. Buber then spoke about genuine dialogue and the possibility of peace and of the fight between the human and the contrahuman. He came because he wanted to fight for the human within each people. Buber opposed the execution of Adolf Eichmann, not only because he did not believe in capital punishment but more importantly that he was afraid that the young people in Germany would take Eichmann's execution as a symbolic evening of the ledger, that they would not live with the guilt of their fathers as he felt they had to do.

Buber's philosophy of the "demarcation line" is an important aspect of his "narrow ridge." We cannot live without doing injustice—no community can, said Buber. Yet every hour anew we have to examine to see that we take on no more guilt for ourselves than we must. Those who say, "We do it for the sake of our children," their children grow up to be tormented or hypocrites.

In "And if Not Now, When?" Buber wrote, "Zion can only be reached *bemishpat;*" with justice (*IW*, 237). We cannot reach a goal by any means except that which is like it. But Buber did not believe in perfection on earth. Not long ago the Russians knocked over the statue of Derzhinski, the head of the original O.G.P.U. In 1918 a Spartacus proponent of the Russian revolution, Derzhinski said he could kill with a clean soul. Buber said, "It is not a question of 'souls' but of responsibility" (*PW*, 119). Buber was not a pacifist. He said you have to truly be in that situation: "No one who counts himself in the ranks of Israel can desire to use force" (*PW*, 145). He was not an absolutist, but he was also not a relativist. This is what the narrow ridge means—the demarcation line which stays close to the concrete situation. Opposed to it is that "realism" that says you cannot meet with the Russians or there is no point in having dialogue with the Arabs.

In 1987–88 I was Senior Fulbright Lecturer at the Hebrew University of Jerusalem and was there when the Intafada broke out in December. In January I gave a lecture before a large audience on Buber's Hebrew humanism applied to Jewish/Arab relations. Here, too, Buber walked the narrow ridge, urging Israel to hold its ground yet to establish relations of good neighborliness with the Arabs. Hebrew humanism meant dialogue within the community and between communities. To Buber, "dialogue" in the first instance is the meeting between I and Thou. He remarked that no one had ever understood the Decalogue, the Ten Commandments, unless he understood the "thou" as addressed to him or herself. If you turn it into a disguised "it"—"One ought not to do this," instead of "thou"—then it addresses everyone and no one. To be a "thou" it has to be really in that situation. In the very passage where

Buber says, "No responsible person is a stranger to norms," he also writes, "I know of a man who was struck by the lightning flash of 'Thou shalt not steal' in such a way that he had to turn and do the exact opposite of what he was going to do and bring all the passion he was going to use into what he now had to do" (*BMM*, 114). "I was that man," Buber told me. "It wasn't 'Thou shalt not steal,' it was 'Thou shalt not kill.' I wasn't going to kill anyone, nonetheless that is the command I heard."

It is as Thou that we hear the command, but we hear it as a part of the group or groups to which we belong. I should not say, "My party right or wrong," or "My country right or wrong." Yet, in contrast to Kierkegaard, who set the crowd in opposition to the "Single One," we should really be in groups of people, but nothing should take away our responsibility. We should not be like a lynch mob (i.e., social without direct interhuman relations).

For Buber, the "essential We" went so far that even if he did not do something personally, he felt great pain and guilt, such as the Kibya raids in Israel, when many Arabs were mowed down because they came home after the curfew. Buber had lived through three wars—World War I and the World War II and then the war that marked the foundation of the state of Israel. Buber did not say, as some imagine, that this third war was the most *significant* war for him—as a result of which mishearing they claim that Buber did not take the Holocaust seriously enough. What he said rather was that it was the most *painful*. The reason it was the most painful was that it was connected with the very Zionism that he had helped bring into being. Because of this he had a great sense of grief.

In contrast to the Ten Commandments, the revelation at Mt. Sinai was to a large people who were gathered there, not just to one person. That too was a genuine revelation, yet Buber wrote me, "The mid-point of revelation is the present. The revelation is not Mount Sinai or the burning bush but our present receiving of it." Buber very much wanted the Yishuv, which later became the state of Israel, to continue the covenant, and that is what he wrote to Gandhi, who accused the Jews in Palestine of inhumanly imposing themselves upon the Arabs. Buber admired Gandhi more than any figure in public life, as someone who combined the political and the religious. Nonetheless, Buber wrote Gandhi a public letter, saying, "Do you know what a universal steam roller is? No one could gather together and organize the way you did in South Africa." You can't ask people to be martyrs for political reasons when it can have no possible political effect. But he also said we cannot give up this covenant which places a demand on us. It is not just our right to the land. It is our duty to make real God's Kingship in social life.

Buber saw three things as connected: the land, the people, and the task. Some people really hated Buber for that because they wanted to be a nation like the other nations. Buber said to Gandhi, "We cannot give up our task on the land." On the other hand, he also said, we can also honor the claim that is ours and know that it is not possible to arbitrate the two claims by having any overarching, universal, or "objective" point of view. But, he concluded, where there is faith and love there can be some reconciliation even in the midst of a tragic contradiction. They love the land, and we love the land. It has not happened so far, yet Buber believed that if the Cold War ended, the situation might change. People no longer talk of a "cold war," and there has been a radical change.

In the Seder service at Passover, the good son asks, "What did the Lord do for *us* when he brought *us* out of Egypt?" The bad son asks, "What did the Lord do for *them* when he brought *them* out of Egypt?" For the good son, it is still present. For the bad son, it is merely a past historical curiosity. "Not our fathers but we here, the living, stand on Mount Sinai to receive the Torah," it says in *Deuteronomy*. Thus the revelation still has to be received individually. Israel as Israel could accept the covenant, but we cannot impose it upon them in the name of some biblical theology.

Paul Mendes-Flohr translated and edited and wrote his helpful comments on Buber's book *A Land of Two Peoples*—the essays and speeches Buber gave on the Jewish-Arab problem from 1916 to 1965. The English edition came out in 1982 (Oxford University Press), but it came out in Hebrew while we were in Jerusalem in 1988. There was a full-page interview with Paul Mendes-Flohr in the *Jerusalem Post*. They asked Mendes-Flohr how Buber would have liked the Gush Emunim, who claim Samaria and Judea for Israel on the basis of the Hebrew Bible. "I don't think he would have liked them," he replied, "first because they have nothing to do with dialogue, and secondly because they are not at all humble."

Buber called the kibbutzim in Israel an experiment that did not fail. Buber pointed to "Jerusalem" instead of "Moscow," because he believed neither in capitalism nor in state socialism but in true communitarian socialism. Everything had become politicized in Israel, Buber complained in 1951. You could not go for an hour without everyone arguing politics. This politicization and polarization again and again stood in the way of true humanity. To call Buber an anarchist or see him as simply opposed to the State is to miss the tension between society and the State, between the social and the political principle that marked Buber's narrow ridge. It is a way of life, and of course it is a hard way.

Reinhold Niebuhr and Buber and I had a three-way correspondence on social justice. Niebuhr always thought Buber was great on the I-Thou relationship between persons, but he thought he was totally naive when it came to politics and the nation. Buber said, "I cannot accept the notion that there is one meaning of justice in the interhuman realm and a whole different meaning of justice on a national scale." Honest men lie and compassionate men torture, Buber said, for the sake of justice, or equality, or the kingdom. That is exactly what he could not accept. Buber added, "I cannot know how much justice is possible in a given situation until I go on and my head hits the wall and it hurts, and then I know, oh! this is the limit" (Rome and Rome, 78–80).

In the German universities in the early 1950s Buber gave a lecture called "The Validity and Limitation of the Political Principle." In this lecture Buber criticized Hegel, Marx, and Heidegger because he thought they had no real understanding and conception of the eternal. He said that we have lost all absolutes except one in the modern world, and that is "the nation."

> I have no warrant whatever to declare that under all circumstances the interest of the group is to be sacrificed to the moral demand, more particularly as the cruel conflicts of duties and their unreserved decision on the basis of the situation seem to me to belong to the essential existence of a genuine personal ethos.

Buber went on to say that the "evident absence of this inner conflict, the lack of its wounds and scars, is to me uncanny" (PW, 217).

Buber was not a systematic philosopher, but he was a genuine and profound philosopher of dialogue. He does belong to the great philosophers and thinkers and spiritual leaders because he had this intuition which illuminates many fields. He was not a saint. But he was in fact someone who lived a life of dialogue.

PHILOSOPHICAL ANTHROPOLOGY

Each of the human sciences is ultimately grounded in a philosophical anthropology. None of the social or psychological sciences in itself deals with the wholeness of the human; for each treats one aspect (e.g., the sociological, the economic, the political, the historical, or the psychological). Yet if they are to be understood as *human* sciences, they must recover their grounding in that human wholeness and uniqueness which is found in the recognition of the varieties of peoples, the types and characters of the human soul, and the stages of human life. Philosophical anthropology tries to grasp human beings in their particularity and complexity, their dynamic interrelatedness with others, and the interplay of possibility, freedom, and personal direction. An important advance in philosophical anthropology was the development of "phenomenology" by the German philosophers Wilhelm Dilthey and Edmund Husserl. Dilthey based his thought on the radical difference between the way of knowing of the "*Geisteswissenschaften*" and that of the "*Naturwissenschaften*." In the former, the knowers cannot be merely detached scientific observers but must also participate themselves; for it is through their participation that they discover both the typical and the unique in the aspects of human life that they are studying. At the same time they must suspend the foregone conclusions and the search for causality that mark the natural scientist in favor of an open attempt to discover what offers itself. Only through this open understanding (*das Verstehen*) can one value the unique that reveals itself in every human phenomenon.

Martin Buber's philosophy of the interhuman—with its twofold human movement of distancing and relating and its twofold human relation of "I-Thou" and "I-It"—has led him, and myself following him, to a more dialogical understanding of the task of the philosophical anthropologist. Philosophical anthropology goes beyond cultural anthropology in that it asks the question not just about human beings but about the human: about our wholeness and uniqueness, about what makes us human. It can only touch on the problem of the human, however, insofar as it recognizes that the philosophical anthropologist himself or herself is a human being and as such is *as subject* and not just as object a part of what he or she seeks to know. To understand the human one must be a participant who only afterward gains the distance from one's subject matter that will enable one to formulate the insights one has attained. Otherwise, one inevitably sees the human being as a sum of parts, some of which are labeled "objective" and hence oriented around the thing known, and some "subjective" and hence oriented around the knower. What is more, one must reject all attempts to reduce the problematic of the human to any single motive or complex of motives or to comprehend the human simply on the analogy of biology or the behavior of animals. Only if as philosophical anthropologist one is a problem to oneself can one understand the human as a problem to itself.

DIALOGUE AND DIALECTIC IN THE HUMAN SCIENCES

What I am pointing to here is an approach, an attitude. It is not a party line. There are people who misunderstand Buber's *Two Types of Faith* as if he's saying, "I'm pro-Judaism and against Christianity." He wasn't saying that at all. He was saying there is a dialectic tension between *emunah*, faith of unconditional trust in relationship, and pistis, which is faith with a knowledge content. This same dialectic applies to all Buber's ideal types—I-Thou and I-It, person and individual, being person and seeming person, dialogue and monologue, prophetic and apocalyptic, *devotio* and *gnosis*. To turn them into opposites between which one must choose, as Walter Kaufmann did, is to make Buber a Manichean dualist, and he was the opposite of that. Thus Buber's narrow ridge means *both* dialogue and the dialectic or, put another way, a dialectic between I-Thou and I-It, a dialectic between dialogue and dialectic when dialogue means a genuine meeting with otherness and dialectic means an alternation of positions within one mind with no real otherness present.

When I wrote my doctoral dissertation, I put forward a scale of attitudes toward evil. When I first met Buber, he told me he had met five days previously with T. S. Eliot. I asked Buber, "Don't you find that your opinions differ from Eliot's?" Buber looked at me and said, "When I meet a person I am not concerned with their opinions; I am concerned with the person." I took it as a reproof, and it was. I had turned the two into a dialectical opposition within my own head.

I had a friend who was on the debating team at Harvard and who argued about everything conceivable. After twelve years he said to me, "You know, I have never yet said to anyone that they were right, not even on the smallest point. But sometimes I go away and think, perhaps on this or that small point, they were right after all." I said nothing, but I thought, "Well, that's better than nothing." Then I thought again; no, it isn't better than nothing because meanwhile the other voice has gotten lost. It is just a dialectic in the end and not a dialogue. In real dialogue something else goes on. It cannot mean that we dispense with dialectic. In a curious way we have to have a dialogue with the dialectic. We have to go back and forth.

For some time I have had the notion of writing a book on dialogue and dialectic in the human sciences in which I would like to show this back-and-forth in such fields as psychology and psychotherapy, sociology and anthropology, literature and religion. That to me is an invaluable approach to the human sciences, if you want to call them that, and in the end I think it is more concrete. Human existence necessarily and properly alternates between the immediate and the mediate, the direct and the indirect. As the prefix *dia* suggests, both dialogue and dialectic imply the alternation between two different points of view. In the case of dialogue, this also means real meeting with the unique otherness of an other, whereas in the case of dialectic the alternation may take place within the head of a single thinker, and the points of view may remain disembodied and hypothetical.

The tendency of by far the largest and most dominant methodologies in most human sciences today is to begin with dialectic and to examine dialogue as a part of that dialectic. Putting this in Martin Buber's terminology, it means that the mutual knowing of the I-Thou relationship is subsumed under the subject-object knowledge of the I-It relation. A radical reversal of this perspective would not mean any rejection of dialectic, which remains essential to the whole human enterprise of connected thought from one generation to another. What it does mean is a shift in emphasis toward understanding dialogue as the source of knowing and dialectic as an elaboration of that source. "The corrective office of reasoning is incontestable," wrote Buber (PI 53). It can be summoned at any moment to adjust the incongruity between my sense perception and what is common to my neighbors. In the I-It relation, what is received in the I-Thou is elaborated and broken up. Here errors are possible that can be corrected through directly establishing and comparing what is past and passive in the minds of others. But reason, with its gigantic structure of general concepts, cannot replace the smallest perception of something particular and unique, cannot by means of it take part in the grasping of what here and now confronts me.

DIALOGUE AND DIALECTIC IN PHILOSOPHY

Starting with the philosophy of dialogue, we can say that the I-Thou relation is a direct knowing that gives one neither knowledge about the Thou over against the I nor about oneself as an objective entity apart from that relationship. It is, in Buber's words, "the genuinely reciprocal meeting in the fullness of life between one active existence and another." Although this dialogical knowing is direct, it is not entirely unmediated. The directness of the relationship is established not only through the mediation of the senses in the concrete meeting of real living persons, but also through mediation of the word. That means the mediation of those fields of symbolic communication, such as language, music, art, and ritual, which enable human beings ever again to enter into relation with what comes to meet them. The word may be identified with subject-object or I-It knowledge while it remains indirect and symbolic. However, it is itself the channel of expression of I-Thou knowing when it is taken up into real dialogue.

Subject-object or I-It knowledge is ultimately nothing other than the socially objectified and elaborated product of the real meeting which takes place between the person and her Thou in the realms of nature, social relations, and art. As such, it provides those ordered categories of thought which are, together with dialogue, primal necessities of human existence. But as such, also, it may be, like the indirect and objective word, the symbol of true dialogue. It is only when the full meaning of the symbolic character of subject-object knowledge is forgotten, or remains undiscovered, as is often the case, that this knowledge ceases to point back toward the reality of direct dialogical knowing and becomes instead an obstruction to it.

In his classic work *I and Thou*, Martin Buber uses Socrates as an illustration of the I which is made real by virtue of sharing in the dialogue between person and person. Yet Socrates is not, for all that, an adequate image of the life of dialogue. Socrates went forth to people, trusted them, met them, never suspended dialogue with them. Yet his emphasis upon dialectic thought often put him in the position of the essentially monological thinker whose dialectic, even when it brings in other people, is little more than a moving forward through the opposition and interaction of different points of view, rather than an interaction between really other persons. Martin Buber's friend, the Jewish existential philosopher Franz Rosenzweig, said that the reason why most philosophical dialogues, including those of Plato, are so tedious is that there is no real other speaker. In a real dialogue the other person has not only ears but a mouth and can say something that will surprise you. That is why real dialogue takes place in time. You cannot know the answer in advance the way Socrates teases the geometrical proposition out of the slave boy in the *Meno*.

In his reply to Robert Maynard Hutchins in the Buber section of *Philosophical Interrogations*, Martin Buber wrote:

> I know of very few men in history to whom I stand in such a relation of both trust and veneration as Socrates. But when it is a matter of using "Socratic questions" as an educational method, I am against it. . . . Socrates overvalued the significance of abstract general concepts in comparison with concrete individual experiences. General concepts are the most important stays and supports, but Socrates treated them as if they were more important than bones—that they are not. . . . Socrates conducts his dialogue by posing questions and proving the answers that he received untenable; these are not real questions; they are moves in a sublime dialectical game that has a goal, the goal of revealing a not-knowing. But when the teacher whom I mean . . . enters into a dialogue with his pupil and in

this connection directs a question to him, he asks, as the simple man who is not inclined to dialectic asks, because he wants
to know something: that, namely, which this young person
before him, and precisely he, knows to report on the subject
under discussion a small individual experience, a nuance of
experience that is perhaps barely conceptually comprehensible,
nothing further, and that is enough. The teacher will awaken in
the pupil the need to communicate of himself and the capacity
thereto and in this way bring him to greater clarity of existence. But he also learns, himself, through teaching thus; he
learns, ever anew, to know concretely the becoming of the
human creature that takes place in experiences; he learns what
no man ever learns completely, the particular, the individual,
the unique. No, certainly no full partnership; but still a characteristic kind of reciprocity, still a real dialogue. (67–68)

This contrast between dialogue and dialectic has much to do with
the importance of the spokenness of speech in which the between
becomes real in the relationship of two persons or more. When the word
really becomes speech, when it is really spoken, it is spoken in the context of relationship, of the meeting with what is other than us, of mutuality. It takes its very meaning from the fact that it is said by one person
and heard by another. The hearer adds a different dimension and relationship to the word that is spoken, even as he or she stands on a different ground from the speaker. One must keep in mind, therefore, the
genuinely two-sided and dialogical character of the word as the embodiment of the between when it is spoken. The mystery of word and
answer that moves *between* human beings is not one of union, harmony, or even complementarity, but of *tension*, for two persons never
mean the same thing by the words that they use, and no answer is ever
fully satisfactory. The result is that, at each point of the dialogue, understanding and misunderstanding are interwoven. From this tension of
understanding and misunderstanding comes the interplay of openness
and closedness and expression and reserve that marks every genuine dialogue between person and person. Thus, the mere fact of the *difference*
between persons already implies a basic dramatic situation as an inherent component of human existence as such, which drama only reproduces in clearer and heightened form.

It is this recognition of *difference* which explains the polarity, the
vis-à-vis *and* the tragic conflict which may arise because "each is as he
is." But this is also at the heart of the distinction between dialogue and
dialectic, even Socratic dialectic. *Dialogue* recognizes differences and

never seeks for simple agreement or unanimity. *Dialectic*, in contrast, begins with the categories of "the same" and "the other," but excludes the reality of "the between" and with it the recognition of real otherness as that which can be affirmed even in opposing it. Thus, both the original assumption and the goal of dialectic is a unified point of view. The dialectician's faith in logic as the arbitrator and common denominator not only of his inner reflections but also of the dialogue between person and person is essentially single-voiced, monological, and pseudo-universal. I like to think (and I admit that this is sheer speculation, since aside from Plato's *Dialogues* we have only Aristophanes' *Clouds* and Xenophon's mention of Socrates to go on) that Socrates himself was a very dialogical person, but that Plato, who bewailed in his epistles that he had to write down Socrates' dialogues, was already moving over to dialectic. Aristotle took over from Plato the categories of same and other on which he built his logic and most of the logic that has followed in the Western world. But for Aristotle even the form of dialogue, which Plato cherished enough to reproduce in literary form, albeit replete with characters who seemed to be there mostly to say, "Yes, Socrates," and "No, Socrates," was no longer important!

DIALOGUE AND DIALECTIC IN SOCIAL PSYCHOLOGY AND SOCIOLOGY

The alternation between dialogue and dialectic also applies to social psychology and sociology, as I shall illustrate with some thoughts from my book *The Confirmation of Otherness: In Family, Community, and Society* (Friedman, 1983). We need to be confirmed by others. They make us present, and this, as Martin Buber points out, induces our inmost self-becoming. One of the paradoxes of confirmation is that we are all too often confirmed with strings attached. Another is that we do and must live in a world in which we have both personal uniqueness and social role. Everyone has to play a social role as a basic prerequisite not only to economic livelihood, but also to relations to other people and families in society. Yet we cannot resolve this tension between personal uniqueness and social role by sacrificing personal confirmation; for that results in an anxiety that can only become greater and greater. To stand in this tension is to insist that one's confirmation in society also be in some significant sense a confirmation of oneself as a unique person who does not fit into a social category.

To be confirmed in personal uniqueness is to be confirmed directly. That is dialogue. To be confirmed only as a certain social role is to be confirmed indirectly. That is dialectic. Both are necessary. We cannot altogether dispense with the idea of social role, though we can guard ourselves against taking it as a reality in itself. We must see it, instead, within the interaction between more or less static conceptions of roles and the actual dynamic of our relationship to them. We cannot deny the specialization of labor. Neither can we deny the continual rationalization of that specialization in terms of job descriptions and problems of decision making and authority. This includes the obvious need to call for people not as the unique persons that they are but as abstractions, such as professor, secretary, machinist, crane operator, doctor, or bank clerk.

What we need not accept is that the convenient label and the social role exhaust the reality of the person for the hours during which he works. On the contrary, his own unique relationship to his work is of crucial importance not only for the success or the meaning of the work but for the human reality that here becomes manifest as event. What is more, we can recognize the necessity for a continual critique of abstractions, to make them more and more flexible and more and more in line with the actual situation at any one time. In terms of this critique, it is a part of the task of man and woman alike to reject the unfair burden of always responding to a situation in a catalogued way. This means rejecting the life in which the human has been all but smothered under the weight of technical, social, and bureaucratic abstractions.

DIALOGUE AND DIALECTIC IN PSYCHOLOGY AND PSYCHOTHERAPY

Dialogue and dialectic are also central to psychology and psychotherapy. Even the patients' sicknesses are part of their uniqueness, for even their sicknesses tell us of the unique life directions to which they are called. If, instead, therapists make patients into objects to themselves, the therapists will have robbed the patients of part of their human potentiality and growth. This is not a question of choice between scientific generalization and the concrete individual, but of which direction is the primary one. Is the individual regarded as a collection of symptoms to be registered in the categories of a particular school, or are the theories of the school regarded as primarily means of returning again and again to the understanding of the unique person and his or her relationship with his or her therapist?

An increasingly important trend in psychotherapy suggests that the basic direction of movement should be toward concrete persons and their uniqueness, and not toward subsuming the patients' symptoms under theoretical categories or adjusting them to some socially derived view of the ideal. This trend emphasizes the *image* of the human as opposed to the *construct* of the human. The image of the human retains the understanding of human beings in their concrete uniqueness: it retains the wholeness of the person. Only a psychotherapy which begins with the concrete existence of persons in their wholeness and uniqueness and with the healing that takes place in the meeting between therapist and client will point us toward the image of the human. In the last analysis, the issue that faces all the schools of psychotherapy is whether the starting point of therapy is to be found in the analytical category or the unique person, in the construct or the image of the human.

The former Jungian therapist Hans Trüb contrasts the dialectical psychological approach with a dialogical anthropological one. He does not ask us to choose between them, but he wants to enclose the dialectical within the dialogical. The dialectical approach of the psychologist entails a methodological and systematic focus on the contradictory multiplicity of the psyche. This approach has to be coordinated with and subordinated to the dialogical attitude of the partner in relationship which rejects both method and system in favor of the person-to-person meeting, each and every time unique, each and every time demanding a decision.

No matter how significant and reliable the self-illuminating insights achieved by the analyst through depth psychology may be in any given case, they demonstrate their curative force decisively only when the patient abandons the stand he took during the analysis and throws himself as himself into the world of real objects and real meetings. The uncovering of these inner psychic defense mechanisms by means of depth psychology can truly succeed only if it recognizes that they are based in the self's personally executed flight from meeting. The reconstruction of the capacity for dialogue must go hand in hand, writes Trüb, with the methodical attempt to loosen and dismantle the complex defense mechanisms in the psychic realm of expression as fast as the recuperating self permits. When the psychological cooperation and dialectical interaction of patient and therapist is conducted dialogically with mutual personal trust between therapist and patient, then there gradually awakens and grows in the patient a new confidence in himself and in the other.

There are two kinds of therapists, Martin Buber asserted at the seminars he gave in 1957 for the Washington (D.C.) School of Psychiatry. One knows more or less consciously the kind of interpretation of dreams she will give to the patient. The other is the psychologist who does not know, who does not want something precise, who is ready to receive what she will receive. She cannot know what method she will use beforehand; for she is, so to speak, in the hands of the patient. "The real master responds to uniqueness," says Buber (*ABH*, 156–173). Such a master uses that type of intuition which Buber calls imagining the real, or "inclusion." Inclusion does not mean empathy but experiencing the other side of the relationship—concretely imagining what the other is thinking, feeling, and willing, while at the same time remaining on your own side of the relationship. Imagining the real is the very stuff of betweenness because it is, in the first instance, the stuff of immediacy that only later becomes something that one reflects upon and thinks about. It is dialogue that only later becomes dialectic.

The therapist with years of experience and with the knowledge of the many case histories that are recorded in the literature will naturally think of resemblances when a client tells her something. But if she is a good therapist, she must discover the right movement back and forth between her patient as the unique person he is and the categories and cases that come to her mind. She cannot know through scientific method when a particular example from case histories, her earlier clients, or even her own experience applies. This is where true intuition, where imagining the real, or "inclusion," comes in.

DIALOGUE AND DIALECTIC IN ANTHROPOLOGY

Let us provide one brief example of dialogue and dialectic from anthropology. Kurt Wolff, a distinguished American sociologist and anthropologist, lived among the Loma Indians for three years, after which he wrote an essay and later a book called *Surrender and Catch*. Instead of coming with his questions and categories already formed, he lived with the Loma Indians long enough to understand from *their* side what was unique to them. The "surrender" was the surrender to their uniqueness. The "catch" was his response. The contrasting and much more usual approach of imposing one's categories on what one is studying is illustrated in extreme form by a distinguished psychoanalyst and direct disciple of Freud. In the late 1950s this man gave a talk about a society where children were raised differently from those of any other society, pointing out all the nefarious effects of such child rearing. Since he was unmistakably talking about the kibbutzim in Israel, I asked him after the lecture about his stay in Israel. "I've never been to Israel," he replied. "I am a Park Avenue anthropologist. I send my students to Israel, and they bring back to me the results of the Thematic Apperception Tests they administer."

DIALOGUE AND DIALECTIC IN PHENOMENOLOGY

The concern for both the typical and the unique in phenomenology may serve as our final example of the necessary interaction of dialogue and dialectic. In true phenomenological research there must be a constant movement between dialogue and dialectic so that the ideal types that evolve can continually be corrected by the particulars and so that there is room for the unique. In contrast to the scientist who is only interested in particulars insofar as they yield generalizations, we can derive valid insights from the unique situations in which we find ourselves without having to claim that they apply to all situations. We take these insights with us into other situations and test the limits of their validity. Sometimes we find that these insights do hold for a particular situation and sometimes that they do not or that they have to be modified. Yet that does not mean that they cannot be valid insights for other situations.

I chaired for five years a phenomenological dissertation in psychology studying Jews who had gone to Oriental religions. Midway through the process the acting dean of the college insisted that the student deal with thirty cases on the grounds that this would help her in her future career. The result was that she could not do an in-depth study but had to limit herself to two out of the ten categories which she had developed in the course of her work. At her doctoral oral I pointed out this loss and with it the fallacy in the notion that thirty would give her more valid "evidence" than six. Precisely because in good phenomenological research the researcher is a part of the knowing involved, real evidence is not a matter of a statistical population and of generalization but of valid insight based upon an in-depth dialogue with each subject and the interplay between ideal types that develop and the uniqueness and particularity of each case.

REFERENCES

Buber, Martin. *ABH*, *BMM*, *EG*, *I and Thou* (Smith), *IW*, *KM* (1966), *LBS*, *Meetings*, *PW*.

Friedman, Maurice. *CO*.

Rome, Sidney, and Rome, Beatrice, eds. (1964). *Philosophical Inter-rogations*. Introduction by Sidney and Beatrice Rome, "Martin Buber" section conducted, edited, and Buber's responses trans. by Maurice Friedman, 13–117. New York: Holt, Rinehart & Winston.

Wolff, Kurt H. (1970). *Surrender and Catch. Experience in Inquiry Today*. Boston: D. Reidel.

PART II

PHILOSOPHY AND RELIGION

INTRODUCTION

SEYMOUR CAIN AND MAURICE FRIEDMAN

In his essay "To Be is to Be Relational: Martin Buber and John Dewey," Arthur Lothstein proposes nothing less than an analogy on human relations and that of the great American pragmatists, selecting John Dewey as the classical example. If experience, for Dewey, is the foundation of thought, art, and action, it is always the experience of relations to what is other, human, and nonhuman (in nature). Like Buber, he also stresses communality, the coming together of human beings, their concrete face-to-face association. But although Lothstein sees a common "communalism" in both men's social thought, he finds Buber far more conscious and profound about what is involved in the making of such a community.

Martin Buber always disclaimed being a theologian and was antagonistic to the very idea of theology, a *logos* of *theos*. Manfred Vogel's essay, "Is a Dialogical Theology Possible?" deals with questions of whether "dialogical theology" is an oxymoron. If theology (for example, "natural theology") is the rational, objective treatment of the divine, essentially an *It*-enterprise, how can there be a *dialogical* theology, dealing thus with what by definition is always *Thou* and never *It*? Vogel rejects the possible alternative of a "revelatory theology" based, for example, on the Sinaitic commands, biblical life-rules, or rabbinic interpretations, as just another *It*-enterprise, with a God who is not an "I" for the human "Thou," nor a "Thou" for the human "I"—the God of monologue not dialogue. The way out, he suggests, is to radically change our notion of theology and have it deal with the "content of faith" in a

29

religious tradition, with its beliefs, rituals, and symbols. He concedes that again we have an "It" as the object of description and analysis, the content of faith, but he argues that now it is not God who is made the "It"-object. Going further, Vogel insists that a dialogical theology must be contentless, anchored in the realm of relation, the in-between, where alone a fully mutual I-Thou relation occurs between God and human beings. The problem remains, however, of just how the latter is to be identified with an essentially contentless dialogical theology. In what sense is content-of-faith theology itself dialogical? Because it is a reflection of the primal I-Thou dialogue?

Daniel Breslauer's "*Into Life*: The Legacy of Jewish Tradition in Buber's Philosophy of Dialogue" shows Buber to have been an outstanding example of those early twentieth-century Jewish thinkers who were concerned with concrete human existence. This concern is directed toward the whole of human life, not at some separate transcendental sphere. The proclaimed unity of God is to be a model for the unity of human life. Buber's interest in Hasidism arose from its emphasis on daily human life and acts as the locus for the holy. Torah is not a text that we read, but a life that we lead. This is a teaching expressible mainly in stories, the Hasidic tales that Buber made world-famous, rather than in abstract discourse. Buber retold the original stories with an emphasis on their universal human meaning—for example, the need to be confirmed in our particular self-existence or the precedence of compassion and human understanding over literal conformity with details of the written Torah.

Richard Freund finds Martin Buber "uniquely suited as a touchstone for a philosophical understanding of Jewish ethics" because he was versed both in general philosophical literature and the contributions of the Bible and Jewish tradition. Freund's "Martin Buber's Biblical and Jewish Ethics" points out in particular that "Buber's insights on I-Thou and dialogue provide us with a window for understanding ethical implications present in modern source critical studies of the Bible." Buber and modern biblical scholarship share the view that the God of Israel is both wholly transcendent and in relationship with us: "Buber's model for Jewish ethics demands that each individual allow for his/her own encounter with the Divine and the experience of the encounter will ultimately determine how one reacts through informed human will."

Freund's presentation of Buber's stance in terms of what Freund describes as "a Buberian dualism" is likely to be confusing to the reader who is used to the simple opposition between monism and dualism. It would help in reading this essay if the reader bears in mind that Freund is actually pointing to Buber's "narrow ridge" between the opposites of what Maurice Friedman has called "non-dual dualism."

Donald Moore, in his essay "Martin Buber and Christian Theology: A Continuing Dialogue," stresses Buber's biblical interpretations of human existence as experienced in his own life and faith and expressed in a language accessible to all who live today. Moore sees Buber's key metaphors of "holy insecurity" and the "narrow ridge" as challenges to Catholic theology to bring the moment of lived encounter to theological reflection and to allow its whole theological undertaking to be permeated by mystery, encounter, dialogue, wonder, and prayer. Moore illustrates this "continuing dialogue" through a comparison of Buber and the Catholic theologian Karl Rahner, who also emphasizes existential trust (the courage to hope), a mystery grasped in the space and time of our human history, the incomprehensibility of God, and a salvation which is an actualization of human potential "*in* and *for* the world, rather than *from* the world."

In "Buber, the *Via Negativa*, and Zen," G. Ray Jordan contrasts the leaving behind of the world of Plotinus, Dionysius, and Buber's own early mysticism with Buber's mature way and Zen, which in their more demanding "way of negation" realize "the nameless mystery in the midst of responding within the everyday realities," without the aid of learned behavioral patterns and ecstatic unconsciousness, and with no confusion of words and the immediate, unmediated reality to which they point.

In his essay "I and Tao: Buber's *Chuang Tzu* and the Comparative Study of Mysticism," Jonathan Herman points out that Sinologists have not taken seriously Buber's selection and translation of the parables of Chuang-Tzu, and Buber scholars have only looked at the concluding essay on "The Teaching of the Tao." Herman, in this essay (which he has now expanded into a book of the same title), not only stresses the influence of Taoism on Buber but also Buber's role as a modern hermeneuticist approaching Chuang-Tzu with a dialogue that brings out much that more traditional scholars have missed. Herman offers Buber's dialogue with Chuang-Tzu as paradigmatic of a creative alternative to the strict disjunction between those who approach mysticism from the standpoint of the "perennial philosophy" and those who see it as always expressed only in a single tradition.

Seymour Cain's "Dialogue and Difference: 'I and Thou' or 'We and They'?" is not an academic paper, but rather an interpersonal address. It calls on us, on you and me, to engage in self-examination on our own antidialogical tendencies. It calls on us to accept and affirm other persons in their otherness—ideological, cultural, ethnoracial, sociopolitical, and ethico-religious—while retaining our own particularity. It refers to concrete situations and daily events in Canada, Israel, and this country to make its point. It cites Buber's attitude toward the Palestinian Arabs and toward alien religious cultures as a model.

CHAPTER 2

TO BE IS TO BE RELATIONAL

Martin Buber and John Dewey

ARTHUR S. LOTHSTEIN

I begin this conversation between Buber and Dewey mindful of the fact that any argument for their joining is prima facie implausible. Although they were nearly exact contemporaries—Buber (1878–1965), Dewey (1859–1952)—who wrote on many of the same subjects, they hardly seemed to know of each other's work; or if they did, each chose to ignore its relevance to his own discussions.[1] Moreover, their apparent ignorance of each other's work has been repeated by their followers, who have generally failed to acknowledge their common interests and concerns.[2] Yet the more I read Dewey and Buber together the more I am convinced of their philosophical kinship; and I am now inclined to read Dewey as a plain-spoken Vermont version of Buber, and Buber as a poetic, Jewish existentialist version of Dewey. If it is not wrong to think of Dewey as Buber secularized and pragmatized—that is, as Buber without God—it is also not wrong, I would submit, to think of Buber as Dewey solemnified and sacramentalized—which is to say, as Dewey divinized.

My reading of Dewey and Buber together has also sharpened for me their respective strengths and weaknesses, and the general lines along which their respective positions may be strengthened and enriched. A Deweyed Buber, I am persuaded, is a metaphysically, aesthetically, and pedagogically fattened Buber, and a Bubered Dewey, I am also persuaded, is a psychologically, politically, and spiritually deepened Dewey. For example, Buber's superb understanding of the worlds of silence, mystery, and love, and his more completely articulated communitarianism, help us to see in what respects Dewey's perspective needs to be filled out. Analogously, Dewey's richer metaphysics of relations, and his profounder grasp of the aesthetic dimension of experience, including the experience of community, teach us how Buber's perspective may be broadened and thickened philosophically.

Dewey and Buber were masters of relations, and their teachings about relations caused them to think philosophically across the lines of traditions, movements, schools, disciplines, and so forth. Neither saw himself as a fussy academic mandarin caught in the lockstep of a single discipline; and neither held any brief for the Cartesian model of philosophy as an insular and claustral practice diced into technical and quarantined discourses, and arrogated unto an *aristoi*. For both, the tendentiously monologist character of modern philosophy (*KM*, 113) was not simply a *deformation professionelle* born of the illusion of technique, but an upward reflection into philosophical discourse of alienated social experience and culturally sanctioned narcissism, as operative in the intellectual realm as it was in society generally. Underneath the problematic of monologism was the fall of public man, the fall into division and fraction, and the relationally bereft experience engendered thereby. Bled dry by relation starvation,[3] the contemporary self had become transmogrified into a shrivelled Seuratian dot, who, in the dark nutritional arithmetic of Emily Dickinson, lived "Zero at the bone." Its regnancy bespoke the eclipse, if not obsolescence, of community and the life of dialogue, and attested to the threadbare character of contemporary experience. Under such dire circumstances, Buber offered, "The glowing deeds of solitary spirits," no matter how incandescent, could be only "spasmodically" rejuvenating. Unless "centered in the living and continually renewed relational event,"[4] there could be no healing, only temporary relief, cauterization perhaps, but no redemption.

I want to begin our conversation between Dewey and Buber by focusing briefly on their metaphysics of relations, which in both cases, and especially in Dewey's case, were framed as alternatives to the divisionism endemic in contemporary culture. It is also my point that their metaphysics undergirded their normative social and political discussions of community, which is the subject of the last part of this paper. Dewey's assertion that "metaphysics is the ground map of the province of criticism" (Dewey 1958, 413) underscored the (to him) inextricable relationship between value theory and metaphysical angle of vision. His claim implied that his own concept of the educative and liberatory value of shared experience and free communication could properly be understood only within the context of his metaphysics of relations.[5] In Buber's writings we find the same marriage of metaphysical and normative discussion, and the same ineluctable dependency of the latter upon the former, even if, as Buber himself also understood, he was not a metaphysician in the strict sense, and that what is called his metaphysics was arguably analyzable without remainder into a collection of impressionistic philosophical anthropological aperçus.[6] I take as essentially correct Charles Hartshorne's reading of Buber as a sage or wisdom philosopher (PMB, 68), but for the purpose of joining Buber and Dewey, I want to identify Buber's central metaphysical aperçus or impressions about relations, and connect them to the formulating insights of Dewey's naturalistic metaphysics of relations, in the belief that there are strong family resemblances between the former and Dewey's doctrine of relations, and that, as in Dewey's case, Buber's metaphysical insights fed and helped to ground his normative discussions of community and communication.

There are three metaphysical propositions of Buber's that I take to be central to his thought, and which also belong to the core of Dewey's naturalistic metaphysics: (1) "In the beginning is relation," (2) "We live our lives inscrutably included with the streaming mutual life of the universe," and (3) "Not things but situations are primary" (I and Thou, 18, 16; KM, 116). Retrospectively, and primarily in response to the French philosopher Gabriel Marcel's criticism of (1), Buber thought his "phylogenetic" formulation unfortunate, arguing that "it is too rich in associations," the result, he hypothesized, of its having been inscribed "in an overpowering inspiration" ("Replies," 706). Over-rich or not, (1) underscores the primacy of relations, which Buber never flinched from asserting, and which he, like Dewey, took to be conducive to something like a Copernican revolution in philosophy. There are two places in I and Thou where we find (1) asserted, and it is in its second occurrence that its full meaning comes to the fore: "In the beginning is relation—as category of being, readiness, grasping form, mould for the soul; it is the a priori of relation, the inborn Thou" (27). I want to focus on Buber's use of the words "category of being" and "a priori of relation," because such language underscores his affiliation with Dewey, although, I am aware, of course, that the game Buber was really hunting was the realization of "the inborn Thou" in one's "living with the world" (69–70). Buber's phrase, "the inborn Thou," when connected to the two other phrases I have isolated for discussion, brings out his Hebraicized Kantianism: the capacity for saying Thou, I read him as meaning, is constitutive of our human essence; we are the kind of beings who can say "Thou" to the world and its inhabitants and by the same token say "Thou" to the God who has endowed us with this epistemic and spiritual capacity for saying "Thou." But for the purpose of bringing out his kinship with Dewey, I want to read (2) as an instantiation of (1). And here, the words "inscrutably included within" and "streaming mutual life of the universe" are what I want to call attention to because they italicize Buber's metaphysical observation that we are not strangers in a strange land, but insiders, indwellers, whose mode of tenancy is organic, not mechanical, and one suffused by mystery. Likewise, Dewey analogized our human mode of inhabitation to embryos within a womb, or to events in history, emphasizing thereby that we are not pariahs or refugees bereft of a home, but transient nesters within earth's cornucopial household, who, if capable of Olympian feats of mind and body, are also brittle Prometheuses condemned to be eaten by omnivorous time. And it is against the background of their inclusive metaphysical understanding of human inhabitation that we find Buber and Dewey breaking their respective lances against the alienative condition of contemporary society, in which fraction, not relation, ruled the roost, and the solipsistic "I" crowded out the salvific "We."

Constraints of space do not allow me to address in detail Dewey's metaphysical discussion, so I offer the following summary of the relevant main points of that discussion; and in this context I shall recur not only to Buber's propositions (1) and (2), but also to (3), which I read also as quintessentially Deweyean.

The first thing I want to bring out about Dewey's metaphysics is its dialectical and processive character, what I like to refer to as its Heraclitean coefficient. Like Aristotle, Dewey began with the natural world as culturally mediated (hence his expressed regret in later years that he titled his book on metaphysics *Experience and Nature* and not *Culture and Nature*, a not unimportant admission for our joining of Buber and Dewey, since we know that Buber read the word "experience" pejoratively, claiming that it enshrined the proprietary logic of the world of It), emphasizing thereby the priority of the culture of experience and its incorrigibly naturalistic status. Consequently, Dewey spoke of persons as "Organism-Environments," the left side of the hyphen asterisking the desiderata of biology, the right side the exigencies of social ecology, and the hyphen the dialectical character of their interaccommodation. His nature was Hegel's Darwinized, or more exactly, it was a distinctively American version of the Greek *physis*. Organic, developmental, and redolent with possibility, it was also pockmarked by loss and setback, allowing for a full spectrum of experiential options, ranging from breakdown to breakthrough.

I cited earlier Buber's reference to our inclusiveness in the world's streaming mutuality as "inscrutable"; and Dewey wrote similarly about the fundamental intractability, if not inscrutability, of nature, not as an American nature mystic, but as a naturalist and radical empiricist respectful of nature's evolutionary superiority to the Herculean efforts of men to hostage her to their specific agendas. His version of Buber's (1) was that the basic elements or primitives of existence are ensembles of relations, not the simply located and reified ephemerals of the tradition. Fields and streams of relational process, interstitched and serially entwined particulars, were Dewey's metaphysical posits, not the atomic, granulated simples or discreta of Hume and Locke. Consequently, Dewey read individuals as clusterings of interactivity, as cooperations of relational process. He rejected the broken, fissive world of the tradition as a chimerical fiction of the modern philosophical imagination. Relations, to him, were not, then, engraftments from without or above; they were not mental or divine interpolations made to cast or splint a fractured world, to weld ideationally or epiphanically what failed to cohere *au naturel*. Rather, he viewed them as inhering within the tissue of ordinary experience, and so multifariously constellated as to form a veritable Hopkinsian kaleidoscope of things fickle, freckled, and dappled. Buber's (3) was simply a more prosaic way of making the same metaphysical point. Or put differently, and in language which is more consonant with Buber's phenomenological account of *dazwischen* experience, the realest loci of genuine nutrition, for Dewey, were the in-between, tertiary spaces, the spaces of co-nutrition and co-fructification, the spaces, we may say more simply, of situation and relation. But also like Buber, Dewey understood that relations were fragile efflorescences within the streams of experience, requiring, like Penelope's mythic web, continual protection and reconstitution. Buber's famous reference to "the narrow rocky ridge" (*BMM*, 184, 204) as the locus of encounter and meeting emphasized the tenuity or "holy insecurity," as he liked to say, of all fructuous relational experience. In stressing the priority of situations over things, Dewey and Buber meant to replace the substance-oriented metaphysics of Aristotle with an event-centered conception of existence. Their point was that what we normally call things or objects are better described as affair*ings*, occasion*ings*, or happen*ings*. I have intentionally used such participial constructions because, as Dewey insisted, they accurately depict, as nominal constructions do not, the processive and situational logic of existence; and if they are graceless locutions that go down hard, that is only because our ordinary language of description and explanation has been so badly perverted by substantive or entitative bias.

The other three dimensions of Dewey's metaphysics that I want to address here briefly are: (a) its embodied aesthetic, (b) its "secular liturgy,"[7] or nearly liturgical celebration of ordinary experience, and (c) its figuration of communication as "the sense of community, communion actualized" (Dewey 1958, 166, 206, n. 41). For Dewey, ordinary experience was "art in germ" (McDermott, *PJD*, 540) and the description of the "dramatic setting" of his metaphysics as delineating an aesthetic ecology is exactly right (xxv). I shall claim later that Dewey's normative ideal of aesthetic community was extrapolated from his aesthetic understanding of the rhythms of vernacular experience; and here the opening chapters of *Art as Experience* are central to an understanding of that relationship. They not only aesthetically worded his formulating metaphysical insights, they also aesthetically grounded the articulating concerns of his social and political thought. Everything he wrote on the subject of education, politics, and ethics celebrated the primacy and centrality of the aesthetic dimension of existence, and the singular importance of constructing an optimal environment for "the realizing and sanctioning of the aesthetic processes of living" (ibid.). I read Dewey's pedagogy, politics, and ethics as different kinds of environmental sculpture,[8] and concomitant with this, as comprising a seminal three-headed critique of the triumph of the anaesthetic over the aesthetic in contemporary society.

The other dimension of Dewey's metaphysics that I want to address here briefly is his nearly hymnal appreciation of ordinary experience. Buber, we know, figured daily life reverentially, and in his ethics admonished us to hallow, to sacramentalize, the everyday. Dewey analogously spoke of "natural piety," putting his tarbrush to philosophers and others for whom the ordinary was *infra dig*. His metaphysics, like his ethics and social philosophy, argued the primacy of colloquial experience, and redemption for him was a function of the en-route accumulation of sacramental moments, not a transfiguration from above. Buber's reference to "a moment God" (*BMM*, 15), I would argue, is but a theological cameo version of Dewey's concept. It is true that Dewey spoke more about ameliorating problematic situations than about consecrating the ordinary, but the two took in each other's wash for him. Moreover, Dewey's concept of the Great Community, which I discuss below, and which he viewed as the social and political representation of the religion of shared experience, of what he called in his plain, Quaker-style mode of speech, "common faith," he took to be a social corollary of the logic of relations choreographed in daily experience. It was not a deus ex machina construction, or the social vision of a political elite. It socially named and institutionalized that "sense of the whole" which Dewey located "within the flickering inconsequential acts of separate selves," in whose presence, he said, "we put off mortality and live in the universal" (McDermott, *PJD*, 723).

In a nearly scriptural tone of voice, Dewey spoke of "a deep-seated memory of an underlying harmony, the sense of which haunts life like the sense of being founded on a rock" (539). But he did not see the appropriation of that harmony as paradise regained, nor did he suggest that we ought to live our lives backward, nostalgically hankering after a prelapsarian Eden. Consistent with his doctrine of social melioration, he held to the differential and inchmeal restoration of the pacific and the harmonious; and the serenity his Great Community instanced was an "edged" serenity, a "peace in action," continually menaced by the press of historical circumstance, and so requiring continual mending and amendment. It neither attested to a marmoreal calm or bespoke an Oblomovian passivity. Processive and situational, it implied a continual enfleshment, not a final solution. A kind of Vermont Heraclitus, Dewey wanted to say, "It rests by changing"; and indeed he worked out a doctrine of aesthetic recurrence, which cast the Great Community as a checkerboard type of experience answering "the organic demand for variety." The Marcusean recapitulation of "a static that moves in its own fullness," or any other doctrine of the cycle or eternal return, was anathema to Dewey.[9] "Cumulative relationships," not "repetition of units," described the lineaments of his Great Community; and consistent with his doctrine of aesthetic recurrence, he pictured the former as an aesthetic democracy in-the-making, requiring continual resculpting and perfecting, lest fossilization ensue and the energies of men peter out. Writing about the aesthetic object and presumably also about the Great Community qua aesthetic object, he wrote: "Fulfilling, consummating are continuous functions, not mere ends, located at one place only" (McDermott, *PJD*, 573). Thusly envisaged, I am inclined to see Dewey's Great Community as the pragmatic meliorist version of the radical political concept of permanent revolution. Those of his critics who have wanted to read him as a bourgeois apologist have completely missed this dimension of his social thought, which, as I have argued elsewhere, is a central part of any case to make for Dewey as a radical social philosopher.[10]

Pragmatizing Hegel, Dewey glossed universals as local occurrences, as interstitial affairings of neighborhood experience. But, like Buber, he also wanted us to see the metaphysical fact of our cosmic confraternity behind the back of local universals, and its potentially "infinite religious significance" (McDermott, *PJD*, 710). Community, for him, was the "fit symbol" of the inter-energizing of the individual and the universal, of the finite and the infinite, "its only rites and ceremonies" being "the acts in which we express our perception of the ties which bind us to others" (723). His concept of the Great Community no doubt was churned from the indigenous American experience of *Gemeinde* or local community, and it represented, he offered, "as near an absolute as exists" (Dewey 1954, 215). And his understanding of the Great Community was, as I indicated above, essentially connected to his understanding of experience as an embodied aesthetic. The Great Community was the prototypical aesthetic Medium, the Medium of aesthetic media, which like any work of art was framed for "enjoyed receptive perception." Indeed, its distinguishing marks were identical with those of a work of art, as Dewey enumerated these in *Art as Experience*. What he wrote there about lines, colors, masses, etc., seemed to apply without qualification to his Great Community. Unfortunately, he never synthesized his metaphysical, aesthetic, and social and political writings, and so the full meaning of his concept has rarely been grasped. It remains for Deweyeans to complete that task, a task which Dewey himself never even began, and which I have tried elsewhere to begin to think about beginning.[11]

The third dimension of Dewey's metaphysics I want to discuss briefly, and in the context of Buber's understanding of the educative and redemptive value of intersubjectivity, is his concept of communication. He devoted the middle chapter (5) of *Experience and Nature* to that subject probably because he meant it to be read as the linchpin of his metaphysics. His concept of communication was a function of his doctrine of relations, and in particular of his transactional understanding of existence. We find his concept synopsized in the proposition that "Shared experience is the greatest of human goods" (Dewey 1958, 202), which, as I read it, is practically synonymous with Buber's assertion that "Genuine life is united life" (*PW*, 34). For Dewey, communication was both instrumental and consummatory; he assigned to it the leading function of extending the relational reach of experience, and claimed that in its most superlative instances it rendered experience both pregnant and poetic.[12] Indeed, when the instrumental and consummatory functions of communication are married in experience, he wrote, "there exists an intelligence which is the method and reward of the common life, and a society worthy to command affection, admiration, and loyalty" (Dewey 1958, 205).

But Dewey, like Buber, was no Pollyannaish optimist. He understood that contemporary society was essentially communicatively incompetent, and like his Frankfurt School Marxist and left-Freudian contemporaries he understood the umbilical connection between alienated subjectivity and social domination. And he knew that if this connection was not broken, the Great Community, which he judged to be the guarantor of such communication, was nothing more than an idealistic nostrum solution. Always the pragmatist, Dewey read the dealienation of subjectivity as a possible positive result of social contestation, never as a *de novo* construction. Unlike the totalistic solutions proffered by his Marxist and other contemporaries, Dewey's proposed solutions were incremental and contextual. He held that in the continual sculpting and resculpting of the cultural frame as locally manifest, new and emancipator habits, habits of community, of freer and more open communication, would, like a slowly developing Polaroid, quietly coagulate around sustained efforts to deinstitutionalize power, forming therearound the lineaments of a new and more communicatively competent self. Such a dealienated self, he understood with Buber, could be framed "only as a world of related objects is constructed";[13] and Dewey's Great Community enfleshed such a social environ, just as his pedagogy created the necessary characterological preconditions for its humanizing inhabitation. Like Buber's, Dewey's dealienated self was a post-factum construction, implying the political transcendence of proprietary society and its ideology of possessive individualism. Both viewed the recovery of the self and the regeneration of community as correlative features of a counter-hegemonic social practice beyond the limits of hierarchy, domination, and class division. But unlike Buber, Dewey seemed to have no understanding of solitude as a necessary precondition of dealienated selfhood. He seemed to make no distinction between solitude that redoubled alienation and solitude that broke it back and matured the spirit. Dewey was so concerned with criticizing the affirmative cultural stance of pathological inwardness that he failed to see that solitude could be, as Buber wrote, a "place of purification," which freed oneself from the entrapments of objectification, and opened a "gate" to the world of relation.[14]

I turn now to a summary and brief evaluation of Dewey's and Buber's communalism, which to me clinches the case for their philosophical kinship. I read Dewey's concept of federation, and specifically his understanding of the Great Community as a confederation of localisms, as practically identical to Buber's, even if Buber's is the more fully fleshed construction.

In the 1946 afterword to *The Public and Its Problems*, Dewey argued the centrality of "the idea of Federation, as distinct from both isolation and imperial rule," eschewing statist formations other than experimental ones as purely mythical. The key that turned all the locks for Dewey was the local, neighborhood community, which, owing to the "close and direct intercourse and attachment" it allowed for, he took to be the "home" of democracy. "In its deepest and richest sense a community must always remain a matter of face-to-face intercourse" (Dewey 1954, 211), he offered; and presumably the Great Community would instance such a permeatively intimate social environ. But nowhere in Dewey's writings do we find a sustained discussion of the compatibility of the liberal democratic state with the ideal of face-to-face community. Nor do we find him ever concretely addressing the strategic question of building such communities, claiming that that question "is outside the scope of our discussion" (213). Indeed, Dewey never formulated a political technology or program of specific transitional proposals for bringing about the Great Community. The fact that there was not a single chapter of *The Public and Its Problems* devoted to the question of power made tolerably clear the naïveté and incompleteness of his discussion, and hence its arguable practical inutility.[15] It has been claimed that Dewey's concept is best instantiated by the anarchist concept of "non-isolated localisms joined by concentric circles of federation."[16] But Dewey himself failed to instantiate his concept thusly or in any other way. Instead, he contented himself with reciting the virtues of face-to-face communalism and with lamenting their increasing obsolescence. Hence the abstractness, some would say disabling abstractness, of Dewey's construction. By contrast, Dewey's defenders have wanted to read his concept as an approximative ideal whose empirical content could not be specified in advance of concrete efforts undertaken on its behalf. But the criteriological question remains: absenting clearly specified criteria for identifying the Great Community, how would one be able to distinguish between actions which catered for the Great Community, and those which did not? His assertion that the conditions of the Great Community would be brought into being by intelligence alone was more than merely naive. It was, as C. Wright Mills persuasively argued, subjective idealism in spades;[17] and it seemed a perfect illustration of Hegel's definition of bourgeois liberalism as "the philosophy which sticks to the abstract and is defeated by the concrete."[18]

This notwithstanding, Dewey's communalism was clearly a clarion call for a politics of generalized self-management based on local, face-to-face "associations." And, in language reminiscent of Buber, he wrote that under such circumstances logic "recurs to the primitive sense of the word: dialogue" (Dewey 1954, 218). But unlike Buber's anti-institutional understanding of dialogic communication, Dewey's paradigm was patently institutional. For Buber, institutions were "animated clods without soul," which rendered obsolete the possibility of authentic "public life." He spoke of them as paradigmatic instances of "the separated (world) of It" (*I and Thou*, 44). Dewey, on the other hand, figured institutions experimentally; capable of atrophying, or worse, fossilizing, they nevertheless constituted the cultural matrix of our human experience, and were viable and energizing when they enshrined "the cooperative consensus of multitudes of cells, each living in exchange with others" (McDermott, *PJD*, 614). As I read their discussions of institutions, Dewey's seems the more empirically insightful of the two, if only because he seems more sensitive to the complexity of institutional experience; whereas Buber, by contrast, seems to bevel the edge too sharply between what is and what is not objectifying. Dewey's language of "cells" and of their metabolic exchange is especially significant for our discussion, because we find the same language in Buber's description of his own communalism. And it is to the latter that I now wish to turn.

At the very beginning of his author's Foreword to *Paths in Utopia*, Buber argued that societal renewal is conditional upon the "renewal of its cell-tissue." His use of cellular and tissue language was consistent with his imaging of society as a body as opposed to an edifice, and his organicism led him to ask about the conditions of fecund societal embodiment. The term *cell-tissue* indicated that the societal renewal of which he spoke was from within, not an imposition from without, apocalyptic or otherwise. He read the term pluralistically, speaking about "small socialist realties," "small organic units," i.e., communes and cooperatives, each of which he glossed as a social microcosm of autonomous and voluntary "consociation." And he envisioned these molecularly, not atomically, in the form of "a far-reaching complex of interlocking magnetic foci" (*PU*, 79) which, taken as a whole, ideally constellated an organic commonwealth—"the Full Cooperative," "a new *consociatio consociationum*" (*PU*, 78, 139, 136).

Now, there is nothing in any of this that Dewey also did not say or imply. But where he was vague and irresolute, Buber was clear and decisive. Both argued the priority of the culture of experience, and, corollary with this, the derivative value of politics. And for both, societal renewal or reconstruction, not eschatological transformation, was the operative transformational ideal. If Buber opted for utopia, as opposed to an inchmeal meliorism, his utopia, however, was not a bloodlessly reified "schematic fiction." Paths to it were plotted and paths in it were carved and traversed. As evidenced by their understanding of community, both Buber's and Dewey's social visions transcended the limits of traditional liberal democratic thinking about freedom and culture. The communalism they both plumped for was substantive, *Gemeinschaft*-type community, not functional, *Gesellschaft*-type association; and for both, the entering wedge into community was the perception of a common humanity, a perception, both saw, which was not coextensive with the identification of common interests. As Buber observed, only cooperatives based primarily on the lives of their inhabitants were "suited to serve as cells of a new structure." Absenting a "continually renewed relational event," which cut across the separate lives of its inhabitants and bound them in community, there could be no cooperatives, only functional agglutination at best. Not tender-minded sentimentalists, both Dewey and Buber understood that mere community of feeling was not a sufficient condition for community proper; "a deeper and more vital bond is required" (Buber), one which flows from a common relation to a center overriding all other relations, and one which "organizes all elements by a common integrating principle" (Dewey). Buber's center was divine and fixed ("built up out of living mutual relation, but the builder is the living effective Centre" [*I and Thou*, 45]), whereas Dewey's was aesthetic and processive. Indeed, Dewey preferred to speak about center*ings*, wanting to call attention by that locution to the fact that the putative center of a community, like the putative center of a painting, should not be construed spatially, but rather as the focus of interpenetrative energies, subject to continual sharpening and enlargement. Despite their differences in language and emphasis, both clearly meant to be understood as saying that the center of a community should not just be an element among other elements, but the keystone in its arch. As Buber put it: "A real community is one which in every point of its being possesses, potentially at least, the whole character of community" (*PU*, 145). Like the Judeo-Christian God, its center would be everywhere, and its circumference nowhere. What needs to be noticed here also is that despite their assertion of the primacy of a center or of centerings, neither Dewey nor Buber wished to invest power in a central authority. Both figured charisma as horizontally diffused and power as popularly held; which is to say both treated the question of form or structure democratically and nonhierarchically.

And because macrosocial structural richness, to them, was conditional upon the existence of viable and fecund microsocial prestructures, both argued the centrality of prestructural forms, even if, as I said earlier, Dewey fudged the question about the framing of prestructures. Their understanding of the importance of "pre-revolutionary structure-making," as Buber called it, was a function of their organic and developmental understanding of transformational social practice generally. Authentic prestructures, they believed, would dissolve into the body of the revolution (i.e., Buber's Full Cooperative, Dewey's Great Community), like surgical thread into a healing wound. Such a view of prestructures presumed the organic interrelationship between means and ends, and the pedagogical value of what Buber called "the real filled Present." His obstetrical formulation of the issue was *non pareil*: "revolution is . . . a delivering force whose function is to set free and authenticate . . . the hour of revolution is not an hour of begetting but an hour of birth—provided there was a begetting beforehand" (*PU*, 44–45). On Buber's account, radical social change, if it is to be real change and not just changeover, must occur incrementally, melioristically; "on dove's feet," in the metaphor of Nietzsche, never cataclysmically. "The continual becoming of humanity," Buber wrote in a Deweyean tone of voice, is the litmus test of democratic social experience. Consistent with their developmental and organic understanding of structure-making, both held, then, that a society is a bona fide community *if and only if* it is "a community of communities," if and only if it is permeatively communitarian, or as Buber put it, "community all through"

Although Buber and Dewey rejected a vulgar economistic understanding of communalism, neither of them denied that voluntary and egalitarian economic relations were a necessary condition of Gemeinschaft-type community. Communal autonomy without generalized economic self-management was, to both, an arch built on one side only. As Buber told a socialist meeting in 1928, real community presumes democratic administration of a common life, that is, "real fellowship and real work Guilds" (*PU*, 15). And this included, he did not back off from saying, holding "the real things of their common life in common"; in other words, a kind of primitive communism, like that prescribed, say, by the Book of Acts.[19] Fellowship to him was not a sonorous title or something merely honorific. It described the mutualism and "reciprocity of service" inscribed by free economic relations, and by, as I argue below, the politics of federation. Indeed, for Buber economic mutualism and political federation were the two sides of the same Jovian medal of community; and through their pacific dovetailing, he offered, "the whole nation will become a body" (*PU*, 33). Analogously, Dewey asserted the essentiality of dealienated economic relations to the Great Community, even if he also, like Buber, believed that economic results by themselves did not constitute a sufficient condition for radical social change. Rarely given their due, even by his followers, Dewey's concepts of aesthetic labor and worker self-management, were central, if underdeveloped, features of his social philosophy, and specifically of his understanding of the meaning of community. And they implied, or at least were consistent with, as I have written elsewhere, an anarcho-communal vision of a federated concert of self-managed eco-democracies.[20]

Dewey argued the dependency of economic factors on what Buber referred to as "the social principle—the principle of inner cohesion, collaboration and mutual stimulation" (*PU*, 80). His graceless utilitarian language often led his untutored readers to misconstrue him as a homemade American version of Jeremy Bentham. But community without common faith, faith in the ameliorative and redemptive possibilities of shared experience, he wanted to be understood as saying, was but a pale simulacrum of the Great Community. He would have agreed with Buber's judgment that "No disturbances on the periphery can serve as a substitute for the living relation with the Centre" (*I and Thou*, 49), even if he figured, as I have indicated, the center differently from the way Buber did. Readers of Dewey who claim that he failed to grasp the existentiality of the social principle confuse his linguistic infelicity with conceptual incapacity. Like Buber, Dewey knew that the ties that bind nutritiously in any community are born from the "texture of friendships and attachments" that accrue therein. His celebratory description of a small Wiltshire village, whose members were bound by reciprocal solidarity and mutual aid, and not just commonly shared interests, recalled, in its recitation of the educative moral and social virtues of such a polity, the ancient Greek concept of *paideia* shorn of its insularity and disequalities (Dewey 1954, 41). Unfortunately, Dewey's often impersonal and reified mode of speech tended to obscure his personalism and dialogicism. But a close and unbiased reading of his major philosophical writings argues, I believe, the case for Dewey as a kind of genteel, Yankee personalist, for whom, like Buber, community was a redemptive dialogic alternative to classical liberalism's bifurcated world of private satisfactions and public virtue.

Earlier, I remarked on Dewey's flirtation with "the idea of Federation," an idea, I said, which he did not clearly instantiate. When we turn to Buber, however, we find a fully articulated social philosophy premised on the idea of federation. Indeed, his important normative ethical notion of directly willed realization was inextricably connected to his idea of federation. Buber began with "small organic units and their organic-federative growth," "a network of Settlements, territorially based and federatively constructed . . . allowing the most diverse social forms to exist side by side, but always aiming at the new organic whole" (*PU*, 79). Following Gustav Landauer, he figured his Community of communities at the other end of a "great arch" constructed by the continual self-expansion of small, organic groups (48). And like Dewey, he understood that the construction of such an arch was contingent upon the eradication of introjected or internalized "statehood," that is, entrenched statist psychical mechanisms. If "broken open, the slumbering, immemorial reality," "the long memories of communal units" of which Landauer spoke, Buber hypothesized, would come to the fore, and energize the communitarian socialist deconstruction of statist society (49). Like Dewey, he reasoned that only self-managing persons could be expected to successfully undercut and subvert established power on behalf of a social vision of generalized self-management. In particular, Buber's admonition that representation "from outside," even when voluntary, decommunalizes, disempowers, and disenfranchises "a human group" (133), seems today especially prescient in light of recent global political history, from Gaza to Goma.

The gist of this short discussion of Buber's and Dewey's communalisms is that there is arguably a convergent set of hypotheses about self and society in their writings, notwithstanding differences in emphasis—Dewey's is more aesthetic, Buber's more prophetic. Clearly, Buber's social vision was less schematic or abstract than Dewey's, and we find in his writings a more concretely and consistently developed concept of a communitarian socialist practice. Beyond this, there was no soul in Dewey, by which I mean no real understanding of love as the binding and fructifying agency of community. For him, "communication can alone create a great community" (Dewey 1954, 142), and his meaning here was semiological, not agapistic, erotic, or filial. The construction of "signs and symbols" commensurate with the press of history was, for Dewey, a desideratum of an emancipatory social practice. As the conclusion to *The Public and Its Problems* made tolerably, if also paradoxically clear, the dominant sensory mode in a Deweyean visual and dialogic polity was hearing, not vision. Now, hearing, of course, like the other proximate sensory modes, is more participatory, less spectatorial, than vision. Dewey apparently wanted to remind his readers that the abstract sensory mode of vision could open a Pandora's box of monologism, and ought not to be, then, the perceptual center around which a liberatory communal experience is themed. But if he traded the soliloquizing, spectating eye (I?) of narcissistic self-absorption for the participatory democratic ears of free and open communication, Dewey did not seem to grasp the open heart of love below the open ears of dialogue, which arguably assured the possibility of pedagogical and redemptive hearing. By contrast, love was at the center of Buber's social vision; and indeed his vision of the Full Cooperative is best read, I would offer, as a vision of love's body, communally reinvented. Moreover, Buber did not merely talk about dialogue and the central role it plays in communal experience. He worked out its "basic movements" as part of his ontology of the interhuman. Dewey, on the other hand, did not seem to see the profound psychological and spiritual ramifications of the dialogical, nor did he possess Buber's extraordinary ear for its "wordless depths" and subtle epiphanies. Yet both their voices, I would submit, were healing contributions to a broken world, albeit in different ways; and both, it is not irrelevant to point out, remain models of sanity and wisdom in a century bereft of both, a century lacerated by daemonic evil and political madness, whose bequests include Auschwitz, Hiroshima, the Soviet gulags, Vietnam, Johannesburg, and, more recently, Somalia, Bosnia, and Rwanda. Dewey's Enlightenment over-belief in reason perhaps blinded him to the existence of daemonic evil, relegating him to the status of a pre-Holocaust thinker.[21] But even if, in this respect, Buber is the more contemporary thinker, Dewey still remains for us a mine of moral courage and social insight as this century comes to a close and the next one begins. At a time when communities everywhere are hanging by their teeth, and the right to privacy is debated ad nauseam in bourgeois political circles, Dewey and Buber remind us that there is perhaps a prior and more precious, if also traditionally politically unarticulated, right to community that deserves our philosophic attention; and that the building of a new Ark of the Covenant is perhaps also the desideratum of a free human future everywhere.

NOTES

1. Buber's *Between Man and Man* contains a minor reference to Dewey's concept of habit (111), a reference which is repeated by Maurice Friedman in *Martin Buber: The Life of Dialogue* (182), and by Ernst Simon in "Martin Buber, The Educator," in *PMB* (549). Dewey's ignorance or disregard of an important contemporary thinker was not unusual. Despite the emphasis he placed on history as a matrix of inquiry, he often seemed completely oblivious of the work of his contemporaries, including those, like Buber, with whom he shared common intellectual ground.

2. We find, for example, in the indices to *The Library of Living Philosophers* volumes on Dewey and Buber, no references to Buber in the Dewey volume and only four incidental references to Dewey in the Buber volume, two of which occur in an article on "Buber and American Pragmatism," by Paul Pfuetze, which, like his book on Buber and Mead, joins them, but only incidentally mentions Dewey. One would have thought that Pfuetze's assertion of the identity of Mead's and Dewey's "general position" would have encouraged Buber and Dewey scholars, who were persuaded by Pfuetze's linking of Buber and Mead, to begin to think at least about the possible philosophical kinship of Buber and Dewey. But this has not happened. See Paul Pfuetze, *Self, Society, Existence: Human Nature and Dialogue in the Thought of George Herbert Mead and Martin Buber* (New York: Harper Torchbooks, 1961), 356 n. 18. Even more striking is the almost complete absence of any reference to Buber in

the secondary literature on Dewey's social philosophy, including his discussion of community.

3. Especially relevant here was Dewey's discussion of the molluscan self in *Freedom and Culture* (New York: Capricorn Books, 1963), 166. On the concept of relation starvation, see John J. McDermott, *Streams of Experience* (Amherst: University of Massachusetts Press, 1986), 141–56.

4. Martin Buber, *I and Thou* (Smith), 54. To which we should add Dewey's observation that "individuals are overwhelmed and emotionally confused by publicized reverberation of isolated events." Cited in *The Philosophy of John Dewey*, ed. John J. McDermott (Chicago: The University of Chicago Press, 1981), 691 (n.b., cited in text as McDermott *PJD*).

5. Recent positivistic rereadings of Dewey by Richard Rorty and others, which argue for a de-metaphysicalized Dewey, fatally misread him, and bequeath to us a positivistic fiction blown by the winds of contemporary doctrine, but not the Dewey Dewey thought he was, nor the Dewey I mean to speak about here.

6. Martin Buber, "Replies to my Critics," in *PMB*, 704: "Since I have never succeeded in grasping a metaphysical totality and accordingly in building a metaphysical system, I must content myself with impressions."

7. I owe this reading of Dewey's metaphysics to John J. McDermott.

8. See my "The Affective is the Effective: Politics as Environmental Sculpture," Dewey prize essay awarded by the Center For Dewey Studies 1977, unpublished.

9. See *The Culture of Experience*, 118–149, for a Deweyean argument against Marcuse's concept. As Dewey wrote: "The effort to maintain directly a consummatory experience or to repeat it exactly is the source of unreal sentimentality and of insincerity." See *The Quest For Certainty* (New York: Minton, Balch & Co., 1929), 236. Dewey's concept of aesthetic recurrence is found in *Art as Experience* (New York: Minton, Balch & Co., 1934), 166.

10. Arthur S. Lothstein, *From Privacy to Praxis: The Case for John Dewey as a Radical Social Philosopher* (Ann Arbor: University Microfilms International, 1980).

11. See *From Privacy to Praxis: The Case for John Dewey as a Radical Social Philosopher*.

12. *Experience and Nature*, 360. Buber's version of this is: "Were there no more genuine dialogue, there would also be no more poetry" (*KM*, 111).

13. *The Philosophy of John Dewey*, 520. And: "The sick cannot heal themselves by means of their disease, and disintegrated individuals

can achieve unity only as the dominant energies of community life are incorporated to form their minds" (605).

14. *I and Thou*, 63–64; 103–4. The concept of affirmative culture derives from Herbert Marcuse. See his *Negations*, trans. Jeremy J. Shapiro (Boston: Beacon Press, 1968), 88–133.

15. See my "Salving from the Dross: John Dewey's Anarcho-Communalism," *The Philosophical Forum* 10 (1), 99.

16. See Peter T. Manicas, "John Dewey: Anarchism and the Political State," *Transactions of the Charles Sanders Peirce Society 28* (2) 133–58.

17. See C. Wright Mills, *Sociology and Pragmatism* (New York: Oxford University Press, 1966), for the most sophisticated version of this reading of Dewey.

18. Cited by Herbert Marcuse, *Reason and Revolution* (Boston: Beacon Press, 1960), 397.

19. The injunction of Acts 2:44 and 4:32 to hold all things common was the scriptural basis for many of the celebrated nineteenth-century American communal experiments. See Arthur Bestor, *Backwoods Utopias* (Phila: University of Pennsylvania Press, 1970), 6.

20. "Salving From the Dross: John Dewey's Anarcho-Communalism," 98.

21. See John Dewey, *The Later Works, 1925–1953, 2: 1935–1937*, ed. Jo Ann Boydston, intro. John J. McDermott, xxxi–xxxii.

REFERENCES CITED IN TEXT BUT NOT IN NOTES

Buber, Martin. *BMM, I and Thou* (Smith), *KM, PU, PW*, "Replies."
Dewey, John. (1958). *Experience and Nature*. New York: Dover.
———. (1954). *The Public and Its Problems*. Denver: Alan Swallow.
Schilpp, Paul Arthur, and Friedman, Maurice. *PMB*.

CHAPTER 3

IS A DIALOGICAL THEOLOGY POSSIBLE?

MANFRED VOGEL

The objective of this paper is to examine whether it is feasible to pursue the theological enterprise in the context of the philosophy of dialogue and, if so, what form the enterprise must assume. This examination is especially needed, seeing that Martin Buber, the most profound and insightful formulator of the philosophy of dialogue, seems to have had a basically negative evaluation of the enterprise of theology and, indeed, refused to call himself a theologian.[1]

At first sight, Buber's position regarding the enterprise of theology may seem puzzling. After all, much of what he has to say impinges on various facets of the phenomenon of religion: describing, analyzing, and criticizing the structure of faith in its various manifestations and expressions—e.g., his study of the Prophetic and Hasidic expression within Judaism, of the faith of Jesus and the religion of Paul within Christianity, or of the mystical expression in both the religious experience of the East and of the West. What he has to say about all these topics is articulated ultimately in rational discourse. And is not the enterprise of theology—broadly and generally speaking—rational discourse regarding the various facets of the phenomenon of religion?

Buber's somewhat negative response to the enterprise of theology and his rejection of the role of theologian must rest on his particular understanding of theological pursuit. It seems that he understands this enterprise in terms of the literal signification of the word "theology" and, even more specifically, of "natural theology." Thus, he understands the enterprise of theology to be the endeavor to establish a "logos" (i.e., a body of discourse or of knowledge) with regard to the "theos" (i.e., to the divine being); and furthermore, to establish it through the method of inference and projection from the human experience of itself and its world (this being the signification of the qualification "natural" attached to the enterprise called "natural theology"). But if Buber rejects the enterprise of theology because he understands it specifically as natural theology, then his rejection is understandable and justified. For a good case can be made that the enterprise of natural theology, as here delineated, is basically incompatible with Buber's dialogical philosophy.

The incompatibility lies essentially in the fact that in Buber's dialogical understanding the only God that is viable is the God to whom one says "Thou" (the Thou-God), whereas the enterprise of natural theology can deliver at best only the God about whom one speaks—an It-God. In dialogical relationship then, only a Thou-being (the realm of ontology is here, by definition, exclusively the realm of Thou-beings) can be the focus—God who by his very essence is a personal being, conscious and aware. He cannot be an It-God (i.e., an impersonal being devoid of consciousness, the mere expression of blind power). Now, a Thou-being, by its very ontological constitution, can only be an ontological subject and not an ontological object, which is to say that in its interactions with others it can be implicated only as an end-in-itself and never as a means to some other end. This further implies that it can only be encountered and addressed but never inferred or described. Natural theology, however, by the very essence of its methodology can only arrive at a God that is inferred and described, that is, an It-God, a God that is an ontological object. There is thus an unbridgeable gulf between the God of dialogical philosophy and that of natural theology. We have here not merely a quantitative but a qualitative difference, expressed so poignantly by Pascal, as between the God of the philosophers and the God of Abraham, the God of Isaac, and the God of Jacob. From the perspective of dialogical thinking, the enterprise of natural theology is not only totally irrelevant and valueless, it is actually misleading and counter-productive, seeing that its It-God is a false god, an idol. As such, dialogical thinking must reject natural theology in no uncertain terms, as indeed Buber does.

This incompatibility between natural theology and the philosophy of dialogue can also be seen to be reflected in those religious traditions which are delineated and informed by dialogical teaching; namely, the religious traditions of biblical faith. Here, the clearest and foremost instance that would readily suggest itself is Judaism or, more precisely, the biblical prophetic strand and the rabbinic-halachic strand within this tradition. And, indeed, there can be no question that historically speaking there has been essentially no expression of the enterprise of natural theology within these strands. This is no accident, for these strands reflect dialogical thinking. Christianity, too, or more precisely, that strand within it which is essentially grounded or anchored in the *Weltanschauung* of biblical faith—the Hebraic-grounded strand—has also eschewed the enterprise of natural theology. At the same time, however, it must be admitted that the explicit articulation of this strand within the course of the history of Christian thought was, with a few exceptions, rather minimal (the most notable exceptions being Reformation theology in the sixteenth century and neo-Orthodox or Crisis theology in the twentieth century). We cannot deny, however, that the biblical dialogical thought is present and essential to the life of Christianity. Thus, Buber's rejection of the enterprise of natural theology is not only dictated by his philosophy of dialogue but is in consonance with important strands within both Judaism and Christianity.

But if pursuing the enterprise of theology along the line of natural theology is not compatible with dialogical thinking, can one pursue the enterprise along a different line that would be compatible? The alternative that would naturally suggest itself is to pursue the enterprise of theology along the line of what may be called "revelatory theology," for this method of theology seems to escape the problematic that arises between the enterprises of natural theology and dialogical philosophy.

How so? Revelatory theology is the enterprise which endeavors to establish a body of knowledge regarding the divine, starting not from the human experience but from divine revelation. We can have such a body of knowledge regarding the divine because the divine chose to impart it to us. Both revelatory theology and natural theology endeavor to establish a body of knowledge regarding the divine. The change that revelatory theology introduces is only with respect to the starting-point of the enterprise—while natural theology locates it in human experience, revelatory theology locates it in divine revelation.

But precisely by virtue of this change revelatory theology escapes the problematic that natural theology precipitates for dialogical thinking. For revelatory theology does not implicate a God that is inferred, demonstrated, or proven, that is, an object, an It-God. On the contrary, the God implicated in revelatory theology, far from being an object, is clearly a subject. After all, it is a God who reveals, imparts, and discloses, and only a Thou-God and never an It-God can reveal or disclose Himself. Thus there is no discrepancy between the kind of God required by dialogical understanding and the kind implicated by revelatory theology; if anything, it is the one and the same kind of God—the Thou-God.

And as such, doing theology along the lines of revelatory theology should be eminently acceptable to dialogical thinking. Dialogical philosophy, therefore, excludes only the doing of natural theology, not *all* theology.

Indeed, one can see the stance of revelatory theology manifest itself in significant segments of the theological thought of our century. This is particularly noticeable in the theology pursued within Protestant Christianity, especially by Karl Barth and the whole school of neo-Orthodox or dialectical theology. Under the impact of rediscovering the Weltanschauung of biblical faith, this theology uncompromisingly rejects natural theology and turns instead to the pursuit of theology along the lines of revelatory theology. In Catholic theology, too, one can detect some tendencies (under the impact, perhaps, of Existentialism and the consequent mitigation of the influence of neo-Thomism) of moving away somewhat from that tradition; long and venerable pursuit of natural theology towards some form of revelatory theology (one thinks, for example, of Karl Rahner or Yves Congar).

Judaism has pursued natural theology very little to begin with. Indeed, the theology that manifests itself in the religious tradition of Judaism is revelatory from the onset of Rabbinic Judaism. I make this claim on grounds that in the context of Rabbinic Judaism, the content of faith that the community is supposed to possess is clearly claimed to be grounded in a revelation, namely, the Sinaitic revelation. And as such, this content of faith must be qualified as revelatory even though it may not be so decisively clear that it can be characterized as constituting a theology. The reason for this unclarity is that while Rabbinic Judaism clearly claims that the body of knowledge in its possession is ultimately *derived* from the divine, it does not, in turn, equally claim that it ultimately also *refers* to the divine—indeed, it does not. What Rabbinic Judaism knows comes from God but has to do with matters relating to man. This body of knowledge consists merely of the divine's intentions for and expectations of human beings; it says nothing about the ontological nature of the divine. Now, whether or not the *interpretation* of such a disclosure (i.e., what would constitute the enterprise of the *Halacha* in Rabbinic Judaism) can properly qualify as an enterprise of theology is open to debate. But clearly, if one were to conclude that it does, then the enterprise of Halacha in Rabbinic Judaism would certainly have to be taken as an enterprise in *revelatory* theology. And inasmuch as Rabbinic Judaism by its very essence constitutes itself in terms of the Halachic enterprise, Rabbinic Judaism must be taken to pursue and possess a *revelatory* theology.

Still, notwithstanding these important instances of revelatory theology within religious traditions that clearly reflect the dialogical orientation, the enterprise of revelatory theology also runs into a serious problem with the dialogical orientation. Indeed, Buber clearly saw and identified this problematic. The problematic lies in the fact that the enterprise of revelatory theology must imply the transfer of content from the divine to the human; after all, this is precisely what the notion of revelation signifies. And this, in turn, means that the relation involved here is a relation moving in a one-way direction, a direction from the divine to the human. But this relation cannot possibly be an I-Thou relation since an I-Thou relation cannot be a one-way relation, but only a relation of mutuality, a relation oscillating between the two poles of the relation, thus moving simultaneously in both directions. But then the divine implicated in this relation cannot be a Thou-God (and, indeed, the relation itself cannot be a relation of authentic revelation) but only an It-God. However, as we have seen, dialogical thinking cannot countenance an It-God; by its very essence it requires that the divine be a Thou-God.

Thus, revelatory theology comes to present for dialogical thinking the same kind of problematic that natural theology presents; namely, in both cases the divine can constitute itself only as an It-God. The only difference between the two theologies is that in natural theology the relation is a one-way relation by virtue of being a relation of inference (a relation in which the divine is the object, the action of the relation) while in revelatory theology the relation is a one-way relation by virtue of *contentful* revelation that is transmitted (a relation in which man is the object of the action of the relation). In natural theology, the being that perpetrates the It-action (inferring and demonstrating) is man, while in revelatory theology the being that perpetrates the It-action (transmitting content) is the divine. But in both cases the God that is implicated is an It-God. Thus, not only natural theology but also revelatory theology cannot be acceptable to dialogical thinking.

Thus, it would seem that the mere change in source and direction within the enterprise of theology is not enough to render the enterprise acceptable to dialogical thinking. Indeed, it is not so much a case of not doing enough of the right thing, as of doing the wrong thing, of applying the wrong remedy. The problem does not lie in the source from which the theological enterprise proceeds, but in there being such a one-way enterprise to begin with. For with respect to the philosophy of dialogue, God cannot be a direct and immediate object of a body of knowledge at all. Changing the source from which theology proceeds will not help us. What is needed is a change in the very signification of the noun *theology*, away from the literal signification of it as a body of knowledge regarding the divine. As long as we retain the literal signification we cannot avoid the consequence that the divine is a direct and immediate object of a body of knowledge.

In line with these considerations I will suggest, therefore, that we change the signification of the term *theology* in the following way: it is to signify a body of knowledge or discourse with regard to the content of faith of a religious tradition. Such a proposed change is by no means arbitrary or, indeed, radical; if anything, it is a natural and readily appreciated stretch of the original signification. For in the content of faith of practically every religious tradition the notion of the divine occupies a prominent position, and consequently any body of knowledge that impinges on such a content of faith would inescapably also impinge on the notion of the divine. As such, the notion of theology proposed here would still signify a body of knowledge that impinges on the divine but not exclusively so—it may also impinge on other notions, entities or activities that the content of faith of a religious tradition may encompass (for example, the community of faith, its worship, rituals, and institutions). It would appear, therefore, that the proposed new signification is eminently acceptable. After all, notions and terms when taken in the context of a living language are flexible, malleable, and capable of being stretched. And clearly, the stretch proposed here is very minimal, less prescriptive even than descriptive. For clearly in many instances the actual object of the theological enterprise is extended beyond the divine to the various other entities and practices that constitute the content of faith.

But the weighty advantage of our proposed definition lies in removing the divine from being the direct object of the activity that the term *theology* is to signify. Now the direct object of the activity constituting the enterprise of theology is no longer the divine but rather the content of faith of a religious tradition. And this should present no problem whatsoever for dialogical thinking. Certainly, the content of faith in this context can only be related to an It-entity. But a philosophy of dialogue does not require that the content of faith not be an It-entity. After all, the content of faith, unlike the divine, cannot be anything but an It-entity. For a content of faith is a body of beliefs and not a concrete personal being. Philosophy of dialogue is fully cognizant and accepting of this.

But not only does dialogical teaching have no problem relating to the content of faith as an It, it has no problem to relating to the divine when the divine is taken as a constituent entity of a content of faith. For then the relating to the divine is not direct but, so to speak, in a once-removed context. The once-removed context makes all the difference in the world. By means of it, the theologian is spared reducing the divine, in its objective ontological reality to an It-being. God remains the pure Thou-being beyond the content of faith that is the theologian's immediate object. Clearly, such a "content-of-faith theology" differs from natural theology in that its activity is not inference or demonstration. It is much closer to revelatory theology in that its core activity is interpretation. Both revelatory theology and content-of-faith theology constitute themselves through the pursuit of interpretation, except that for revelatory theology the body of material which is to be interpreted comes from the divine while for content-of-faith theology it comes from a community of faith. Now, there is no denying that the act of interpreting is an act in the It-domain. But because the direct object of interpretation here is not the divine being in its objective ontological reality, but a body of material, either disclosed by the divine (as in the case of revelatory theology) or established by a religious tradition (as in the case of content-of-faith theology), no problematic arises for dialogical thinking.

Revelatory theology, however, must still face the charge that, by the one-way relation of transmission it posits from the divine to the human, it reduces God to an It-being. And it is precisely at this point that the advantage of content-of-faith theology over revelatory theology, as far as dialogical thinking is concerned, can be clearly seen. For by shifting the source of the content that is to be interpreted by the theological enterprise away from the divine-being toward a religious tradition, content-of-faith theology avoids precipitating a problematic for dialogical thinking. Dialogical thinking can easily accept the It-status of religious traditions, for this in no way compromises the ontological reality of the divine as a Thou-being. So, there should be no problem whatsoever with the dialogical mode accepting the enterprise of theology when it is formulated in terms of a content-of-faith theology. Thus, one can conclude that there is after all a sense in which one can pursue the enterprise of theology within the context of the dialogical mode.

But even more, it seems to me that philosophy of dialogue actually gives rise to considerations that bring forth the pursuit of content-of-faith theology. This can be seen by focusing on the starting-point implicated in the pursuit of the theological enterprise.

Thus, clearly the starting-point of natural theology is the human being, the human experience of oneself and one's world. Here the theological enterprise infers claims regarding the divine from human experience; it proceeds from the human pole to the divine pole. As against this, it is equally clear that the starting-point of revelatory theology is the divine (i.e., the divine's revelation, disclosure, of Himself). Here the theological enterprise interprets a content impinging upon the divine which is transmitted from the divine to the human; it proceeds from the divine pole to the human pole. But if the problem for the dialogical mode lies in the very placing of the starting-point in one pole or the other, then the only possibility left here for pursuing the theological enterprise is when the starting point is to be located in the between, in the very relation subsisting between the human and the divine.

But for this alternative to be truly valid, the relation must be a relation of true mutuality, of true reciprocity. This implies that the relation must at one and the same time oscillate in both directions between the two poles. It certainly cannot be a one-way relation from one pole to another. Indeed, it is precisely because such a one-way relation characterizes the formulation of both natural and revelatory theology that dialogical teaching objects to these theologies. But neither can the relation be constituted by two opposing one-way relations proceeding simultaneously. The difficulties which pertain to a one-way relation must also apply here. To escape these difficulties, the relation must originate in itself, in its own betweenness, moving simultaneously in the opposite directions of both its poles (or, more accurately, the relation that arises is but an oscillation between two poles, the poles being constituted secondarily by the relation as its demarcation at either end). Only where the relation is ontologically prior to its poles is it a relation of authentic mutuality.

And lastly, it follows from the preceding observations that a relation of authentic mutuality cannot possibly have content. For the moment content is injected, the relation per force becomes the transmitter of that content and as such is inescapably reduced to a one-way relation—relation moving from the giver of the content to its receiver. If the starting point, then, is to be validly placed in the between, the relation implicated must be a contentless relation.

These, then, are the characteristics of the relation that can serve as the alternative locus for the starting point of the theological enterprise in contrast to the human and divine loci—the relation must be a relation of authentic mutuality, it must have ontological priority, and it must be devoid of content. But clearly, such a relation is feasible only in the context of the Thou-domain; indeed, the characteristics of the relation delineated here are identical with the definitive characteristics of the I-Thou relation. For it is of the very essence of the I-Thou relation to be authentically mutual, ontologically prior, and free of transmitted content. So, if the starting-point of the theological enterprise is to be placed neither in the human nor in the divine but in the relation between them, this relation can only be an I-Thou and not an I-It relation. It must be a relation whose poles constitute themselves as Thou-beings, not It-beings; and this, in turn, means that such a theological enterprise (seeing that the enterprise is determined, in an essential sense, by the nature and location of its starting point) can arise only in the context of the Thou-domain. As such, it is clear that the pursuit of this kind of theological enterprise not only precipitates no problematic for dialogical thinking but is the only theological enterprise consistent with it. And in view of this, it may not be inappropriate to refer to this kind of theology, in contradistinction to natural and revelatory theology, as *dialogical theology*.

But, granting the feasibility of what we called dialogical theology, what is its connection, if any, to content-of-faith theology? In fact, dialogical theology necessarily implies a content-of-faith theology, indeed, to such an extent that the two become really one and the same. Because dialogical theology starts in the relation which oscillates between the human and the divine, and because this relation, as necessarily an I-Thou relation, cannot have anything to do with content, dialogical theology cannot really signify an enterprise of theology. For clearly, the enterprise of theology must contain content. The content can be generated by the enterprise itself (as, for example, is the case in natural theology) or it can be presented from the outside and merely interpreted by the enterprise (as is the case in revelatory theology). But content must be present if the enterprise is to be a theological enterprise. Since dialogical theology, as delineated here thus far, cannot come to possess content in either of these two ways—an I-Thou relation cannot possess, let alone generate, any content—it falls into being a self-contradictory notion. It cannot fly as a theological enterprise. It negates itself; it unravels or explodes before it can take off.

It would be wrong to go to the other extreme and conclude that dialogical theology is a complete nonstarter. For it clearly points to the possibility of a very valid and important experience—the encounter between the human and the Thou-God. While the relation in which dialogical theology wants to place the starting point of the theological enterprise cannot, on its own, give rise to the theological enterprise, it can constitute the original, primal experience which, when elaborated and interpreted by other agents, can give rise to a tenable theological enterprise. Briefly delineated, the following scenario can be supposed: a contentless encounter of pure mutual confirmation between the Thou-God and the human takes place which, communicated and remembered, gives rise to a community of faith. This community then generates narration, beliefs, symbols, and rituals—in short, a religious tradition—which serves to transmit the memory of the encounter to future generations. Now, it is this religious tradition which can be taken as the content which, by lending itself to interpretation, generates a theological enterprise. So, dialogical theology, though it has its starting point in the primary relation that subsists between the human and the divine, cannot and does not begin to function as an enterprise of theology until it has content placed at its disposal by a community of faith. But as such, what we have here is nothing else but what we referred to as content-of-faith theology. Dialogical theology, when it functions as a theological enterprise, is nothing else but content-of-faith theology.

Thus, there is one formulation of the theological enterprise which should be acceptable to dialogical thinking, namely, the formulation we referred to as content-of-faith or dialogical theology. For if a dialogical position is to express itself at all through the intellectual medium (and clearly, such expression is an essential and fundamental need for it), it can do it only in terms of content-of-faith or dialogical theology. As such, the dialogical position can not only accept a dialogical or content-of-faith formulation of theological enterprise, it actually calls it forth.

Still, before accepting this conclusion, we must dispose of a difficulty raised for us in Malcolm Diamond's excellent essay "Dialogue and Theology" (Schilpp and Friedman, PMB, 235–47). He tries to determine what kind of theology, if any, Buber could pursue. Diamond argues that neither what he refers to as ontological theology (i.e., that enterprise which undertakes to delineate in a rational and systematic discourse the ontological structure of the divine [241, 243–44]) nor what he refers to as apologetic theology (i.e., that enterprise which directs itself "towards the philosophically oriented non-believer" and attempts to defend "the faith in philosophical terms" [247]) are consistent with Buber's dialogical philosophy. The only kind of theology that Buber could possibly pursue is what Diamond refers to as confessional theology (i.e., that enterprise which attempts "to reformulate the faith in contemporary terms for those who are already passionately engaged" [247]).

Diamond observes that while ontological and apologetic theology are by their very essence constituted as rational discourse, confessional theology is not; neither does the dialogical orientation lend itself to rational discourse.[2] Indeed, its notion of the divine as the Eternal-Thou is by its very essence paradoxical. For the notion of the Eternal-Thou signifies an absolute personality—that is, it combines "the absolute with the particular, with the concrete . . . unlimited Being becomes, as absolute person, my partner" (EG, 51–61; quoted in PMB, 242–43). The notion is paradoxical because the adjective "absolute" denotes a being that is infinite, while the noun "person" denotes a particular being reduced "to the finite level as a person among persons" (PMB, 246). Thus, we have here in the notion of the Eternal-Thou a reality representing "a unity of contraries" where the "contradictoriness . . . is transcended in the dialogic character of the lived experience" and can be expressed not in rational terms but "only in the language of paradox" (246). And this is precisely what confessional theology (but not ontological or apologetic theology) can do because it is not concerned with systematic consistency in presenting its view of God but rather with evoking the memory of past encounters and pointing the way to future ones (241). So, according to Diamond, Buber's presentation of the dialogical mode would countenance the enterprise of theology only if it is to be taken as a kind of poetry, distancing the criterion of logical consistency and accepting the language of paradox.

But, if this is so, then there is no theological enterprise whatsoever that is really applicable to the dialogical context. For no enterprise that rejects the canons of logical consistency can by definition be an enterprise of theology, seeing that the "logos" that theology aims to establish is necessarily rational. A theology that acquiesces in paradox is a contradiction in terms. And as such, it follows that Diamond's notion of a confessional theology is self-contradictory.

True, I also altered the strict literal signification of the notion of theology. But my alteration impinged upon the signification of the "theos" and not upon the signification of the "logos" as these operate in the notion of theology. My alteration impinged upon the object (i.e., the parameters) of the enterprise and not upon the nature of its activity, of its method. One can change the parameters or even the object and still retain the same enterprise; but Diamond would change the nature of theological activity itself. While my alteration was merely one of stretching the literal signification of the notion of theos, the alteration of logos implicated by Diamond is a complete reversal and undermining of that signification. Thus, I have to conclude that because of its incompatibility with the nature of the theological enterprise, Diamond's confessional theology is not theologically tenable. Consequently, it cannot be taken as a valid *theological* alternative or substitute to the content-of-faith theology that I have advanced.

But this rebuttal does not as yet dispose of the real challenge that Diamond's essay presents. The real challenge lies in its clearly implied contention that confessional theology is not just another alternative formulation of the theological enterprise that is viable in the context of dialogical thinking but that it is the *only* formulation that could possibly be viable in such a context. For it claims that no formulation that rejects paradoxical or nonrational discourse can validly capture or articulate Buber's dialogical philosophy. But this means that if the theological enterprise is essentially rational, then the dialogical mode can countenance no theological formulation whatsoever. For, according to Diamond's contention, whatever is theological should be unacceptable to the dialogical position; while, according to my claim, paradoxical formulations, however acceptable to the dialogical mode, cannot belong to the theological enterprise. Thus, Diamond's contention, if valid, would force us to conclude that there is indeed an unbridgeable incompatibility between the dialogical position and the theological enterprise.

But is Diamond's contention valid? Clearly, the answer to this depends on whether Diamond is right in claiming that dialogical philosophy is, in its very delineation of the divine, inescapably paradoxical. Diamond bases his claim on the fact that by its very essence the dialogical position can constitute the divine only as an Eternal Thou, that is, as an absolute person (absolute corresponds to "eternal", and "person" corresponds to "Thou" [PMB, 242]). And such a constitution characterizes an entity that is, by its very nature, finite (i.e., "person"), by an adjective that signifies infinity (i.e., the adjective "absolute"). Thus, the characterization of absolute person states that a finite being is infinite, and this is clearly the stating of a paradox (242, 246).[3]

Of course, there can be no quarrel with the claim that to ascribe to one and the same entity, at one and the same time, both finitude and infinitude is paradoxical. To the extent that "absolute" is to signify infinite and "person" is to signify finite, the expression "absolute person" states a paradox. But is it really the case that "absolute" can only signify infinite and "person" can only implicate a being that is finite? I do not think so.

I would submit that such significations apply only when these terms are taken in the context of the It-domain. For in the It-domain every entity is inescapably quanticized; an It-being, any and every It-being, is per force a quanticized entity, and consequently a quantitative comparison of greater and smaller or of more and less would always be applicable to It-beings. Inasmuch as "absolute" signifies ultimacy, and everything within the It-domain is quanticized, ultimacy is also per force quanticized and comes to signify the infinite. And by the same token, since "person" in its own terms does not in this context signify the ultimate, it must per force signify an entity that is finite—"a person among persons." Thus, when grasped from the perspective of the It-domain, the notion of an absolute person is indeed paradoxical—it does signify that a finite entity is infinite. In the context of the Thou domain, however, "absolute" and "person" cannot possibly have these same significations. For the Thou-domain is by its very essence nonquanticized. Therefore, comparisons in terms of more and less or greater and smaller are simply not feasible here; consequently, the notions of infinite and finite are not applicable either. As such, "absolute" cannot signify here infinite nor can "person" implicate finitude. In the context of the Thou-domain, "person" signifies a being that is constituted as a Thou and what "absolute" signifies is the characterization of totality and exclusiveness. Therefore, what "absolute person" signifies is a being that is constituted totally and exclusively as a Thou, a being that is a pure Thou, a being that is only a Thou and cannot be anything but a Thou. Evidently, such a notion is in no way paradoxical.

The notion of absolute person is paradoxical only if "absolute" is taken in a quanticized sense and "person" is taken in the sense of a *human* person, which is to say as signifying not a pure Thou-being but rather an It-Thou being, a being where the Thou is refracted through the It-domain. But it is precisely the point of our argument that these moves are unjustified—"absolute" need not be taken in quanticized terms, and "person" should not refer here to the human person but to the divine person—therefore not to an It-Thou being but to a pure Thou-being. When "person" refers to a pure Thou-being and "absolute" signifies exclusivity of kind and not quantization within a kind, there is no paradox involved in the notion of absolute person.

If the notion of the divine as absolute person is not paradoxical when its signification is delineated in the context of the Thou-domain, then dialogical philosophy as such is also not paradoxical. But if it is not inherently paradoxical, it need not confine itself only to formulations that are amenable to paradoxical discourse. Indeed, just the reverse is the case—seeing that its notion of the divine is not paradoxical, the dialogical mode can readily accept formulations that exclude any turning to paradoxical discourse and insist on a discourse that is exclusively rational. Now, given my contention that rational discourse constitutes the very essence of the theological enterprise and that, therefore, any formulation that claims to be theological must consist of rational discourse, the dialogical position can readily countenance and accept formulations that are bona fide theological (theological in our sense of resorting exclusively to rational discourse). Diamond's claim that it can countenance only formulations that resort to poetic discourse (i.e., to discourse that is amenable to paradox) and as such are, according to my contention, nontheological, evaporates. Indeed, as I have tried to show, dialogical philosophy can authentically and validly accept what we called content-of-faith theology.

NOTES

1. See, for example, Martin Buber, *I and Thou*, 1958 (Smith), 79–81, 112, 115–16; *BMM*, 1955, 184; *EG*, 1957, 28, 68, 128; "Response" in *Philosophical Interrogations* (Rome & Rome), 97; "Replies to My Critics" in *The Philosophy of Martin Buber*, 689–91, 713–14. See

also Paul E. Pfuetze, *Self, Society, Existence* (Harper Torchbooks), 276, 277, 279, 280, 295, 296; Donald J. Moore, *Martin Buber: Prophet of Religious Secularism*, (Philadelphia: JPS, 1974), xxii, 121, 122, 131, 170–73, 232.

2. As Diamond approvingly reminds us, Ronald Gregor Smith referred to *I and Thou*, the "bible" of dialogical philosophy, as a "philosophical-religious poem" and, "a poem should not mean but be" (*PMB*, 235, 238).

3. Diamond further suggests that this basic paradoxical description of the divine as being at one and the same time finite and infinite pervades the whole dialogical enterprise and gives rise to any number of other paradoxical stances, such as grace and freedom or the description of the divine as being at one and the same time both the wholly Other and the wholly Same (243).

REFERENCES

Buber, Martin. *EG.*
Diamond, Malcolm. (1967). "Dialogue and Theology." In Schilpp and Friedman, 235–47.
Schilpp, Paul Arthur, and Friedman, Maurice. (1967). *PMB.*

CHAPTER 4

INTO LIFE

The Legacy of Jewish Tradition in
Buber's Philosophy of Dialogue

S. DANIEL BRESLAUER

INTRODUCTION: TOWARD A LIFE OF UNITY

The phrase "into life" is associated with Martin Buber's friend and collaborator Franz Rosenzweig, who uses it to conclude his work *The Star of Redemption*. Despite the highly theoretical discussion within that book, Rosenzweig called his theology "empirical" since it pointed to the evidence of lived human experience. Whether studying the principles of God, humanity, and the world or expounding the meaning of the Jewish festival calendar, Rosenzweig intended his writings as a point of departure for daily Jewish existence. Nahum Glatzer notes this and uses the fact to emphasize the central theme of Rosenzweig's work: "The distant vision of truth does not lead into the beyond, but *into life*" (Glatzer 1961, xxvi). Too often theology gets lost in its own world of intellectual constructs. It forgets its connection with everyday existence. Rosenzweig stresses his rejection of such theology, which subsists only in abstraction.

Early twentieth-century Jewish thinkers bequeathed a legacy well represented by Rosenzweig's motto. While that motto derives from Rosenzweig's book, however, it fits many other Jewish thinkers who, as Bernard Martin recognizes, evince a common "existentialist concern" that always keeps in mind "the particular individual whose conflicts and struggles cannot, in their endless complexity and contrariety, be reduced to precise definition." The life at the heart of religious teaching, then, is the life of the individual. This life reflects the variety of experiences and forces out of which the individual draws strength in his or her recognition of the diversity and spontaneity characterizing human existence. No single formula or recipe exhausts the meaning of a tradition or a religion. Without a single definition, life tends toward the chaotic.

Bernard Martin considers Martin Buber to be an exemplar of Jewish existentialism. Buber's special contribution to the existentialist vision, however, emphasizes the unity that Judaism provides to life-experience. Buber comments that the theological notion of divine unity becomes the anthropological recognition of the wholeness of human life. "The Jewish teaching of the wholeness of life," he declares, "is the other side of the Jewish teaching of the unity of God" (OJ, 93). What distinguishes Jewish theology, according to Buber, is its refusal to accept limitations. No area of human life stands outside the range of divine concern. The biblical deity demonstrates an all-embracing involvement in civil and political action, in ritual and ethical legislation, in national, international, or private relationships. When a king such as Solomon seeks to redefine the spheres of the holy and the profane and confine the deity to a prescribed realm, prophets arise to oppose such a view. In opposition to the politics of the kings they reaffirm the unity of God by affirming the unity of public life.

Buber emphasizes a similar concern for unity in the life of the individual. While "in the first place" Jewish theology recognizes that God requires the sanctification of the entire culture of the Jewish people, "in the second place" it incorporates "the whole of the individual"—the mind and emotions, affairs of the marketplace and the sanctuary, of home life and public life. Judaism teaches every person how to unify life and to give it a single goal. The temptation to restrict religion and divinity to an isolated sphere arises in the life of the individual as in that of the community. Here too the prophets spoke out against disunity. They insisted on the coherence of every aspect of human life. Defenders of democracy sometimes mistake the anarchy of personal desires for freedom. Buber notes that the prophets spoke against "false emancipation of civilization" which liberates into meaninglessness (OJ, 194–96).

The prophetic protest against fragmentation continues as the genuine message of Judaism in the modern world. Buber notes that modernity testifies to continued Jewish religious life—flashes of spiritual insight illuminate Jewish existence. However, he hopes for a new synthesis which will once again unify the Jewish people and the individual Jew. He seeks a new expression of what he calls "the immortal Jewish unitary drive." In the name of this drive he embraces Zionism as a restatement of the original Jewish message. Returned to their own land, Jews can once again fulfill a "vocation among the nations" consisting of a realism that produces a unified nation in which individuals live a good life unified by commitment to a single ideal (*OJ*, 76–77).

Buber recognizes the problematic nature of this Jewish vocation. Not every Jew or Jewish community acclaims what Buber considers the immortal Jewish drive. Buber, therefore, calls for a renewal and self-transformation. A new Judaism will in fact be a restored Judaism, not a new creation but a return to the earlier principles. Buber seeks to reestablish the process of unification that characterizes Jewish religion at its start and at its most authentic. His basic call is for Jewish preparation. He demands that Jews express what he calls "the human attitude," and he considers "the molding of it and the renewal of Judaism" as two sides of a single process, essential for modern humanity (*OJ*, 52–55). His work may be understood as a programmatic plan that expresses each side of this process. Buber teaches humanity how to stand prepared for life. He teaches Jews how their tradition summons them into a unified life. The Jewish ideal of unity, its demand to be prepared for life, motivates every aspect of Buber's varied interpretations of Jewish religion. He sets forward a "program of Jewish revival" not by supplying a blueprint for a new religious order, but by reminding Jews of their original duties, of their primal responsibility of going forward into life. Whether reconsidering Jewish religious thought, the meaning of Jewish practice, or the structure of the Jewish community, Buber emphasizes an orientation toward life and the practical realities of daily experience.

HASIDIC TALES AND BUBER'S PRESENTATION OF JUDAISM

Buber embraced Hasidism as a vehicle for conveying the Jewish message to a humanity in need of it. He rejected the form that message took in traditional Jewish legalism because the rabbinical leaders often ignored the imperative to unify life in their understandable desire to maintain continuity of tradition. Rabbis fail, he thinks, because they preserve the outward form of the Jewish teaching without renewing the life toward which that teaching points (*HMM*, 25–26). Hasidism, however, preserves in its stories and lore the central message of Judaism. Humanity today can find in Hasidic stories the lesson that Judaism has conveyed through the centuries: Human life takes shape as a unified whole.

Hasidism transforms the central concepts of Judaism—God, Torah, and Israel—to make their inner message transparent. Traditional Jewish religion expresses a yearning for the divine, a quest for God. Buber suggests that for Hasidism this quest takes place in the mundane sphere of daily life. The true religious quest prepares for a meeting with the divine in daily life. For Hasidism, yearning for God entails a continual expectation and readiness for the holiness within ordinary existence (HMM, 94). Torah, the second central concept in Judaism, undergoes a similar change. Traditionally, Torah refers to the accepted canon of Jewish teachings, the texts of the written and oral law. Buber argues that in Hasidism Torah takes the form of life; true religion appears as the living Torah of the person with a unified soul. Torah in this sense consists not of a book that a person studies but a way in which a person lives. Hasidic tales identify Torah with people who "realize it in the simple unity of life" (HMM, 60). Torah stands for more than a written book; it takes shape as the book of a human being's life.

Buber affirmed the reality of the Jewish people, of the community of Israel. He understood this ideal in a peculiar way. True community emerges where people join together with a common goal and a central value. Hasidism associated this aspect of community with the Zaddik, the leader. The Hasidic anecdote focuses on the Zaddik as an exemplar, an image of the life of unity which provides the goal and model for every member of the community. Buber identifies the inspiration for Hasidic tales with the objective reality of true community as experienced by the Hasidim when associated with their leader. Israel, so understood, represents in its objectivity the unity that teachers convey to their students through their living relationship with one another (HMM, 25–26). Thus Hasidism teaches a three-fold lesson: true religiosity consists in preparing to meet God in every sphere of life, true education consists in living as a model of self-unification, and true community emerges from fidelity to a leader who teaches unification by example. These three lessons revive the inner message of Judaism even while apparently challenging the accepted forms of Jewish tradition.

Buber comments that Hasidism uses its tales to transmit the message of Judaism. It expresses its conviction about the importance of these tales through metaphors drawn from the myths of the Jewish mystical tradition. These myths, claims Buber, recognize the limits of discursive language. They realize that a central type of knowledge "is communicable only in images, not in concepts" (HMM, 33). Buber, no less than the Hasidim, realizes the limits of conceptual knowledge, knowing that images often serve when concepts fail. Not unsurprisingly, then, Buber turns to Hasidic tales to illustrate the basic message of Judaism. As he retells the stories he helps clarify for modern readers the lessons taught to older generations. A study of his renditions of the tales show how he refashioned his material to retain what he found to be its pristine meaning.

THE RETURN OF THE DEAD TO KEEP A PROMISE

In *The Legend of the Baal Shem*, one of the stories that Buber retells is called "From Strength to Strength," in which is found a common folk-motif—that of "Return of the Dead to Keep a Promise."[1] The story ultimately derives from an original tale in one of the first Hasidic collections of stories: *In Praise of the Baal Shem Tov, Shivhei Ha-Besht*. While basing his retelling on this tale, however, Buber introduces significant changes. He accurately reproduces the story's structure, its framework, and three-fold development. He includes important details from the original tale but transforms them to illustrate his orientation toward life. Although Buber wrote the tales included in *The Legend of the Baal Shem* in an early stage in his retelling of Hasidic stories, the narratives still reveal the main aspects of his approach. In this case, he uses the story to suggest two types of religiosity, to characterize the progress of human life through which Torah unfolds, and to derive a means of testing the nature of a religious community. Each part of the story suggests Buber's own way of interaction with Jewish tradition.

Each element in the story points to a different aspect of Jewish thought as refracted in the light of Hasidic insight. Four such elements constitute the basic structure of the tale. Three derive from the narrative plot itself as it moves from its problematic beginning to a final resolution. These derive from the motif of the return of the dead to fulfill a promise which develops through three stages. The first stage focuses on the promise made by a dying man to reveal the secrets of life after death. The first stage offers Buber an opportunity to contrast a narrow concern for external propriety to the life-affirming concern for all existence. In his description of the second stage Buber shows how education leads a person along the path of self-development, how Torah develops from life. The final stage focuses on the practical duties of the living, duties that Buber realizes entail attachment to a community. The three movements in the motif of the promise made by the dead combine to describe an ideal religiousness for modern Jews. This ideal influenced and shaped many modern Jewish thinkers, and its presence unifies the three parts of the tale by providing a framework for the story. Buber's use of such a framework echoes that of the original story itself. The early Hasidic writers also set their narrative within a wider context. Buber's characterization of the Jewish ideal draws upon, while changing, that of the first Hasidic narrators.

THE FRAMEWORK OF THE STORY

The creation of an ideal or a model religiosity often takes place in a polemical setting. Both Buber and *Shivhei Ha-Besht* place the story in just such a context. Buber portrays the conflict as that between two human types. He describes two friends who study together and seek to discover the meaning of truth. One friend follows the guidance of the Baal Shem Tov and affirms the value of life. The other, an inveterate skeptic, sees the multiplicity behind the apparent unity of appearance. While the first declares "It is," the other counters with "It is not." One friend acknowledges his need for advice and leadership; the other considers loyalty to any system inevitably misleading and a rejection of freedom.

The story, however, moves beyond describing this basic conflict between religious types. Its drama lies in the transformation of the second friend. By the end of the tale that friend has become a follower of the Baal Shem and has learned to affirm life. The circle completes itself as the Baal Shem uses the same words to orient the living friend to life as he had to comfort the dying friend in his last hours: move from goal to goal, from strength to strength (*LBS*, 173, 178). The story, then, traces the development of a human personality and how the conflict between two human types becomes reconciled through an orientation to life.

The traditional tale, like Buber's, relates how conflict becomes reconciliation. The original authors, unlike Buber, sketched the social and political tension engendered by the rise of Hasidism as a viable alternative to rabbinic types. The tension they describe arises from the confrontation between two teachers who oppose the Hasidic way and one of their students who yearns for the Baal Shem Tov. The story begins by declaring that when the Besht settled in his main headquarters of Medzhiboz, the leading mystics, Rabbis Zeev Kotses and David Forkes, considered him an insignificant magician. These teachers had a student who became ill and sought permission to seek advice from the Besht. The teachers at first refused, but when the student was on the verge of death they relented on the condition that he tell them everything the Besht might tell him. That condition sets up the framework of the story. Through the information they receive they eventually learn to honor and respect the Besht. After the Besht gives them clear signs of his miraculous power they accept him as their master. "From that day on they followed the Besht" (Ben-Amos and Mintz, 175). The point of the story, then, is that miraculous knowledge of life after death validates authority.

The difference between the two versions appears greater on the surface than in their meaning. Certainly Buber emphasizes interhuman relationships while the traditional text focuses on a particular historical problem: that of legitimating Hasidism in the sight of the authoritative leaders of Jewish tradition. A study of the context in which Hasidism took shape, however, shows that they, like Buber, sought a way to renew the quest for God without rejecting inherited forms. For the early Hasidic community such legitimation provided the basis of their self-understanding and appeal. The Hasidim did not consider themselves upstarts or revolutionaries. They were champions of the continuing tradition and required the verification which acceptance by authoritative leaders could afford. Buber, however, looks beyond the historical situation to an enduring human one: the need to confirm the meaning of existence. The Hasidic desire for acceptance merely mirrors that desire in an institutional form. Buber focuses on this underlying and universal concern rather than the historical guise it took in the original tale.

Nahum Glatzer recognizes this aspect of Buber's work when he contends that Buber "responded above all not to scholarly problems but to human needs, not to issues of history but to the challenge of the present day" (Glatzer, 13). This focus presents one way the Jewish heritage functions in Buber's work. It provides a concrete example of more universal truths. While Buber remains within the framework of the tradition, he extrapolates from the particularity of that tradition to a general fact of human existence. The need for authenticity and legitimation which animates the original tale becomes for Buber a sign pointing to the basic human requirement of confirmation. This ability to transform the particular into a symbol of the more general influences modern Jewish thinkers to the present. The model Buber provides in his rewriting of the Hasidic tale shows how a modern Jew can utilize an ancient theme to express a universal message. What Grete Schaeder calls Buber's "passion to salvage for the European spirit its lost legacy" infuses this reshaping of the framework of the Hasidic story (Schaeder, 17). By recapturing the impulse behind the original story while changing the details of its narrative, Buber provides modern Jews with a viable model for their own quest for the divine. The ideal of self-renewal links with the original tale the various motifs that Buber weaves into the story of the Besht's intervention in the affairs of the afterlife. That story traced the reconciliation of those leaders whose conflict tore apart the fabric of Jewish life in the eighteenth and nineteenth centuries. When establishment leaders learn that the Besht protects rather than destroys tradition they heal the breach that has opened in the Jewish community. When the skeptical friend learns to trust the Besht he begins healing the tear in his own soul. The theme of a healing unity standing as both the goal of the personal quest and as the basis for a transformed Jewish religiousness unites Buber's intention with that of his Hasidic predecessors.

THE IMPORTANCE OF JEWISH OBSERVANCE

The traditional story concludes on a strange editorial note. The editor remarks that the rabbi of his community claimed that the Besht could not insure the dead man's ascension into paradise but only that at each new ascension his soul would find a place by the gate from which the light of paradise would shine upon him (Ben-Amos and Mintz, 175) . That additional note weakens the magical element of the tale and grants a concession to the rules of propriety laid down by rabbinic Judaism. The story as originally told emphasizes rabbinic propriety and observance of the commandments of the Torah. The young man who is dying fears because he has not corrected one of his deeds. The rabbis suspect the Besht because he takes a name that is "not considered proper for a pious man." When they hear what the Besht has told the student they wonder whether anyone has the power to change the divine decree (Ben-Amos and Mintz, 174). When the teachers reluctantly allow the dying disciple to see the Besht, they demand to know what transpired because they fear impropriety. When the youth reveals his conversation with the Besht, his masters think their concern justified. They fear that the Besht's concern with Torah and life has replaced the details of Torah law which they revere. The Besht makes a promise that seems to transcend the obligations of Torah and replace them with a duty for personal loyalty to himself. Only the conclusion of the tale shows that they have been misguided. The Besht has indeed fulfilled what he promised but not by negating the ways of Torah. His exemplary life reinforces adherence to the Jewish way of life. Thus he convinces the rabbis that he has kept within the bounds of propriety. The story shows that while the Hasidic leader may appear to flout customary practice, in fact he upholds traditional Torah and the customary demands of propriety in the force of his life's example.

Buber shifts the focus of this part of the story so that it centers on interhuman relationships. For Buber the youth does not worry about observances unfulfilled or misdeeds uncorrected. In his version the youth accepts his destiny, recognizing in his illness "the message of a power which must bring his earthly life to its end." He only wonders whether he can still proceed from strength to strength, and the Besht reassures him that this is possible (LBS, 173). Not the fulfillment of commandments but rather the fulfillment of the inner drive to self-development motivates the youth. The promise he gives the young boy to return from the grave also entails an affirmation of life. While the dying lad reconciles himself to death his friend cannot find comfort as easily. The youth tells his friend what the Besht has said to him and promises to return not to justify the Besht but rather to reassure him that life's path continues and that even after death he can "return to behold the beautiful earth" (*LBS*, 174). The Torah for which the youth yearns speaks from within his own soul. It does not stand outside of him. The Besht's assurance draws its power from the knowledge that the Torah comprises the movement of life and not a set of details appropriate for only one time or place.

The promise of assurance, in this case, arises from genuine interhuman concern. The traditional tale depends on suspicion and doubt, on religious self-scrutiny. Buber's tale emphasizes compassion and human understanding. Obligations grow out of relationships not out of arbitrary rules of propriety. This approach to Torah often disturbs traditionalists. Eliezer Berkovits criticizes Buber's view of Torah obligations as a serious deviation from Jewish values. Berkovits emphasizes that "tradition affirms that God explicitly reveals his Torah and his law. Buber's dialogical revelation is altogether foreign to the spirit of the Bible" (Berkovits, 110). Certainly obligations born of encounters entail a spontaneity and unpredictability not found in those associated with traditional laws and customary propriety. Buber's rendering of this tale displays his so-called "antinomianism," his willingness to replace the written laws of custom with the unwritten obligations arising from true meeting. At first glance such an approach separates Buber from the tradition he uses.

Nevertheless, Buber's insight suggests an important lesson already adumbrated in the Hasidic tale. Appearances may deceive. What looks impious and improper may disguise deep piety and concern for others. Buber applies the lesson of the Hasidic tale for a modern purpose. The original author intended to show the slow-witted nature of the Besht's opponents. Buber goes a step beyond. He shows that slow-wittedness is rooted in a lack of caring for others, in a misunderstanding of the obligations of tradition. When traditional law becomes a replacement for interhuman meeting, when people accept dogma rather than hear the actual needs of others, then they lose touch with the meaning of the very laws and dogmas they revere. The true teacher revives the meaning and relevance of Torah by reestablishing its roots in the individual's quest for the unity of life.

TORAH EDUCATION AND PERSONAL DEVELOPMENT

The Hasidic tale as originally told summarizes the youth's ascension into the heavenly world briefly. He indeed entered paradise but could not find a place there: "When he sat in one place somebody else came and pushed him away and sat down there" (Ben-Amos and Mintz, 174).

The soul itself did not know what happened. He continued wandering from place to place until he chanced upon a yeshiva where the Baal Shem Tov engaged students in debate. When the students returned to their places, the wandering soul asked the Besht to explain his predicament. The Besht responded by noting that he could not find a place because his unfulfilled promise to his teachers obstruct his way and prevent his advancement. The soul should then descend to fulfill this task.

The point here seems to be that education consists in learning one's proper place. Each person has an appropriate role both in this life and in the world to come. The educator, in this case the Besht, understands where everyone is and should be. When someone cannot find his own place, the teacher helps. In the example of the wandering soul the teacher helps the student discover what prevents his attaining of his proper place. While one naturally comes to one's own place, external causes, such as an unfulfilled vow, obstruct the process. Teaching removes those obstructions that interfere with finding one's appropriate place.

Buber tells the story differently. He describes how the man's soul ascended with his teacher's sign on his forehead, moving from goal to goal and from holiness to holiness, receiving the meaning of life. Eventually, however, he reached a place from which he could not move "and he knew that his forehead no longer bore the sign." Buber tells of an encounter, not with the Besht, but with an old man who tells him that "all the life of the world to come is this: to move from strength to strength unto the abyss of eternity" (LBS, 174–75). The old man, consulting the sanctuary, discovers the forgotten promise and advises the youth to appear in his friend's dream.

Here, as in the earlier sections, Buber emphasizes both interhuman concern and self-development. Unlike the original story, Buber's tale does not focus on finding one's proper place. The opposite is true—the meaning of existence consists in moving from place to place, from goal to goal. Buber describes a dynamic rather than static pattern of human meaning. Secondly, Buber leaves the Besht in the shadow of this part of the story. A lost soul needs a concerned friend, not an authoritative mentor. The old man of Buber's tale provides compassion and advice, not a definitive pronouncement on the youth's proper role and what prevents his attaining it. This approach typifies Buber's view of education, which, as Alexander Kohanski explains, is not an "implement" but a process. The old man in the tale, as Kohanski says Buber does, "lets the spirit itself do the work, which indeed is the primary act of entering into relation" (Kohanski, 83).

Such a view of education allows individuals to develop dynamically in dialogue with their tradition and heritage. While the static image of the original story fit the necessity of Hasidism's social and political agenda, it can not provide the basis for a renewal of Jewish life today. The modern Jew seeks a religion that allows experimentation and growth, not one that relegates people to an unchanging status. Buber, however, did not find the modern and Hasidic viewpoints antithetical. As Ernst Simon points out, Buber consistently discovered "in his Zionistic patterns of ideals each basic trait of Hasidic pedagogy" (Simon, 555). Buber's sense of fidelity to the Hasidic original can be defended. Jewish leaders in the eighteenth and nineteenth centuries couched their own innovations in different terms from the liberal theologians of the twentieth century. Behind both positions, however, stands a similar discontent with the status quo. Both Hasidic storytellers and Buber sense the inadequacy of official leadership to meet the crisis of their times. They both seek to revive the tradition by returning to its primal roots. The commonality which Buber and the original story share lies in the sense of discontent that both consider central to understanding the meaning of Torah. Both versions of the story contend that learning begins with discomfort. When a person feels out of place, when disturbed by lack of progress, then education commences. This recognition of the root of learning in dissatisfaction links Buber to the tradition on which he builds. Both Buber and Hasidism study Torah motivated by frustration and the demand for an improvement of the self.

Buber succeeds in translating the concerns of the Hasidic legend into modern concerns, and therein lies his contribution to modern Jewish religiousness. As one who sets alternatives before us, Buber acts like a Hasidic master in his use of the tales of the Hasidim, thrusting his readers *into life* by demanding a decision about the model to choose and the path to follow.

NOTES

1. See Martin M. Buber, *The Legend of the Baal Shem* 172–78, and compare it to the story in *In Praise of the Baal Shem Tov*, Ben-Amos and Mintz, 173–75. Ben-Amos and Mintz (296) note that this corresponds to Stith Thompson's motif number E374.1 in his *Motif-Index of Folk Literature*.

REFERENCES

Ben-Amos, Dan and Mintz, Jerome R., trans. and eds. (1972). *In Praise of the Baal Shem Tov (Shivhei Ha-Besht)*. Bloomington: Indiana University Press.

Berkovits, Eliezer. (1974). "Martin Buber's Religion of Dialogue." In *Modern Philosophies of Judaism*. New York: KTAV.
Buber, Martin. *HMM* (1958), *OJ, LBS*.
Glatzer, Nahum N. (1981). "Aspects of Martin Buber's Thought." *Modern Judaism* 1:1.
————. (1961). *Franz Rosenzweig: His Life and Thought*. 2nd rev. ed. New York: Schocken.
Kohanski, Alexander S. (1982). *Martin Buber's Philosophy of Interhuman Relation: A Response to the Human Problematic of Our Time*. Rutherford: Fairleigh Dickenson University Press.
Martin, Bernard. (1970). *Great Twentieth Century Jewish Philosophers: Shestov, Rosenzweig, Buber*. New York: Macmillan.
Schaeder, Grete. (1973). *The Hebrew Humanism of Martin Buber*. Trans. Noah J. Jacobs. Detroit: Wayne State University Press).
Simon, Ernst. (1967). "Martin Buber, the Educator." In *The Philosophy of Martin Buber*, ed. by Paul Arthur Schilpp and Maurice Friedman. The Library of Living Philosophers, Vol. 12. La Salle, IL: Open Court Press.

CHAPTER 5

MARTIN BUBER'S BIBLICAL AND JEWISH ETHICS

RICHARD A. FREUND

"Jewish ethics" has been defined as the systematic analysis of good and evil according to Jewish sources. It can be a difficult subject because of the lack of a single, authoritative Jewish text which maps out the parameters of Jewish ethics in systematic format. While one can point to medieval attempts to compare and contrast some Aristotelian and neo-Platonic ideas to biblical and rabbinic texts in the writings of Maimonides, Saadiah Gaon, and Ibn Pequdah, for example, these attempts generally fall short of providing a philosophical framework which is loyal to the rather diverse and nonsystematic rabbinic and post-biblical (non-rabbinic) writings of Judaism. What is essentially missing in these attempts is a philosophical system which begins not from comparison and contrast with Greek and Roman ideas but begins with uniquely Jewish texts and creates a framework which accounts for the vast diversity in these texts and attempts to find the unifying philosophical principles within them. One might say that this method begs the entire question of Jewish ethics. Ethics is a Greco-Roman philosophical concept and is therefore comparative with that tradition.

While methodologically this may be true, in point of fact behind the Platonic and Aristotelian assumptions lies another layer of ethical discourse. This layer of discourse assumes only that there is an "ethos" or habitual custom which the human being strives to inculcate into his

or her personality. This custom is conditioned by often unique expressions, which may be radically different in their assumptions about the
nature of the world and the human being, which in turn affect what is
the goal of moral behavior.

In the course of the investigation of different Jewish thinkers and their
systematic investigations of Judaism in the modern period, one thinker
stands alone in his presentation of Jewish ethics as unique but not necessarily in line with Greco-Roman ethical assumptions. That thinker is
Martin Buber. Therefore, we investigate Martin Buber and Jewish ethics.
As Maurice Friedman has written concerning Buber's concept of ethics:

> The traditional approach to Ethics is Greek; Martin Buber's is
> Biblical. In the *Crito* and the *Republic*, the good is intrinsic to a
> person's being but not to the relations between man and man
> themselves. One is just not for the sake of justice but in order
> not to injure one's soul. Justice is primarily a reality of the soul
> rather than of the interhuman. In the *Psalms*, in contrast,
> man's very existence is set in relationship with reality that
> confronts him, and this relationship transcends 'ethics' in the
> usual understanding of the term.[1]

Buber considered the Bible and biblical ethics to be the basis for the
rest of Judaism's ethics. Unlike other writers who considered the
Talmud and rabbinic ethics to be the sum total of Judaism's ethics, and
other writers who used Platonic and Aristotelian categories to determine what was ethical for Judaism, Buber returned to another source for
Jewish ethics: the Bible. As he stated in one of his earliest lectures to
Jewish students in Prague in 1918:

> The reader of the Bible must attempt to understand the spirit of
> its original language, the Hebrew—an understanding that is
> service; he will approach it not as a work of literature but as
> the basic documentation of the unconditional's effect on the
> spirit of the Jewish people.[2]

A substantial part of Buber's life work was devoted to the Bible and
its meaning for the Jewish people.[3] This essay, therefore, will deal with
one specific facet of the topic of Martin Buber's biblical and Jewish
ethics which may be important to scholars of the Bible, Jewish ethicists,
and the writings of Martin Buber. This topic can be defined as the
insights of Buber on the Bible and the implications of these insights for
the study of Jewish ethics.

Martin Buber is uniquely suited as the touchstone for a philosophical understanding of Jewish ethics.[4] His training, his life experience, and

his interest in many aspects of Judaism, Jewish life, Jewish texts, and general philosophy allowed him to consider Jewish ethics as an expression of more than just rabbinic decisions. If anything, it is Buber's non-emphasis upon Talmudic and medieval rabbinic traditions (and especially the halakhic tradition) which is crucial for an understanding of Buber's Jewish ethics. Buber's Jewish ethics is clearly not intended to be "normative" rabbinic ethics. It is representative of a tradition which Buber saw as inherent in rabbinic Judaism but not necessarily supported by the particulars of rabbinic Judaism. Buber's system is simultaneously a critique of Greco-Roman ethics and rabbinic ethics. For Buber, the basis of ethics is dialogue, which was and continues to be the source for Judaism's constant renewal and possibilities for revival. Buber's views, therefore, strike at the most basic philosophical questions of ethics (the sources of ethics) and fit the definition of Jewish ethics used in this essay.

One of his earliest formulations of these basic philosophical questions is found in the 1923 work, *I and Thou*. *I and Thou*, however, is only a general expression of what Buber saw as the specific view of the biblical and Jewish ethics, even as Michael Fishbane observed in his article, "Martin Buber as an Interpreter of the Bible":

> I am reluctant to dismiss his [Buber's] Biblical work as a gloss on his life-thought. One must judge each case independently, but also appreciate the deep relationship between Buber's "I-Thou" thought and his Bible studies; the one confirmed the other; and each acted on the other reciprocally. Buber intuited the Biblical soul of Judaism long before *I and Thou* was a literary germ-cell. . . . *I and Thou* is itself a deeply Biblical work.[5]

I and Thou and other writings of Martin Buber are devoted to creating a philosophical understanding which is indicative of what he found in the pristine beginnings of Western thought, presumably before the advent of Plato and Aristotle, but still utilizing the rich vocabulary and categories of classical Greek philosophy. Buber may be seen as the ideal type of investigator of the philosophical origins of Jewish ethics, since he was versed in the vocabulary, the implications, and inadequacies of general philosophical literature and so interested in the contributions of the Bible and Jewish tradition. He appreciated both the philosophical and the biblical-Jewish traditions for what they had contributed, and was seeking an understanding of Judaism's unique contribution to civilization as part of his own search for Jewish identity. Like other contemporaries of his time, Buber sought a theory which unified the apparently divergent thought systems in which he found himself. Judaism's lack of a single, authoritative text devoted wholly to the systematic investigation of Jewish ethics led Buber back to the Bible rather than the rabbinic tradition for a basis for Jewish ethics. He recognized the important differences between the Jewish system of ethics and other systems of ethics.[6] His investigations seem to have passively noted and accounted for the lack of a single, authoritative "human" role model in Jewish ethics. This lacuna prompted Buber to investigate Jewish ethics as a system which resulted from the relationship or dialogue in the individual's encounter with the Divine rather than a single individual's authoritative, historical experience with the Divine. He, like Rosenzweig, believed that revelation was an ongoing and individual event, although unlike Rosenzweig, who found God's disclosure in actual ritual laws, Buber found this experience to be without formal structure.[7]

Buber's understanding of Jewish ethics provides a unique insight into Jewish ethics from the Bible through later postbiblical (rabbinic) Judaism. This essay will concentrate on Buber's unique insights on the Bible and ethics and how these insights can be used to elucidate issues present in modern biblical criticism. In particular, Buber's insights on I-Thou and dialogue provide us with a window for understanding ethical implications present in modern source critical studies of the Bible. While these insights may not have been anticipated by Buber, modern biblical scholars might do well to familiarize themselves with Buber's ideas, since he seems to have captured part of the elusive spirit of some of the biblical writers. In addition, Buber's insights on the Bible and biblical ethics also have implications for the way that postbiblical Jewish ethical (and rabbinic) texts might be understood.

I. BUBER AND THE BIBLE

Gershom Scholem's comments at the celebration of the completion of Buber's translation of the Bible in February 1961 map out some of Buber's unique contributions to biblical studies and Judaism in his translation of the Hebrew Bible into German. In his comments, Scholem stated:

> Finally, there is one last consideration which has determined the special character of your translation in both versions. It is one of the grand paradoxes of this undertaking that in a translation which in the final analysis renders the Bible as the word of God, the name of God as such should not appear. It is replaced by the emphatic and prominent use of I, Thou, and He. By these pronouns alone may we apprehend God, with great clarity, though only mediately as befits us. This is not the least sig-

nificant of the numerous and bold innovations of the translation. It rests on the conviction that in a book that speaks of the rule of God in creation and in history, the name of God which was available to the ancient authors need only appear indirectly. In this way you have found a creative compromise between the traditional Jewish awe that forbids the pronouncing of the name of God and the obligation to make the biblical word readable, i.e., audible.[8]

Scholem's comments reveal the essence of the Buberian system in the Bible. For Buber, the Bible contained expressions of humans' dialogues with God and as such the I-It and I-Thou relations Buber had outlined in *I and Thou*. Buber's reading and translation of the Hebrew Bible was an attempt to reveal the basic meaning of the text. This attempt parallels, in part, the task of the modern critical Bible scholar. Buber attempted to read the text as a unity, the way the final edited version of the Bible was intended to be read. His entire approach to the translation and subsequent studies is either consciously or unconsciously a reaction to the Graf-Wellhausen forms of source criticism practiced in the early twentieth century in Protestant seminaries in Western Europe and especially in his native Germany.

Buber did not directly search for the so-called text-behind-the text or Ur-text so sought by those early pioneers of modern biblical criticism. Modern biblical critics, especially Graf-Wellhausen and their followers, found that the doublets and triplets of narratives in the Bible were indicative of different sources. The sources/authors of the Hebrew Bible (and especially the first five books of the Bible) described the same events often in widely different ways. Early source critics attributed these variations to the differing historical backgrounds and agendas of the writers themselves, but recently some source critics have recognized wholly different ethical perspectives, theologies, and relationships present in the different locutions of the authors.[9] Buber, similar to other modern bible scholars, listened intently to the different types of dialogues and relationships between God and the human being in the text.[10] Buber was sensitive to the same stylistic changes and dynamics of the received Massoretic Text (MT), which early source critics had explained in historical terms. Buber's biblical scholarship and I-Thou/I-It categories elucidate another level of understanding apparent in the changes and dynamics of the MT narratives. This level of understanding anticipates many modern source critics, who have only recently made similar observations about the implications of the differences which have been noted for over a century.

Martin Buber's philosophical observations on the Bible also eluci-date basic elements of the Jewish system of ethics from the Bible to the rabbis. His insights differentiate Jewish ethics from other philosophical systems of ethical inquiry that indirectly use biblical references to bol-ster their arguments. More importantly, Buber established a philosophi-cal matrix for Jewish ethics that is both authentically philosophical in nature and intimately aware of Jewish and biblical tradition. His approach allows comparison with other philosophical systems as well as textually oriented religious ethics. His sensitivity for the complex nature of the text of the Bible and his recognition of varying theological stances of different characters anticipates or parallels the results of oth-ers in critical Bible and rabbinic text scholarship. His differentiation between biblical and Greco-Roman thought is particularly important because not only did Buber contend that the Bible contained a complex expression of the human-Divine relationship within its pages, but that this expression was different from the way that the Greco-Roman philosophers conceived of the relationship between the human and the Divine.

II. FROM THE BIBLE TO THE GREEKS

For Buber, the essential differences between the Greek ethical tradition and the biblical ethical tradition represent an important distinction. Buber clearly defines the biblical ethical system as one in which the human being is in a constant state of interrelationship with God. There is no differentiating the individual as apart from God, apart from the world, apart from another human being. The human's existence is so dependent upon the existence of these interlocking pieces of reality as to make his/her own existence meaningless without relationship to the others.

The tension between the human's apparent autonomous existence and the interrelated "auto-heteronomous" existence suggested by the I-Thou is the key. I-Thou is a dualistic term, suggesting two elements, in the words of Buber "a complex, hyphenated concept." For the purposes of explanation in this essay, this type of "complex, hyphenated concept" which recognizes two elements in an interlocking dependency and interrelationship will be defined as a *Buberian dualism* to distinguish it from classical dualism of the Greeks and later Christian scholastics.

Buberian dualism suggests a tension between two elements which are intimately linked in a holistic way. What the term *Buberian dual-ism* implies is a tension between a view which sees the universe as one (monism) and a view which holds that the (physical) universe is only one part of a greater and/or dualistic reality (dualism). This view of Buberian dualism is opposed by classical dualism on the one hand and classical monistic traditions on the other. In the Bible, Buber perceived that the realm of God and the human being were not totally separate from one another. In Buberian dualism, the human being is not estranged from the world but a part of it. Buber perceived that this was one part of the biblical relationship of the human and God. Buberian dualism presents the human as capable of having an ongoing dialogue with God. This dialogue is a necessary part of the world's existence. The human being is not God, nor is God "in" the human being. They are separate entities which exist in relation to one another, and this relationship affects the human being's relation to other human beings. For Buber, the absence of absolute separation between God and the human being in the Bible translates into an extremely important role for ethical behavior. Buberian dualism applies "almost" cosmic/redemptive/divine purpose to human behavior. Instead of separating the "idea/l" from the"form", as is done in most Greek philosophy, this dualism suggests an ethical system which directly takes into consideration what the human being can do ("form") in the formulation of what one ethically "ought" to do ("idea/l").

The Greek view of the world, in general, from the time of Plato and Aristotle, is wholly dualistic. The Greek worldview sees as inherently separate the soul and the body, the form and the idea, the Ultimate Creator and the created, the world of sensations and the world of the mind. It is this idea of separation which transforms itself in the Greek tradition of philosophy into the"gap" between the "thing-itself" and "the thing."

In the ethical traditions of the West, it is this "gap" which may lead the religious thinker to despair. The human being is in search of a "leap of faith" to bridge the great abyss between the human and the reality which is "out there." Dualism also leads to a concept of ethics which is instrumental to human existence but which is only a vague approximation of the "true" values. Curiously, this dualism led to a concept of conforming to the laws of nature for lack of a better, more exalted model of ethical behavior. It is this same dualism which emphasized "human justice," but only as a poor copy of "eternal Justice." Ethics were general characteristics of human behavior which were analyzed and then subsequently, through a form of logical reductionism, minimized.

It is this same dualism which denigrates the body and elevates the soul as the seat of "true" humanity. Classical Greek dualism characterized parts or all of the works on ethics produced by Aristotle, Aquinas,

Alfarabi, and Maimonides. The dualism which developed in the West and which became the general basis for our concept of ethics, both in Judaism and Christianity, sees God as "out there" and generally dictating to the human being a conduct for life. Ethics is the process of interpreting these "dictates." Any system modeled entirely upon dualism will eventually, no matter how creative the interpreter, be subject to serious social challenges as "the dictates" become increasingly disjointed from the reality of the world. Systems which raise their laws to the level of Eternal Ideas residing in an imperfect World of Forms will eventually find that the nondynamic character of "the laws" will be subject to decay.

As Buber describes the biblical concept of ethics it is an integrated system of philosophy. The human being is a psycho-physical unity of spirit and action. The body and soul are linked. The emphasis is also upon this World, a World in which God and the human being are not separate from one another but enmeshed in each other. The human's duty is to conform to the dictates of the Creator and Absolute Reality, which are continually active in this world. Ethics is not only instrumental but central to the human enterprise. Nothing is more central than the directed human activity which the Bible describes. In short, Buber has found a way of describing the ethics of the Bible in a way which gives meaning to what some bible source critics have called the "tension or synthesis of the combined/redacted sources" (R. Friedman, 240–42). Buberian dualism explains the "tension or synthesis" of redacted sources by explaining the different relationships of God and the human being in general. Buber's observations are certainly reminiscent of much of the Bible. Citations can be drawn from throughout the prophetic materials and poetry of the Bible to advance this argument.

Buber emphasizes the personal and close relationship of the human being of the Bible (identified by source critics with the J source—see discussion below), but he also recognized the existence of another relationship. While on the one hand there is the God who "meets" the human being, there is another "wholly Other" *mysterium tremendum* which is not totally knowable. While Buber emphasizes the first as an I-Thou model for human relations, he is aware that there lurks another encounter of the human and the Divine which is also apparent in the Bible (identified by source critics with the P source—see discussion below). Buber would acknowledge that these are human encounters with the Divine and not really different concepts of God. Buber was keenly aware of a complex I-Thou/I-It relationship which is developed in the pages of the Bible. His ideas bear a remarkable resemblance to aspects of modern biblical criticism and especially the results of recent source criticism. Buber's insights, however, not only enlighten philosophical observations about the Bible, but also illumine aspects of modern biblical criticism and its implications for an understanding of biblical and postbiblical Jewish ethics.

III. THE BIBLE AND DIALOGUE:
THE THREE MEETINGS WITH GOD

Recent biblical scholarship has yielded some important new observations about the ancient question of God's relationship to the human being. Many of the results of modern critical Bible studies coincide with some of the conclusions which Buber reached using philosophical inquiry and a careful reading of the biblical text. Professor Richard E. Friedman's recent book *Who Wrote the Bible?* for example, which uses modern biblical criticism, concludes:

> The combination of the sources did more than just affect individual Bible stories. It had an impact on the biblical conception of God. J, E, and D pictured God in very personal ways: moving around on earth, taking visible forms, engaging in discussion and even debate with humans. P's conception was more of a cosmic, transcendent deity. . . . Not to overstate the case, God is sometimes pictured as personal in P, and he is sometimes pictured as transcendent in J, E, and D. But the difference overall is still blatant and profound. When the redactor combined all the sources he mixed two different pictures of God. By doing that, he formed a new balance between the personal and the transcendent qualities of the deity. It was a picture of God as both universal and intensely personal. Yahweh was the creator of the cosmos, but also "the God of your Fathers." The fusion was artistically dramatic and theologically profound, but it was also filled with a new tension. It was now picturing human beings coming into close personal dialogue with the all-powerful master of the universe. It was a balance that none of the individual authors had intended. But that balance, intended or not, came to be at the heart of Judaism and Christianity (236ff.).

What emerges from the biblical investigations of Friedman and also Buber was the mixed nature of biblical theology. If modern biblical scholarship is correct, there are actually multiple concepts of God which emerged from the earliest biblical texts and correspond to Buber's different relational models of I-Thou and I-It. Biblical critics identify one concept of God as an almost wholly cosmic and transcendent God, one which is not directly related or interrelated with human beings. This was the God of P.[11] J and E present a personal and immanent God which the Bible chronicles with highly personalized accounts and intimate Divine contact with humans. The narratives which Buber quotes in much of his works relate to this highly personal and intimate God. Finally, however, the Redactor wove these two concepts which could be denominated I-It (P) and I-Thou (J/E) respectively into a single concept that reflects a hybrid relationship between the I-It and the I-Thou. These three concepts appear together in the overall codified and edited Hebrew Bible, and therefore the Hebrew Bible represents at once the I-It and almost simultaneously (a parallel) I-Thou. It is this tension which Buber writes about in his books. P, who has been identified as the Priestly author, presents a God who was only in dialogue with specific appointed individuals during specific experiences. J, E, and D represent other religious authorities in different periods and seem to allow for a greater interchange with God by larger numbers of the public on a more regular and constant basis. The Redactor seems to present a mixed theological position that allows for both simultaneously. This tension of competing theologies and conceptualizations is the basis of both the confusion and the continuing strength of the Bible. On the one hand, P presents a God who created the universe and has left a clear legacy of his "official" representatives. This Cosmic God cannot and does not directly relate to the general populus. The basis of authority for both Law and Ethics in the system of P appears to be:

a. God is The Cosmic and All-powerful Creator of the Universe and one must follow God's dictates for this reason alone.
b. God has appointed "official" representatives (the Aaronite Priests in Jerusalem) which will be in contact with God and determine how humans are supposed to act.

J/E and D present an ever-present, personal, accessible, and involved deity who communicates with a variety of different souls who seek Him out (and sometimes those who do not). The authority for the Law and Ethics of this God is God alone, and nonfulfillment of divine dictates will be directly punished by God.

The Redactor seems to have been split on this issue of God's participation and role in daily life, presenting both in sometimes parallel, sometimes mixed fashion. This overall mixed theology also implies an overall mixed ethical system. It implies that, overall, God is both immanent and transcendent, both personal and impersonal. It implies that God communicates personally both to the many and to the "official" representative. It implies that the authority of biblical ethics is a mixture of God's personal threat of retribution and the human's fear of not fulfilling the mandates of a cosmic, impersonal Creator and of being punished.

In short, the mixed theologies of the biblical text provide room for human and divine roles in a shared relationship. Buber and modern biblical scholarship actually share the view that the God of Israel is in a relationship that implies both a wholly Transcendent and Eternal Thou which can still, almost impossibly, be known by Man. Buber is in good company when he challenges the commonly held philosophical view that the Eternal Thou is totally separate from the temporal Thou. The position that God is separate and beyond common, human comprehension and reach was the position taken by P over 2500 years ago. J, E, D, and the Redactor of the Bible tempered this view by declaring that God was reachable and knowable. While P held that revelation was a part of selected individuals at specific places and times, J, E, D, and the Redactor seem to imply that revelation was not limited to certain individuals in certain locations and periods. It is this view of revelation which is an inherent part of Buber's biblical view and more specifically his view of ethics. Like the majority of the authors of the Bible and the Redactor, revelation was a consequence of the relationship between God and the individual. The fact that the accounts of P, J, E, and D are all interwoven and interdependent may imply that there existed differing concepts of how revelation was understood in biblical times. The view that revelation was a community event in which each community senses God's unfolding response in varying and clearly different manifestations seems to be a key factor in the Bible. Buber is right in saying that revelation and the "fundamental ethical" are not just directed to the Patriarchs, the religious leaders, or the appointed (EG, 118). The "fundamental ethical" is not an ideal apart from life but rather a practical imperative directed to everyone.

To sum up: Buber's model of the "I-Thou/I-It" encounter with the Divine and especially Buberian dualism, explain much about the process of biblical and postbiblical Jewish ethical decision-making.[12] Buberian dualism preserves God as distinct from the human being but fundamentally linked to the reality of the individual. Instead of ethics emerging as a result of a Divine ideal imposed upon the human being for his/her own good, Buber's concept of ethics makes ethics a result of the individual's encounter with the Divine Thou. According to Buber's philosophical understanding of Jewish ethics, the Divine relationship with the individual may be intimate or not, intensive or not, recognized or not. The individual may feel at one moment estranged and in another moment connected. Whether the relationship is intimate, intensive, or recognized, the existence of this "encounter with the Divine" is the defining factor in Jewish ethics. It is fundamental to why humans choose to be Good or Evil and are able to perform good and evil actions. This philosophical orientation of Buberian dualism allows Jewish ethics to reflect more accurately the reality of human intercourse and decision making rather than an idealized view of how Jews should act. God does not thrust God'self into individual decisions except where invited. Although it is an exaggeration to say that Jewish ethics is fundamentally humanistic in orientation, as a rule, Jewish ethics does not derive its ethical stances from a direct Divine Command theory or even a single authoritative text or human role model. Buber's model for Jewish ethics demands that each individual allow for his/her own encounter with the Divine and that the experience of the encounter will ultimately determine how one reacts through informed human will.

NOTES

1. Maurice Friedman, "Martin Buber's Concept of Ethics," *Judaism* 14 (Summer, 1965): 274. A full-scale discussion of this problem is found in Maurice Friedman's essay "The Bases of Buber's Ethics" in *The Philosophy of Martin Buber* volume of *The Library of Living Philosophers*, ed. by Paul Arthur Schilpp and Maurice Friedman (LaSalle, Illinois: The Open Court, 1965).
2. "Herut: On Youth and Religion," in Buber's *On Judaism* 1967, 172.
3. Some of these writings in English are

    a. *Israel and the World: Essays in a Time of Crisis* (New York: Schocken, 1948)
    b. *The Prophetic Faith* (New York: Harper, 1949)
    c. *Moses: The Revelation and the Covenant* (New York, Harper, 1958)
    d. *Kingship of God* (New York: Harper, 1967)
    e. *On the Bible* (New York: Schocken, 1968)

These studies are part of the larger project of the translation of the Hebrew Bible into German begun with Franz Rosenzweig in 1925 and completed in 1961 by Buber himself. Rosenzweig's and Buber's ideas about this undertaking, need for a retranslation of the Hebrew Bible into German, and their techniques in translations are found in *Die Schrift und ihre Verdeutschung* (*The Scriptures and their Translation into German*) (Berlin: Schocken, 1936).

4. See S. D. Breslauer's article entitled: "Decoding the Jewish Elements of I and Thou," in *Conservative Judaism* 33 (Winter, 1980): 34–45; and especially footnote 1 on page 34 for more on the controversy.
5. M. Fishbane, "Martin Buber as an Interpreter of the Bible," *Judaism* 27, (Spring, 1978): 194.
6. See my introduction in R. A. Freund, *Understanding Jewish Ethics* (San Francisco: Mellen, 1990), 1–40.
7. For Buber's view, see "Herut," 166. For F. Rosenzweig's view, see *On Jewish Learning*, ed. N. N. Glatzer (New York: Schocken, 1955), 116.
8. G. Scholem, *The Messianic Idea in Judaism* (New York: Schocken, 1971), 317.
9. R. E. Friedman, *Who Wrote the Bible?* (New York: Harper and Row, 1989).
10. Buber, *Die Schrift*, "Zur Verdeutschung der Preisungen," 168.
11. Friedman and most other Bible scholars hold that P is later than J and E. Friedman places J in the South of Israel in the period between 848 and 722 B.C.E. and E in the North between 922 and 722 B.C.E. P wrote in the period after 722 and before 609 B.C.E. See R. E. Friedman, *Who Wrote the Bible?*, 86–87, 210.
12. There is evidence to suggest that the I-Thou/I-It concept delineated by Buber in the Bible continues in early and medieval rabbinic literature. Early rabbinic literature contains two separate foci. Many identify these two foci as the differences between the *Aggadah* and the *Halachah*, the "lore" and the "law." In fact, what is more striking are the two separate forms of rabbinic literature rather than the contents. Early rabbinic literature presents revelation in two distinct forms.

   One can be called the "Midrashic" form; the other can be called the "Mishnaic" form. Midrash (literally, "exposition"; the general conclusions here apply to Midrash Halachah as well as Midrash Aggadah) is a collection of rabbinic interpretations of biblical verses. Many different collections of Midrash are found independent of the Mishnah and Talmudic collections from the 3rd–10th century C.E. The Mechilta, Sifra and Sifrei, some of the earliest collections, apparently came in parallel versions edited by the students or school of Rabbis Yishmael and Aqiva in the second century (see H. L. Strack, *Introduction to the Talmud and Midrash*, 6th ed. [New York: Atheneum, 1980], 206–207). It has been noted by many scholars that the Midrashic format (Midrash Halachah, for example) is a word-by-word or phrase commentary on the Pentateuch and other Hebrew Bible books used liturgically by the Jews. This commentary seeks to directly interpret or often continue the Divine text in order to clarify and establish the basis for much of rabbinic Judaism's vision for personal conduct. This type of ongoing revelatory experience of the Midrashic form often continues the narrative "I-Thou" personal relationship between God and the individual. Direct quotes from Scripture are used as the basis for the ongoing narratives and the explanations are seen as the logical conclusion of the scriptural references. In general the early Midrashic collections have been edited by different schools and often include varying methods and final conclusions.

The Mishnah (literally, "study"; the general conclusions here concerning the Mishnaic form includes Mishnah, Tosefta, and Baraitot of Tannaitic origin) is another early, written collection of rabbinic materials which includes many of the same sayings, ideas, and rabbinic sources, as the Midrash and was finally redacted by Rabbi Yehuda HaNasi (Rabbi Judah the Prince) about 200 C.E. While this collection often contains the same laws and customs found in the Midrashic form it does not regularly cite scripture, and although the Bible is understood as its indirect source of authority, the Mishnaic form suggests a different relationship to the text of the Bible. This literature emphasizes *an indirect relation* to the source of authority (the Divine), which suggests an "I-It" relationship to the Divine.

In the Bible the different relationships between God and the human being present in the different sources were combined together by redactor(s) who created a new and perhaps unanticipated third view of the relationship between God and the individual. The later redactors of the Babylonian and Palestinian Talmuds (in the fifth and sixth century C.E.) brought together the Mishnaic and Midrashic formats of early rabbinic literature and created a third view, whose very form suggests a new and perhaps unanticipated perspective on the relationship between the Divine and the human being. This third, more complex theological relationship is suggested by the format of the Talmud. The Talmud schematically begins with the Mishnaic format but moves quickly to incorporate Midrashic materials and other later questions. This is all developed by the redactors together in the context of a dialogic interaction between earlier and later rabbis which often never took place in history. While the format of the Talmudim is not generally understood as being representative of a theological position, the mixing of very different types of literatures which synthesize direct Divine commandments together with human dicta unlinked to Divine writ can be seen in theological terms with ethical implications. One example will suffice. The Mishnah contains an entire tractate dedicated to the study of the laws of the Sotah found in the Bible in Numbers 5.11ff. In the Mishnah there is a simple listing of the different laws associated with the "unfaithful wife." In the Midrash Halachah, Sifrei-Numbers, a similar collection of laws is found, but this time connected directly to "extended narratives" which parallel and comment upon the Numbers 5 reference. In the Babylonian Talmud tractate Sotah in the gemara commentary on these same laws, the Mishnaic formats (including Tosefta and Baraitot) are freely mixed and associated together with the Midrashic materials. The overall impact for the reader of the Talmud, therefore, is a sensation of theological "motion" from a direct to indirect, intimate to nonpersonal, ongoing revelation to indirect commentary on revelation, I-Thou to I-It relationship with the Divine (and the sacred text) all in the space of the same page. The ethical import and authority of such a text is one of combined human and Divine authority and decision-making. Personal autonomy and Divine input. What might be characterized as auto-heteronomy.

Early and late Mishnaic and Midrashic sections referring to the same laws and ethical views were often recorded one after another or transferred to new and often unanticipated connections (as in the biblical redaction process) by later rabbinic redactors in the Talmudim. This type of achronological sequencing of words and ideas from different periods and contexts may imply that the Talmudic redactors were faced with the same dilemma as the biblical redactors; i.e., to create a cogent whole out of disparate but authoritative traditions. Later medieval rabbinic law and ethics is a byproduct of this third hybrid synthesis of the Talmudic redactors. God is at once immanent and transcendent in the world. The God of the rabbis is similar to the redacted theological positions of the Bible.

The ongoing I-Thou and I-It encounter with the Divine is evident even in the forms of medieval rabbinic literature. Much medieval (post-Talmudic) rabbinic literature appears in two radically different formats. One type of medieval rabbinic literature is based in mysticism and the other in a nonmystical format. The literature of medieval rabbinic responsa and commentaries and such writings as the *Sheiltot and the Mishneh Torah* are clearly nonmystical in nature. They characterize the relationship of God and the human being in a very indirect way.

The mystical and nonmystical medieval rabbinic literature often contains the names of the same rabbis but their words and actions are radically different. In works such as the *Heikahalot Rabbati*, *Sefer Yetzirah*, parts of *Seder Eliyahu Rabbah*, and *Shi'ur Qomah*, the relationship between the human being and the Divine is characterized in very intimate and realizable terms (I-Thou). In the *Shi'ur Qomah*, for example, the knowledge of the measure of the "body" of the Creator has the ability to affect Divine action. In other rabbinic works of the same period this type of encounter between God and the human being is not generally possible (I-It).

CHAPTER 6

MARTIN BUBER AND CHRISTIAN THEOLOGY

A Continuing Dialogue

DONALD J. MOORE, S.J.

Martin Buber's simple, ingenious elaboration of the twofold manner in which we relate to the world around—I-Thou and I-It—has been hailed by Karl Heim as a "Copernican Revolution" in the thinking of human-kind. Emil Brunner has referred to this twofold attitude as a "profoundly revolutionary fundamental insight."[1] Buber explicitly rejected meta-physics as a foundation on which to build his understanding of reality. Steven Katz refers to this "failure" as a "disservice" to the philosophy of dialogue (1984, 108).

BUBER'S METHODOLOGY

In place of metaphysics Buber makes an appeal to experience—the expe-rience of faith. "I give my faith experience the conceptual expression necessary for its being understood, but I posit no metaphysical thesis." He communicates his own experience of faith, and he speaks to the experience of faith of his readers, recognizing that some will understand, while others will be left unsatisfied (PI, 97). Writing a few years before his death in 1965, Buber pointed out:

> No system was suitable for what I had to say . . . I witnessed for experience and I appealed to experience. The experience for

which I witnessed is . . . not to be understood as a "subjective"
one. I have tested it through my appeal and I test it ever anew. I
say to him who listens to me: "It is your experience: recollect
it . . ."
    I must say it once again: I have no teaching. I only point to
something . . . in reality that had not or had too little been
seen. I take him who listens to me by the hand, and I lead him
to the window. I open the window and point to what is outside.
(PMB, 693)

It is important to point out that Buber's experience of faith is also
an experience of the human. Authentic faith and authentic humanity
can never be divorced in Buber's thought. In his last great public address,
the acceptance of the Netherland's Erasmus Prize in 1963, Buber
insisted that humanity and faith penetrate each other so completely
that we may say that "our faith has our humanity as its foundation and
our humanity has our faith as its foundation" (ABH, 117). Furthermore,
Buber designated as central to all his writings the basic insight that "the
I-Thou relation to God and the I-Thou relation to one's fellow man are
at bottom related to each other" (PI, 99). Every particular Thou brings
with it a breath from the eternal Thou. All of Buber's writings on religion and society and politics, his work on Hasidism and the Bible, his
approach to Zionism and to the problems of Jews and Arabs, ultimately
served to clarify and expound this central theme and basic insight.
    The experience to which Buber points is the experience of lived
relation, of a dialogical relation which is, for Buber, at the heart of all
human reality. In this lived relation one does not and cannot have the
certainty of metaphysical truth but only the experience of mutual
knowing that springs from genuine meeting, from wholehearted presence to the other, and ultimately from wholehearted presence to the
One who is eternally Other, eternally Thou. Buber describes this experience of lived relation as the "narrow ridge," an understanding of reality
that is not rooted in any philosophical or theological system of objective
truths but on "a narrow rocky ridge" between the abysses, where there
is no metaphysical certitude but only "the certainty of meeting what
remains undisclosed" (BMM, 184).
    Closely associated with this theme of the narrow ridge is that of
"holy insecurity," a theme rooted in Buber's early work, Daniel:
Dialogues of Realization (1913), and which permeated his thought for
the last six decades of his life. "You must descend ever anew into the
transforming abyss, risk your soul ever anew, ever anew vowed to the
holy insecurity" (Daniel, 99). Holy insecurity implies a trusting response

when confronting the shattering abyss that enters into life, the insecurity involved in not reducing to general categories and principles the unique and irreducible situation in which one finds oneself but rather entering into it with openness and trust and answering it with one's whole life. Maurice Friedman describes the person of holy insecurity as the one who "meets every new situation with the quiet and sureness out of the depths of his being, yet he meets it with the fear and trembling of one who has no ready-made answer to life" (Friedman *LOD*, 136; *MBLW: Early*, 150–176). Buber constantly contrasts holy insecurity with "gnosis" which "not only offends the transcendent but also human existence because it constructs a structure of knowledge which passes from now on as complete" ("Replies," in *PMB*, 743). Gnosis is ultimately destructive of a life of dialogue.

In a 1934 article entitled "Symbolic and Sacramental Existence," Buber contrasts the certitude of the Kabbalists with the holy insecurity of the Hasidim. It is the contrast between an attitude of self-assurance that "almost never stops short, almost never shudders, almost never prostrates itself" as opposed to a profound recognition "of the impotence of all 'information,' of the incongruence of all possessed truth." The truth of Hasidic piety for Buber lies precisely in "stopping short," in allowing oneself to be disconcerted by ever new demands—it is rooted in holy insecurity. We are called to live in "the world of contradiction." If we seek refuge in the general truths and principles of theology or metaphysics, then we forsake our mission. For Buber it would be contrary to both Hasidic faith and Hasidic humor to try to lift ourselves to a plane of being above or beyond the problematic of everyday existence. We are plunged into the absurd in order to "endure and sustain it" with our lives. This "enduring and sustaining of the absurd" is the one meaning which we can experience and discover (*OMH*, 179).

The final aspect of Buber's methodology, closely allied to the narrow ridge and holy insecurity, is the *coincidentia oppositorum*—the paradoxical unity of the coincidence of opposites which is the mystery at the innermost core of dialogical existence. Religion for Buber is the lived coincidence of opposites; he describes the religious situation, our "*being there* in the Presence," as one characterized by this "indissoluble antinomy." The only way one can carry through the conflict of this coincidence of opposites is with one's life. The significance of the religious situation, which is at the same time the significance of life on the narrow ridge, of a life of holy insecurity, of existential trust, is simply that "it is lived, and nothing but lived, continually, ever anew, without foresight, without forethought, without prescription, in the totality of its antinomy." Logically, only one of the two contraries can be true, but in the reality of authentic life, of life on the narrow ridge, one knows the contraries are inseparable. Buber gives the example of necessity and free-dom where one standing before God knows "I am given over for dis-posal," and yet at the same time one also knows "It depends on myself." One cannot escape the paradox; one is compelled to take both contraries to oneself "to be lived together, and in being lived they are one" (*I and Thou*, 95–96).[2]

The best known expression of Buber's life on the narrow ridge, of holy insecurity, is his *I and Thou*. Here, as well as in his later writings on dialogue, Buber underscores the *Ur-humanum* religious experience of Moses and the prophets as the universal model of humankind's encounter with God. He is giving a biblical interpretation of human existence, taking the language and teaching of the Bible as experienced in his own life of faith, and expressing it in a way that is accessible to men and women of all faiths or of no faith. Buber warns that our ever-increasing ability to use and experience, manipulate and control, while often of benefit to humankind, is stifling our ability for encounter, for life on the narrow ridge, for community, for prayer. The more that the I-It attitude dominates our lives, the less human we are, and the less we are open to God Who is eternally Thou, eternally present, eternal Presence. Authentic humanness is achieved through the sharing that is at the heart of the lived encounter with the Thou; the deeper the shar-ing, the more actual or real the I becomes. That is why all real living is meeting. Only through encounter with the Thou is there sharing and presence: only through the Thou do we "know" presence and come to a glimpse, a breath, of the Thou revealed as to Moses as eternally present, eternal Presence: "I will be there as I will be there" (Exod. 3:14).[3]

Buber's world of It is not evil; on the contrary, it is necessary for life, for progress, for civilization. Through the knowledge and understanding of I-It, one may come to a deeper sharing in the encounter with the Thou. Yet one must take care lest I-It become dominant in one's life. One must not allow oneself to drift toward Buber's pole of individuality, toward the I of alienation, of unreality. The whole of *I and Thou* might be viewed as an urgent plea on the part of Buber to center our lives more and more on the life of dialogue, on the holy insecurity of the narrow ridge.

APPLICATIONS OF BUBER'S METHODOLOGY

The experience of dialogical relationship, of holy insecurity, of the lived coincidence of opposites is for Buber the very core of biblical revelation. Israel's prophets constantly frustrate the people's yearning for security.

They preach instead the holy insecurity of "the unwished-for-God" who is at once a demanding God and at the same time a confounding God for those who are looking for a once-for-all certainty (*EG*, 73). Such certainty, such security, is not to be found in the God of Israel.

Buber is representative of that group of scholars who have attempted to reestablish what is essential from a Jewish perspective for biblical exegesis and scholarship. Both in his translation of the Bible into German, a project which occupied him for forty years, and in his interpretation of the Bible, Buber sought to go beyond the oral tradition to the primordial moment of the spoken word. "Is it a book we mean?" Buber asks. "We mean a voice: and do we believe our task is to read? We believe our task is to listen for the spoken word. We want to reach the word in its moment of utterance."[4]

One can say that for Buber the fundamental reality is speech—the speech or address of God to humankind. The very act of God's creation is speech, dialogical relationship. "In the beginning is relation," writes Buber (*I and Thou*, 18); each lived moment carries on this dialogue so that all that happens, all that befalls a person, is taken as a sign of address. In seeking to recapture the origins of the Bible, then, Buber wants to make audible again the living Voice of the message, a Voice that addresses and challenges, with humankind answering through prayer and action. The Bible is to be understood acoustically, for Scripture has primordially an oral character rooted in the spokenness of the word. Through address and response the dialogue between God and human beings, between I and Thou, must once again be made experienceable behind the self-interest and familiarity which so often stifle the Voice for us in our time. The meaning of the word, insofar as it concerns the relation between God and humankind, cannot in Buber's mind be grasped objectively; it offers itself "not to our discursive understanding, but to our contemplation" (Buber, "Abraham," 297). The Bible must always be read in living Presence; we must listen faithfully to the Voice that addresses us.

This effort of Buber to recapture the lived moment of encounter, this effort to live in the holy insecurity of the narrow ridge, had manifested itself earlier in his approach to the texts of the Hasidim. Buber perceived that Hasidism was pointing to a fundamental Jewish and human reality—namely, that our being created in the image of God must be grasped "as deed, as becoming, as task." Buber was convinced that at the heart of Hasidism was the simple message that we cannot approach the divine in any other way than by becoming human. To become human is what each individual person is created for. Buber recalls the words of Rabbi Zusya to his disciples: "In the world to come I shall not be asked: 'Why were you not Moses?' I shall be asked: 'Why were you not Zusya?' " In Buber's understanding of Hasidism the world is not an illusion from which we must turn in order to find God; rather it is the arena in which reciprocity manifests itself, bearing the message of creation to us and bearing in return our response, our service in the redemption of the world (*HMM*, 59, 140).

In the now famous controversy with Gershom Scholem over the interpretation of Hasidic texts, Buber insisted that his purpose was to recapture the power and vitality of Hasidic faith, to preserve the dialogical character of this living faith, and to return to the moment of lived encounter rather than to convey and analyze the teachings that arose from this faith. The theoretical teachings are not at the center of Hasidism's religious and historical development, as Scholem had insisted, but rather the legends and the tales. The Hasidic relationship to God, in Buber's mind, was so clearly existential that no theoretical teaching can do it justice. Only the anecdote or legend can suitably convey this relationship. Buber's success in accomplishing this task was indirectly acknowledged by Abraham Heschel who, when, in his presence, a disciple suggested that a group of South Africans read Scholem, responded: "If you want to know Hasidism as it was, begin with Buber" (cited in Friedman, *MBLW: Later*, 299).

Buber's methodology in approaching Jesus and the New Testament likewise seeks to recapture, as it were, the primordial moment of the spoken word and the dialogical character of Jesus' living faith. In listening to the Voice that speaks ever anew from the Gospels, Buber concluded that there was one dominant characteristic of Jesus, one that marked his essential Jewishness, namely, his desire to persevere in immediacy with God. The very person of Jesus is defined by this immediacy. The "I" of Jesus, powerful and overpowering, as Buber points out in *I and Thou*, is rooted in total openness to the One who is eternally Thou. Jesus is so fully turned toward God in unconditional relation that he calls his Thou "Father," and he himself becomes nothing but Son. Everyone, says Buber, can speak the Thou and thus become I; everyone can say "Father," and thus become son (*I and Thou*, 66–67). Romano Guardini echoed Buber's thought on this point when he wrote that the ultimate Thou for each Christian is the Father, and Jesus alone is the one who speaks the true Thou to God. The individual Christian is invited to share in this Thou-saying of Jesus to the Father, thus Jesus remains ever the way for the Christian (Guardini 1950). Buber also sees the Jesus of the gospels as the one who calls men and women to this unconditional relationship with God. This teaching of Jesus is eloquently expressed in the prayer he gave to his disciples: the Lord's

Prayer expresses the concern of Jesus, not for the revelation of divine mysteries, but for the life of *emunah*, a life lived in holy insecurity before the face of God.

In his appreciation of Jesus, Buber has probably gone as far as any Jew, as Jew, could possibly go. In some quarters Buber has been reproached for seemingly being too Christian, for exhibiting a tendency to "christianize" his thoughts. Buber admitted that he found in Jesus his "great brother" and that his fraternal relationship to Jesus continued to evolve in his lifetime. "I am more than ever certain that a great place belongs to him in Israel's history of faith and this place cannot be described by any of the usual categories" (*TTF*, 12–13).

On many occasions Buber underscored the common spiritual patrimony of Jew and Christian, with special emphasis on the "book" and the "expectation" that they share in common. Despite the very real differences, Jew and Christian can together listen to the Voice that speaks from the pages of the Bible and together "redeem the imprisoned living word." Both Jew and Christian can wait together for the One who is to come, and together they may prepare the way. Buber acknowledged the abyss that divides Christians and Jews, but he argued that this should not prevent them from looking forward to that common unity which can come only from God and which will replace all the credal truths of the religions with the one transcendent truth of God's Presence. The many advances in Jewish-Christian relations over the last several decades evidence the truth of what Buber stated forty years ago: if Judaism and Christianity maintain a genuine dialogical relationship with one another, they would then have something "as yet unsaid to say to each other and a help to give one another—hardly to be conceived of at the present time" (*TTF*, 174).

APPLICATIONS TO CATHOLIC THEOLOGY

The dialogue between Martin Buber and Catholic theology is still in its early stages. There is a growing realization that Buber represents for Catholic thought a profound challenge. I would submit that his challenge to Catholic theology is above all the challenge to theologize from the "holy insecurity" of the "narrow ridge." Buber challenges us to bring more to the center of our theological reflection the moment of lived encounter, to recapture those moments of meeting, of address, which form the marrow of all revelation and which are the basis of the Scriptures, the teachings, the creeds, the symbols, the rites, the practices—at the basis of all those elements that comprise the biblical and Christian traditions.

The admonitions and criticisms that Buber so often mentions concerning religion are aptly applied to theology as well. "Degeneration of the religions," he writes in *I and Thou*, "means the degeneration of prayer in them." In other words, unless prayer, the moment of encounter with the eternal Thou, has a central place in religion, then religion becomes mere structure—objectified, immersed in the world of It.

It is this type of religion that Buber had in mind with his stinging words: "Religion can hide from us as nothing else can the face of God" (*BMM*, 18). When we examine Buber's polemic against religion, we must recognize that it is a polemic against the vast structures of beliefs, of rituals, or precepts which at times form a virtual barricade, preventing that critical immediacy or directness between the human being and God. In such a religion there is no place for holy insecurity, for existential trust. Religion in all of its forms and manifestations and structures must be open to the power of the spirit, to the power of the Thou encounter, to the insecurity of the dialogical relationship. In other words, it is not the forms and symbols and structures of religion *of themselves* which are the object of Buber's polemic. As he points out in *I and Thou*, such aspects of religion are necessary because of our nature as human beings; creating them is not done "out of arbitrary self-will." The forms and symbols and structures of religion represent "the passage away from the living God and back again" to God. The changes from the moments of lived encounter with the eternal Thou, from the moments of prayer "to establishment of form, of objects, and of ideas, dissolution and renewal—all are one way, are *the* way." Buber insists that God is near the forms of religion as long as we do not remove them from God. And how do we remove them from God? The answer for Buber is quite simple: by lack of prayer. "The fact that true prayer lives in the religions witnesses to their true life: they live so long as it [prayer] lives in them" (*I and Thou*, 118).

Elsewhere Buber recognizes the need of law and structure in the religions of humankind. Yet structure and law represent two of the greatest dangers to the religious undertaking. Without the spirit of renewal that comes from prayer, from encounter with the Thou, from life on the narrow ridge, then structure and law become the epitome of all that is harmful and obstructive in religion. To the point are Buber's words of caution: "Centralization and codification, undertaken in the interests of religion, are a danger to the core of religion, *unless there is the strongest life of faith*, embodied in the whole existence of the community, and not relaxing its renewing activity" (*PF*, 170). And a life of faith for Buber is a life lived before the face of God, a life of unconditional openness and trust to the Thou of one's life.

These cautions and criticisms of Buber concerning religion should also be applied to theology: degeneration of theology means degeneration of prayer among theologians, degeneration of the lived moments of encounter, a failure to recognize or to search for the living voice that speaks to us through Scripture and through tradition. John Courtney Murray spoke of the silence that should befall every theologian as the final product of theological investigation, a silence that bespeaks the language of adoration (1964, 73). The challenge of Buber to theologians is to place such silence and adoration at the center of their enterprise; otherwise theology is indeed in danger of "removing its forms from God" and hence of dealing only with an It-God. Moments of mystery, encounter, dialogue, wonder, prayer should permeate the whole of our theological undertaking to prevent theology from becoming overly immersed in formulae, teachings, speculations, systems that are far removed from the holy insecurity of the narrow ridge and immersed instead in the objectivizing mentality of the It-world. Again, to paraphrase Buber, the fact that true prayer lives in our theologies witnesses to their true life. Conceptualizations and systematization must remain open to the spirit of renewal that comes from a living faith, from moments of prayer and worship, from life on the narrow ridge.

BUBER AND RAHNER

It would be very difficult to ascertain whether Martin Buber and Karl Rahner were ever cognizant of one another's writings, but there is clearly in Rahner's thought enough similarity to form the basis of dialogue with Buber. I will limit myself to a few key points.[5]

It is unfortunate that Buber did not live to see the fruits of Vatican II in Catholic theology. For Rahner the significance of Vatican II lies not so much in the content of its various decrees and constitutions, important as these might be, but in the fact that for the first time in its history the Roman Catholic Church began to become a world church—that is, it began to take a few crucial steps toward becoming a truly catholic or universal church. This change is so major that one can liken it only to that moment early in its history when Christianity moved from being a Jewish church, a sect within Judaism, to being a church of Gentiles and pagans outside of Jewish observance. It is difficult for us to grasp how much rethinking of what had been held to be "immutable" truths must have taken place for the primitive Church to reach this understanding of itself. If Rahner is correct, if the Church has become less Roman and more catholic, then so much that has been considered profane, secular, ungraced must now be viewed in a different manner. We need both a new image of the secular as well as a new image of Christianity. This "conversion" of the Church's attitude toward the world is not unlike that conversion in his own religious outlook that Buber describes for us—the change from considering the "religious" as something set apart from our everyday life in the world, as "extraction, exaltation, ecstasy," as that which lifted one out of everyday affairs, to considering the religious as being "just *everything*, simply all that is lived in its possibility of dialogue" (*BMM*, 13–14). For Buber, too, his conversion implied a wholly new attitude toward the world. What was fundamental to Buber's attitude toward the world was a fundamental or existential trust. There is no movement towards encounter or meeting without this existential trust. The world is that which mediates God's presence to us. When Rahner speaks of the "mediated immediacy" of God, he means that this immediacy of God is mediated by the world, so that humanity's highest spiritual goal is reached "not by the negation of history, but by its being raised to a new and divinized level. That such a mediated immediacy of God does exist is testified by existential experience" (Viladesau, 226). Only the self-communication of God, this mediated immediacy of God, can explain for Rahner the courageous hope, the existential trust, we manifest in our absolute commitments of love. Rahner's position presupposes the continuity of "nature" and "grace." The human achievement of intimate union with God does not abolish the finite, conditional world in which we live but gives it eternal validity—our lives take on ultimate and divine significance. Rahner's affirmation of the continued mediation of the world even at the highest point of genuine immediacy to God "implies a vision of salvation in which the historical and personal are of essential and eternal value; a salvation which is therefore *in* and *for* the world, rather than *from* the world" (ibid.).

One could say of Rahner that he, like Buber, remains in the holy insecurity of the narrow ridge. His was in no way a theology that unveiled the mystery of God. Rather he continually points out that we live always in the presence of a holy and absolute Mystery, a Mystery that has drawn so near to us that we can discover this Mystery in the depths of our own spirit and in the space and time of our human history. To live this Mystery, which is grasped only by faith, is to be open to the presence of God in all things. Nicholas Lash describes the basically simple vision underlying Rahner's theology as "a vision of the uncontrollably diverse darkness of human existence which is, nevertheless, at all points 'graced' by the Spirit of God and illuminated by the Cross of Christ. From that dark place and in that light, we may learn appropriate obedience, which is our freedom, to the incomprehensible mystery of God" (1988, 241–42).

Given this absolute incomprehensibility of God, Rahner poses the question: "How can the incomprehensible and nameless be the meaning that *we* have?" In other words, if absolute incomprehensibility is the answer to our quest for meaning, how are we to live so as to "allow for the incomprehensibility of God without being broken by that incomprehensibility or putting it aside as irrelevant?" (Or, as he later adds, without taking refuge in the banality of some kind of gnosis or clear knowledge?) Rahner responds that we live in such a way as to allow for and accept God's incomprehensibility as the comprehensive meaning of our own existence without being broken by it, by "the act of self-surrendering love trusting entirely in this very incomprehensibility, in which knowledge surpasses itself . . . and is aware of itself only by becoming love" (Rahner 1984, in Lash, 222–23).

Elsewhere Rahner affirms his position on the narrow ridge of insecurity when he writes that the human person is "someone who dares to hope, and shows that hope is possible *in* the very act of this courageous hope [what Buber would refer to as existential trust], that his existence is borne by this all-pervasive mystery." We hope that this mystery gives itself to us as the fulfillment of our claim for absolute meaning. "Consequently, the finite, the conditional and the plurality which we are inescapably does indeed remain, but nevertheless it participates in the infinite itself, in the unity of the fullness of meaning, in a Thou who is absolutely trustworthy" (Rahner 1985, 209).

Christians have often given the impression (an impression shared by Buber) that the revelation of God in Christ renders the mystery of God less incomprehensible, or that this incomprehensibility is a temporary condition which will cease when we see God "face to face" in the beatific vision. In either case, this would reduce divine incomprehensibility to a function of our ignorance, whereas for Rahner (and for Buber) this incomprehensibility pertains to the very being of God. For Rahner God's revelation in Christ *deepens* the perception of God as mystery, and when Christianity proclaims the immediate vision of God as the one fulfilling goal of the human person, Rahner says that we probably forget that this vision means coming immediately into the presence of the *incomprehensibility* of God (Lash, 222).

There is good reason for Buber to argue that, while the relationship of Israel to its God is so exclusive and so immediate that it can be a relationship only to a God who cannot be represented or confined by any outward form, such is not true of Christianity, for Christians, at least in the actual living of their faith, assign to God a definite human countenance: "The God of the Christian is both imageless and imaged, but imageless rather in the religious idea and imaged rather in actual experience. The image conceals the imageless One" (*TTF*, 131). Christians are indeed guilty of this distortion of faith; the correction of Buber is needed here (as well as in many other areas of Christianity). Once again, Rahner's theology parallels Buber's thought. For Rahner the Christian doctrine of Incarnation does not imply that God ceases to be Absolute Mystery or that God can in any way be contained in the finite phenomena of the life of Jesus. Moreover, for Rahner the humanity assumed by God at the Incarnation "neither is nor can be graced in itself with a closeness to God and an encounter with God which is essentially different from *the* encounter with God which is essentially different from *the* encounter and self-communication of God which in fact is intended for *every* person in grace" (cf. Viladesau, 229). Although Rahner means something quite different from Buber, his words echo the thoughts of Buber in *I and Thou* cited earlier. Jesus calls his *Thou* Father in such a way that he himself is simply Son and nothing else but Son. Everyone can say *Thou* and is then Son or Daughter. The opportunity and the need for dialogue should be evident.

For Rahner all theology must also be anthropology: every statement about God is also a statement about humankind. God is grasped or encountered only as a dimension within our experience of the human. Rahner's theory of the "supernatural existential" serves as the theological foundation for saying that all authentic human existence is in touch with the realities denoted by the theological terms of grace, salvation, revelation, faith (Rahner 1985, 126ff.). These are realities that take place with the realm of the human and the secular, within the lived concreteness of everyday life. When divorced from the lived situation of our lives, these theological realities are objectified into a separate realm, creating the false problem of relating these two realms—the supernatural and the natural, the sacred and the secular. What theologically we call revelation and salvation and grace take place within the human as an actualization of human potential, not as something added on extrinsically to what we are as human beings.

One encounters God, not primarily through some kind of explicitly religious experience but through one's encounter with the world and with humankind. In Rahner's thinking, Christianity does not deal with eternal truths or with immutable situations but with historical realities, with events which occur in time (138ff.). There is an ever-present temptation in Christianity toward doceticism and gnosticism, to see Jesus not as a being in time who became who he was by living through each stage of life in freedom, but rather as a God who merely pretended to be human. Should Christianity ever lose its roots in the concrete life of Jesus of Nazareth (or, might I add, in Judaism), it would lose its roots also in the here and now. It would become a gnostic doctrine whose truth is no longer dependent upon being discovered ever anew in the lived concrete, in the ever new particularities of time and space. It would become instead a religion employed to help us escape from the responsibilities, from the existential trust required by the here and now.

We might say then that Rahner developed in his theology a theme central to the thought of Ignatius of Loyola and central to the thought of Martin Buber: "finding God in all things." This does not mean, as it could for some, imposing one's God on all things, a God who represents an absolutized set of concepts and rules. Rather one finds God in all things by letting all things reveal God, each in its own way, each revealing a facet of God by what it is in its own concrete and particular reality, each by its own face, its own words, its own time. For each of God's creatures carries within it, in Kabbalistic terms, a divine spark. Buber warns us in *I and Thou* that there is no such thing as seeking God, for there is nowhere where God cannot be found. It should not be surprising that the first of the many dozens of Rahner's books translated into English was a volume of his meditations (Rahner 1960). Those who worked closely with him testify to the centrality of prayer in the life and work of this German Jesuit. For Rahner, faith is never a possession but rather an attitude and a search that carries us through all the variety and detail of the finite world. Rahner's theology leaves us not with a content but a process, a way of thinking, of encountering, of being free, and of believing. If Buber's thought could be called an interpretation of human existence from a biblical perspective, then Rahner's theology might be termed an interpretation of human existence from a Christian perspective. The untheological Buber and the rigorous theologian Rahner would have much to say to one another.

"I have no teaching, but I carry on a conversation" ("Replies" in *PMB*, 693). This is the invitation that Buber addressed to his readers as he neared the end of his life. Catholic theology, especially since the end of Vatican II, has been at least indirectly ever more caught up in this conversation generated by Buber. It is a conversation carried on wherever two or three are gathered together in dialogue, present to one another, open to one another. I would suggest that Martin Buber and Karl Rahner would have made, and it is hoped will yet make, very interesting conversation partners.

NOTES

1. See Emil Brunner, "Judaism and Christianity in Buber," in *PMB*, 309–10.
2. Cf. Maurice Friedman, *Martin Buber: The Life of Dialogue*, new ed. (1960), 136; cf. also Friedman's *MBLW: Early*, 150–76.

3. Martin Buber, *I and Thou* (Smith), 95–96. Cf. M. Friedman 1981, 369–70, and also his "Martin Buber's Approach to Contemporary Religion" in *Martin Buber: A Centenary Volume,* 367–80.
4. Cf. Martin Buber, *The Prophetic Faith,* 28–29, and *Moses: The Revelation of the Covenant,* 51–55, for an analysis of Buber's exegesis of *Exodus* 3:14.
5. This section owes much to the perceptive article of my colleague, William Dych, "Moving on to Fresh Horizons: The Discoveries of Karl Rahner and William Lynch" in Catholic Mind LXXVII (Sept. 1979): 8–19, and to Nicholas Lash, *Easter in Ordinary,* especially pp. 13–15.

REFERENCES

Buber, Martin. (1955). "Abraham the Seer." *Judaism* 4.

———. *ABH; BMM; Daniel; EG; HMM; I and Thou* (Kaufmann); *IW; OJ; OMH; PF; PW; TTF.*

———. (1964). "Interrogation of Martin Buber." Edited by M. Friedman. In S. Rome and B. Rome (eds.), *Philosophical Interrogations* (113–117). New York: Rinehart and Winston.

Friedman, Maurice, *LOD; MBLW: Early; MBLW: Later.*

Guardini, Romano. (1950). *Welt und Person.* 3rd ed. Wurtzburg: Werkbund Verlag.

Katz, Steven. (1984). "A Critical Review of Martin Buber's Epistemology of I-Thou." In Haim Gordon and Jochanan Block (eds.), *Martin Buber: A Centenary Volume.* Hoboken: KTAV.

Lash, Nicholas. (1988). *Easter in Ordinary.* Charlottsville: University Press of Virginia.

Murray, John Courtney. (1964). *The Problem of God.* New Haven: Yale University Press.

Rahner, Karl. (1960). *Encounters with Silence.* Westminster: Newman Press.

———. (1985). *Foundations of Christian Faith.* Trans. by William Dych. New York: Crossroad.

———. (1984). "The Human Question of Meaning in Face of the Incomprehensible Mystery of God." In *Theological Investigations,* vol. 18, trans. by Edward Quinn. London: Darton, Longman and Todd.

Schilpp, Paul Arthur, and Friedman, Maurice. *PMB.*

Viladesau, Richard. (1988). "How is Christ Absolute? Rahner's Christology and the Encounter of World Religions." In *Philosophy and Theology* 2(3).

CHAPTER 7

BUBER, THE *VIA NEGATIVA*, AND ZEN

G. RAY JORDAN, JR.

Martin Buber tells how in his earlier years "religious experience" was for him ecstatic and lifted him out of everyday reality (*BMM*, 13). I believe that this type of experience is similar to the ecstatic experience of union with the Divine referred to by Plotinus (Mackenna II, 9) and selected Christian mystics beginning with the late-fifth-century writer who used the pseudonym Dionysius the Areopagite (Gandillac, 7, 14). The *via negativa* is Dionysius' "Negative method," which he says he prefers because it

> lifts the soul above all things cognate with its finite nature, and guiding it onward through all the conceptions of God's Being which are transcended by that Being, exceeding all Name, Reason, and Knowledge, reaches beyond the farthest limits of the world and there joins us unto God Himself, in so far as the power of union with Him is possessed even by us men (Rolt, 189).

Although Buber gave up ecstatic religious experience, or was given up by it, his way in the midst of the everyday (*BMM*, 14) is itself a via negativa which is more demanding than the "Negative method" of Dionysius. Along the path of Mahayana Buddhism, particularly the way of Zen, masters and teachers have left signposts which can sharpen understanding of everyday life as a via negativa which is the most radically positive way possible.

In what respects are Buber's ecstatic experiences of his earlier years similar to those described by Plotinus and Dionysius? First, the most important, most valued reality (realities) is (are) different from everyday realities. Porphyry, Plotinus' biographer, says that:

Plotinus, the philosopher our contemporary, seemed ashamed of being in the body.
So deeply rooted was this feeling that he could never be induced to tell of his ancestry, his parentage or his birthplace.
He showed, too, an unconquerable reluctance to sit to a painter or a sculptor, and when Amelius persisted in urging him to allow of a portrait being made he asked him, "Is it not enough to carry about this image in which nature has enclosed us? Do you really think I must also consent to leave, as a desireable spectacle to posterity, an image of an image?" (Mackenna I, 1)

Porphyry, who was "in close relation" with him for the last six years of Plotinus' life, describes him as "sleeplessly alert . . . pure of soul, ever striving towards the divine which he loved with all his being," and as one who "laboured strenuously to free himself and rise above the bitter waves of this blood-drenched life." And, says Porphyry, "four times, during the period I passed with him, he achieved [union with all-transcendent God]" (Mackenna I, 23–24). Dionysius says that:

If it happens that, seeing God, one understands what he sees, one has not seen God himself, but some one of those knowable things which gain being from him. For in himself he surpasses every intelligence and every essence (Gandillac, 327).

As this passage implies, actual contemplation of the true God is a state of "Unknowing" or "Divine Ignorance." C. E. Rolt says that Dionysius is "unquestionably speaking of a psychological state to which he himself has been occasionally led" (Rolt, 33). For Plotinus, also, the supreme God is beyond all knowing (Mackenna II, vi, 8, 11). Plotinus' experiences of union with the Supreme, mentioned by Porphyry, must be moments or events of realization which are "above the bitter waves of this blood-drenched life."

For Buber, also, the religious experiences of his earlier years "were hours that were taken out of the course of things":

"Religious experience" was the experience of an otherness which did not fit into the context of life. . . . The "religious" lifted you out. Over there now lay the accustomed existence with its affairs, but here illumination and ecstasy and rapture held without time or sequence. (BMM, 13)

Did Buber's ecstatic religious experience go so far as to include the
Divine Ignorance referred to by Plotinus, Dionysius, and others? Maybe.
Certainly there is an "unknowing" which is basic to Buber's way in
"the everyday out of which," he says, "I am never taken. The mystery is
no longer disclosed; it has escaped or it has made its dwelling here
where everything happens as it happens" (*BMM*, 14). Since it is "no
longer disclosed," this "mystery" must have been at one time "disclosed" in special ecstatic moments. Surely what is referred to is "the
essential mystery" which "comes when our existence between birth
and death becomes incomprehensible and uncanny, when all security is
shattered through the mystery" (*EG*, 36).

Buber *may* once have thought experience of this "essential mystery" to be an experience of absolute unity. That, at least, is a possible
implication of his remark in *I and Thou* that he at one time confused
the nonduality of "the soul's becoming a unity" with the *apparent* nonduality of a supreme encounter with God (*I and Thou* [Smith], 86).

Whether or not Buber's earlier religious experiences of the Divine
included immersion in (apparent) radical nonduality, their ecstatic
nature removed him from ordinary, everyday realities as surely as the
unitive experiences of Plotinus and Dionysius leave behind what are
regarded as lesser realities. The leaving behind of the lesser and the
incomplete is the way of negation—the via negativa.

The fact that the way of contemplation (ecstatic experience of God)
seems to be self-validating as the highest good and that such ecstasy literally removes one from the activities of the everyday world led, in the
history of Christianity, to the distinction between the active life and the
contemplative life—the way of Martha and the way of Mary—at least as
early as St. Augustine (Reinhold, 173–82). The active way of helping
others in the world is a necessary good, "but," writes Augustine, "still
sorrowful; the other [the life of contemplation] is better and perfectly
blessed. . . . The one laboureth here even unto the end, and findeth its
end hereafter; the other stretcheth out into the hereafter, and in eternity
findeth no end" (Reinhold, 174). The subsequent history of Christianity
in medieval times and right down to the present in religious orders and
among some Protestant pietist groups records intense discussions as to
how the two ways—action and contemplation—are or should be related
to each other. Whatever the view as to their correct interrelation, each
traditional idea assumes that here on earth both ways are necessary.
One often repeated idea is that contemplative experience may charge
the spiritual battery of an individual so that what is taken in during
withdrawn prayer aids one in actively helping one's neighbors. And, as
Augustine suggests, when our doing attains "a calm peacefulness

instead of degenerating into a restless hurry," our very actions help toward a fuller, freer contemplation of the eternal (Reinhold, 176).

However one perceives the interrelation of the active way and the contemplative way, the very distinction between the two is not there in Buber's mature way. Nor is it present in the mature way of Zen. In *I and Thou* Buber says:

> I know nothing of a "world" and a "life in the world" that might separate a man from God. What is thus described is actually life with an alienated world of *It*, which experiences and uses. He who truly goes out to meet the world goes out also to God. Concentration and outgoing are necessary, both in truth, at once the one and the other, which is the One. (95)

In *Eclipse of God* Buber makes clear his view that "all religious reality" begins when, immediately aware of one's own finitude, one encounters

> the essential mystery, the inscrutableness of which belongs to its very nature; it is the unknowable. Through this dark gate (which is only a gate and not, as some theologians believe, a dwelling) the believing man steps forth into the everyday which is henceforth hallowed as the place in which he has to live with the mystery. (*EG*, 36)

Although Buber speaks of such an encounter with "the essential mystery" (which he equates with the Biblical "fear of God") as passage through a gate, one's "passing through" does not leave the mystery behind. Rather the mystery "has made its dwelling here where everything happens as it happens" (*BMM*, 14). And each I-Thou meeting with an individual, though it brings no objectified knowledge (*BMM*, 4) "is a glimpse through to the eternal Thou; by means of every particular Thou the primary word [of I-Thou] addresses the eternal Thou " (*I and Thou*, 75).

Who is this eternal Thou we meet in every particular I-Thou encounter? Buber warns his reader:

> It would not avail us to give for reply the word "God," if we do not give it out of that decisive hour of personal existence when we had to forget everything we imagined we knew of God, when we dared to keep nothing handed down or learned or self-contrived, no shred of knowledge, and were plunged into the night. (*BMM*, 14)

Clearly "the essential mystery" is recognized in "unknowing." Encounter with it is a "way of negation" wherein we must forget all we imagine we know of God whether learned from others or "self-contrived."

As we enter daily life the mystery is still with us. All that we can therein know of God "is what we experience from time to time from the signs themselves" (*BMM*, 15). What are these "signs"? They are given not in extraordinary or great events. Rather:

> Each concrete hour allotted to the person . . . is speech for the man who is attentive. Attentive, for no more than that is needed in order to make a beginning with the reading of the signs that are given to you. For that very reason . . . the whole apparatus of our civilization is necessary to preserve men from this attentiveness and its consequences. For the attentive man would no longer, as his custom is, "master" the situation the very moment after it stepped up to him: it would be laid upon him to go up to and into it. Moreover, nothing that he believed he possessed as always available would help him, no knowledge and no technique, no system and no programme; for now he would have to do with what cannot be classified, with concretion itself. This speech has no alphabet, each of its sounds is a new creation and only to be grasped as such.
>
> . . . . .
>
> But the sounds of which the speech consists—I repeat it in order to remove the misunderstanding, which is perhaps still possible, that I referred to something extraordinary and larger than life— are the events of the personal everyday life. In them, as they now are, "great" or "small", we are addressed, and those which count as great, yield no greater signs than the others. (*BMM*, 16)

The way of concrete, daily reality is clearly a way of negation (via negativa) because no learned habit or custom, no knowledge, no learned behavioral pattern will help. All such devices—habit, knowledge, learned behaviors, etc.—constitute the "whole apparatus of our civilization" which preserves us from "this attentiveness and its consequences." This negation, however, does not involve either an ecstatic unconsciousness or a non-ecstatic blank mind condition. As Buber says when speaking of an I-Thou encounter (becoming bound up in relation) with a tree:

> There is nothing from which I would have to turn my eyes away in order to see, and no knowledge that I would have to forget. Rather is everything, picture and movement, species and type, law and number, indivisibly united in this event. (*I and Thou*, 7)

A Zen teacher would observe that words and knowledge can be very valuable but must not be confused with the immediate (unmediated) reality. Shibayama Roshi says that:

An old Zen Master . . . warns us, "Be sure to detach yourself from all your clingings. Be sure not to attach yourself to non-clinging either."
It is, however, an unfortunate tendency of man that he clings to traditional labels. . . . Names and words are nothing but the result of man's discriminating intellection. To cast away our attachment to all such labels is to live the One Truth right in front of us just as it is. . . . In your going and in your sitting, in the redness of flowers and the green of the willows, live the Truth as it is. When you do so, your true self works freely. (Shibayama, 16–17)

The "True Self" which "works freely" is at least similar to the "I" of "I-Thou." It may or may not be the same in all respects. In any case Buber points out that "the I of the primary word I-Thou is a different I from that of the primary word I-It " (I and Thou, 3). The I of I-It is the atta (atman) or ego self described in Buddhist teachings. This latter I is always grasping and mastering, or trying to master, things, situations, and events. In reality—Buddhist vathabhutam, Buber's I-Thou relation where "no deception penetrates . . . the cradle of Real Life" (9)—one cannot grasp or master "a newly-created concrete reality" which "cannot be classified." One can turn away from it by becoming busy or inattentive (BMM, 16) (Buddhist ignoring or not seeing—avija/avidya). Or one can respond with one's being. Buber says:

The words of our response are spoken in the speech untranslatable like the address ["the signs that are given to you"], of doing and letting—whereby the doing may behave like a letting and the letting like a doing. (BMM, 17)

Becoming aware of the "signs that are given to you" is not enough. One must really respond (BMM, 16). This distinction is at least paralleled by the Mahayana Buddhist distinction between the awakening or "seeing" of prajna and the compassionate responding to others of karuna (Suzuki, 46–82; Thurman, 3–9, and throughout). Buber's description of genuine responding "whereby the doing may behave like a letting and letting like a doing" is very much like descriptions in Mahayana Buddhist literature of the Bodhisattva's tireless helping of others, a helping which is "no helping" because it is rooted in the groundless ground of shunyata (literally, "emptiness," "voidness") (Thurman, 43–49, and throughout).

Near the beginning of this paper I described the implicit via negativa of Buber's way (the way of Zen) as more demanding than the traditional "Negative method" of Dionysius. Now we can see why it is more demanding, more radical. The via negativa of Plotinus and Dionysius leads to an alternate state of ecstatic consciousness which is removed from the ordinary time-space world. The way of Buber and Zen (and the Bodhisattva) realizes the nameless mystery in the midst of responding within the everyday realities. In the words of a Zen teacher, one who lives this way

> is neither worldly nor holy, dwelling neither in passions nor wisdom. . . . He comes from the place of Nothing, non-difference, into the world of various differences. When a person enters it after going through Nothing, it becomes a world of unending freedom and inexhaustible creativity. He lives an "enlightened life without enlightenment." (Trevor, 93)

He has attained the final Unity which, according to Tozan Ryokai, as well as various commentators on the tenth ox-herding picture, is "the current of ordinary life" which "all men [aspirants to a better life, or to "the spiritual life"] want to leave. . . . But he, after all, comes back to sit among the coals and ashes" (Miura and Sasaki, 71). Detached from all clingings, and not attached to non-clinging either, such a one has no special signs by which he can be identified. Thus "even the wisest cannot find him" (Kapleau, 323–25).

This Unity is the same Unity approved by Buber as earlier cited. Buber's words bear repeating:

> I know nothing of a "world" and a "life in the world" that might separate a man from God. What is thus described is actually life within an alienated world of *It*, which experiences and uses. He who truly goes out to meet the world goes out also to God. Concentration and outgoing are necessary, both in truth, at once the one and the other, which is the One. (1958, 95)

REFERENCES

Buber, Martin. *BMM*; *EG*; *GE*; *I and Thou* (Smith).

Kapleau, Roshi Philip. (1980). *The Three Pillars of Zen*. Revised and expanded edition. Garden City, NY: Anchor Press/Doubleday.

Gandillac, Maurice de (ed. and trans.) (1943). *Oeuvres completes de Pseudo-Denys l'Areopagite*. Paris: Aubier, Editions Montaigne. [English in text is my translation from the French.]

Mackenna, Stephen (trans.). *Plotinus* [The Enneads]. Vols. 1 and 2. Boston: Charles T. Branford Company [n.d.].

Miura, Isshu, and Sasaki, Ruth Fuller. (1967). *Zen Dust, The History of the Koan and Koan Study in Rinzi (Lin-Chi) Zen.* New York: Harcourt, Brace & World.

Peers, E. Allison (trans.). (1945). *The Complete Works of St. John of the Cross.* Vol. 3. Westminster, MD: The Newman Bookshop.

Post, L. A. (trans.). (1925). *Thirteen Epistles of Plato.* Oxford: Clarendon Press.

Reinhold, H. A. (ed.). (1947). *The Spear of Gold: Revelations of the Mystics.* London: Burnes Oates.

Rolt, C. E. (trans.). (1940). *Dionysius the Areopagite on the Divine Names and the Mystical Theology.* New York: Macmillan.

Sensaki, Nyogen, and Reps, Paul (trans.). *101 Zen Stories.* London: Rider and Co. [n.d.].

Shibayama, Zenkei. (1974). *Zen Comments on the Mumonkan.* New York: Harper & Row.

Suzuki, Daisetz Teitaro. (1957). *The Essence of Buddhism.* 2nd ed. London: The Buddhist Society.

Thurman, Robert A. F. (trans.). (1976). *The Holy Teaching of Vimalakirti.* University Park: Pennsylvania State University Press.

Trevor, M. H. (trans.). (1969). *The Ox and His Herdsman.* Tokyo: Hokuseido Press

CHAPTER 8

I AND TAO

Buber's *Chuang Tzu* and the Comparative Study of Mysticism

JONATHAN R. HERMAN

In 1909, Martin Buber began work on an essay addressing ancient Chinese thought in general and Lao Tzu's *Tao Te Ching* in particular, thus initiating an ongoing involvement with Chinese philosophy and religion. He soon expanded the essay to include discussion of Chuang Tzu, the other great philosophical Taoist of the Chinese Classical Period, and of the text that bears his name. The following year, the entire document appeared as the "afterword" to Buber's *Reden und Gleichnisse des Tschuang-tse*, an unreferenced selection of fifty-four passages from *Chuang Tzu*, translated into German by way of two English versions as well as uncredited, unspecified advice from Wang Chingdao, a visiting lecturer at the Berlin Seminar for Oriental Languages. Buber's Chinese output continued over the years, notably with his 1911 collection, *Chinesische Geister- und Liebesgeschichten,*[1] and a second, unpublished commentary on the *Tao Te Ching* in 1924.[2]

Originally, Buber's *Chuang Tzu* received uncritical accolades from his peers, was cited on the title page of a German Youth Movement periodical,[3] and had enough popularity to merit several printings and two major revisions. However, in the two academic areas where it would be most likely to find an audience, those of Chinese studies and Buberian studies, it has been an underdeveloped subject of discourse. On the one hand, the sinological academy has commented on Buber's work only through conspicuous disinterest, no doubt because of his lack of historical and linguistic competence; in fact, in the eighty-year stretch following the volume's first edition, only one sinologist had dignified the text with more than a footnote.[4] This sinological indifference is summarized by Irene Eber, who opines, "From the perspective of Chinese philosophy, Buber's work on the Chuang Tzu text, whether in the translated portions or as commentary, is not sufficiently rigorous to be taken into account."[5] On the other hand, a small number of Buber scholars have given some attention to the work, though all have ignored the text translation in favor of the commentary, examining the latter only in as much as it espouses a perspective similar to that of *Daniel* and marks a transitional phase in Buber's movement toward the life of dialogue.[6]

It is my contention not only that there is significant room in both disciplines for further discourse, but also that their respective concerns—Buber's contributions toward explicating *Chuang Tzu* and the role of *Chuang Tzu* in Buber's philosophical development—are more closely related than one might anticipate, and that this relationship carries important implications for the modern comparative study of mysticism. In brief, the dominant methodological orthodoxy, identified most with Steven Katz, though owing an obvious debt to Gershom Scholem, is based on the quite reasonable epistemology that mystical experiences are historically and culturally bound phenomena, and that any rigorous study should situate them in their appropriate contexts. As a self-consciously historical response to perennialism, this particularistic approach nevertheless lends itself to two overly severe corollaries: (1) that mysticism does not exist as a sui generis category and, consequently, (2) that an understanding of a particular historical occurrence of mysticism cannot contribute to an appreciation of a separate occurrence. Taken together, these two points render somewhat suspect the entire enterprise of a "comparative" study of mysticism. While this concern for historical fidelity is well taken, the dogma of historicity has often been misapplied in order to shut inconvenient or undesirable topics out of the discourse; one salient example is the recurring argument that comparison or dialogue between Hasidic mysticism and Buber's I-Thou relation is inappropriate, on the basis that the two are historically discontinuous, that the former is true Jewish mysticism while the latter is renegade existentialism.[7] This essay will demonstrate that despite the apparent temporal and spatial disconnection of Chuang Tzu and Buber, it is nevertheless crucial to place the mysticism of the former and the dialogical principle of the latter in relationship to one another, using Buber's early text translation and commentary as the locus of the investigation.

MARTIN BUBER AND CHUANG TZU:
THE TEACHING AND ITS PARABLE

The text of *Chuang Tzu*, the authentic portions of which date back to the fourth century B.C.E., already had a rich interpretive history long before Buber's translation. It had been variously identified as a mystic's chronicle, an epistemological treatise, a philosophical plea for freedom, and simply brilliant pastoral literature. It contributed to the legacies of Taoist asceticism and landscape painting, and is currently employed by a Taiwanese monastic community as a meditation manual. Thus, it is not surprising that modern western sinologists, not unlike two millennia of Chinese thinkers, have been unable to agree upon a coherent or consistent interpretive strategy; even the best recent translations and studies hardly appear to be addressing the same text. Interestingly, the most important thesis that Buber's commentary brings to *Chuang Tzu* has its strongest ramifications in the areas of methodology and textual self-definition, where he addresses not specific interpretations of Chuang Tzu's philosophical tenets or the text's didactic qualities, but the broader significance of Chuang Tzu and his text in relation to the whole of Chinese spirituality.

Building on a theme pulled from a dated translation of the *Tao Te Ching*,[8] Buber asserts that *Chuang Tzu* is a poetic parable-presentation of the "teaching" (*die Lehre*), a "foundational power" which continues to define the collective identity of the East. In demarcating the teaching, Buber distinguishes it from science and law to emphasize that it represents neither existential knowledge nor moral imperative. For Buber, both science and law resolve into discrete bodies of categorical propositions, the former to "information" about "existence," the latter to "command" born from "obligation," both of which are scrutable and objectifiable. That is, the principles of science and law are intellectually abstractable from both the disciplines themselves and the objects to which they refer. Science describes the totality of phenomena, and these descriptions are processed as bits of data; law normalizes the totality of responsibility, and these norms are processed as statements of duty. On the other hand, the teaching cannot be reified; it cannot be reduced to propositions or conceived apart from its actualization in life. Buber attributes this conceptual inaccessibility not to any esoteric character of the teaching, but to an "all-quenching oneness," a unity so encompassing that no specific property can be separated from the whole and that the whole cannot be separated from life:

> The teaching comprises no subjects, it has only one subject, itself: the one that is necessary. It stands beyond existence and

obligation, information and command; it knows only to say one thing, the needful that is realized in the truthful life. The needful is by no means an existence and accessible to information; it is not found either on Earth or in Heaven but rather possessed and lived. The truthful life is by no means an obligation and subject to command; it is not taken over either from man or from God, but rather it can only be fulfilled out of itself and is utterly nothing other than fulfillment. Science stands on the duality of reality and cognition; law stands on the duality of demand and deed; the teaching stands on the oneness of the one that is necessary.[9]

Here the unified teaching—which addresses the whole, and yet is inseparable from it—cannot be expressed in descriptive or normative statements, each of which would necessitate a dialectical distancing between subject and object. Any attempt at reification thus presents a dualism that ultimately misrepresents the unity of the teaching. One cannot describe the "needful," for that would suggest a chasm between its existence and the perception of it; it does not exist apart from its being lived. Similarly, one cannot advocate the "truthful life," for that would suggest a chasm between its imperative and the enactment of it; it makes no obligation apart from its being fulfilled. As such, the teaching has no didactic intent to promote beliefs or actions; it simply proclaims itself in its oneness and is consequently experienced and embodied only in its totality. It should be noted that for Buber, this pervasive oneness is the defining characteristic of Eastern experience—"the Orient forms a natural oneness"—and he hazards a "genetic explanation" for this phenomenon in his impressionistic essay, "Der Geist des Orient und das Judentum."[10] Buber suggests that the Oriental is a "motor-type man" for whom "the basic psychic act" is a "centrifugal" process, whereby "an impulse emanates from his soul and becomes motion." As such, there is no dichotomy of perception and action; the latter is not the deliberated result after a period of cogitation, it occurs as though it were identical to the former. For Buber, this totality of experience for the eastern man "does not grow in him, but strikes through him" (OJ, 58).

An important corollary is that the teaching cannot be presented through conventional speech—"the naked oneness is silent"—but only through what Buber calls a speech of "images," that which occupies a liminal ground between silence and speech, between wordless solitude and spoken sermon. Buber identifies Lao Tzu's cryptic Tao Te Ching as such a compendium, as it chronicles "the immediate word of fulfillment awakening in the central man," thus embodying the "elemental oneness." By contrast, he views Chuang Tzu as "one to whom the teaching has been delivered already in its fulfillment," and his "attained oneness" begs purposive expression to "the simple persons, his impoverished brothers in spirit." Buber's crucial point is that for the teaching to be brought into speech, there must occur an engagement of this oneness with "things, events, and relations" (*Beziehungen*), and that such a meeting necessitates the expression of the teaching through "parable" (*Gleichnisse*). That is to say, the parable does not arise directly from the oneness, but is mediated through the existential multiplicities in which the oneness inheres. This, I would argue, already represents "proto-dialogical" thought, as it develops a concept of unity that is compatible with and actually demands a world of individuated phenomena in genuine relation with one another. As such, parable embodies both oneness and relation; it is unitary as white light passing through a smooth pane of glass, spectral as colors emanating from a prism.

Most importantly, Buber views the parable-speech of Chuang Tzu as not merely a moment incidental to the life of the teaching, but as a necessity—in tandem with the *Tao Te Ching*—to its actualization in the world. "But only both together give us the perfect form of the teaching in its purest fulfillment, as they proclaim Tao, 'the path,' foundation and sense of the unified life, as the universal foundation and the universal sense." Thus, it is Buber's assertion that the significance of *Chuang Tzu* lies not in its descriptions or norms but in its potential as a vehicle for transformation as it "carries the oneness of the teaching into all the world" and "allows each now to discover and animate the teaching in oneself." The irony here is that those who hear this parable are called to do nothing more than to realize existentially that which is already ontologically so, the oneness that is manifest in all being. "For indeed the teaching brings nothing to man, but it says to each person that he has the oneness when he discovers it and animates it in himself." Thus, *Chuang Tzu* elicits a unique transformation; it enables those who understand it simply to realize their actuality.

CHUANG TZU AND THE TEACHING:
TEXTUAL INTERPRETATION AS SPIRITUAL REALIZATION

While several Buber scholars have been struck by his use of the "teaching,"[11] no sinologist has yet taken seriously the possibility that the concept may apply to Chinese thought and experience. Nevertheless, while Buber's historical information is the product of dated scholarship, his

basic assertion—that *Chuang Tzu* is a transformative parable of a unified and unreifiable primordial teaching—does provide some useful and
compelling insights. Of course, the question of whether China possesses
a "foundational power" called "the teaching" is impossible to verify, but
it is appropriate to explore whether the authors of *Chuang Tzu* demonstrate any sense of being heir to such a legacy. A reasonable place to
begin this part of the investigation is with Buber's text translation,
where the isolated noun *Lehre* appears only twice, with a striking contrast between the two instances. In the first case, the term is actually
used pejoratively, in juxtaposition with the higher knowledge of Tao:

> One cannot speak of the sea to a fountain frog; he cannot see
> out over his hole. One cannot speak of ice to a summer fly; it
> only knows of its own season. One cannot speak of Tao to a
> pedagogue; he is immured in his teaching. But now, since you
> have come out from your narrowness and have seen the great
> sea, you know your unimportance and I can speak to you about
> the primordial foundation.

Here, the teaching is a set of explicit propositions, which, in the context
of this episode, is portrayed as a static refuge for the shallow and self-
absorbed, that inhibits one from learning of the "primordial foundation." This conventional teaching is certainly not the unified teaching
expounded in Buber's commentary.

On the other hand, the second occurrence of the term concludes the
vignette about a hunchbacked catcher of cicadas who easily performs
his task to perfection while indifferent to other existential circumstances. "Where the will adheres to one thing, the spirit collects its
power. This is the teaching of the hunchback." In this case, the one who
possesses the teaching is marked by his experience of subject-object continuity, singularity of intent, and total attendance in the mundane
world; certainly a glimpse of what Buber calls "the oneness of the truthful life." And as illustrated in the segment, the unified teaching is not a
reifiable doctrine or specific set of instructions but an evocative parable
of the human life in achievement of its potencies. Other episodes in the
text translation provide similar aesthetic metaphors; "The Wheel-
wright" labors with a "secret skill" that he "cannot teach" (*lehren*) even
to his own son, while "The Mutilated Man" somehow claims the
regional teaching authority (*Lehregewalt*) and "teaches information that
finds no expression in words." This latter phrase corresponds to the
Chinese tetrad, *pu yen chih chiao*, "wordless teaching" or "unspoken
teaching," which appears repeatedly in both *Chuang Tzu* (5/2, 22/7) and
the *Tao Te Ching*.[12] The Chinese character lying behind most appear-

ances of the German *Lehre* or *lehren* is the noun or verb *chiao*, which appears more than forty times in the text of *Chuang Tzu*.

As a noun, *chiao* is the most appropriate literary Chinese equivalent to "the teaching," and its varied usages in *Chuang Tzu* and other texts of the period parallel the tension between Buber's two applications of *Lehre*, the conventional teaching and unified teaching. In Confucian classics, the term is analogous to the former, though with positive connotations, referring to a specific set of moral or literary lessons.[13] As Buber's single pejorative use of *Lehre* correctly demonstrates, it is this understanding of the teaching that is satirized in portions of *Chuang Tzu*. By contrast, even in the morally charged Confucian texts, there is an occasional use of the term that is considerably more delicate. A salient example is from the metaphysical *Doctrine of the Mean*, which begins with a series of definitions: "That which Heaven charges is called the nature; the following of the nature is called the way; the cultivating of the way is called the teaching; as for the way, it cannot be deviated from for even an instant."[14] Here, the author makes the interesting existential statement that the teaching is the lived fulfillment and realization of that which is ontologically so—the way that is inseparable from human existence and, paradoxically, entails the human execution of Heaven's charge. In Buberian terms, it addresses nothing more than "the needful that is realized in the truthful life." Again, the reference point for the teaching is the way as not a fusion but a whole, though the text certainly has in its background the full gamut of specific Confucian duties. Chuang Tzu takes this a step further by making explicit that the realization of the teaching differs from conventional learning: "As for the (perfect man's) teaching, there is no learning; to receive its intent is not that" (26/37). The most striking appearance of *chiao* in *Chuang Tzu* occurs in the following:

> The great man's teaching is like form to shadow, sound to echo. If there is a question he answers it, drawing out all that is in his bosom, and becomes a match to all-under-Heaven. He finds a place in the echoless, travels in the directionless. So move beyond the annoyance of going and returning, and by this journey the borderless, with no margin between coming and going, each day renewing the beginning. In your extolling and discussing form and body, harmonize in the great sharing. In the great sharing, there is no self; and without self, how could one obtain and have? The one who perceives as having is the "gentleman" of former times; the man who perceives as not having is the friend of Heaven and Earth (11/63–66).

In many ways, this passage captures the heart of what according to Buber one can and cannot say about the teaching. As Buber regards the teaching as a primordial lore "in the beginning" that "eternally begins anew"; here the great man is "each day renewing the beginning." Likened to form and sound, the essences at base of shadow and echo respectively, the teaching is the "foundational power" that underlies and permeates existence in Heaven and Earth. And just as shadow and echo follow immediately upon that which engenders them, the "truthful life" is neither experientially separable nor intellectually abstractable from the teaching. Where Buber states that "the fulfilling person has nothing but his life," here the one who fulfills the teaching is portrayed as embodying pure unity, of himself as a whole being ("drawing out all that is in his bosom"), of the world as an undifferentiated totality ("journey the borderless, with no margin between coming and going"), and of himself as an integrated part of the world ("a match to all-under-Heaven" who will "harmonize in the great sharing"). Still, the specific details of the unified life are evoked only in parable, as the great man is depicted simply as "the friend of Heaven and Earth." While this hardly gives explicit confirmation to the historical reality of the teaching and the role of its parable, it is interesting to note how a number of modern sinologists have begun to approach the text in the same spirit, thus testifying indirectly to Buber's interpretive credibility. Using language that recalls that of Buber, Harold H. Oshima writes, "The exact understanding of most of its ideas . . . lies buried . . . in the parable and imagery of the text, and must be salvaged from them."[15] Wu Kuang-ming, a critic of undiluted historical-philological method, elaborately describes the text's inner dynamic:

> The *Chuang Tzu* is poetic in that its thoughts cluster in a web—one thought points to another which explains it, then the pair point to another, and the movement goes on—and back. Clusters of thought co-mirror, co-imply into layer after layer of meaning. A spiral of thought loops in loops, twisting back to itself only to start over again in a new direction, from a fresh perspective. "Loop" sounds linear. It is rather a co-deepening co-resonance; to enter its pulsing rhythm is to enjoy life.[16]

But more importantly, what establishes Wu and Buber as kindred spirits is that the former represents an emerging network which argues that any attempt at systematization—any analysis that seeks a supposed philosophical position underlying the document—is ultimately untrue to both the intent of the author and the history of the text. Wu claims that *Chuang Tzu* does not simply use metaphors to represent some other ideas that could have been made discursively intelligible, but that it creatively applies them through "evocative indirection" which induces a unique experiential state in those who receive it:[17] "In metaphorical indirection, the author does not state but, by silences or by irrelevancies, evokes in us the desire to create something significant ourselves. Sometimes the author states things so obviously atrocious that they provoke our own discoveries in the light of what is said, and often in revolt of what is said" (Wu 1982, 15). In a sense, Wu is arguing what Buber has already implied, that a correct interpretation would not explicate what the text says, but would *demonstrate what it inspires*, what spiritual response it elicits. This is a fascinating position with serious hermeneutic ramifications, as it maintains that true historical reconstruction in the case of *Chuang Tzu* entails not an archaeological expedition through an archaic discourse, but an enterprise bent on exploring, in the words of Paul Ricoeur, "the horizon of a world toward which a work directs itself."[18] Wu does not actually justify his hermeneutic beyond the internal consistency and raw aesthetic appeal of his interpretations, though other scholars affirm the implication that textual interpretation and spiritual realization are here one and the same. Guy C. Burneko, for example, states that "*Chuang Tzu* welcomes us to a guerrilla hermeneutic whose practice alters our consciousness."[19] Robert E. Allinson claims that the text's parabolic nature is the crucial ingredient in its transformative powers, that "the disconnectedness of the text and the highly oblique literary form of the text have a systematic correlation with the technical means of accomplishing the goal of self-transformation."[20] And as Buber would suggest that such a transformation is to nothing other than the truthful life that already exists in potentiality, Wu claims that this text which "imaginatively reconstructs . . . human actuality" (Wu 1990, 24) serves "to goad the reader into self-scrutiny and awaken him into becoming himself in the world" (Wu 1982, 24). In essence, these scholars are continuing a discourse that Buber began eight decades ago.

THE READER IN TRANSFORMATION:
THE EMERGING I-THOU RELATION

Interestingly, an understanding of Buber's approach to *Chuang Tzu* may be further illuminated by his other works of the same period, specifically the translations and interpretations of Hasidic material, which methodologically parallel his Chinese studies in many ways. It is relevant not only how Buber's Hasidic texts continue to inspire fervent debates on matters of hermeneutic freedom and historical fidelity, but also how the scholarly arguments are analogous to those that are central to this study. As mentioned earlier, the early Hasidic studies have been criticized for methodology lacking in historical and philological grounding, the same reason why Buber's Chinese work has been ignored. Scholem rebuked Buber for "present(ing) Hasidism as a spiritual phenomenon and not as a historical one," evidenced by how "he combines facts and quotations to suit his purpose," a point echoed by Katz, Jacobs, and others.[21] All base their opinions on a "reconstructionist" interpretive model assuming that textual "meaning" is the exclusive domain of the historian.

However, in a series of articles, Steven Kepnes has attempted to liberate Buber from this particular interpretive paradigm, by employing rigorous hermeneutic theory to demonstrate that Buber and his critics simply labor under different, though equally valid, models of meaning. In brief, Kepnes establishes Buber's debt to the *Verstehen* hermeneutic school of Friedrich Schleiermacher and Wilhelm Dilthey, who likened textual interpretation to "thought transfer" and broadened "understanding" to include "divinatory" components as well as grammatical and stylistic analyses. While such an enterprise still amounts to a type of historical "reconstruction," its focus, particularly in Dilthey's model, does not end with the discernment of a frozen authorial intent, but continues on to the re-creation and re-living of the life-experience of the author. Within this framework, Buber sought contemporary significance for the timeless messages latent in the Hasidic texts, the essences that find modes of manifestation and transmission appropriate to the given exigencies, but which are not to be identified with the actual manifestations: "Using Dilthey's principles, Buber took old tales into his imagination and attempted to re-imagine them, to discover new continuities, and to complete them in a new way."[22] In effect, Buber's model of meaning is predicated on the hypothesis that mystical insights have some essential quality that transcends historical context, thus suggesting that textual "meaning" is here more the domain of the fellow mystic than of the historian.

While this does make it difficult to find objective criteria by which one may judge the validity of interpretations stemming from Buber's alternative hermeneutic position, Kepnes suggests that the solution may be found within the later developments of the *Verstehen* school, particularly those of Hans-Georg Gadamer's "philosophical hermeneutics" and Buber's "dialogical hermeneutics."[23] Both approaches share the breakthrough of granting equal respect for the integrity of text and reader and locating the gist of interpretation within the interactive "conversation" or "play" between the two, a process which both Buber and Gadamer predicate on distancing between subjects and liken to the I-Thou relation. This represents a major paradigm shift in the hermeneutic science, as it moves the locus of inquiry away from the supposedly fixed body of "authorial intent" onto the flexible "meeting of horizons, the horizon of the text and that of the interpreter" (Kepnes 1988, 208). Buber's interpretations would thus be judged not exclusively by their historical objectivity, but by the integrity of the process that informed them, the degree to which his presentation represents an actual transformation before the text, an enlargement of self catalyzed by the text.

Buber's association with Dilthey's hermeneutic school reached its apex in the years when he was preparing the Chinese texts (Kepnes 1988,195), and his place in the sinological discourse is analogous to his place in the Hasidic discourse, that of romantic exegete whose works, despite their popularity, would eventually be met with skepticism or disinterest from a discipline increasing in historical rigor and sophistication. Also, there is one more compelling reason why the evaluative criteria suggested by Kepnes are even more appropriate when applied to Buber's *Chuang Tzu*. By establishing the text as the parable of a primordial teaching, Buber finds the historical grounding he needs to justify examining the text ahistorically. That is to say, a crucial ramification of Buber's argument is that it implicitly defends his exegetical approach as not merely an alternative hermeneutic position, but the most appropriate hermeneutic position, given the intent of the text.

So, Buber's interpretation is best understood as a personal reception of the teaching through its parable, his own participation in its transformative influence, and an evocation and transmission of the wholeness of the unified life. In short, interpretation is here defined as the transformation of self occurring during the good-faith engagement with the text. There are a number of interesting aspects to Buber's response, but the most relevant for this discussion are those that express what I have previously termed "proto-dialogical" thought. This is not to deny that the general thrust of Buber's essay is the experience of pure unity—"the making whole that heals all separation and fragility"—which does seem quite discontinuous from Buber's mature dialogical principle.[24] However, it is too often overlooked that Buber does display many indications that he is discerning in *Chuang Tzu* a concept of unity predicated on relationality, as though he were on the threshold of breaking free from a self-annihilating pantheism. This is most evident in his discussions of Tao. Buber begins by portraying an undifferentiated totality, a uniform and eternal presence; but in a crucial elaboration, he then addresses Tao as it is concretely manifested within the phenomenal world. "Tao is the path of things, their manner, their proper order, their oneness; but as such it exists in them only potentially; it first becomes operative in its contact with things." What is striking is that Buber regards this as a necessary development, that manifestation entails relation, as "the Tao of the thing becomes alive and manifest only though its contact with other things." More specifically, the oneness of Tao is only realized in relation, anticipating how "*I* become through my relation to the *Thou*" (*I and Thou*, 1958, 11). "The oneness of the masculine and feminine elements that exist not for themselves but only for one another, the oneness of antitheses that exist not for themselves but only through one another, the oneness of things that exist not for themselves but only with one another. This oneness is the Tao in the world."

Moreover, the identification of the immediate and the absolute is also a prominent feature here. Just as "every particular *Thou* is a glimpse through to the eternal *Thou*," (ibid, 75), so too "there is no thing in which the whole Tao is not as this thing's self." The key point here is that Buber's engagement with *Chuang Tzu* represents more than a transitional philosophical stage that anticipates his later dialogical principle. Rather, it is my contention that the fundamental ingredients of the I-Thou relation are, in fact, already present within this encounter, although they have admittedly not yet coalesced or found articulate expression. Much of this is more evident in the body of the text translation, where Buber's choice of material and his use of interpolation are both quite telling. In one instance, Chuang Tzu argues that a tree is deemed "useless" when it is made a utilitarian object of experience, and that its worth is recognized only when it is approached as a subject in its own right. He also affirms the integrity of apparently insignificant entities (ants, weeds, dung, etc.), and one of his characters finds the eternal in a friend's transformation, having "leaned one single time shoulder to shoulder." Without a doubt, the most striking example of proto-dialogical thought occurs in the following passage, a liberally interpolated account of one ascending the steps toward an enlightened state:

> After three days, the separation of things ceased for him. . . . After seven more days, the external ceased for him. And after another nine days, he stepped out of his own existence. After that, his mind became radiant like daybreak and he beheld being [*Wesen*] his I, countenance to countenance. When he had seen this, he became without past and present. Finally, he entered the realm where death and life are no more, where one can kill without causing to die, and engender without causing to live. The one who is in Tao thus accompanies, thus finds, thus destroys, thus builds all things. Its name is Shattered-Unbruised, and its path is completion.

The climax is a revelation of sorts, depicted as not an absorptive identification of the self with the absolute, but a personal interactive encounter, where self-awareness is catalyzed through the direct apprehension of and meeting with the eternal. Here, only by beholding being can one behold oneself, just as Buber would soon write that "through the *Thou* a man becomes *I*" (*I and Thou*, 28). The continuity suggests that *I and Thou* is in part an extension of Buber's process of textual interpretation that completes the transformation of self he had begun in his initial engagement with *Chuang Tzu*. In Buberian language, his Taoist volume is the chrysalis to *I and Thou*'s butterfly.

BUBER AND CHUANG TZU: INTRAWORLDLY MYSTICISM AND THE I-THOU RELATION

Of course, the claim that *I and Thou* represents the climax of an ongoing reception of *Chuang Tzu* could be simply dismissed as postmodernist sophistry were it not that the dialogical principle brings much to an understanding of the latter, that the I-Thou relation may indeed be latent in the pages of the original Chinese. More to the point, rigorous sinological method demonstrates the value of Buber's reception, as it sheds new light on *Chuang Tzu* through the lens of dialogical philosophy. Specifically, this conceptual framework provides an important link between Chuang Tzu's complex philosophical discussions of theoretical relation and his playful mystical vignettes illustrating personal relationship, which are otherwise tenuously related. As Buber correctly notes, Chuang Tzu is well aware of a dialectical tension between the unity of Tao and the multiplicity of its manifestations. An important ingredient to Chuang Tzu's resolution of this is his perspective on ontology, as he affirms the reality of Tao, yet invokes it only in the language of nonbeing:

As for Tao, there is actuality, there is reliability; there is no doing, there is no form. It can be transmitted but cannot be received, can be gotten but cannot be seen. It is itself the basis, itself the root. When there were not yet Heaven and Earth, it existed firmly since antiquity, making spiritual the ghosts, making spiritual the gods, engendering Heaven, engendering Earth. It is in precedent of the ultimate extreme, but is not deemed high; it is beneath the six extremes, but is not deemed deep. It was born before Heaven and Earth, but is not deemed longstanding; it is elder to antiquity, but is not deemed old. (6/29)

Chuang Tzu regards Tao as a genuine, ineffable, spontaneously self-generating and self-perpetuating, inexhaustible source of power and creativity. It straddles a conventional demarcation between transcendence and immanence, as Tao is independent of temporal and spatial categorization, yet is immediately pervasive and totally embodied in all levels of existence. Most importantly, this formulation provides the ontological basis for Chuang Tzu's principle of equality. Since all being is rooted in a oneness that defies affirmative categorization, all apparent opposites—existence and annihilation, cosmos and chaos, life and death—participate equally in a fluid and impartial life-process. "Heaven and earth exist together with me; the ten thousand things and I amount to one" (2/52–53). Still, it is essential to note that this equalizing does not preclude the possibility of and necessity for diversity with the phenomenal realm: "To see things from their difference, there is liver and gall, Ch'u and Yueh; to see them from their sameness, the ten thousand things are all one" (5/6). More succinctly, Tao is the progenitor of existential multiplicity, and that which it engenders has individual integrity, by virtue of participation in the underlying unity. For Buber, the I-Thou relation is the ontological basis for the sacrality of the world—"in the beginning is relation" (*I and Thou*, 18)—as it signifies the perfect, undifferentiated state that can be continually realized "in the sanctity of the primary word" (9). For Chuang Tzu, relation is inextricably bound to the whole, as the ultimate resolution to the tension between unity and diversity lies simply in "carrying out both" (2/37–40), the realization that all entities are legitimately diverse manifestations of Tao, thus embodying both oneness and distinctness.

The primary implication of this is that one should ideally approach the world in a manner that unravels the habituated tendencies to objectify, utilize, and superimpose hierarchy onto an ontologically integrated existential order. In Chuang Tzu's words, one should strive "to embrace the ten thousand things and, by this, deem as one" (1/31). Thus, every appropriately ordered relation is for Chuang Tzu a microcosmic experience of Tao. This adds a fascinating nuance to his repeated illustrations of exemplars who execute the most mundane tasks effortlessly, almost magically; what on the surface appear to be hyperbolic illustrations of the sense of freedom that supposedly accompanies Taoist enlightenment are actually vivid depictions of enlightened beings who engage all constituents of reality as subjects in themselves. The most memorable account is of the ox-carver who never has to sharpen his blade, as he simply discerns the configurations of matter and energy so clearly that he can slide the knife edges through the spaces between the joints:

That which I devote myself to is simply Tao, which extends beyond skill. At the time when I first began to carve oxen, I could see nothing but oxen. Three years later, I was still not yet seeing the ox as a whole. And now, I meet it by way of spirit, and do not look with my eyes. The senses and cognition know to stop, and the spirit carries out as it deigns to. I trust in Heaven's pattern, strike in the large seams, cleave through the large openings, and follow what is inherently so. Thus, I never touch the smallest ligament or tendon, much less a main joint. (3/4–5).

Other examples include the woodcutter whose bellstand virtually carves itself (19/54–59) and the ferryman whose boat glides across the water (19/22–26). It is crucial that all of these characters shunt aside suggestions of demonic possession or self-dissolution, professing instead simply to know Tao. Most importantly, they describe a new orientation toward their tasks, one characterized by presence of the whole being and attentiveness without attachment, analogous to Buber's "power of exclusiveness" (I and Thou, 7). In each instance, the subject retains his full identity but without reducing other entities to objects of experience. Lee Yearley characterizes this as an "intraworldly mysticism" where "each new moment is grasped as it comes and surrendered as it goes," as one recognizes that "life is a series of new beginnings."[25] And for Chuang Tzu, each new beginning is a moment of integration, a moment to be engaged as a legitimate frame in the process of transformation, which is why one character embraces his own terminal illness (6/45–60) and Chuang Tzu himself faces his wife's death with equanimity (18/15–19). Clearly there seems to be sufficient resonance between intraworldly mysticism and the life of dialogue to conceptualize them as variants of one typology of mystical experience.

Finally, the hypothesis that Chuang Tzu was, in a manner of speaking, the original dialogical philosopher twenty-four hundred years ago necessitates revisions in the current understanding of Buber's later writings, reflecting the insight that the I-Thou relation is a dynamic and innovative development of Taoist mysticism within a totally different intellectual and spiritual milieu. As I and Thou may reflect a particularly subtle layer of interpretation, a protracted transformation of self before the text of Chuang Tzu, it is reasonable to consider that the full extent of Taoist influence may not be evident in Buber's original essay, the area on which Buber scholars have most tended to focus. More plainly, it is no longer plausible to try to gauge the importance of Taoism in Buber's development without a considerable understanding of Taoism itself; the text of Chuang Tzu, particularly the portions Buber translated as well as the English sources that he used, may contain crucial bits of information heretofore overlooked. Clearly, this opens up a daunting scholarly enterprise, though I would venture that topics of likely interest for Buber scholars would be the nature of meditation in Chuang Tzu's dialogues and perhaps the actual practice in Taoist monastic communities, especially since Buber offers so little concrete direction as to how one can break free of the "I-It" orientation and begin to speak the "I-Thou" groundword. For example, one recurring theme in Chuang Tzu is the "fasting of the heart-mind" (4/26–28), the process of figuratively starving one's faculties and attenuating one's vital energies in order to bring nothing less than the whole being to each encounter. Here one neither perceives nor contemplates things—"I do not experience the man to whom I say Thou" (I and Thou, 9)—but meets them as a whole being, with one's differentiating powers of sensation made tenuous to the point of vacuity.

Another similar meditative technique evidently derived from Chuang Tzu is "sitting and forgetting," the process of progressively diminishing evaluative discrimination. In Yearley's account of "intraworldly mysticism," he suggests a concrete method. "The ideal state sought by the radical Chuang-tzu is an intraworldly mysticism where you focus intently on the perception that is directly present before you but pass on to another perception when a new perception comes or the old one fades. This 'hold and let go' approach sees life as a cinema show, a series of passing frames, a kaleidoscope of ever-changing patterns" (Yearley, 130). Of course, just as there is continuity (rather than identity) between Buber's essay on Chuang Tzu and the mature formulation in I and Thou, so too Chuang Tzu's implied instructions for meditative technique may resonate with (rather than define) the quest for the life of dialogue. However, the nature of the scholarly question is now somewhat transformed. No longer can this be understood solely as a matter of "influence," of what Chuang Tzu contributed to Buber's philosophical development; now it is partly a matter of "transformation," of how Buber transformed a brilliant and subtle philosophy, and how textual interpretation plays an operative role in that transformation.

CONCLUSION: BUBER, CHUANG TZU, AND COMPARATIVE MYSTICISM

The intent of this study has been not simply to conflate Buber and Chuang Tzu, but to argue that an understanding of each can be enhanced by an appreciation of the other, and that Buber's Chuang Tzu provides the crucial pivot in supporting this claim. That is to say, this essay offers a theoretical justification for two new avenues of inquiry which, admittedly, are here only presented in their germination. Sinologists now have reason to consider Buber as a worthy interpreter of *Chuang Tzu*, and Buber scholars may begin to explore the complete role of Taoist thought in dialogical philosophy. If the purpose of the current paradigm in the study of mysticism has been to rescue mysticism from the entropy of philosophical speculation and return it to its rightful place as a topic in the "history of religions," then it is important to recall Wilfred Cantwell Smith's caution that these "religions" should be thought of not as discrete, easily compartmentalized entities, but as dynamic historical complexes that are in constant interaction with one another, often overlapping in unexpected ways.[26] In essence, this essay does not seek to undermine Katz's particularistic paradigm for the study of mysticism; rather, it argues that if we are to "regionalize" the study of mysticism, then we must recognize that a number of factors are involved in informing and determining each "region." And part of this determination is the historical role of interpretation, for Buber and Chuang Tzu are now part of each other's hermeneutic-historical contexts. It may thus be premature to discard a comparative study of mysticism; in fact, this essay may establish some workable parameters by which such a study may be conceived.

NOTES

1. The preface to this volume appears in English translation as the introduction to P'u Sung-ling, *Chinese Ghost and Love Stories*, Rose Quong, trans. (New York: Pantheon Books, Inc., 1946).
2. This essay, evidently transcribed from a series of lectures, is titled "Besprechungen mit Martin Buber in Ascona, August 1924 uber Lao-tse's Tao-te-king."
3. *Freideutsche Jugend* 4: 8 (August 1918).
4. O'Hyun Park, "Chinese Religions and the Religions of China," *Perspectives in Religious Studies* 2 (1975): 160–90.
5. Personal correspondence from Eber, 15 April 1990. Eber authored the introduction to a recent English edition of Buber's two Chinese volumes. *Chinese Tales* (Atlantic Highlands: Humanities Press International, 1991) includes translations by Alex Page, whose fine abilities with German texts are muted by his lack of familiarity with Chuang Tzu or Buber and a general disinterest in mysticism.
6. See, for example, Maurice Friedman, "Martin Buber and Asia," in *Philosophy East and West* 26 (1976): 411–26; James Moran, "Martin

Buber and Taoism," in *Judaism* 21 (1972): 98–103; Robert Wood, "Oriental Themes in Buber's Work," in *Martin Buber: A Centenary Volume*, Haim Gordon and Jochanan Bloch, eds. (Negev: KTAV Publishing House, Inc., 1984).

7. Steven Katz, "Martin Buber's Misuse of Hasidic Sources," in *Post-Holocaust Dialogues* (New York: New York University Press, 1985), 74–86; Gershom Scholem, *The Messianic Idea in Judaism* (New York: Schocken Books, 1971).

8. Victor von Strauss, *Lao-tse's Tao Te King* (Leipzig: Verlag von Friedrich Fleischer, 1870).

9. All unannotated citations appearing in this essay are my own translations of passages from *Reden und Gleichnisse des Tschuang-tse*, which are drawn from my forthcoming volume, *I and Tao: Martin Buber's Encounter with Chuang Tzu* (Albany: SUNY Press, 1996).

10. The essay appeared originally in *Vom Geist des Judentums* (Leipzig: Kurt Wolff Verlag ,1916), later translated as "The Spirit of the Orient and Judaism," in Buber's *On Judaism*, 56–78.

11. Carl Kerenyi, "Martin Buber as Classical Author," in *PMB* (Schilpp and Friedman), 629–38.

12. Lao Tzu, *Tao Te Ching*, D. C. Lau, trans., (Middlesex: Penguin, 1963), 58, 104. All translations of *Chuang Tzu* are my own, referenced to their location in Chuang Tzu, *Harvard-Yenching Institute Sinological Index Series*, no. 20 (Cambridge: Harvard University Press, 1956).

13. See, for example, *Mencius*, D. C. Lau, trans. (Middlesex: Penguin Books, 1970), 51–52.

14. The translation is my own. One is also available in James Legge, *Confucian Analects, The Great Learning, and The Doctrine of the Mean* (New York: Dover, 1971).

15. Harold H. Oshima, "A Metaphorical Analysis of the Concept of Mind in the *Chuang Tzu*, " in *Experimental Essays on Chuang Tzu*, Victor H. Mair, ed. (Honolulu: University of Hawaii Press, 1983), 64.

16. Wu Kuang-ming, *The Butterfly as Companion* (Albany: SUNY Press, 1990), 23.

17. Wu Kuang-ming, *Chuang Tzu: World Philosopher at Play* (New York: Scholars Press, 1982), 23.

18. Paul Ricoeur, *Hermeneutics and the Human Sciences*, John B. Thompson, trans. (Cambridge: Cambridge University Press, 1981), 178.

19. Guy C. Burneko, "Chuang Tzu's Existential Hermeneutics," in *Journal of Chinese Philosophy* 13 (1986): 396.

20. Robert E. Allinson, *Chuang-Tzu for Spiritual Transformation* (Albany: SUNY Press, 1989), 3.

21. Scholem, 1971, 230–231; Louis Jacobs, "Aspects of Scholem's Study of Hasidism," from *Modern Judaism* 5 (February 1985), 95–104.
22. Steven D. Kepnes, "Buber as Hermeneut: Relations to Dilthey and Gadamer," in *Harvard Theological Review* 81 (1988), 199.
23. Kepnes, "A Hermeneutic Approach to the Buber-Scholem Controversy," in *Journal of Jewish Studies* 38 (Spring 1987), 92—98.
24. It is well documented that Buber would later repudiate the essay as representing a "mystical" phase. (*PW*, ix–x).
25. Lee Yearley, "The Perfected Person in the Radical *Chuang-tzu*" in Mair ed., *Experimental Essays on Chuang-tzu*, 135. (University of Hawaii Press, Honolulu, 1983).
26. Wilfred Cantwell Smith, *The Meaning and End of Religion* (New York: Harper and Row, Publishers, 1962).

CHAPTER 9

Dialogue and Difference

"I and Thou" or "We and They"?

SEYMOUR CAIN

In memory of Martin Buber (1878–1965), master and friend.

I direct my thoughts and yours to the I-Thou model of human related-ness as it is confirmed or denied in the all-too-human realm of ethnic, national, religious, and ideological differences. Any honest and wide treatment of how we behave in such circumstances is bound to cause some discomfort, since we may recognize ourselves in some of the horrible examples of nondialogical relatedness. What I have to say here is not directed at someone else, at *them,* those other guys, whom we scan with a critical eye. I'm talking about us, about you and me. Indeed, what I have to say applies to Buberians as well as non-Buberians or anti-Buberians. We cannot enter the kingdom of dialogue by a rote recitation of phrases from Buber's works, while engaged in non-dialogical relations with our ideological adversaries in politics, religion, and philosophy.

Let us talk together about dialogue and difference, what the deep existential and phenomenological thinkers call "otherness" (why not "others"?). One stance towards distinctive others is to consider them abnormal, inferior, alien, as, say, Orientals compared with us Occidentals—as Africans or Blacks compared with us Euro-Americans or

Whites, as primitives compared with us civilized persons. It is "We" as versus "They," us good guys as versus those bad guys, we the advanced versus they the backward, we the developed versus they the undeveloped, we the dominant versus they the dominated. This imperialist view of other human beings is targeted in Edward Said's *Orientalism*. Although his presentation may seem strident and exaggerated at times, on the whole it is a correct picture of Western attitudes towards the peoples, cultures, and religions of the Middle East, particularly the Arabs and Islam. Read it and weep or gnash your teeth, according to your respective allegiances.

There is a clear distinction, however, between what Said has to say and what Buber teaches. Said wants us to see the other as same, not as other, in his generality as a human being, to see her in a sense as "one of us." Buber wants us to confirm the other in his particularity, in his difference, in his *haecceity*, if you'll pardon me that useful medieval Latin term, not in his partaking in a general, abstract humanity. The dialogical relation, for Buber, is one of "I" or "We-uns" in our own cultural and spiritual heritage to "Thou" or "You-all" in your particular culture and traditions. As opposed to the "We" versus "They" stance, which Said sees as the dominant response of Euro-American culture to the non-European peoples, the way of dialogue points to the meeting of two realities—two selves or two communities—each in its ownness, its concrete particularity.

Far from being unrealistic, as some anti-Buberians allege, this is the height of realism, insisting that we address real beings in their actual concrete situation, not treat them as ethnic stereotypes or remote abstractions—which are outside the realm of address and response. The dialogical stance does not foreclose the possibility of conflict or division. In fact, it includes it as real possibility, that which we see actualized almost every day. But it steers us away from the demonization of the other person, nation, religious community, or socio-political party, from the dehumanization of our adversaries, of those who differ with us.

That is the way of dialogue. The way of nondialogue, the non-I-Thou stance is opposite. It says, "I'll affirm you and allow you to exist if you become like me, think like me, do as I do, are my mental-spiritual clone." Its motto is, "Nothing alien is human to me." This is not simply the stance adopted by uneducated, backward, unenlightened persons. It is the stance very often adopted by people like you and me, the so-called liberal, tolerant, enlightened, cultivated persons. It plays a prominent role in intellectual circles, where people skewer one another with verbal swords. Many of us, intellectual or not, are imprisoned in ideological stances which act as iron maidens against any real human intercourse. Abstract reductionism prevails in the differences between liberal and conservative, socialist and free-marketeer, atheist and theist, right-to-lifer and free-choicer, feminist and patriarchalist, etc. There is no interhuman meeting, no real dialogue between human beings, just barrages of abstract ideas or ideals, partisan slogans, condemnations, and fanaticisms which block off even the possibility of encounter. We sanctify ourselves as the repositories of right and virtue, and demonize our adversaries as evil incarnate. Fanaticism and bigotry, we should note, are by no means the monopoly of organized religion and its adherents. They are universal human failings indulged in by disputants on all sides.

I recall the story about a meeting between Buber and T.S. Eliot that may exemplify my general point here. It seems that Buber and Eliot met and talked with one another at some length and with mutual respect. Later Maurice Friedman asked Buber, "How come you were able to have a friendly meeting with a man like T. S. Eliot, who is so opposed to you in his opinions?" (Eliot had once described himself as an Anglo-Catholic in religion, a classicist in literature, and a monarchist in politics.) Buber replied pithily, "I met with another man, with another human being, not a set of opinions" (Friedman, *ENR*, 334, 419).

How many of us can say the same for our encounters with persons who have ideas and ideals opposed to our own? Do we open up to the other in his difference, take his views seriously, or rather seek to win an argument, substituting debate for dialogue, domination for meeting? Of course, you and I don't meet a T. S. Eliot every day, but how about someone on our own level? I'm afraid many of us act badly most of the time when we meet persons with radically different commitments and allegiances. We seek to subdue rather than to understand. Often what most moves us are the intense passion, resentment, and hatred evoked by dialectical differences. "How dare this other person believe utterly different than I do! Let's demonize the bastard!" That is our kneejerk response to a radical difference in opinions. Recall that in the Christian tradition (which a lot us tend to demonize) there is a doctrine that one should condemn the sin but not the sinner. Assuming that we view a radical difference in viewpoint from us as a serious failing, do you or I make that salutary distinction?

By sheer chance, while I was on a week's holiday in Vancouver, B.C., a few years ago, I came across a newspaper column titled "Hatred of All the Things We Aren't." The author, writing from an Indian reservation, cites a contemptuous letter from a Canadian Caucasian, expressing his scorn for the primitiveness of the Indian aborigines who, he maintains, have nothing of value to contribute. He is especially scornful of the alleged spirituality of their rituals and myths, which he attributes to bunk about the "noble savage" who he claims existed only in Rousseau's imagination. In rebuttal the columnist cites early missionaries as witnesses to the nobility and spirituality of the aborigines they encountered. He calls for the preservation and enhancement of the traditional spiritual culture to maintain the Indian essence and identity. He realizes that the man who wrote the contemptuous letter does not understand this and is not even interested in trying. That man exemplifies the "Orientalist" vice, treating what is non-European or premodern as inferior, worthless, contemptible, bypassed in the progressive unrolling of history. He also exemplifies the failing highlighted by Buber of treating what is other as "It" rather than "Thou," as an object of disregard rather than a being to be met, of closing oneself off from the realm of the *Zwischenmenschlich*, the interhuman.

Let's turn our attention now to the always tensile topic of religious difference, which provides a good take-off point for analogies with other fields. What is involved here again is the relation to what is other—other basic beliefs, sacred acts, communal forms—what is unfamiliar to us, strange, sometimes abrasively so. Should any of you feel left out, I assure you that I am including naturalism and humanism among the basic stances towards reality and the attitudes developed in their support.

Let me suggest a typology of response to religious differences.[1] There have been three main historical responses: complete disregard, polemical attack or defense (apologetics), and syncretism. The first is the way of ignorance, of not-knowing, of shutting ourselves off in a sectarian enclave or ghetto, unstained by physical or mental contact with the awful, threatening others and their sinful, pagan ways and beliefs. "Ignore them" is the maxim about others: "Act as if they don't exist." This was a far more practicable alternative in former ages.

As against this passive, insulating reaction there is the active, aggressive way of attack upon other religions as "untruth" or "unfaith," in comparison with our own religion, which we proclaim contains the whole and only truth. This polemical response may involve considerable study and knowledge of other faiths, but solely as a means to extol one's own faith while denigrating that of others, and, above all, to become the victor in intellectual debates, *contra Gentiles*, against the Gentiles, the Pagans, the Unbelievers.

The third way, called variously "syncretism," "synthesis," or "eclecticism," has a great appeal to liberal humanists in religious communities. It seeks to open up to whatever is deemed holy and good in other religions and to incorporate it with one's own faith. This approach has been subjected to ridicule as well as praise. It risks a certain shallowness, inauthenticity, or irresponsibility when it tries to put things together that don't belong together or are clearly contradictory. It may also descend to a merely aesthetic appreciation, a nonexistential spectatorial stance, without engagement or commitment. Yet it points us to real contacts with other religions and their adherents, to real mutual influences, and to the effects of such contacts on our religious attitudes, assuming that there can be growth and development in religious existence.

I should point out that there has been a good deal of syncretism in Judaism and Christianity, however the orthodox may deny it. Ralph Marcus, the eminent scholar in Hellenistic Judaism, used to say that the Israelites stole far more than the jewels of the Egyptians from the ancient Near Eastern cultures. Similarly, early Christianity was enriched by various patterns of Greek thought and culture, and Greek and Islamic philosophy had an enormous effect on medieval Jewish and Christian philosophical theology. W. E. Hocking, the American philosopher of religion, noted that the capacity to assimilate from other sources may be the sign of health and vitality in a religion. A religion already has to be something definite before it can assimilate anything from external sources.

The possibility of mutual influence between religious communities and cultures brings us to a fourth way, beyond the traditional three ways: the way of dialogue. Here we assume a real difference, which cannot be ignored or blotted out, and a real relation, a mutual address and response. A real dialogue openly and unreservedly engaged in (and I don't mean just talking together) may lead to mutual understanding and to self-realization. In coming to understand and appreciate the other in his or her particular religious existence, we may come to realize what we are in ours. This is the way to do away with the dividing, distorting stereotypes that proclaim the defects and shortcomings of other faiths and extol the virtues and perfections of our own. There a religious term for these stereotypes—*idolatry*—and it takes many forms: idolatry of ourselves, our nation, our "race," our political ideology, our religious community.

Let's take the example of the encounter or misencounter between Rabbinic Judaism and Christianity. The two movements arose out of the same historic situation in first-century Palestine and soon went on their separate paths, each claiming lineal descent from the biblical patriarchs and prophets, from the religion of Israel. While the "elder brother" proclaimed itself to be the true Israel, entrusted with the one and only Torah, the "younger brother" proclaimed itself to be the new Israel with a new Word, to be preached to all the peoples of the world. The old Israel looked down on the new Israel as at best an inferior imitation fit only for the uncircumcised Gentiles and considered the incarnational theology that developed as sheer blasphemy. The new Israel looked down on the old Israel as superseded and made obsolete by the new dispensation through Christ. The seeds for conflict, anger, and resentment were present from the beginning. The struggle for domination or survival, physical or spiritual, went on for the next 1,900 years. The war of Christendom against Judaism, a living alternative in its midst, became a cruel and horrible one, inevitably directed against the Jewish people, who were the bearers of the targeted religion, and was one of the main contributors to the European anti-Semitism which culminated in the Holocaust.

"With these senseless exterminations something quite different has begun," declared Hans Joachim Schoeps, a mourner for parents and a brother murdered in the Nazi death camps. He saw genuine, open dialogue as made possible by the Holocaust, not only because it shocked the civilized world, but because it was the product of twentieth-century totalitarianism and racism, not of the religious conflict between Judaism and Christianity (Schoeps, xi). Certainly there have been all kinds of institutional attempts, going as high as the Vatican, in which the term "dialogue" has been copiously used. I myself attended a conference at Loyola University in Chicago celebrating the tenth anniversary of the Vatican declaration on the opening of dialogue with Judaism. Rather than examining in detail and depth the work of these rabbinical and priestly representatives, let us try to map out what real dialogue would consist of between Christian and Jew, as for the members of any two faiths.

First, each must accept the whole historical sweep of the other's faith. Christians must not limit their view of Judaism to what is recorded in the Hebrew Bible, but must understand that it has had a 2,000-year postbiblical history, is a living faith, not superseded by Christianity in actual reality. They should have at least a dim awareness of the Talmud, the rule of the Oral Law, the development of mysticism, messianic movements, philosophical theology, the Jewish Enlightenment, and latter-day Reform, Conservatism, and Neo-Orthodoxy. And they should not view the religion of the Jews on an ecclesiastical model like their own.

Similarly Jews must view Christianity in all its forms, from the primitive Palestinian church to Roman Catholic, Eastern Orthodox, Protestant, and independent communities. They should not make similarity to Judaism the norm of authentic Christianity, a requirement for acceptance and dialogue. Christianity is what it became in the whole world through 1,900 years, not what it was in first-century Palestine, in the Jewish-Christian church. My old classmate Schubert Ogden, the eminent Protestant theologian, once said to me that Judaism and Christianity are historically bound together, but theologically distinct, an observation to remember.

What is required for Jewish-Christian dialogue is that the two peoples (I use the term "peoples" advisedly) deal with each other as they really are, not as the cardboard figures and stereotypes that have so long prevailed. Judaism must be understood as it really is, not as a preparatory, inadequate stage superseded by Christianity. Nor can the latter be taken merely as an adulterated form of Judaism for the inferior, lax, indulgent Gentiles. These concoctions lead only to self-satisfaction, not to dialogue.

The truth is that there has been very little dialogue between Jews as Jews and Christians as Christians. To a large extent, the relationship has been one of mutual not-knowing and not-caring, of not taking the other seriously in his religioethnic particularity, of the opposite of dialogue. This is not to say that there have not been friendly relations between Jews and Christians. This has been true even in medieval times. But it has most often occurred with disregard for the other's faith, for his religious existence, the presumed center of his being. We approach the way of ignorance that I first enumerated, but now without the physical restriction of a sectarian enclave or ghetto. I have heard from religious Jews this comment on dialogue: "Who needs it?" Who indeed? I have heard similar remarks from Protestants opposed to ecumenical ties even among themselves. Whether real dialogue is possible between the Christian as Christian and the Jew as Jew (not those who merely list themselves as such on informational forms) remains an open question.

Dialogue, open encounter, is not only a problem between religions but also within religions. European history is full of the intramural conflicts that have often resulted in bloody warfare between adherents of the Prince of Peace. Such hostility and undialogical stances exist flagrantly in present-day Israel between secular and Orthodox Jews, as well as between Reform and Orthodox Jews.

An article in the *Jerusalem Post International Edition* (September 14, 1991) tells us of the existence of an organization called *"Gesher"* ("Bridge") that works to establish a meeting between secular and Orthodox high-school students that will open them to an understanding of their varying humanistic and theistic approaches to the Judaic tradition. An effort is made through mixed secular-Orthodox seminars to divest the two groups of the facile stereotypes they have about one another, such as that the Orthodox are simply narrow, repressive, and draft-dodgers, or that the seculars are merely pleasure-seekers, without any ethical values or knowledge of Judaism. This divestiture of stereotypes is done through ingenious exercises, such as cooperation in building a model city and making decisions affecting secular and religious needs, including tough ones as to which project must be scrapped in a budgetary crisis. If one side is not sensitive to the other's needs, the seminar leader switches the advocacy roles, the seculars acting as religious spokesmen and vice versa. Other ingenious paideutic devices are used to make the two groups see how things look from the other side and avoid demonizing one another. The director of *Gesher*, Daniel Tropper, aims not at mere tolerance, leaving the two sides in separate enclaves, but at closing the gap between the secular and religious in an increasingly polarized and politicized society. His basic assumption is that both the theistic and humanistic stances are part of the Judaic tradition.

Coincidentally, a *New York Times* report in 1991 uses the term "bridges" (*Gesher*, again) about the endeavor to bring about mutual understanding between conflicting Orthodox Jews and African Americans in Teaneck, N.J. This supposedly model integrated suburb erupted into a white-black conflict in 1990 at the killing of a black youth by a white police officer. The building of "bridges" between blacks and whites following that tragedy, through the efforts of the Teaneck Clergy Council, is credited with coping with the crisis caused eighteen months later by the anti-Jewish remarks of Leonard Jeffries, a black New York City College professor and resident of Teaneck. Threats of demonstrations and counterdemonstrations by Jewish and black groups ensued. Ugly confrontations seemed imminent. A meeting between African Council and Jewish Community Council representatives reached a mutual understanding of good will, and a planned Black march past local synagogues to counter a threatened militant Jewish march past Professor Jeffries' house, was canceled. The potentially incendiary marches did not take place. The "bridges" stayed intact.

"A year ago," said the head of the Teaneck Clergy Council, "it wouldn't have been possible *because the level of trust was not there*" (italics added). An official of the African Council noted that they had never spoken directly before with the Jewish Community Council. Hitherto the state of relations between Orthodox Jews and African-Americans had been one of mutual disregard and ignorance. Now they got together to talk about ways in which to reach mutual understanding of their differing cultures and religions, and further to share the joys and problems of bringing up children, their common experience. I need not belabor the point I have made previously on the potentiality of dialogue between differing and even conflicting groups. This is by no means a magic once-for-all nostrum, for in Teaneck, as elsewhere in the world, mutual suspicion, distrust, and demonization may arise again. As in Camus' Oran, "the plague" may come again and again. Hence the price of dialogue is eternal vigilance and flexibility in the concrete situation.

Buber's own dialogue with Christianity, Zen Buddhism, Taoism and other non-Judaic religions is well known. His attitude can be summed up in a remark he once made, that he stood on the threshold of his "ancestral house" and faced the world outside that house, in openness to what was there. This is not the stance of a Mr. Zero at Point Nowhere, but of a proud son of Israel, an "arch-Jew" (his own designation) ready to meet persons from other houses—from other peoples, cultures, religions—ready to listen and to respond.

Perhaps the most important application of Buber's philosophy of dialogue to group relations was to the conflict between the Jewish resettlers of Palestine and the resident Arab population. Buber insisted on just and sensitive consideration of the claims and aspirations of the longtime Arab residents of the land (there were also longtime Jewish residents). He held that the Jewish resettlement must ultimately be judged by moral norms, not by the purely pragmatic standards of power politics. Mainline Zionist leaders, on the contrary, though they were reluctant to act unjustly towards the Arab residents, decided that the interests of resettlement were of higher ethical priority. They opted for what Max Weber called the "ethics of responsibility" over the "ethics of conscience." (It was my friend, the late Ernst Simon, who called Weber's dichotomy to my attention.)

Buber, along with a minority of irenic Zionists, rejected both the morality and the practical wisdom of this position. He held that the main task was to gain the trust of the Palestinian Arabs, who were alarmed by the incursion of European newcomers under the aegis of the British Crown, a longtime imperialist opponent of Arab interests. Only if the Arabs were assured that the Zionists were not aiming for dominance in Palestine and eventually a Jewish national state, would they drop their mistrust and be inclined to compromise—this was the thesis of Buber and his friends in the B'rit Shalom (Covenant of Peace) group. This would require restriction of *aliyah* (Jewish immigration) and giving up the idea of a Jewish national state, requirements that were anathema to majority Zionists. The alternative, Buber held, would be continual conflict with the local Arabs and the surrounding Arab World. Judah Magnes, a co-worker with Buber for Jewish-Arab amity, warned that if the Zionists established a national state against the will of the people of the region, it would tie a Gordian knot that would inaugurate fifty years of intense Arab-Jewish conflict. These predictions seem to have been confirmed by the ensuing events in the past four decades.

Buber's advocacy of these views incurred great disfavor among the leaders of the *Yishuv* (Jewish settlement) and their supporters abroad, exposing him to intense criticism as a traitor to Zionism or an impractical idealist. Granted that Buber's vision of a binational Jewish-Arab entity, shared with some illustrious Zionists, never had a real chance of being fulfilled, expecting unusual imagination and flexibility from Arab and Jewish leaders and their followers. Yet it is inaccurate to dismiss him as a mere moral idealist, devoid of practical realism. He understood that some injustice was to be expected in intergroup conflicts. What he advocated was doing as little injustice as possible in the concrete situation, as against the amoral idolatry of *Machtpolitik*. It is important to recall that Buber was no absolute pacifist. On the contrary, he held that in some cases it is necessary to resort to armed violence (e.g., for the survival of a community or to resist greater evil) while praying for forgiveness for the slaughter and suffering inflicted on our fellow human beings.

I am one of those who believes that Ben-Gurion, the practical statesman, was right in advocating a national state for the Yishuv in 1947–48. It was a moment of opportunity and decision that probably would never come again, to save a part of Palestine as a refuge for the survivors of the Holocaust. This assured a much different kind of community than that envisioned by the humanistic, cultural Zionism of Buber and Ahad Ha-Am, eventuating in a state like other states and an eating once again of the apple of state power, with all the consequences that flow therefrom. That it did not solve the problem of Jewish-Arab conflict is obvious. Once again Jewish leaders seem to be opting for unlimited immigration, this time into the West Bank with its population of over 1,500,000 Arabs. Do they intend to create a binational entity under Jewish hegemony decades after they rejected the binational entity of equal partners advocated by Buber and Magnes? We are reminded again that the historical dialectic is as perverse as can be.

It is interesting to note that, while accepting the existence of the State of Israel after 1948, Buber envisioned a confederation of Israel and the Arab states of the Middle East. An impossibility now? Of course, but maybe a possibility by the year 2048. What we require of prophets is far-reaching vision, not immediate satisfaction. Buber once remarked to a critical younger scholar that while the young man's thought aimed at today, his own thought aimed at the day after tomorrow. (It was the younger scholar who told me the story.)

That the way of dialogue between different religious and ethnic groups is not an airy philosophical speculation somewhere up in the heavens is indicated by the two news stories I have noted. The impulse to engage in dialogue is a fairly common one, impeded though it may be by contemporary society, culture, and ideology. Human life—a really human life—demands it. One need not know what Buber taught in order to do it. But after we do it, intercourse with Buber's writings may lead to an understanding of the meaning and importance of what we have been engaged in.

Now Buber belongs to the ages. He is no longer with us in the flesh. But just as the way of dialogue preceded his life and works, it remains after him, leaving us ready to walk that path—or to go the other way.

NOTES

1. I have used this typology before in classes on "The Jewish Christian Encounter: Conflict and Dialogue" and in a published article carrying the same title in *FORUM: On the Jewish People, Zionism and Israel* (Jerusalem), Fall/Winter 1979.

REFERENCES

Friedman, Maurice. (1991). *Encounter on a Narrow Ridge: A Life of Martin Buber*. New York: Paragon.

Schoeps, Hans Joachim. (1963). *The Jewish-Christian Argument: A History of Theologies in Conflict*. Trans. by David E. Green. New York: Holt Rinehart Winston.

Said, Edward. (1978). *Orientalism*. New York: Pantheon Books.

PART III

THE WRITTEN AND THE SPOKEN WORD: HERMENEUTICS, AESTHETICS, AND LITERATURE

INTRODUCTION

JOHN STEWART

Ultimately, all the human sciences have to do with language. Research in philosophy, religion, history, economics, politics, and psychotherapy must somehow attend to the word. This is because, as Buber clearly knew, language is the human's way of being in the world, when "language" labels our written and spoken, verbal and nonverbal ways of effecting articulate contact. Buber's originary insight was that in the flowing present, humans may embody either of two orientations to what confronts us, that each manifests in our speaking, and that our choice is *ontologically* consequential. As he put it, "I require a [Thou] to become; becoming I, I say [Thou]. . . . And in all the seriousness of truth, hear this: without *It* a [human] cannot live, but [one] who lives with *It* alone is not a [hu]man."[1]

These seven essays limn disparate facets of linguisticality and in the process reveal how Buber continues to speak to scholars grappling with some of the human sciences' most basic problematics. John Stewart demonstrates first how Buber's writings contain responses to two basic questions incompletely answered by contemporary human scientists. The first concerns the "object of inquiry" of human scientific research and the second focuses on how the findings of this research may best be validated. Stewart argues that Buber's concept of spokenness offers a new understanding of "text," and that Buber's suggestions about how his insights might be tested may be read as outlining an approach to validity as "resonance." Stewart shows how several of

Buber's *Autobiographical Fragments* and his essay "The Word that is Spoken" point toward the centrality of language as spoken-and-heard. Then he briefly reviews some recent conversation analysis research to illustrate how human science may be enriched by defining its text as oral-aural articulate contact. In the second half of the essay Stewart reviews three currently influential conceptions of validity and demonstrates how Buber extended the most recent of these approaches with his principle of "resonance." Approaches to validity developed by such philosophers as Hans-Georg Gadamer and Charles Taylor may be sharpened and made more applicable, Stewart claims, when they are supplemented by Buber's encouragement, "I say to him [or her] who listens to me, 'It is your experience. Recollect it, and what you cannot recollect, dare to attain it as experience.'"[2]

Gadamer also figures prominently in Steven Kepnes' essay, but as foil. Kepnes argues that Gadamer is one of several contemporary hermeneuticians who believe that the Bible and other texts must be approached exclusively as Thou, and that "scientific" methodologies from the realm of I-It must be avoided. Kepnes claims that the Buber-Rosenzweig German translation of the Hebrew Bible and Buber's *Zu einer neuen Verdeutschung der Schrift* show how Buber employed *both* I-It and I-Thou contact to produce the most appropriate translation of the text. In this way Buber demonstrated the complementarity of what Dilthey treated as distinct methods of the *Geisteswissenschaften* and the *Naturwissenschaften* and anticipated by at least several decades Paul Ricoeur's argument for the complementarity of "explanation" and "understanding."

Gadamer might not recognize himself in Kepnes' essay as a hermeneutician who "argues that one blocks access to the truth that can be disclosed in a text by employing scientific explanatory methodologies." Although Gadamer does argue that the methods of the social sciences and psychology are incomplete and that a fuller I-Thou relation affords the "highest type of hermeneutical experience," he explicitly acknowledges the utility and partial adequacy of all three modes of relating to the text.[3] But Kepnes does not need Gadamer to make his central point: that both Buber's hermeneutic principle of the *Leitwort*, or "theme word," and his blend of historical–critical and dialogic hermeneutics contribute significantly to contemporary biblical scholarship.

Virginia Shabatay's brief discussion of deception shows how Buber speaks directly to a concern as real for laypersons as for scholars. Like Sisela Bok's best-seller *Lying: Moral Choice in Public and Private Life,* Buber's writings offer guidance to each of us in our struggles with white lies, demands of dissimilar cultures, and the tensions between maxim and situation. Shabatay reviews several of the guidelines Buber provided to those involved in these struggles, including his discussion of the differences between "seeming" and "being" and his advice to do all one can to unify one's saying, being, and doing. Shabatay also reviews Buber's descriptions of the effects of lying on the liar and his or her community.

Aslaug Kristiansen's essay is another that demonstrates the direct applicability of Buber's writings to contemporary issues. One of the most influential recent accounts of the ethics of teaching is included in a collection of essays titled *Education for Judgment: The Artistry of Discussion Leadership.*[4] This book chronicles the experiences of nearly twenty skilled and successful teachers who discovered, as Buber might put it, that I-It knowledge-dispensing was ineffective and demeaning, and that forms of genuine dialogue appropriate for the classroom promote greater retention, higher student and teacher satisfaction, and an enhanced sense of ethical community. Kristiansen finds more confirmation of this fact in the work of the Danish philosopher and theologian Knud E. Løgstrup. She documents Løgstrup's relational philosophical anthropology and complementary ethics grounded in existential trust. Kristiansen traces several of the similarities between Løgstrup's ethics of education and Buber's and emphasizes the importance of Buber's exhortation to the teacher, "Trust, trust in the world, because this human being exists—that is the most inward achievement of relation in education." To the degree that teaching is ideally dialogical, trust is the core of entering into this dialogue, and to the extent that dialogue is an act of mutual creation, trust must be "the access to this mutuality."

Mutuality is also of focal interest to Kenneth N. Cissna and Rob Anderson, two human scientists who study Buber's works from the perspective of speech communication. For several years Cissna and Anderson have been working with the 1957 dialogue between Buber and psychotherapist Carl R. Rogers. In this chapter they argue that previous commentaries about this event have ignored at least three dimensions of this dialogue that become apparent only when one views it as a *communicative* event: the effects on mutuality of the roles taken on by both Buber and Rogers, the coauthoring influences of the two audiences that were being addressed, and Buber's and Rogers' different interpersonal styles. What Buber would call "the situation" defined his role as "interviewee" and "visiting expert," and Rogers' as "interviewer" and "junior colleague." These roles, Cissna and Anderson claim, affected seven aspects of the dialogue. The Buber-Rogers exchange was also influenced by not only the four hundred listeners who were present but also by the audio tape recorder, which potentially implicated an audience of hundreds more.

Cissna and Anderson list several features of the dialogue that may be traceable to the presence of these two audiences. Finally, these authors find in the transcript and audio tape of the dialogue that Rogers' style served mainly to invite Buber to explain his ideas, clarify Rogers' understanding of Buber, and highlight his own experience in relationships. Buber's style, on the other hand, was much less provisional, much more precise, and marked by what Cissna and Anderson call a "rhetoric of cannot." They argue that future work on this dialogue should take into account these important speech communicative features.

Goutam Biswas' "Martin Buber's Concept of Art as Dialogue" returns to some of the topics that interest Steven Kepnes in chapter 11. Biswas draws extensively on Buber's writings to describe his understanding of the ideal relationship between the human and his or her objects of art. He argues that, for Buber, "both anthropological knowledge and aesthetic cognition require a Thou-orientation." In order to enter into a dialogical relation with one's image-work, Biswas summarizes, one must be open to immediacy, trust the meeting, and engage fully. If Kepnes were to extend his argument in the direction of Biswas' topic, he might claim that this is only one important moment in Buber's view of aesthetic experience, and that I-It relating is also part of any full contact with an art object. But Biswas focuses on a different tension: that between the degree to which the art object has "a life of its own" and the degree to which its being is "parasitic upon the being of the human." He argues convincingly that "in fact, these two senses of being are knitted together in Buber's writings." In the final section of his essay, Biswas provides a fruitful and illuminating sketch of connections between Buber's account of a work of art and the account developed by Mikel Dufrenne. He also contrasts Buber's view with those developed by Richards, Croce, Collingwood, Langer, and Gadamer.

The final chapter in this section is an essay that would lose more than it would profit from extensive introductory remarks. Pat Boni deftly illustrates how a Buberian reading of Shakespeare's *King Lear* reveals that the two authors clearly glimpsed parallel human truths. Both Buber and the Bard knew that awareness comes only to the one who stands "before the void" and is called to him or herself, who understands this as a call to relation, who takes the risk of being, who transcends "vulgar conscience," who speaks plainly, and who responds wholly. They also knew that even though such a one's entire world may be turned upside down and the person experience great tragedy, he or she "could begin to live a genuine life of dialogue, to know and love others."

NOTES

1. Martin Buber, *I and Thou* (Kaufmann, 68; Smith, 34).
2. "Replies to My Critics," 693.
3. Hans-Georg Gadamer, *Truth and Method*, 2nd rev. ed., trans. J. Weinsheimer and D. G. Marshall (New York: Crossroad, 1989), 358–362.
4. C. Roland Christensen, David A. Garvin, and Ann Sweet, *Education for Judgment: The Artistry of Discussion Leadership* (Cambridge: Harvard Business School Press, 1991).

CHAPTER 10

TWO OF BUBER'S CONTRIBUTIONS TO CONTEMPORARY HUMAN SCIENCE

Text as Spokenness and Validity as Resonance

JOHN STEWART

Especially since the mid-1970s, scholars in several disciplines have decried the "crisis in the human sciences."[1] This crisis has been keenly felt in psychology, sociology, and communication—three disciplines which, especially in North America, have historically embodied the tension between the *Naturwissenschaften* and *Geisteswissenschaften* because of their interests in both understanding (interpreting) and explaining (predicting, controlling) human behavior. For most of the second half of this century, science has been the dominant paradigm in all three of these disciplines. Communication scholars, sociologists, and psychologists with "interpretive" or "qualitative" interests have often been marginalized, and their work has been viewed as "speculative" at worst, or at best capable only of laying the groundwork for the real task of hypothesis-testing.

In the 1970s this imbalance began to change, partly because some scholars, clinicians, educators, and practitioners became impatient with the narrowness and triviality of some social scientific research findings. The "softer" sciences and humanities began to influence sociology, psychology, and communication both substantively and methodologically. Scholars returned to qualitative questions, and field studies, participant observation, grounded theorizing, and ethnography all became increasingly respectable. One reason interpretive human science has been able to achieve a measure of scholarly respectability is that its focus and its methods have been legitimated by influential philosophers. Jurgen Habermas, Hans-Georg Gadamer, Karl-Otto Apel, Paul Ricoeur, Richard Rorty, and Charles Taylor have all inveighed against the physics envy of positivist social science and have proposed alternative perspectives and approaches. Gadamer's *Truth and Method* is among the most influential works. He argues that scholars have been misled by the claim that rigorous scientific methods can insure truthful findings. "The certainty achieved by using scientific methods does not suffice to guarantee truth," he writes.

> This especially applies to the human sciences, but it does not mean that they are less scientific; on the contrary, it justifies the claim to special humane significance that they have always made. The fact that in such knowledge the knower's own being comes into play certainly shows the limits of method, but not of science. Rather, what the tool of method does not achieve must—and really can—be achieved by a discipline of questioning and inquiring, a discipline that guarantees truth.[2]

Although Gadamer's program is explicitly not methodological (Gadamer, xxviii–xxix), many scholars have celebrated his significant contributions to current post-Cartesian or postmodern approaches to the human sciences.[3] But two central problems lead many human scientists with both "hard" and "soft" orientations to remain unconvinced of the viability of Gadamer's alternative "discipline." The first is that Gadamer's main interest is in written texts, while sociologists, psychologists, and communication scholars are primarily interested in the oral-aural event of human meeting—"human interaction," the "social construction of reality," "social accountability and selfhood," "speech communication," or "interpersonal communication."[4] The second is that Gadamer's discussion of validity is incomplete. He decisively critiques the claim that human scientific insights or findings can be validated by determining the extent to which they "correspond to" or "fit" some objective reality. But his account leaves many concerns unaddressed; in the final analysis, he only characterizes in a general way how the findings of human scientific research are or can be validated.[5] This is understandable, in that, as I noted earlier, Gadamer explicitly chose not to write a methodology. But because of these two shortcomings, human scientists who wish to adapt his work to their concerns are left without completely coherent and workable accounts of (a) texts as *spoken* events and (b) the full human experience of validating understanding.[6]

Martin Buber's work offers accounts of both that can be used to flesh out the human scientist's understanding of the nature of what is being studied and the most appropriate way to validate findings. Sociologists, psychologists, and especially communication scholars influenced by post-Cartesian thinking could thus profit from integrating Buber's insights into their work. In this essay I hope to facilitate this integration by clarifying how Buber's works reformulate the human scientist's "object of study" and how he outlined a process for validating social theories or the insights of human scientific research.

TEXT AS SPOKENNESS

In "Replies to My Critics" Buber made it clear that the primary goal of his "mature" (post–World War I) scholarship was to "insert the framework of the decisive experiences that I had at that time into the human inheritance of thought" (*PMB*, 689). The "framework" of this "decisive experience" is expressed in the first seven sentences of *I and Thou*:

> The world is twofold for the human in accordance with our twofold orientation.
> The human orientation is twofold in accordance with the two basic words humans can speak.
> The basic words are not single words but word pairs.
> One basic word is the word pair I-Thou.
> The other basic word is the word pair I-It, but this basic word is not changed when He or She takes the place of It.
> Thus the I of the human is also two-fold.
> For the I of the basic word I-Thou is different from that of the basic word I-It. (my translation)

The most widely noted, at that time revolutionary, feature of this "framework" was Buber's claim that, in Allen Clark's words, "alongside and in tension with the subject-to-object directed consciousness-*of*-something [Buber] discovered a primal capacity of [the human] for a consciousness-*with*-another that is in its pure form objectless.[7] In other words, Buber's most widely recognized and influential claim was that, contra most modern philosophers through Husserl and Sartre, subject-object analyses of the human world are incomplete.[8] There is another "fold" of the uniquely human world, the "I-Thou," which cannot be understood as any form of subject-object relating. This insight is expressed in the first sentence.[9]

The second sentence is potentially just as revolutionary, but its significance has not yet been widely acknowledged. It focuses the attention of those who would understand human life in its wholeness not on Weber's "society," Freud's "unconscious," or Skinner's "behavior," but on *speaking*, on the *word pairs* whose utterance manifests our human being. Like the claim in the first sentence, this one moved Buber to the forefront of philosophical anthropology in the 1920s. Philosophers rooted in several traditions were beginning at that time to take what is now known as "the Linguistic Turn."[10] But their interests in language manifested in projects such as Bertrand Russell's logical atomism or the picture-calculus that Ludwig Wittgenstein attempted to work out in the *Tractatus*.[11] Buber's insight was anchored much more directly in the existential human experience of living language. The human's world, he wrote, is directly connected to human *speech*, oral-aural lived experience.

Notice, too, that this "fold" of the human world manifests not just in *utterance* but in a kind of *oral-aural* experience. As Buber clarified at the end of "What is Man?" his program differed from Kant's, Hegel's, Marx's, Feuerbach's, Nietzsche's, Heidegger's, Kierkegaard's, and Scheler's in its focus not on the individual or the social but on the "between" (*BMM*, 202–3), the realm he later called "the interhuman" (*KM*, 72–75). He acknowledged in "What is Man?" that this realm or sphere "is conceptually still uncomprehended." But he also argued that it is "a primal category of human reality," and the place where his "genuine third alternative" to prior accounts of the human condition "must begin" (203). This realm, sphere, or category of human reality is constituted in speaking-and-listening or address-and-response. Thus, in his post–*I and Thou* work, Buber laid out an approach to studying humans that was revolutionary in two senses. Like many subsequent postmodern thinkers, Buber broke the shackles of subject-object thinking, and he also pointed human scientists to the event of speech communicating as the primary site of human being.

Two of Buber's works are especially informative about what he meant by this non-objectifiable mode of speaking-and-listening—certain of the "Autobiographical Fragments" and the essay "The Word that is Spoken." Fragment 1, "My Mother," is Buber's account of his first memory of the lived experience of the primal, oral-aural category of human reality. It describes how he experienced spokenness as a four-year-old when he learned from his babysitter that his mother "will never come back." "I know that I remained silent," he wrote, "but also that I cherished no doubt of the truth of the spoken words. It remained fixed in me; from year to year it cleaved ever more to my heart" (*Meetings*, 18). One of the notable features of this fragment is Buber's focus on the spoken-and-heard quality of this watershed experience. Buber's memory here is of what was spoken by the babysitter and heard by the boy. Later in the fragment he describes the other central event as his coming to an abstract understanding of what had happened in his encounter with the babysitter, but this too is grounded in his *hearing* the word *"Vergegnung"* as if it were being spoken to him. And not only are the memories focally about speaking-and-hearing, his certainty is also anchored in the lived-event quality of these moments of contact. He was convinced that what was spoken-and-heard was true because of the way it was spoken-and-heard. In short, this first fragment suggests that from an early age Buber was unusually both aware and trustful of certain lived events of speech communicating.

The "Languages" fragment helps flesh out Buber's concept of spokenness when it emphasizes how his fascination with German, French, Hebrew, and Latin went beyond "nuances of meaning" identifiable in the written texts. As a learning tool, he reported, he devised two-language conversations between a German and a French speaker and between a Hebrew speaker and an ancient Roman. These taught him to feel "half in play and yet at times with beating heart . . . the tension between what was *heard* by the one and what was *heard* by the other" (21, emphasis added). This insight about the tension of lived speech doubtless contributed to Buber's later development of the concept of "the between."

Spokenness is also focal in "The School" fragment. This childhood experience of objectification occurred as the Catholic teacher *"spoke* the Trinity formula, and [the teacher and Catholic students] prayed *aloud* together," while Buber and the other Jewish boys were forced to stand *"silent* and unmoving" "in the room *resounding* with the strange service" (24, emphasis added). Here again, the distinctive features of these events are not the meanings of the terms used (semantics), nor the structures of the liturgy's language (syntactics), but something closer to the pragmatics, the phenomenological event of contact-in-speech-and-heard-speech.

"Vienna," too, is a fragment that clarifies the nature and function of spokenness and the between. Here Buber identified three settings that influenced him precisely because they were occasions where world was co-constructed in talk. In his studies, Buber was affected most by the "regulated and yet free intercourse" of the seminar, which manifested "more intimately than anything that I had read in a book, the true actuality of the spirit, as a 'between'" (31). Importantly, Buber's term "spirit" does not designate any theological category here, but highlights the presence of what I have called turn-toward-ability, the inclination and the capacity to encounter another as other and as person.[12] One *has* "spirit" insofar as he or she acknowledges and manifests this inclination and capacity. The second setting was the Burgtheater, where he experienced the distinction between "recitation," which calls attention to itself as monological performance, and "genuine spokenness," which builds the very world that a play invites its audience to enter (31). In the theater, playwright, director, actors, and audience facilitate together their focused *Welt*-building. The third setting is mentioned only in passing in this fragment but in a highly evocative way. The "argument over falling prices by two market wives taking a rest" is poignantly identified as embodying "the spokenness of speech, *sound becoming 'Each Other'*" (32, emphasis added). Here Buber's almost paradoxical formulation enables the careful reader of the fragment to acknowledge what Buber noticed: that in even the most mundane event of speech communicating, persons co-construct who-they-are-for-one-another. This is the ontological facet of communicating, the complement of its instrumental and expressive facets. There is an explicit connection between the lived oral-aural nexus and the event of human being. Humans *become* in speaking-and-listening.

"The Walking Stick and the Tree" adds an additional element to Buber's description of spokenness by underscoring the centrality of the palpable in what is said-and-heard. When, near the end of a mountain hike, Buber's walking stick contacts a tree, he has a vision of dialogue, because "the speech of [the hu]man is like that stick wherever it is genuine speech, and that means, truly directed address." He explains, "'I' am here . . . where ganglia and organs of speech help me to form and to send forth the word. . . . But also there, where he is, something of me is delegated . . . pure vibration and incomprehensible; that remains there, with him . . . and takes part in the receiving of my word" (42). In other words, "I" am *between*, in spokenness. As spokenness, "speech [is] the manifest proclamation of existing reciprocity between the one and the other"(58).

All these passages point toward the ontological significance of the oral-aural nexus and thus the necessity, for any study of the whole person, of focusing on spokenness. Although Gadamer argues persuasively that the most fruitful study of texts treats them as analogues to living conversation, his general acknowledgment of the centrality of this process is overshadowed by Buber's ability to thematize the specific event of living contact in speaking-and-listening.

"The Word that is Spoken" (*KM*, 110–20) is Buber's most thorough discussion of this event. He begins by arguing, as did Saussure, that there are "three modes-of-being of language." But unlike Saussure, Buber anchors all three in speaking. "Present continuance" is the reservoir of that which can be spoken by members of a language community, but its place is "the being-with-one-another of all the speakers of this realm of language. . . . Every attempt to understand and to explain the present continuance of a language as accessible detached from the con-

text of its actual speakers, must lead us astray" (110). "Potential possession" is the language's history, but again Buber describes it as anchored
in concrete utterance: "nothing belongs to it except what can still today
be lifted by a living speaker into the sphere of the living word" (111).

The third mode of being of language is "its actual occurrence—its
spokenness, or rather being spoken—the word that is spoken." It presupposes the human's "will to communicate" which "originates in [persons']
turning to one another." This turning-toward facilitates creativity; the
speaker "receives his [or her] creative force in fief from [the] partner in dialogue" (111). To further emphasize the relational, transactional, or medial
quality of the phenomenon he is describing, Buber emphasizes that "the
importance of the spoken word . . . is grounded in the fact that it does not
want to remain with the speaker. It reaches out toward a hearer, it lays
hold of him [or her], it even makes the hearer into a speaker, if perhaps
only a soundless one" (112). He also reaffirms the connection between
spokenness and the between that I noted in "What is Man?" above: "The
word that is spoken is found . . . in the oscillating sphere between the persons, the sphere that I call 'the between' and that we can never allow to be
contained without a remainder in the two participants" (112).

Buber develops this relational emphasis by addressing the counter
claim "that thinking is essentially a [person's] talking to [one]self" (112).
He argues here, as he does elsewhere, that dialogue is primary and
monologue derivative, and therefore that the thinker does not want to
be heard by oneself, for he or she

> knows it already as the person uttering it. Rather he [the speaker]
> wants to be heard by the nameless, unconceived, inconceivable
> other, by whom he [or she] wants to be understood in [this
> speaker's] having understood. (113)

In this context, Buber offers "the moment of surprise" as a distinctive feature of language-as-spoken. In other words, he points out that
one characterizing property of language-as-spokenness is its occasional,
"indexical,"[13] context-dependent quality, the degree to which one cannot predict or control exactly what is uttered, the extent to which the
speaking escapes formula and contributes to novelty. To be fully spoken
in Buber's sense is to supersede, to transcend, and sometimes to violate
expectations, not only of the utterer but also of the hearer. Surprise is
thus one indicator of the presence of spokenness.

Another quality follows directly: "it is not the unambiguity of a word
but its ambiguity that constitutes living language" (114). Insofar as life
itself can be characterized as change, living language at once embodies
and encourages change. Spokenness manifests several tensions—

between the context that situates it and its contribution to this context (i.e., between past and present); between the meaning-world it helps construct and the meaning-world that can be built on it (i.e., between present and future); between one person and his or her other; between the said and the unsaid. All these tensions contribute to the unresolvable ambiguity of living speaking.

Buber's next move in the essay is to remake his anthropological argument that spokenness establishes human being. As he puts it here: "A precommunicative stage of language is unthinkable. [The hu]man did not exist before having a fellow being, before [living] over against him [or her], toward [the other], and that means before [the human] had dealings with him [or her]. Language never existed before address; it could become monologue only after dialogue broke off or broke down" (115). He cites the polysynthetic or holophrastic character of primitive languages as evidence for his claim and speculates that the move from inarticulate to articulate being came as hominoids experienced calling-and-answering between one another. Again he emphasizes that "the mystery of the coming-to-be of language and that of the coming-to-be of [the hu]man are one" (117).

In the final section of the essay Buber elaborates another dimension of spokenness by distinguishing between two conceptions of truth. On the one hand, a correspondence view of truth is consistent with the belief that language is a system of symbols which represent objective reality. From this perspective, truth is a function of how faithfully language symbols do their job of representing. Insofar as they accurately represent reality, they are "true." The alternative conception of truth is consistent with a view of language as oral-aural articulate contact, that is, language as spokenness. When the spokenness of language is focal, the nature of truth changes. Under these circumstances truth emerges as, to borrow Buber's formulation from his work on Hasidism, speech expresses a unity among one's saying, being, and doing.[14] This truth, he argues, is not the *aletheia* of the Greeks but the Hebrew *etymon*: "faithfulness" (120). And this faithfulness is threefold:

> It is . . . faithful truth in relation to the reality which was once perceived and is now expressed. . . . faithful truth in relation to the person addressed, whom the speaker means as such . . . faithful truth in relation to its speaker, that is, to his [or her] factual existence in all its hidden structure. . . . This concrete person, in the life-space allotted to him [or her], answers with . . . faithfulness for the word that is spoken. (120)

Thus, speaking is true insofar as it is faithful in relation to the speaker's perceptions, faithfully addressed to the actual other, and a faithful embodiment of the speaker's being. At the risk of obscuring this point with jargon, it might be said that this truth emerges from a synthesis of the psychological, the communicative, and the ontological.

The perspective on spokenness available in Buber's works can guide the sociologist, psychologist, and especially the communication scholar and teacher toward a new understanding of his or her "object of study." Much has been gained by the post-1950s decision to approach human events as "texts,"[15] and Buber's perspective enables human scientists to continue to exploit all the richness of this metaphor, including its suggestions of woven warp and woof, co-construction, and emergent design. But even more can be done by treating *text as spokenness*, by attending freshly to oral-aural articulate contact itself, by experiencing, observing, and reflecting on the verbal and nonverbal happening of language in speaking and listening. The talk itself, as that which happens between persons, can become the focus for both study and teaching.

Currently the work of one interdisciplinary group of scholars suggests some of what might be achieved by focusing on text as spokenness. These scholars are known as conversation analysts, and they have roots in sociology and communication. They share a central interest in "how speakers and hearers routinely use, rely upon, and shape language to accomplish daily activities." They eschew studies based on "individuals' perceptions, interpretations, attitudes, and related self-report data" in favor of "the examination of what speakers and hearers noticeably provide and make available to one another conversationally."[16] Some conversation analysts emphasize the structure of "sequential organization" of conversation; these are more influenced by the enlightenment desire to systematize and formalize human doing.[17] But others want to explicate what one calls "interactants' world as culturally shaped."[18] These conversation analysts are, it seems to me, engaged in one kind of systematic, empirical research on what Buber might call text-as-spokenness. Insofar as they attend directly to talk itself—verbal/nonverbal articulate contact—and approach it as the site of the co-construction of world, they are clarifying the event Buber labelled "sound becoming Each-Other." These conversational analysts are attending to verbal/nonverbal talk as the palpable "between" and are working out ways to make more comprehensible this "conceptually still uncomprehended" domain.

VALIDITY AS RESONANCE

Buber's writings also offer the contemporary human scientist a fresh approach to a problem that has traditionally vexed scholars of the

Geisteswissenschaften: the problem of validity. Even lay people concur that validity is something which good advice, sound organizational policies, and worthwhile research findings should "have," but there is no universal agreement among scholars or laypeople about what it "is" or how one "gets it." The research literature, for example, includes dozens of discussions of validity as a construct, and almost as many definitions as definers.[19]

Part of the problem is that there are at least three different conceptualizations of validity reflecting two different philosophical positions. The classical social scientific conceptualization is that

> validity is concerned with the accuracy of scientific findings. Establishing validity requires determining the extent to which conclusions effectively represent empirical reality and assessing whether constructs devised by researchers represent or measure the categories of human experience that occur. Internal validity refers to the extent to which scientific observations and measurements are authentic representations of some reality. External validity addresses the degree to which such representations may be compared legitimately across groups. (LeCompte and Goetz, 32)

From this perspective, validity is assessed by checking the "match" or "fit" between a "representation" (theory, finding, etc.) and some "reality."

A second, pluralist conceptualization of validity acknowledges distinctions among construct, content, convergent, criterion-related, discriminant, ecological, explanatory, external, face, internal, methodological, predictive, and statistical conclusion validity, and offers different definitions to match the various types. Brinberg and McGrath, for example, argue that "the concept of validity takes on fundamentally different meanings in each of the three stages" of research. In the preparatory stage, "validity means *value* or *worth*"—how important, significant, useful, or desirable the research is. In the central stage—data gathering, analysis, and interpretation—"validity means *correspondence* or fit" between elements of the substantive, conceptual, and methodological domains. In the third, follow-up or replication stage, "validity means *robustness* [or] *generalizability*" (Brinberg and McGrath, 16–20).

A third conceptualization of validity distinguishes between "positivist" or "hypothesis-testing" and "naturalistic" or "interpretive" research, and argues that, for the latter, validity is synonymous with "trustworthiness" (Mishler; Lincoln, and Guba). As one proponent of this conceptualization argues:

First, no general, abstract rules can be provided for assessing overall levels of validity in particular studies or domains of inquiry. Second, no formal or standard procedure can be determined either for assigning weights to different threats to any one type of validity, or for comparing different types of validity. These assessments are matters of judgment and interpretation. And these evaluations depend, irremediably, on the whole range of *linguistic practices, social norms and contexts, assumptions and traditions* that the rules had been designed to eliminate. (Mishler, 418; emphasis added)

Thus, the third, interpretive approach holds that, for all but "positivist" researchers, validity assessments are situationally and communicatively accomplished. On this view, validity is a rhetorical outcome which is established when one is *persuaded* that a social theory or set of research findings or interpretations is trustworthy.

The first two conceptualizations of validity are consistent with Enlightenment or Cartesian ontology and epistemology. A basic assumption underlying these two conceptualizations is that there is a distinction between the subjective and the objective, that humans exist over-against a world of objects which their linguistic formulations and knowledge claims more or less accurately represent. Thus, the correspondence model of truth critiqued by Buber at the end of "The Word that is Spoken" governs these approaches to validity. This orientation obviously grounds the classical conception and also the pluralist conception of validity as "correspondence." Moreover, it also underlies the pluralist treatments of validity as "generalizability" or "robustness," because there remains the assumption that theoretical propositions or findings are fundamentally different from the realities they are "about."

Interpretive approaches to validity, on the other hand, are consistent with post-Enlightenment, post-Cartesian philosophizing. From this perspective, what counts as human "reality" or the human "world" is socially constructed or communicatively accomplished. Utterances, social theories, knowledge claims, and research findings do not *represent* reality so much as they help *construct* or *constitute* it. As philosopher Charles Taylor puts it, humans are uniquely "self-interpreting animals," and thus, "if we are partly constituted by our self-understanding, and this in turn can be very different according to the various languages which articulate for us a background of distinctions of worth, then language does not only serve to *depict* ourselves and the world, it also helps *constitute* our lives."[20] This constitutive function of language affects how, in practice, we actually arrive at validity assessments. Taylor argues that the process goes roughly like this:

Our conviction that the account makes sense is contingent on
our reading of action and situation. But these readings cannot
be explained or justified except by reference to other such readings, and their relation to the whole. If an interlocutor does not
understand this kind of reading, or will not accept it as valid,
there is nowhere else the argument can go. Ultimately, a good
explanation is one which makes sense of the behaviour; but
then to appreciate a good explanation, one has to agree on what
makes good sense; what makes good sense is a function of
one's readings; and these in turn are based on the kind of sense
one understands.[21]

This is how and why validity is a rhetorical and hermeneutic phenomenon: The process is circular, but not viciously, because there is no way
to break out of our linguistic home to connect with "brute data."
Ultimately we validate findings and social theories by testing them in
practice to determine which enable "practice to become less stumbling
and more clairvoyant" (Taylor 1985b, 111).

There are obvious similarities between Taylor's account of validity
and the sketch of Gadamer's view that I offered earlier. Both begin from
the conviction that human reality is thoroughly linguistic, that, in
Heidegger's terms, language is the human's way of being-in-the-world.
Both emphasize that validity judgments cannot simply be the outcome
of following certain methodological procedures. Both also emphasize the
importance of practice and application. But neither specifies the *kind* of
practice or application that can be most fruitful. Each points the human
scientist away from reliance on *methods* for determining *correspondence*, but the person who wishes to validate a finding or theoretical
proposition is left to determine just how to engage in the necessary
"practice" or "application."

Buber usefully extended this interpretive conceptualization of validity
with what I call his principle of *resonance*. The principle is an extension of
Buber's distinction between "critical" and "personal" scholarship. In
response to challenges of his Hasidic interpretations, Buber distinguished
between scholarship which treats its topic as an object of knowledge to be
advanced exactly and comprehensively and that which "seeks primarily to
re-present to the reader the force and vitality of the past tradition in such a
way that its former spirit will reinfuse itself into the present."[22] As he
explained in "What is Man?" when engaged in personal scholarship: "Here
you do not attain to knowledge by remaining on the shore and watching
the foaming waves, you must make the venture and cast yourself in, you
must swim, alert and with all your force, even if a moment comes when

you think you are losing consciousness: in this way, *and in no other*, do you reach anthropological insight" (124, emphasis added).

Buber's comments early in "Replies to My Critics" about those who doubt the validity of his insights directly extend this conceptualization of personal scholarship. As he explained there, throughout his life as a scholar, writer, and teacher, he "witnessed for experience and appealed to experience." Though his experience was naturally limited, it should not be understood as "merely subjective." Why? Partly because he "tested it through my appeal and test it ever anew." And the primary test of the validity of his findings is this:

> I say to him who listens to me: "It is your experience. Recollect it, and what you cannot recollect, dare to attain it as experience." But he who seriously declines to do it, I take him seriously. His declining is my problem. (*PMB*, 693)

The term *resonance* comes in part from my own experience with Buber's challenge. As I read Buber's reply to the person questioning the validity of his work, I picture two tuning forks or two of the strings of a violin or acoustic guitar. We know that when one fork or one string is made to vibrate at a certain pitch, the nearby one will also vibrate, even thought the two are "not touching." Moreover, the vibration of the second one will be significantly different from, yet mathematically related to, the vibration of the first. This is what it means for the second to *resonate* with the first. This phenomenon is analogous to a significant part of Buber's challenge. If you are searching for a way to validate my anthropological claims, he urges, let yourself be affected by what I write or say. Be moved as the second fork or string is moved by its adjacent partner. Then, he continues, see if your experience is analogous to that against which it is juxtaposed; test whether my ways of talking render articulate aspects of your lived experience. Insofar as my ways of describing are faithful to your experience, you can trust them; they have attained a level of *trustworthiness* that marks them as "valid."

In a recent discussion of validity, communication scholar Scott Jacobs argues for a view of resonance very similar to Buber's. Jacobs contends that the examples which a scholar describes as part of a research report can function substantively, not just to make the report more vivid and interesting, but to facilitate validity testing. Jacobs writes: "Because examples are assumed to more or less publicly exhibit properties generated by the rule of language, any reader who has mastered those rules can elevate the prima facie adequacy of any characterization of an example by inspecting that example and comparing the characterization to his own native intuitions."[23] Jacobs cites other accounts of the

same criterion functioning in philosophers' analyses of ordinary language: "The ground of my analysis . . . is my appeal to the reader's
native sense of the concepts in question: if my intuitions . . . are idiosyn-
cratic or skewed . . . [they] will not ring true to the reader's ear." And
later in the essay he speaks of cases "that strongly resonate with the
intuitions of any reader" (155–56).

Jacobs' account of resonance highlights the dynamic that Buber
pointed toward. It also responds to a central problem faced by post-
Cartesian human scientists who affirm the necessity of turning away
from correspondence views of validity and truth. As I suggested earlier,
the problem is that many fear that this turn leads into the abyss of relativism. If one cannot test findings against "reality," then it appears that
"anything goes." Taylor, Gadamer, and others have shown that this fear
is unfounded, that there are "standards," and that interpretive tests of
validity are genuine and rigorous tests. But their accounts stop one step
short of being as helpful as they could be. Buber's primary contribution
to this discussion of validity is to suggest specifically *how* one might
"apply" (Gadamer) or "put into practice" (Taylor) the claims, research
findings, or social theories that one wants to test.

The process Buber advises goes something like this: As one reads or
listens to the claim one wants to test, one should initially and tentatively
be open to its coherence and legitimacy. Initially enter, in other words,
the world constituted by the theory or claim. Then search your own
experience ("Recollect it") and juxtapose the claim the text makes
against what your search of your own experience reveals. As you compare the claim with relevant parts of your experience, notice the degree
to which the claim and the experience "resonate" or "vibrate" in distinct
but interconnected rhythms. If there is some dissonance, you may well
want to reserve judgment and to continue juxtaposing the claim against
your ever-widening base of experience. If you can find no experience
against which to juxtapose the claim, consider searching out or at least
opening yourself to such experience ("Dare to attain it as experience"). If,
on the other hand, there is little or no resonance between your experience and the claim you are testing, it may be best to reject it as invalid.

CONCLUSION

Surely Martin Buber never considered himself primarily a philosopher of
the human sciences. Yet his commitment to spokenness can sharpen the
human scientist's focus on the event of oral-aural articulate contact. Ever
since the so-called Linguistic Turn, many western scholars have acknowl-

edged that the study of humans must first be a study of language. But under the influence of Saussure, structuralism, contemporary linguistics, and British language philosophies, "language" has often meant language-as-system. In various ways Humboldt, Heidegger, Bakhtin, and Gadamer have worked away from that emphasis toward a focus on language as it is lived. But no philosopher has developed as consistent and strong a commitment as Buber did to studying the event of becoming and worlding in concrete address and response. Under Buber's influence, the "text" of the human scientist can become text as spokenness.

Buber's work can also encourage the human scientist already committed to an interpretive conceptualization of validity to take a final step away from tests grounded in subject-object analyses. Buber modeled this approach by welcoming those who were initially unwilling to accept his claims and by describing simply how they could most fruitfully and profitably be assessed. Resonance is the key. As he put it, what he describes "is your experience. Recollect it, and what you cannot recollect, dare to attain it as experience." This is the best way to determine whether Buber or another human scientist is making an invalid claim or whether he or she is actually pointing "to something in [human] reality that [has] or [has] too little been seen."[24]

NOTES

1. Fred R. Dallmayr and Thomas A. McCarthy, eds., *Understanding and Social Inquiry* (Notre Dame: University of Notre Dame Press, 1977), 3.
2. Hans-Georg Gadamer, *Truth and Method*, 2nd rev. ed., trans. Joel Weinsheimer and Donald G. Marshall (New York: Crossroad, 1989), 490–91.
3. See, e.g., Susan J. Hekman, *Hermeneutics and the Sociology of Knowledge* (Notre Dame: Notre Dame University Press, 1986); Richard E. Palmer, *Hermeneutics* (Evanston: Northwestern University Press, 1969); and Richard J. Bernstein, *Beyond Objectivism and Relativism* (Philadelphia, University of Pennsylvania Press, 1985).
4. Bavelas, Janet Beavin, "Nonverbal and Social Aspects of Discourse in Face-to-Face Interaction," *Text* 10 (1990), 5–8; Peter Berger and Thomas Luckmann, *The Social Construction of Reality* (New York: Doubleday Anchor, 1967); John Shotter, *Social Accountability and Selfhood* (Oxford: Blackwell, 1984); Robert J. Kibler and Larry L.Barker, eds., *Conceptual Frontiers in Speech Communication* (New York: Speech Association of America, 1969); John Stewart and

Carole Logan, *Together: Communicating Interpersonally*, 4th ed. (New York: McGraw-Hill, 1995); John Stewart, ed., *Bridges Not Walls: A Book About Interpersonal Communication*, 6th ed. (New York: Hill, 1995).

5. See John Stewart, "An Interpretive Approach to Validity in Interpersonal Communication Research," *Interpretive Approaches to Interpersonal Communication*, ed. K. Carter and M. Presnell (Albany: State University of New York Press, 1994), 45–81.

6. If space permitted, I would argue that other philosophical works are similarly incomplete. Apel, Habermas, Ricoeur, Rorty, and Taylor all comment on the nature of the "text" which the human scientist "reads," and/or on validity issues. But, like Gadamer, none explicates text as spokenness or fully operationalizes hermeneutic validity.

7. Allen L. Clark, "Martin Buber, Experience and Dialogue," written in dialogue with Helen Martin Felton, ed. John Stewart, unpub. ms.

8. Michael Theunissen clarifies the relationship among Husserl, Sartre, Heidegger, and Buber in *The Other: Studies in the Social Ontology of Husserl, Heidegger, Sartre, and Buber* Trans. Christopher Macann (Cambridge: MIT Press 1984).

9. This dissatisfaction with subject-object analyses is now recognized as one central feature of "postmodern" philosophy. See Thomas McCarthy, "General Introduction," in *After Philosophy: End or Transformation*, eds. Kenneth Baynes, James Bohman, and Thomas McCarthy (Cambridge: MIT Press, 1987), 1–18.

10. Richard Rorty, *The Linguistic Turn* (Chicago: University of Chicago Press, 1967).

11. Ludwig Wittgenstein, *Tractatus Logico-Philosophicus*, trans. D. F. Pears and B. F. McGuinness (London: Routledge and Kegan Paul, 1961).

12. John Stewart, "Martin Buber's Central Insight," *Dialogue: An Interdisciplinary Approach*, ed. Marcelo Dascal (Amsterdam: John Benjamins, 1985), 325.

13. Harold Garfinkel, "What is Ethnomethodology," *Studies in Ethnomethodology* (Engelwood Cliffs, NJ: Prentice-Hall, 1967), 1–34.

14. See Martin Buber, "Beginning with Oneself," in *Hasidism and Modern Man*, 154–61.

15. See, e. g., Paul Ricoeur, "The Model of the Text: Meaningful Action Considered as a Text," *Social Research* 38 (1971), 529–55.

16. Wayne Beach, "Foreword: Sequential Organization of Conversational Activities," Special Issue of the *Western Journal of Speech Communication* 53 (1989): 85.

17. For example, Harvey Sacks, Emmanuel Schegloff, and Gail Jefferson, "A Simplest Systematics for the Organization of Turn-Taking for Conversation," *Language* 50 (1974): 696–735.

18. Anita Pomerantz, "Epilogue," *Western Journal of Speech Communication* 53 (1989): 242–46.
19. See, e.g., H. M. Blalock, *Conceptualization and Measurement in the Social Sciences* (Beverly Hills: Sage,1982); D. Brinberg and J.E. McGrath, *Validity and the Research Process* (Beverly Hills: Sage, 1985); D. T. Campbell, and J. C. Stanley, *Experimental and Quasi-Experimental Designs for Research* (Chicago: Rand McNally, 1966); T. D. Cook and D. T. Campbell, *Design and Analysis of Quasi-Experiments for Field Settings*, (Chicago: Rand McNally, 1979); L. J. Cronbach, *The Dependability of Behavioral Measurement* (New York: John Wiley, 1972); M. D. LeCompte and J. P. Goetz, "Problems of Reliability and Validity in Ethnographic Research," *Review of Educational Research* 52 (1982),31–60; Y. S. Lincoln and E. G. Guba, *Naturalistic Inquiry* (Beverly Hills: Sage, 1985); E. G. Mishler, "Validation in Inquiry-Guided Research: The Role of Exemplars in Narrative Studies," *Harvard Educational Review* 60 (1990): 415–42.
20. Charles Taylor, *Philosophy and the Human Sciences: Philosophical Papers*, vol. 2 (New York: Cambridge, 1985b), 9.
21. Charles Taylor, *Human Agency and Language: Philosophical Papers*, vol. 1 (New York: Cambridge, 1985a), 24.
22. Hilary Evans Bender, *The Philosophy of Martin Buber* (New York: Monarch, 1974), 18.
23. Scott Jacobs, "How to Make an Argument from Example in Discourse Analysis," in D. G. Ellis and W. A. Donohue, eds., *Contemporary Issues in Language and Discourse Processes* (Hillsdale, NJ: Lawrence Erlbaum, 1986), 155.
24. Martin Buber, "Replies," 693. The added term "human" clarifies that Buber was not using the term "reality" to refer to a Cartesian "external world." That interpretation would be inconsistent with many of Buber's other writings.

Works of Buber's cited in text include *ABH*; *BMM*; *HMM*; *KM*; *Meetings*; *PMB*.

CHAPTER 11

MARTIN BUBER'S DIALOGICAL
BIBLICAL HERMENEUTICS

STEVEN KEPNES

To Man the World is Twofold, in accordance with his twofold attitude. The attitude of man is twofold is accordance with the twofold nature of the primary words which he speaks. . . . The one primary word is the combination I-Thou. The other primary word is the combination I-It.[1]

Thus Martin Buber's book *Ich und Du* (1923) begins. Two basic attitudes, two modes of language, two ways of life are delineated. The I-Thou mode addresses the whole of a being, the I-It only a part. I-It objectifies, analyzes, categorizes, establishes differences. I-Thou draws relations between subjects, seeks the common ground, draws out the total gestalt, and affords a glimpse of the divine, the "Eternal Thou." Most scholars of Martin Buber have used his philosophy of I-Thou to talk of the necessary prerequisites for genuine dialogue and ethical relations between persons. Some have also used his philosophy to speak of human relations to the divine and others to the natural order. But in *Ich und Du* Buber delineates another application of the philosophy of I-Thou, an application that has important implications for the way in which we approach literary works. For Buber tells us that the I-Thou attitude must penetrate not only our relations with fellow humans, with animals, and the divine, but with works of art, what he calls *"geistige Wesenheiten"* (*Ich und Du*, 12). What I want to suggest is that the philosophy of I-Thou provided Buber with a hermeneutic to approach all geistige Wesenheiten from plastic to written arts, secular to sacred arts. Most specifically I want to argue that the philosophy of I-Thou provided Buber with philosophy to read, translate, and interpret the Hebrew bible, what the Jews refer to as "*Tanakh*." This hermeneutic, at once literary and theological, helped him to develop extreme sensitivity to the Hebrew Bible. Approaching the text as "Thou" required Buber to see it as a whole gestalt and not a series of separate and unrelated literary strands or historical documents. Approaching the Tanakh as Thou heightened his appreciation for the particularities of Hebrew language and biblical rhetoric. What is somewhat ironic about this move to biblical language and rhetoric, however, is that it required Buber to develop certain techniques and methods of translation and interpretation that seem to contradict the meditative attitude of I-Thou. Indeed what he seems to come to realize is that in order to preserve the biblical text as Thou certain "scientific" methodologies from the realm of the I-It must be employed. What I conclude from this is that a contemporary biblical hermeneutic requires a mixed discourse, an interpretive tool which includes both the techniques of I-It and the attitude of I-Thou.

Among leading philosophers of interpretation today, it is Paul Ricoeur who has most eloquently argued for the hermeneutical imperative of a mixed discourse. To make his argument Ricoeur challenges the romantic hermeneutics of Schleiermacher, Dilthey, and the Heideggerian hermeneutics of Gadamer. What I will try to show is that Buber's attempt to include technical methods of interpretation in his biblical hermeneutic foreshadows Ricoeur's argument with Schleiermacher, Dilthey, and Gadamer and, in my view, further supports Ricoeur's position. If contemporary biblical hermeneutics is to help us to most fully appreciate the Bible it must employ a large array of methods which includes both I-It and I-Thou modes.[2]

BUBER'S DIALOGIC AESTHETICS

In the aesthetics in *I and Thou* we can clearly see the conceptual underpinnings of a hermeneutical philosophy. In the beginning of *I and Thou*, Buber develops a view of the human relation to all creative works. He refers to creative works in his discussion of the three "spheres in which the word of relation arises" (6). These three spheres are nature, humanity, and geistige Wesenheiten. This later term is translated as "spiritual beings" by Kaufmann and Smith, but a better translation is offered by

Robert Wood—"forms of the spirit"—and Buber, himself, suggests, "spirit in phenomenal forms.[3] Buber associates the term with human creative activities—art, language, knowledge, and action—of which art is the "prime analogate."[4]

In *I and Thou* Buber presents art as the expression, not of a human experience but of a relationship between an individual and a suggestive artistic form, Gestalt. This is the eternal source of art: a man is faced by a form which desires to be made through him into a work. This form is no offspring of his soul, but is an appearance which steps up to it and demands of it the effective power (*I and Thou*, 9–10).

Buber makes the crucial point, however, that the production of a work of art, the fashioning into relief of the world, requires a "restriction" of endless possibility. In the language of I-Thou, the artist turns the limitless Thou into a thing, an object. The artist "leads the form across—into the world of It"(10). Thus the work can be carried about, categorized, and viewed by others.

But the work as "It" can be brought to life as Thou again. Here we can see the grounds for a dialogic hermeneutic in Buber's work. A form of spirit, which ostensibly is an "It," can be brought to life again if the form is approached by a viewer with the attitude of I-Thou. I quote from two different places in *I and Thou*:

> The work produced is a thing among things, able to be experienced and described as a sum of qualities. But from time to time it can face the receptive beholder [*empfangend Schauender*] in its whole embodied form. (10)

> Again and again that which has the status of object must blaze up into presentness and enter the elemental state from which it came, to be looked on and lived in the present by men. (40)

In these quotations, we have the rudiments of Buber's dialogical hermeneutic philosophy. First we have the realization that a geistige Wesenheit, a work of art or form of spirit, although an It, can "blaze up into presentness," into the status of a Thou, again. The work of art which was produced by an I-Thou relationship between an artist and a sensed form can become a Thou again through a new I-Thou relationship. To properly interpret the work, the interpreter must take the attitude of a "receptive beholder" who finds him or herself "bodily confronted" by the work.

Louis Hammer, remarking on the relevance of Buber to contemporary aesthetics, suggests that this attitude of receptiveness requires some restraint on the part of the interpreter: "The critic must exercise restraint, he must cause the work to step forward, not obstruct it by his own interpretive constructions."[5] Encountering a form of spirit as a "Thou," we find ourselves encountered. The work addresses us, confronts us, says something that "enters our life" (*BMM*, 9). The work, as "Thou," has a "reality character" (*KM*, 150). It discloses a truth that forms our relation to truth.[6] Encountering a work as a "Thou" one respects the integrity of the work. Hammer argues that Buber's notion of the interpretation of a work of art involves an encounter with "other being." To have interpreted "a work of art is to have reached out and encountered other being by giving oneself over to form within the spheres of sight or sound or human speech" (Hammer, 614). Here, we can begin to understand Buber's use of the curious term, *Wesenheit*, to refer to a work of art or form of spirit. To the extent that the work "blazes up" and becomes a Thou, it is capable of addressing another and appears as a *Wesen*, a being, addressing its viewer or reader. One cannot remain passive in facing a form of spirit but must become active. In clarifying the I-Thou relationship with "geistige Wesenheiten," Buber states, "The You [Thou] encounters me. But I enter into a direct relationship to it. Thus the relationship is election and electing, passive and active at once" (*I and Thou* [trans. Kaufmann], 62).

An I-Thou relationship with a form of spirit engages us in a conversation. Maurice Friedman states that the interpretations of these works "like the I-Thou relationship with nature are modified forms of dialogue" (Friedman in *KM*, 53). Interpreting a form of spirit requires us to face the work as we face another being. We open our senses to it, to its particularities and to its total gestalt. We allow it to move us, to confront us, to speak to us. We try to perceive its special message and disclosure of reality. And we also respond to it. We present our reactions, we mirror back our reading and look to see if the work confirms it.[7]

In his groundbreaking work, *Wahrheit und Methode* (*Truth and Method*), first published in Germany in 1960, the contemporary hermeneutical philosopher Hans-Georg Gadamer gives us a very helpful model to conceptualize the dialogic hermeneutical method. Gadamer suggests that the process which takes place between the interpreter and the text can be appreciated by considering the dynamics of play (Gadamer, 91ff.). In a game truly played, the players relinquish some of their control. The players are taken over by the game in such a way that they live in the challenges, the ups and downs, the back and forth movements of the game:

> Play obviously represents an order in which the to and fro
> motion of play follows of itself. It is part of play that the move-

ment is not only without goal or purpose but also without effort. It happens, as it were, by itself. . . . The structure of play absorbs the player into itself, and thus takes from him the burden of the initiative. (94)

Gadamer asserts that the proper subject of play is not the player but "instead, the game itself." Thus "all playing is a being played" (95). When one reads a good text attentively one is similarly overtaken by it. The subject matter is neither the author nor the reader but, properly, it is the content of the text, the truth of the text, which enthralls, challenges, and educates the reader. Gadamer asserts that the interpreter must "subordinate" him or herself to "the text's claim to dominate our minds" (278). And the text has this claim because, as Gadamer says without quoting Buber," it expresses itself like a "Thou"[!] (321).

In his dialogic hermeneutics Gadamer directly addresses the issue of the efficacy of technical methods of interpretation. He argues that technical methods, like the attitude of I-It, block, instead of open, avenues to understanding cultural products. He does not refer to Buber but he uses the language of I-Thou to clarify different hermeneutical relations to a text (or Gadamer generally uses the broader term "tradition").

Gadamer delineates three types of I-Thou relationships with texts. Two of these are not fully mutual and have the quality of what Buber calls the "I-It" relationship. In the first, we study a text as the scientist studies objects of nature, attempting to place it in categories which render it suitable for analysis. Here we are interested in the text only as an "instantiation of a general law" (Gadamer, 323). Here the "Thou" is treated as a mute "object," and the "I" exercises a practiced neutrality refusing to be affected or involved in any way with the Thou.[8] This is typified, for Gadamer, by a social-scientific approach to a tradition or text.

In the second type of I-Thou relationship with a tradition or text, the I is concerned with the Thou not as a type but as a historically unique entity. Yet the relationship is fundamentally one of "self-relatedness." The interpreter is not really open to the otherness, the "strangeness" (Gadamer, 262), of the Thou and immediately seeks to understand the other in his or her own terms. Here, the goal is to "understand the other better than the other understands himself" (322). This is the approach, in Gadamer's view, of "historical consciousness," which is exemplified by the romantic hermeneutics of Schleiermacher and Dilthey.

The third, authentic type of I-Thou relationship, is based on an initial "separation," and "temporal distance" (262–63), what Buber called "the primal setting at a distance" (KM, 60), which guarantees "an acceptance of [the] otherness" (69) of the Thou and prepares the way for genuine relationship. Gadamer asserts that the crucial thing in an I-Thou relationship with a text is to "experience the 'Thou' truly as a 'Thou,' i.e., not to overlook his claim and to listen to what he has to say" (Gadamer, 324). This requires a "fundamental sort of openness" which allows that the "criteria of our own knowledge" can be put into question (325). This attitude, he says, allows the "truth" of a text to be disclosed. Here, following Heidegger, Gadamer intends a notion of truth as *aletheia*, or "disclosure: "The presence of the being itself . . . as it presents itself" in an artistic work (414, 443).

What we thus find in Gadamer's hermeneutics is a strict interpretation of the separation of I-Thou and I-It spheres and the modes of interpretation that are peculiar to each. Following Kant's separation of the phenomenal world from the noumenal and Dilthey's separation of the *Geisteswissenschaften* from the *Naturwissenschaften*—the human sciences from the natural sciences, Gadamer sees an ontological gap between I-Thou and I-It hermeneutics. Dilthey puts the distinction in this way: natural science employs methods of causal explanation, *erklaren*, and the human sciences employ the hermeneutics of understanding, *verstehen*. Following on this, Gadamer argues that one blocks access to the truth that can be disclosed in a text by employing scientific explanatory methodologies.

BUBER'S DIALOGICAL BIBLICAL HERMENEUTICS

Turning now to Martin Buber's methods of translating and interpreting the Hebrew Bible, we can see the direct relevance of the issues surrounding the hermeneutical methods of explanation and understanding for biblical criticism. It is very clear from his remarks on the way in which the modern reader should interpret the biblical text that Buber sees his I-Thou model as the proper paradigm. Many of Buber's remarks on methods of translation and interpretation are found in his "Zu einer neuen Verdeutschung der Schrift" ("Toward a New German Translation of Scripture"), a supplement to the 1954 German translation of the Hebrew Bible which he began with Franz Rosenzweig in 1925 and finished after Rosenzweig's untimely death in 1929. In this supplement Buber describes the attitude which he hopes the reader will take toward the biblical text in ways which parallel his description of the attitude which the individual must take toward the "Thou" as geistige Wesenheit. This is the attitude of the patient waiter or "empfangend Schauender" ("receptive beholder") (*Ich und Du*, 84):

He, too, especially when he makes the subject truly important to him, can open himself to the Bible and let himself be struck by its rays wherever they happen to strike him; he can wait without preconception and without reservation surrender himself, let himself be tested; he can take up, with all powers take up and await what will happen to him, await whether or not a new uninhibitedness to the Bible sprouts up within him.[9]

Buber stresses the need for the biblical text to be approached as "unfamiliar," as "other." This is the prerequisite for seeing the biblical text as Thou:

The "man of today". . . must approach the scripture as if he had never seen it before; as if he had not had it presented to him in school and after that in the garb of "religious" and "scientific" certainties; as if he had not all his life experienced it as all kinds of illusory concepts and propositions which are based on those certainties; he must place himself anew before the book which has become new. ("Neue Verdeutschung," 4)

When the Bible is approached as other—even as "alien"—readers can have fresh encounters with the text, encounters which, like all I-Thou encounters, will have transforming effects on them:

He must place himself anew before the book which has become new, withhold nothing and allow what happens between it and himself to happen. He does not know which saying, which image from this source will seize and remold him, from where the spirit will rush in and penetrate him in order to embody itself anew in his life; but he is open. (2)

That the receptive attitude of I-Thou and the concomitant hope for a dialogue with the biblical text is a central element in Buber's biblical hermeneutics is certain. But how is the modern reader to come to regard the biblical text which has been made so familiar by its ubiquitous presence in Western cultural products, as other, as Thou? Here Buber has one simple answer: the reader must return to the original Hebrew text. For the Hebrew with its peculiar semantics and syntax is bound to appear to the Western reader as alien. But what if the reader does not know Hebrew? Here he or she is offered a new translation—a German translation that attempts to bring the modern reader to the Hebrew text by mimicking Hebrew rhetoric and style.

In stark contrast to Buber's early Hasidic translations in which he strays far from the written texts, the Buber-Rosenzweig German translation of the Hebrew Bible may be one of the most literal translations that was ever produced. Everett Fox points out that in the Buber-Rosenzweig translation "each man was taxed to the utmost (*especially Buber*) in the effort to restrain poetic enthusiasm in favor of strict adherence to an existing text" (Fox, 6).

Buber criticizes other translations of the Hebrew Bible—the Septuagint, the Latin of Jerome, the German of Martin Luther—for not proceeding from "the purpose of preserving the original character of the Bible" ("Neue Verdeutschung," 6). He suggests that all these translations were executed with the desire of transmitting "a reliable foundation charter to a community" to the Jews of Hellenism, to the early Christian world, to the Protestants of the Reformation. The translators often altered the "brittle form" of the Hebrew to make it more comprehensible to its target community (ibid.). Buber is particularly critical of these translations for transforming the concrete "sense and sensuality" of the Hebrew vocabulary into abstract philosophical and theological terminology. These translations stand like "palimpsests," (5) writings which cover over the original Hebrew and prohibit access to it. Buber laments that the Hebrew has been "encrusted" not only by abstract theological terms and a desire to make the text amenable to certain communities, but also by aesthetic and literary concerns. In contrast to his early "romantic" and "aesthetic" translations of Hasidic tales, and in a direct challenge to his teacher Dilthey, Buber tells us that in his Bible translation one will find no "aestheticizing":

> It would be a false, superfluous, questionable, late romantic unfelicitousness if the translation were inspired by aesthetic or literary reflections; or if the choice of word were determined totally or even partially by taste. (9)

Buber allows that the translation be dictated solely by "the demands of the [Hebrew] text" (9). The translation must "proceed with the purpose of preserving the original character of the book in choice of word, sentence structure, and rhythmic arrangement" (6). He stresses the import of the "*Von wo aus,*" that through which the biblical message arises. For Buber, the biblical "content" cannot be separated from the "form" (*Moses*, 9).

His translation is directed toward presenting the overall unity of the Bible. If the Bible is to be regarded as a "Thou" it must be seen as a unity. "The Bible demands to be read as *one* book" ("Neue Verdeutschung," 13). Buber admits that there were various traditions and a variety of writers or schools that contributed to the writing of the Bible, but there was a final redaction of these writings and a canon was produced.

He is thus primarily interested in translating the text "which has become a whole no matter out of how many and varied fragments it has grown" (ibid.).

But how is Buber to disclose this unity in the biblical text to his reader? Here he cannot only count on the attitude of I-Thou. To present the biblical text as a whole he has to develop a way of imitating the Hebrew literary techniques through which the Bible became whole—techniques such as assonance, alliteration, repetition of cadence, and, most importantly, repetition of words or roots of words. To do this he develops his most famous translation and hermeneutic principle and technique, the principle of the *Leitwort*, the theme word.[10]

LEITWORTE

Buber argues that Leitworte give the biblical text rhythm and accentuate meaning. They are the defining attribute of biblical rhetoric. He defines the term as "a word or word-root meaningfully repeated within a text, series of texts, or collection of texts" ("Neue Verdeutschung," 15). His translation attempts to follow the biblical use of Leitworte by translating each Hebrew word or root consistently with one German word or root. Buber found that in doing this he not only was able to produce a more Hebrew-sounding German but he also found a key to the meaning of biblical passages and sections. Thus, the leading word technique became not only a principle for translation but also a principle of interpretation that was used to discern the meaning of the biblical text. Buber came to believe that it was through Leitworte that a unity of style and content could be found not only through the Torah, the first five books, but through the entire Tanakh. The leading word, in his view, was the tool through which the last redactor forged a unity and established a canon for the Hebrew Bible.[11]

Because the use of Leitworte is so pervasive throughout the Hebrew Bible, examples can be found on every page. Take, for example, the Tower of Babel story in Genesis 11:1–9. The word *safah* ("language") is repeated four times. The phrase *kol haretz* ("all the earth") is repeated five times, and the words and word stems *habah, banah, ir, patz,* ("come," "build," "city," "scatter") three times each. Despite the fact that German and English style would suggest that one not repeat the same words over and over again, Buber translates the words of the Tower of Babel story directly into German as they appear in the Hebrew. The repetition and mirror arrangement of the Leitworte not only give the Babel tale a rhythm and unity of sound but also quickly bring the hearer to the central theme and meaning of the tale: There was one language over all the earth and the people said, "Come let us build a city, lest we be scattered." But precisely from the hubris of the thought that unity and domination could be built by human power alone, the people lost the unity and were scattered over all the earth.

HISTORICAL CRITICISM

Although Buber's unique contribution to biblical hermeneutics can be found in his Leitwort principle he did not eschew the leading biblical critical principle of his day, historical criticism. In the introduction to *The Kingship of God*, Buber tells us that his aim is to "establish anew, upon the basis of critical research, the thesis of an early direct-theocratic tendency in Israel" (*KG*, 15). The "critical research" which he depends upon is philology, historical documents, and comparative analysis of kingship systems of the ancient Near East. Buber tells us that "the historical bias" of texts—its historical context, its audience, its original purposes—are "fundamentally decisive" (17) to his method of analysis. Regarding the documentary hypothesis he does not believe one can clearly isolate and date sources J, E, P, and D, but he does believe that there are "trends of literature," "manners of manipulating traditional material," and that knowledge of these "traditions" can be very helpful in interpreting the Bible.[12]

In his later books, *Moses* and *The Prophetic Faith*, Buber further outlines his use of historical criticism. He tells us his aim is to unearth the "tradition which we may regard legitimately as being near to the historical events" (*PF*, 6). His goal is to "penetrate beneath the layers of different redactions of tradition and their tendencies" (6–7) to "separate the early from the late here, and then to advance, as far as possible, from the reworking of tradition to what may be presumed to be tradition, orally preserved (*Moses*, 8). To these historical critical methodologies Buber adds the literary methodology of the leading-word so that he believes he is able to "treat . . . the Hebrew text in its formal constituents more seriously" (ibid.) than most historical critics.

A good example of the way in which Buber complements historical criticism with the leading-word technique is found in *The Kingship of God*. The entire book is dedicated to proving the historicity of the Judges passage of Gideon 8:23,"I will not rule over you, neither shall my son rule over you: the Lord shall rule over you."[13] Protestant biblical scholars Budde, Moore, Gressman, and Wellhausen have suggested that this saying of Gideon's is "too lofty" for the period of the Judges; it does not correspond with the development of Israelite faith which at this time had not arrived at the point of conceptualizing such a potent God that could supplant the need for human rulership. What actually happened with Gideon, these critics argue, is that he did accept the offer for him to be king, and this is confirmed by the statement of one of Gideon's sons, Abimelekh (9:2). Abimelekh, in an effort to usurp the power of his brothers who were ruling after their father Gideon, says: "Which serves you better, that seventy men rule over you, all sons of Jerubbaal [Gideon], or that a single man rule over you? [i.e., me, Abimelekh]."[14] Thus 8:23 is actually later than Judges 9:2.

Buber uses the leading word technique to show that 8:23 and 9:2 cannot be so easily severed. In both of these passages a Hebrew word, *mashal* (the German *walten*, "to rule"), which occurs only two other times in the entire book of Judges, occurs many times (three times in 8:23, two times in 9:2). This repetition not only prohibits the attempt to disconnect the passages but also provides a way to harmonize their seemingly contradictory meanings. Buber notes that the root *malakh*, "to be king," is not used here, but, instead, *mashal* is used, which signifies the "factual possession of power" and not the dominion of a "ruler's office." Thus, Abimelekh is acknowledging that Gideon and his seventy sons had practical power but never assumed the office of king. Gideon and his sons ruled (i.e., exercised power), yet all the while knowing full well that God was ultimate king.

Buber complements this leading-word analysis with a comparative historical analysis reviewing the kingship systems of Babylon, Egypt, and South Arabia to show that the germ of a notion of an "immediate, unmetaphorical, unlimitedly real theocracy" suggested by Gideon existed at his time and was not necessarily developed after him (*KM*, ch. 3).

Thus, in summarizing Buber's biblical hermeneutic we can say that though the I-Thou paradigm was essential to establish the proper attitude, added to or inserted within the I-Thou paradigm is a variety of technical operations and biblical critical methods. In an ironic turn away from the pure hermeneutic principles that appear in *I and Thou*, Buber appears to have become convinced that in order to insure an I-Thou relationship between the reader and the Bible, technique and method need not be eschewed, as a strict dialogical hermeneutical approach such as Gadamer would suggest. Buber seems to be convinced that in the case of the Hebrew Bible it is precisely techniques and methods that insure that an I-Thou relationship of the reader with the text is possible. Thus, what we find in Buber's biblical hermeneutics is a model for translation and interpretation that employs both the paradigm of I-Thou and select techniques and methods of explanation.

BUBER'S BIBLICAL HERMENEUTICS AND
CONTEMPORARY BIBLICAL CRITICISM

Given the recent interest in literary analysis and interpretation theory in academic circles in general and religious studies in particular, Buber's exegetical writings are receiving increasing attention. Edward Greenstein has shown that Buber's leading-word analysis continues to have relevance to contemporary biblical criticism. In reviewing five recent books which employ literary analyses of the Bible, Greenstein shows how all employ Buber's leading-word technique (Greenstein, 202). Michael Fishbane[15] and Harold Bloom[16] have also focused on Buber's literary sensibilities. Yet, though there has been a tendency to concentrate on his literary techniques alone, Buber's adept ability to combine literary and historical analysis with dialogical hermeneutics also deserves attention. For it seems that we have arrived at a time in biblical studies where many are realizing that one type of method—be it source criticism, form criticism, tradition criticism, or literary criticism—is not adequate to the complex task of interpreting the Bible. There is a movement away from the use of one methodological approach or one kind of method toward the use of a plurality of methods—methods which have often been opposed to one another and considered mutually exclusive by their original progenitors.

Important Jewish and Christian interpreters have argued that the turn toward the literary dimension of the Bible is not hindered but aided by historical scholarship. Meir Sternberg has stated that compositional issues, dating of texts, and historical studies of ancient Near East "prove indispensable to literary study as such" (Sternberg, 13). David Tracy has argued that, more than any other means, it is historical critical method that establishes a distance between modern readers and the biblical text and thus "preserves the otherness of the text," and allows for a true dialogue with the modern reader (Grant and Tracy, 154).

One helpful way of framing contemporary debates on the use of critical methodologies in biblical criticism is by employing the terms from Dilthey's distinction between the Geisteswissenschaften and the Naturwissenchaften which I introduced earlier. In Dilthey's view the human sciences and natural sciences each utilize different types of methods: methods of *verstehen* (understanding) and *erklaren* (explanation). The controversy in biblical hermeneutics surrounding use of critical methodologies represents a focal question in all of contemporary hermeneutic theory: to what extent do methods of erklaren and methods of verstehen represent epistemologically and even ontologically opposed approaches to the interpretation of texts? In framing the controversy in terms of a larger debate on method we will be able to take advantage of the work of a man who has, perhaps, thought most deeply about the estrangement of the sciences from the humanities—the French philosopher, Paul Ricoeur.

Ricoeur has shown, in addressing the issue of the radical separation between the methods of verstehen and erklaren, that though the methods are certainly different they can be shown to complement each other in the task of interpretation.[17] For example, we can think of a human conversation as a model for human communication. When two people understand one another, statement builds on statement, and creative dialogue rich with intuitive understanding ensues. Yet if one interlocutor suddenly does not understand the other, then free conversation is stopped and the partner is asked for explanations, reasons, exact information, analysis. After this is done the free and creative dialogue can continue. Thus, in the example of conversation, explanation assists understanding. Similarly, when we read a literary text we find that an analysis of the structure of the plot, the rhetorical style of the writing, and the period in which it was written assists us in understanding the meaning in front of the text, the meaning for our life and for our relationship to our world.

To apply this to biblical criticism we could say that questions about rhetoric and the historical status of certain texts need not be regarded as irrelevant to the hermeneutical task. Developing a "dialogue" with the text which opens to an understanding of the "meaning" and modern significance of the Bible can be aided by historical critical investigation. To take this further, we could say that there is no reason why historical critical methodology must be antithetical to a dialogical or a Gadamerian hermeneutical approach.

In his essay "Explanation and Understanding," Ricoeur argues that "explanation *develops* understanding" and "understanding precedes, accompanies, closes, and thus *envelops* explanation" (165). He believes that explanatory methods are especially important allies when we approach a phenomenon that is communicated, not directly, as in the model of conversation, but indirectly, through textual form. Here, where texts are our only form of communication, we need forms of explanation to help us to decipher the cultural codes that the text assumes and is written with: "This exteriorization into material marks, and this inscription in the codes of discourse, make not only possible *but necessary the mediation of understanding by explanation*"(153). Historical critical and rhetorical analysis can be of crucial importance in establishing the preunderstandings of the culture which produced a specific text. Without some information on these preunderstandings it is difficult to even begin a dialogue with a text.[18]

Historical critical methodology approaches texts and historical phenomenon as objects to be analyzed and categorized. The text as "object" cannot "address" a reader as subject. Gadamer, who develops a pure dialogical hermeneutics, attempts to exclude explanatory methods from the hermeneutic process. Utilizing Aristotle's distinction between *Phronesis* and *techne*, Gadamer argues that hermeneutics, as a form of Phronesis, "must attain its true dignity and proper knowledge of itself by being liberated from history" and "the methodological ideal of the natural sciences."[19] For Gadamer, the "truth" which the human sciences seeks cannot be won by a "method," especially a method whose goal is an atemporal objectivity. Yet, as Ricoeur has shown, explanatory methods can be of help to the tasks of understanding. For Ricoeur, explanatory methods must not be seen as obstacles but rather as aids to viewing the biblical text as "Thou." If we return to Buber's biblical hermeneutics we see that in order to approach an ancient text like the Hebrew Bible as Thou, we must out of necessity turn to technical historical and literary methodologies. Although in *Ich und Du* Buber established what some see as a radical distinction between I-Thou and I-It modes, his recognition of the complementary relationship between historical, literary, and dialogical hermeneutical approaches to the Bible represents an important step toward bridging the gap between I-Thou and I-It. Bridging this gap, which can be traced back through Dilthey to Kant to Descartes to Plato and which can be found wherever religions separate the sacred sphere from the profane, is a goal that I am confident many involved in contemporary hermeneutics share and regard not only as important to their work as scholars and teachers in the postmodern world but also as long overdue.

NOTES

1. Martin Buber, *I and Thou*, trans. R. G. Smith, 3. All references to *I and Thou* will be taken from this translation unless otherwise noted.
2. For a more extensive discussion of Buber's biblical hermeneutics in the context of his general hermeneutical philosophy, see my *The Text as Thou: Buber's Dialogical Hermeneutics and Narrative Theology* (Bloomington: Indiana University Press, 1992).
3. From a letter of Buber to Ronald Smith which Smith reported in his *Martin Buber* (Richmond: John Knox, 1967), 16 n.19. For another good discussion of how to translate the term *geistige Wesenheiten*, see Robert Wood, *Martin Buber's Ontology* (Evanston: Northwestern University Press, 1969). 43 n. 38.

4. The expression, "prime analogate," is Wood's, *Ontology* (50). Buber's first mention of *geistige Wesenheiten* in *I and Thou* refers to "forming, thinking, acting" (6). His next reference is to "language, art, and action" (39), which is followed by paragraphs on knowledge, art, and action (40–42). The discussions of art seem primary because it is out of them that Buber develops most fully his notion of a form of spirit that has become concrete.

5. Louis Hammer, "The Relevance of Buber to Aesthetics," in *PMB* (627). Also in *Martin Buber: Philosophen des XX. Jahrhunderts*, P. Schilpp and M. Friedman, eds. (Stuttgart: W. Kohlhammer, 1963).

6. Buber's notion of the "reality" and "truth" which art discloses has some affinities with Heideggerian aesthetics and its "disclosure model" for truth. See Heidegger, "The Origin of the Work of Art," *Poetry, Language, Thought*, trans. A. Hofstadter (San Francisco: Harper and Row, 1971). Also *Martin Heidegger and the Question of Literature*, ed. W. Spanos (Bloomington: Indiana University Press, 1979).

7. We can use Donald Berry's analysis of how it is we can have a "mutual" I-Thou relation with nature to explain the mutual relationship with a work of art. Berry suggests that we establish a notion of varying "degrees" or levels of mutuality. See Donald Berry, *Mutuality: The Vision of Martin Buber* (Albany: SUNY Press, 1985), ch. 1. The I-Thou relation I have with a tree is not the fully mutual relationship I have with my friend, but there are aspects of give and take in the relationship that make it more than a relationship of objectification or I-It. Similarly we could say that we do not have a fully mutual relationship with a work of art but there can be a give and take, a "dialogue" with the work when I approach it with the attitude of Thou.

8. Cf. Buber, *I and Thou* (4) and "Dialogue" (8), where Buber speaks of the objective way of perceiving which he calls "observing."

9. Martin Buber, "Zu einer neuen Verdeutschung der Schrift" [1954], *Beilage* to *Die fünf Bücher der Weisung* (Köln: Jakob Hegner, 1968), 2. This is a supplement to the 1954 and 1968 revised publication of the translation of the Pentateuch, which summarizes many of Buber's earlier essays on the translation from Martin Buber and Franz Rosenzweig, *Die Schrift und Ihre Verdeutschung* (Berlin: Schocken, 1936). Most of these essays are also found in Martin Buber, *Werke II Schriften zur Bibel* (Heidelberg: Lambert Schneider, 1964), 847–71, and 1093–1187 and some in Buber, *Darkho shel Mikra* [Hebrew] (Jerusalem: Mosad Bialik, 1964), 272–307; 344–59). All translations from this supplement are my own.

10. Benno Jacob and M. D. Cassutto used Buber's principle of *Leitworte* extensively in their commentaries on the Hebrew Bible and attempted to discredit the documentary hypothesis and trace out a unity throughout the text by using *Leitworte*.

11. *"Neue Verdeutschung"* (13). Buber refers to the final redactor of the Hebrew Bible as "the consciousness of unity which constructed the great halls of the Bible out of handed down structures and fragments." Rosenzweig refers to this redactor with the reverential term *rabbenu, unser Lerner*—our rabbi, our teacher (7).

12. *KG*, 17. Although Buber was often critical of the documentary hypothesis, he regarded it as a given of modern biblical interpretation. However, he believed that the interpreter had to go beyond the fragmentation of the Bible which the documentary hypothesis caused and seek the hints of unity throughout a section or book of the Bible. See Martin Buber, "Herut" [1919], *On Judaism*, 172. Also Buber, "Abraham the Seer" [1939], *On the Bible*, 25.

13. *Nicht ich will über euch walten. / nicht mein Sohn soll über euch walten* (Richter 8:23) *Bucher der Geschichte*, Verdeutscht von Martin Buber gemeinsam mit Franz Rosenzweig (Heidelberg: Lambert Schneider, 1985).

14. *Was taugt euch besser, dass über euch siebzig Männer walten, alle Söhne Jerubbaals, oder dass einziger Mann über euch walte?* Ibid., Richter 9:2. Thus, as I mentioned in the essay, according to the critics, 8:23 is actually later than Judges 9:2.

15. Michael Fishbane, "Martin Buber as an Interpreter of the Bible," 184–95); see also *Garments of Torah* (Bloomington: Indiana University Press, 1989).

16. Harold Bloom, "Introduction," Buber, *On the Bible*.

17. Paul Ricoeur, "Explanation and Understanding," *The Philosophy of Paul Ricoeur* (New York: Beacon, 1978), 149–67. See also Ricoeur, *Interpretation Theory* (Fort Worth: Texas Christian University Press, 1976), ch. 4.

18. See Bultmann, "The Problem of Hermeneutics," *New Testament and Mythology*, trans. and ed. S. Ogden (Philadelphia: Fortress Press, 1984), 86.

19. Gadamer, *Truth and Method*, 302–303. For Ricoeur's critical comments on Gadamer's attempts to exclude explanatory methods from the interpretation of texts, see Ricoeur, "The Hermeneutical Function of Distanciation," *Philosophy Today* 17 (Summer 1973): 129–30. Jürgen Habermas maintains that certain texts are "systematically distorted" by ideologies and they require critical explanatory theories like those provided by Marx and Freud if they are to be properly

understood. Habermas, *Hermeneutik and Ideologiekritic* (Frankfurt: Suhrkamp, 1971). See also the debates between Habermas and Gadamer in *Continuum* 8, (1970): 77–96; 123–28.

ADDITIONAL REFERENCES CITED IN TEXT BUT NOT IN NOTES

Buber, Martin. *BMM; I and Thou* (Smith; Kaufmann trans. noted in text); *Ich und Du; KG; KM; Moses; OB; OJ; PF.*
Gadamer, Hans-Georg. (1982). *Truth and Method.* New York: Crossroads.
———. (1965). *Wahrheit und Methode* [1960]. Tübingen: J. C. B. Mohr.
Grant, Robert and Tracy, David. (1984). *A Short History of the Interpretation of the Bible.* Philadelphia: Fortress Press.
Sternberg, Meir. (1987). *The Poetics of Biblical Narrative.* Bloomington: Indiana University Press.

CHAPTER 12

DIALOGUE IN PUBLIC

Looking Critically at the Buber-Rogers Dialogue

KENNETH N. CISSNA AND ROB ANDERSON

Martin Buber was renowned for his philosophy of dialogue and was widely known as an adept conversation partner. In this essay, we summarize our studies of one remarkable conversation—an instance of what Michael Oakeshott (1975) aptly termed an "unrehearsed intellectual adventure" (75)—between Martin Buber and the American psychotherapist Carl Rogers.[1]

This 1957 public conversation was significant because through Rogers's writings, especially following this meeting, many thousands of readers in the United States were introduced to Buber's thought. In addition, the dialogue was a critical incident in the careers of both Buber and Rogers. Although it has been cited often to distinguish their approaches to dialogue, all previous commentators have assumed that Buber and Rogers were on equal footing and ignore the communicative process of the meeting in favor of analyzing its content.

APPROACHING THE BUBER-ROGERS DIALOGUE

We became interested in this dialogue through our research into Carl Rogers's "philosophical praxis" of dialogue (Cissna and Anderson, 1990), an approach largely consistent with Buber's thought. After Kirschenbaum and Henderson (1989) published transcripts of Rogers's dialogues with noted intellectuals, we decided that these public conversations could extend our theoretical and philosophical understanding of the process, the "how" of dialogue. We focused temporarily on the Buber-Rogers dialogue in our paper for the 1991 Buber conference and became captivated by the rich implications of this one conversation. We have not yet returned to the broader project (Anderson & Cissna, 1993, 1994; Cissna and Anderson, 1994).

Our study of the Buber-Rogers dialogue has been productive, we think, for four reasons. First, we have demonstrated the usefulness of close rhetorical and communicative analysis of significant face-to-face meetings. Virtually all critical scholarship on dialogue has focused on the concepts of noted philosophers or theorists, charting the implications or distinctions among these ideas. Few studies have engaged in close, critical examination of people's efforts to create dialogue. Despite shelf after shelf of rhetorical analyses of public speeches, social movements, and various mediated events, scholars only rarely attempt to explore critically the rhetoric of a single public conversation. Second, the project has deepened our understanding of both Buber and Rogers, as thinkers and as communicators. They were conceptually similar yet nonetheless very distinct thinkers, and both were known as talented communicators. Existing studies have examined similarities and differences between their *ideas*. We enhance the intellectual portraits of Buber and Rogers by focusing on their rather dissimilar interpersonal styles in action. Third, this research extends scholarly interest in this one revealing event of dialogue. For years, Maurice Friedman almost single-handedly has sustained interest in the Buber-Rogers dialogue as a significant event. Our approach complements Friedman's concern for *what the dialogue teaches* with a concern for *how the dialogue developed*. Finally, by illuminating the internal dynamics of the dialogue itself, we hope to contribute to a broader contemporary scholarly conversation about dialogue. By focusing on a specific dialogic event, we show that dialogue is not "an ideal possibility seldom realized," as R. D. Laing said of confirmation (1969, 98), but a practical achievement coauthored anew in each concrete instance.

Our central argument is that previous commentaries about this event have ignored (a) the roles explicitly assigned to Buber and Rogers, (b) the presence of two non-participating audiences, and (c) the different interpersonal styles demonstrated by the two men. By clarifying the nature and function of these three features, we demonstrate the impact of the event's interpersonal dynamic and the lessons it teaches about dialogue. We discuss each of these issues after briefly reviewing the event's historical and intellectual context and summarizing the conversation itself.

CONTEXT OF THE DIALOGUE

Both participants and observers believed that this encounter was indeed a "dialogue." Immediately after the event, Buber noted that because Rogers "brought himself as a person" to the event it became a "real dialogue" (Friedman, *ENR*, 370). This was significant because in a paper delivered a month before at the Washington School of Psychiatry and published that year in *Psychiatry*, Buber argued that public dialogue was "separated by a chasm from genuine dialogue" (1957, 113). Yet, several years later when this lecture was reprinted in *The Knowledge of Man*, Buber's experience with Rogers had changed his mind (see *KM*, 184), and he directed that this paragraph be deleted.

Rogers also commented immediately following the dialogue that it "went very well" (Pentony 1987), and mentioned in an interview shortly before his death that he and Buber had had "a very good dialogue" (Rogers and Russell, 1991, 201). Friedman, too, called this meeting a dialogue, both in his concluding remarks that evening and subsequently in print (*MBLW: Later*; *ENR*; 1986; 1994). Other critics have expressed similar views (Anderson 1982; Arnett 1982; Brink 1987; Burstow 1987; Seckinger 1976).

The event itself occurred at the University of Michigan on April 18, 1957, during Buber's second U. S. tour. Buber's views on dialogue were influential and respected. Buber was well acquainted with Friedman and his work and had read several of Rogers' papers. By 1957 Carl Rogers, age fifty-five, had published a number of influential works, including *Counseling and Psychotherapy* and *Client-Centered Therapy*, and his "client-centered" approach was an important and distinct theory of psychotherapy. He had become acquainted with Buber's work during his years at the University of Chicago and believed it supported his own emerging theory of the therapist-client relationship. The previous year Rogers received the American Psychological Association's Distinguished Scientific Contribution Award and had the first of his famous interchanges with behavioral psychologist B. F. Skinner. Buber and Rogers met for the first time about an hour before the dialogue began. In 1957 Maurice Friedman was a young professor of philosophy at Sarah Lawrence College and a leading Buber scholar, having translated several of his books and published *Martin Buber: The Life of Dialogue* (1955). Friedman corresponded with Rogers and sent several of Rogers's then-unpublished papers (from *On Becoming a Person*) to Buber.

One highlight of Buber's 1957 tour was the conference devoted to him at the University of Michigan. Friedman describes the evening dialogue, with an audience of four hundred, as the "most notable event" of the several-day conference (1991, 368).

The ground rules for the event were somewhat unusual given Buber's emphasis on spontaneity in dialogue. Friedman described his function as "moderator" as "only, if the occasion should arise, to sharpen these issues or interpret one way or another." He also prescribed the roles of Buber and Rogers very clearly: "And the form of this dialogue will be that Dr. Rogers will himself raise questions with Dr. Buber and Dr. Buber will respond, and perhaps with a question, perhaps with a statement."[2,3]

THE DIALOGUE

The dialogue followed brief introductions by Rev. DeWitt Baldwin, who told the audience to expect a one-hour discussion, and Friedman. It was fueled by six questions, the first four asked of Buber by Rogers, the fifth asked of Buber and the sixth of Buber and Rogers by Friedman.

Rogers began with a slightly light-hearted phrasing of a biographical question, asking Buber: "How have you lived so deeply in interpersonal relationships and gained such an understanding of the human individual, without being a psychotherapist?" The highlights of Buber's response included: (a) a 5.7 second pause by Buber, during which Rogers was silent, (b) Buber's description of a crucial autobiographical episode that was so personal he never was able to write about it,[4] (c) Rogers's summarizing and organizing Buber's response into a "threefold answer" to which Buber responded, "Just so," (d) Rogers's interrupting the flow of the conversation in order to move the table so that he could face Buber and the microphone simultaneously, and (e) first Friedman and then Buber telling stories illustrating the naive ignorance of Jews by Christians.

Buber's willingness to talk about psychotherapy evidently conflicted with advice he had received. Rogers reported that an hour or so before the dialogue Buber had mentioned that his sponsors had "told him not to speak with Rogers about psychotherapy."[5] Rogers said he could not imagine what else they could discuss meaningfully together and decided that although Buber "might not be able to speak to him about psychotherapy, there was nothing to stop him from speaking about psychotherapy to Buber" (Pentony, 1987, 420). In such a context, Rogers's opening question to Buber seems much less whimsical and more assertive. In addition, Buber's willingness to ignore the advice of his sponsors in this and subsequent answers indicates his willingness to engage Rogers.

The second question occupied nearly half the dialogue: "I have wondered," Rogers asked, "whether [3.1] your concept—or your experience—of what you have termed the I-Thou relationship is similar to what I see as the effective moments in a therapeutic relationship." Rogers explained himself at some length, and Buber's response was even longer and rather like a lecture. Rogers interrupted twice to clarify. On the whole, Rogers described his experience as a therapist, while Buber emphasized what he called the "real situation." Halfway through this discussion, Buber observed, "Now, Dr. Rogers, this is the first point where we must say to one another, 'We disagree,'" to which Rogers responded simply, "Okay." But they did not leave it there. Buber continued to explain his objection to Rogers's claim that his therapeutic relationships can be "immediate, equal, a meeting of two persons on an equal basis." Buber illustrated the limits to what he said "interests me, eh, more than anything: human, eh, effective dialogue" by engaging Rogers on the problems of establishing relationships with schizophrenics and paranoiacs. Friedman entered this discussion and attempted to clarify the issue by questioning Rogers.

Rogers then shifted to a question about a "type of meeting which has a lot of significance to me in my work that, as far as I know, um, you haven't talked about"—"the person's relationship to himself." Buber's response was clear and direct: "Now here we approach a problem of language. You call something dialogue that I cannot call so." Rogers indicated his wish to play tapes of therapy sessions to show how surprise, one of the essential elements of dialogue that Buber had mentioned, is present in this form of meeting. Buber identified a more general problem in psychology of not appreciating terms sufficiently.

At first Buber did not appear to understand Rogers's fourth question, concerning "basic human nature." Rogers explained that he saw human nature as trustworthy and wondered if Buber agreed. Buber replied that human nature was polar rather than basically positive. In our judgment, this was the clearest philosophical difference that emerged in this dialogue.

Rogers then acknowledged Friedman, who asked about the relationship of Rogers's concept of "acceptance" and Buber's "confirmation." The difference between them seemed at least partly semantic: Rogers used acceptance as an umbrella term, "accepting the individual *and* his potentiality," while Buber used acceptance more narrowly with confirmation including helping the other "even in his struggle against himself." Rogers then attempted to end the dialogue, perhaps because the announced time limit had passed.

Friedman, however, asked one more question, which concerned whether the locus of value was within the person or between persons. Rogers spoke first; Buber then addressed a problem he found in one of Rogers's articles and explained the difference between an individual and a person. Rogers evidently agreed with this distinction, very softly saying "Correct" as the closing utterance, after which Friedman briefly thanked the participants and the audience. This was the least revealing segment of the dialogue—both in terms of interchange (there was almost none) and content.

ENFOLDED ROLES AND COMPLEMENTARY CONVERSATION

Although this conversation was in many ways dialogical, it also resembled an interview and a classroom lesson. The occasion had been arranged well in advance, and both Buber and Rogers were told what was expected of them during the evening. These expectations are manifest in "roles."

Roles are patterns of behavior that become identified with interpersonal positions and are sometimes distinguished as social (e.g., student and teacher) or emergent (e.g., a person in a relationship who often initiates or terminates conversation). Conversational roles are usually emergent and rarely explicitly structured—especially when genuine and spontaneous dialogue is desired. The roles provided to Buber and Rogers ("Dr. Rogers will himself raise questions with Dr. Buber, and Dr. Buber will respond") are unusually explicit if dialogical conversation was expected. We term them *enfolded roles*, because as real but not always obvious aspects of the dialogue, they seemed to exist in the folds of the conversation's process rather than on the surface of its content.

The dialogue was a small part of a three-day conference held in Buber's honor and devoted to his thought. No doubt it seemed natural to have Buber assume the role of expert. Rogers was younger, from the host country, and had acknowledged an intellectual curiosity about Buber. Further, he was known as a skillful interviewer and facilitator. It must have seemed just as natural to ask him to take a role that was, in comparison with Buber's, secondary and functional. Communication theorists call this a complementary relationship, one based on interactional differences rather than similarities (Haley, 1963; Watzlawick, Beavin, and Jackson, 1967).

The consequences of this choice, however, were significant. Buber (1957) had previously suggested that "genuine dialogue cannot be arranged beforehand," and that each partner in dialogue must be willing "to say what is really in his mind about the subject of the conversation," "without reduction and without shifting his ground," "determined not to withdraw when the course of the conversation makes it proper for him to say what he has to say" (112–13). These suggestions would be difficult for interviewers to follow, especially in front of an audience, because persons in these roles have two somewhat contradictory responsibilities: to contribute as participants to the conversational content, and often to refrain from contributing substantively because they are supposed to be facilitating. Interviewers, in other words, must often enable the other's talk at the expense of their own. Rogers was expected to offer questions and probes to get the conversation started and to sustain it. His enfolded role, by definition, required planning, and indeed, he prepared and brought with him the four questions he asked and five additional questions that he did not ask (Rogers 1957). This responsibility for the *process* necessarily reduced Rogers's potential for spontaneity. Buber's role was to be responsive to Rogers, which, although also constraining, allowed for more ideational creativity.

We would expect, therefore, to find that a questioner in a conversation would tend to speak less than his interlocutor, to develop his ideas with less depth, to defer and yield the floor more often, to facilitate the other's talk with assists and encouragements, to check more often on the other's meanings, to introduce more transitions of topic, and to be less overtly concerned with maintaining face. Conversely, the authority in such a situation would tend to speak at greater length, more often, to develop his ideas more fully, to express his ideas with greater certainty, and to be less concerned with understanding the other's ideas.

We are not suggesting that this interaction was totally one-sided or that Rogers constantly deferred to Buber while Buber always asserted his authority. Far from it. What Haley (1963) called the struggle to define the relationship is evident occasionally. Still, our reading of this dialogue is informed by realizing that their relationship in this dialogue, driven in part by their enfolded roles, is basically complementary. For example, late in the dialogue Buber and Rogers respond to Friedman's question about acceptance and confirmation. Buber responds first, then Rogers; and, in the most commonly cited transcript, Buber appears to get the last word before Friedman changes the topic with another question (*KM*, 183). Actually, in language edited out of that transcript, Rogers terminated their exploration of that topic and attempted to end the dialogue ("I just feel that one, um, difficulty with a dialogue is that there could easily be no end, but I think that, uh, both in mercy to Dr. Buber and to the audience . . ."). Although this could be interpreted as Rogers not wanting to engage Buber fully, a more plausible explanation concerns Rogers's assigned role. As the evening had already lasted more than the promised one hour, Rogers probably chose to enact his functional role—perhaps even assuming some of Friedman's role as moderator as Friedman assumed Rogers's role as questioner—in an attempt to end the event. In this act, we see Rogers's willingness to speak less, to develop his ideas in less depth, to defer to Buber, and to introduce transitions (and conversely, Buber's willingness to accept the positions complementary to those). Were they not constrained by the enfolded roles, we might have heard Rogers's response to Buber's analysis of the difference between acceptance and confirmation.

Thus, any examination of the dialogue that attempts to probe intellectual differences between Buber and Rogers must consider the quasi-political effects of enfolded roles. Unfortunately, this has not happened. Previous accounts presume that Buber and Rogers engaged in a spontaneous and unrehearsed dialogue where each conversant was equally able to articulate his ideas (Arnett 1981, 1986, 1989; Brace 1992; Brink 1987; Burstow 1987; Friedman, *MBLW: Later, HDP*, 1986, *ENR*, 1994; Peterson 1976; Roffey 1980; Seckinger 1976). Although Buber plainly assumed such freedom because he correctly understood the focus of the dialogue to be on him, he was perhaps constrained in other ways. For example, his assigned role made it less likely that his skills as a listener would be fully revealed. Rogers, on the other hand, could be expected to have felt constrained by his role to leave at least some of his own ideas less well developed. Although the dialogue was a significant intellectual interchange, role definitions limited a thorough exploration of Rogers's concepts relative to Buber's, and in many ways—as Buber himself would have predicted—this choice did not serve Buber particularly well either, for the interactional ground upon which his conversation partner could stand was certainly different and in some ways less secure than his own.

AUDIENCE AS COAUTHOR OF THE BUBER-ROGERS DIALOGUE

Audiences are not merely passive recipients of messages but are active coauthors of the meanings of communication. An auditor is an active partner—in some ways a coauthor—of the meanings developed by a speaker. That is, to some extent, messages are not just what someone *wants to say*, but also what one *wants an audience to hear* and what one *believes is "called for" in a particular situation*. Thus, it is misleading to consider ideas apart from audience influences.

Obviously, each man was speaking to his partner and, to that extent, expected the other to be his audience, along with Friedman and DeWitt Baldwin. Less obvious to readers of the transcripts may be two additional audiences who "silently participated," as Friedman put it at the close of the dialogue. The four hundred people who listened in Rackham Auditorium that evening constituted one audience; the tape recorder that functioned to preserve the dialogue served as a marker of an even more distant and far larger potential audience. The influences of these audiences on the dialogue also have not been considered by previous commentators.

Buber came to his meeting with Rogers believing that dialogue could not be conducted in public and apparently having rather low expectations for this encounter. He refused to have his lectures in Washington, D.C., the previous month filmed, despite his host having secured a grant for that purpose (Buber, 1991) or even to have them audio-recorded (Friedman, *ENR*, 362). Buber argued that recording oral discourse would spoil the spontaneity that was necessary for dialogue and that speakers would tend to court favor with the audience rather than to address themselves to one another. Further, he thought that dialogue was compromised when additional people are present but expected to remain silent (Buber, 1957, *KM*).

Conducting a tape-recorded dialogue before a public audience presents unique rhetorical challenges to the participants. While the conversants are expected to be partners in dialogue, open to the other's ideas and willing to examine their own, they are also, in a sense, "performing" for both immediate and deferred audiences. We cannot know with certainty how such audiences influenced this conversation. Research concerning the broadcast news interview, a genre similar in some ways, suggests that the presence of an audience affects how participants frame their own and others' status and how interactants characterize others' talk (see Heritage, 1985, 99–112).

Consistent with such evidence and with Buber's own ideas about audience, we speculate that the presence of observers to a dialogue could foster:

1. *A subtle sense of competition*—which might reduce the likelihood of change or of a speaker acknowledging being changed.
2. *A desire to speak for voiceless audience members*—perhaps encouraging such references as Rogers's "consideration for the audience."
3. *A preoccupation with the permanence of one's remarks*— which would encourage safety and reduce spontaneity.
4. *A concern for the dramatic requirements of the occasion*— which might result in such light jokes, cleverness, and storytelling as are found early in the dialogue.
5. *An exaggeration of both agreement and, at times, differences*—arising from the sometimes competing desires to be

seen as cooperative and to establish one's own identity in the eyes of the audience.

6. *A tendency to take longer conversational turns*—more like mini-speeches, designed to provide conceptual background or amplification for the audience.

7. *A need to satisfy the time requirements of the event*—perhaps terminating the conversation prematurely or extending it past its moment (e.g., "since I see time is going by," said Rogers.)

In this dialogue, a procedural influence of audience was created through the decision to assign Buber and Rogers conversational roles, which undoubtedly would not have happened had they talked privately in someone's living room that evening. In the example discussed earlier, Rogers is acting within his role and on behalf of the audience in his attempt to terminate the event.

The influence of audience on interaction processes can also be found throughout the dialogue, as, for example, in their length of speaking turns. Rogers never asked a short question, and Buber almost never gave a short answer. Their remarks were full of examples and illustrations to help an audience understand their ideas. Another artifact of audience is found in the stories told by Friedman and by Buber in the transition between Rogers's first and second questions. These stories functioned, at least in part, to entertain the audience. Later, in their extended discussion of the second question, Rogers, perhaps puzzled about Buber's position vis-à-vis his own, said: "Well now, now I'm wondering uh who is Martin Buber, you or me, because what I feel . . ." to which Buber and audience responded with laughter. In the remainder of their discussion of this question there were efforts to mark both disagreement (Buber: "Now, Dr. Rogers, this is the first point where we must say to one another, 'We disagree'") and agreement (Rogers: "Well, if we don't look out, we'll agree")—all done with humor and in a way intended to inform and entertain the audience.

INTERPERSONAL STYLE DIFFERENCES OF BUBER AND ROGERS

As we would expect from the enfolded roles, the spotlight clearly was on Buber, and the principals adjusted both the quantity and quality of their talk accordingly. Buber dominated the speaking time, commanding 64 percent of the dialogue compared to 30 percent for Rogers and 6 percent for Friedman. In the final twenty-four minutes, after the event had gone past its allotted hour and Rogers had noted that "time is going by" and that he would "raise one other question," Rogers became even less active, and Friedman assumed the role of questioner. In this segment, Buber spoke 73 percent of the time, Rogers 14 percent, and Friedman 13 percent. Because Buber spoke very slowly and deliberately, the differences are less dramatic when we examine lines of type, which probably reflects more closely the ideational content (Buber spoke 53 percent more words than Rogers). Not only the amount but the kind of talk differed as well.

Rogers's conversational style served primarily to: (a) invite Buber to explain his ideas, (b) clarify his own understanding of Buber's explanations, and (c) highlight his own experience in relationships. As the first two are fairly straightforward, we will focus in more detail on Rogers's style of limiting his claims to his own concrete experience. Rogers frequently qualified assertions with such phrases as these from the dialogue: "it seems to me," "it has been my experience," "I say very tentatively," "I've learned from my experience," "from my point of view," "perhaps," "I wonder if," "I feel that," and "I may be mistaken on that" (cf. Cissna and Anderson, 1990). Such reservations, Rogers believed (1980, 96–108), were consistent with scientific understanding of the limits of social knowledge and exemplified his insistence on accepting responsibility for personal perceptions. Thus, not only was Rogers tentative and provisional in his assertions, he was also offering his psychotherapeutic experience to Buber to be examined as a kind of "data."

Buber's style was quite different. While Rogers' style was provisional, Buber's was certain—perhaps influenced also by audience expectations that he be "the expert." While Rogers's talk emphasized invitation, Buber corrected, insisting on precise terminology. Often when Rogers framed questions in terms of what he believed or had experienced, Buber replied with how that "cannot" be. In fact, Buber used "cannot" and occasionally "can't" to assert certainties thirty-nine times during their conversation (Friedman used "cannot" once; Rogers said "can't" twice). Although the word is reasonable in many contexts, partners in dialogue are unlikely to feel confirmed by repeated suggestions that their feelings and perceptions cannot be valid. Note these examples of Buber's certainty from the dialogue: "He cannot, by far, cannot see you"; "He is not interested in you as you. It cannot be"; "He cannot be but where he is"; "I see you *mean* being on the same plane, but you cannot be"; "You cannot change this"; and "You cannot say." Elsewhere we termed this discourse a "rhetoric of cannot," which is likely to be heard as a request to acquiesce to authority (Anderson and Cissna, 1996). Because this appears inconsistent with what Buber believed about dialogue, we assume he was relatively unaware of this reliance upon authority. Indeed it is similar to the role of many European professors who patiently correct the nascent assumptions and ideas of inquiring students.

Interestingly, we also find evidence in their talk of their influence on each others' conversational styles, which may offer some additional indication of the dialogue's quality. In the second half of the conversation, while answering Buber's claim that dialogue is not present in an intrapersonal encounter, Rogers takes on something of Buber's certainty when he says, "He really is surprised by himself. That can *definitely* happen." Buber, late in his discussion of the second question, says "as far as I see," and somewhat later appears to adopt even more of Rogers's style, repeating "as far as I see," and also saying "My experience is," "I, eh, experience it as," and "I would say that." Further, in his response to the next question, Buber mildly deferred to Rogers's experience as a therapist ("I'm afraid I'm not so sure of that as you are, perhaps because I'm *not* a therapist"). Still, the dominant impressions are that Rogers's talk represented a provisional rhetoric and Buber's a "rhetoric of cannot." Overall, we must emphasize that *their behavior in the dialogue was consistent with the expectations raised by the requirements of enfolded roles and audience presence* that were part of the rhetorical challenge they faced that evening.

CONCLUSION

The 1957 Buber-Rogers dialogue was significant for both men and for the development of Buber's reputation in the United States. Almost forty years after it occurred, this dialogue continues to stimulate intellectual commentaries by scholars interested in how Buber's ideas influence—and can be distinguished from—the work of his followers and coexplorers of dialogic processes. The dialogue also appears to have been a critical incident in the careers of both Buber and Rogers. Following this encounter, Buber changed his opinion about whether audiences could preclude dialogue, and that October he wrote a new afterword to *I and Thou* that appears to address issues raised in the dialogue (see *I and Thou*, Kaufmann's translation, 177–79). Rogers increasingly cited Buber's work in connection with his own therapy and subsequently expanded his focus to human relationships more generally.

This brief chapter only summarizes our investigations of this dialogue. Space limitations prevent us from including much of our argument and evidence or explaining our conclusions regarding such theoretical issues as mutuality or confirmation. We trust we have cautioned readers about interpreting the content of this or any conversation without considering the interactional dynamics that produced it, and that we have referred readers appropriately to other, more detailed studies in which we discuss our critical methodology in detail, and consider additional implications for understanding public dialogue and for understanding Buber and Rogers as thinkers and communicators.

We have much to learn from Martin Buber and Carl Rogers as insightful commentators on the human condition. We hope we have shown that we can also learn from the Buber-Rogers *relationship*.

NOTES

1. Our thanks to Professor John Stewart for providing us a copy of the audiotape of the Buber-Rogers dialogue and helping us revise this essay. Maurice Friedman also encouraged us in this project, shared his impressions of the event, and helped us refine our analysis. Thanks to the staffs of the Martin Buber Archives at the Jewish National and University Library; the Michigan Historical Collection at the Bentley Historical Library and the Harlan Hatcher Graduate Library, both of the University of Michigan; The Carl R. Rogers Collection at The Library of Congress; and especially Nel Kandel and Avis Johnson of the Carl Rogers Memorial Library at the Center for Studies of the Person. The authors also acknowledge the assistance of their institutions in providing research support for this project. Both authors contributed equally to this study.
2. The ground rules for this event were given to Friedman by DeWitt Baldwin, who ran the conference (Friedman, personal communication, December 14, 1991).
3. Our quotations from and references to the dialogue are from the transcript we produced from the audiotape rather than from any of the published transcripts (Buber, *KM*; "Dialogue Between," 1960; Friedman, 1964; Kirschenbaum and Henderson, 1989), or from the original typescript of the dialogue circulated by Rogers ("Dialogue Between," n.d.). We found that much has been omitted and some statements changed in the earlier transcripts; several changes are very significant and alter our interpretations of what Buber and Rogers meant. We do not claim that our transcript is "correct"; by the standards of contemporary conversation analysis, a transcript of this ninety-minute discussion would require a small volume. Specifically, we have added speaking turns, noted audible material not in the transcript, and restored original language where it had been changed. We found some lengthy pauses where none were indicated, and found some indicated pauses quite short. Sometimes we

did not hear the same emphasis as one finds indicated by italics. Upon request, we will provide our transcript to the interested reader.

4. We are referring to the barbaric killing of his friend Gustav Landauer at the end of World War I. Friedman identifies it as one of the three most important events in Buber's life. To the end of his life Buber was "preoccupied" by it and, despite Friedman's urging, "too close to this event to be able to write about it." Although in the dialogue he does not mention Landauer by name, describing him only as "a great friend," he never wrote about this episode and apparently spoke publicly about it and its impact on him only in this dialogue with Rogers (see Friedman, 1991, 114–15; *MBLW: Early*, 257–58).

5. If the reader finds this statement perplexing, perhaps Rogers also was surprised at the time. Actually, the dialogue was almost cancelled. Leslie Farber, then chairman of the Washington School of Psychiatry, suggested to DeWitt Baldwin that the dialogue be omitted because, Baldwin reported in a letter to Buber, it "would concern itself with psychiatry [and] he felt that this subject should be left with your Seminars in Washington since the Washington School of Psychiatry was paying your expenses to this country and paying an honorarium" (Baldwin, 1957b). The correspondence from Baldwin to Buber also showed something of how the topics for the dialogue evolved. In an earlier letter, Baldwin suggested that the dialogue deal "primarily with what you have found out about men and how to affect better human relations" (Baldwin, 1957a). In letters to Buber and Rogers dated nine days before the conference began, Baldwin confirmed Rogers's suggestion that the dialogue concern "the nature of man as revealed in inter-personal relationship" (Baldwin 1957c, 1957d). Surely Rogers would have wondered how psychotherapy could be excluded from such topics.

REFERENCES

Anderson, R. (1982). "Phenomenological Dialogue, Humanistic Psychology and Pseudo-Walls: A Response and Extension." *Western Journal of Speech Communication* 46: 344–57.

Anderson, R., and Cissna, K. N. (1995). "The Martin Buber-Carl Rogers Dialogue: A New Transcript with Commentary." Unpublished manuscript.

Anderson, R., and Cissna, K. N. (1996). "Criticism and Conversational Texts: Rhetorical Bases of Role, Audience, and Style in the Buber-Rogers Dialogue." *Human Studies* 19: 1–35.

Arnett, R. C. (1981). "Toward a Phenomenological Dialogue." *Western Journal of Speech Communication* 45: 201–212.

———. (1982). "Rogers and Buber: Similarities, Yet Fundamental Differences." *Western Journal of Speech Communication* 46: 358–72).

———. (1986). *Communication and Community: Implications of Martin Buber's Dialogue.* Carbondale: Southern Illinois University Press.

———. (1989). "What is Dialogic Communication?: Friedman's Contribution and Clarification." *Person-Centered Review* 4: 42–60.

Baldwin, D. (1957a). Baldwin to Buber, 11 January 1957, Jerusalem. Unpublished letter from Martin Buber Archives, Jewish National and University Library, Arc. Ms. Var. 350/836d:2.

———. (1957b). Baldwin to Buber, 11 February 1957, Jerusalem. Unpublished letter from Martin Buber Archives, Jewish National and University Library, Arc. Ms. Var. 350/836d:5.

———. (1957c). Baldwin to Buber, 8 April 1957, Washington, D.C. Unpublished letter from Martin Buber Archives, Jewish National and University Library, Arc. Ms. Var. 350/836d:8.

———. (1957d). Baldwin to Rogers, 8 April 1957, Chicago. Unpublished letter from The Carl R. Rogers Collection, Collections of the Manuscript Division, Library of Congress, Washington, D.C. (Box 80, folder 13).

Brace, K. (1992). "I and Thou in Interpersonal Psychotherapy." *The Humanistic Psychologist* 20: 41–57.

Brink, D. D. (1987). "The Issues of Equality and Control in the Client- or Person-Centered Approach." *Journal of Humanistic Psychology* 27: 27–37.

Buber, M. BMM; *I and Thou* (Kaufmann); KM.

———. (1957). "Elements of the Interhuman." *Psychiatry* 20: 105–13.

———. (1991). Buber to Leslie H. Farber, 19 February 1957, Jerusalem. In N. N. Glatzer and P. Mendes-Flohr, eds., *The Letters of Martin Buber: A Life of Dialogue* (No. 665). New York: Schocken Books.

Burstow, B. (1987). "Humanistic Psychotherapy and the Issue of Equality." *Journal of Humanistic Psychology* 27: 9–25.

Cissna, K. N., and Anderson, R. (1990). "The Contributions of Carl Rogers to a Philosophical Praxis of Dialogue." *Western Journal of Speech Communication* 54: 125–47.

———. (1994). "The 1957 Martin Buber-Carl Rogers Dialogue, as Dialogue." *Journal of Humanistic Psychology* 34: 11–45.

Dialogue between Martin Buber and Carl Rogers. (1960). *Psychologia* 3, 208–221.

Dialogue between Martin Buber and Carl Rogers. (n.d.). Unpublished typescript, The Carl R. Rogers Collection, Collections of the

Manuscript Division, Library of Congress, Washington, D.C. (Box 46, Folder 6), and Carl Rogers Memorial Library, Center for Studies of the Person, La Jolla, CA.

Friedman, M. *MB:LoD; MBLW: Early; MBLW: Later; HDP; ENR.*

———. (1964). "Dialogue between Martin Buber and Carl Rogers." In *The Worlds of Existentialism: A Critical Reader* (485–97). New York: Random House.

———. (1986). "Carl Rogers and Martin Buber: Self-Actualization and Dialogue. *Person-Centered Review* 1: 409–435.

———. (1994). "Reflections on the Buber-Rogers Dialogue." *Journal of Humanistic Psychology* 34: 46–65.

Haley, J. (1963). *Strategies of Psychotherapy.* New York: Grune and Stratton.

Heritage, J. (1985). "Analyzing News Interviews: Aspects of the Production of Talk for an Overhearing Audience." In T. A. van Dijk, ed., *Handbook of Discourse Analysis: Vol. I, Discourse and Dialogue* (95–117). London: Academic Press.

Kirschenbaum, H., and Henderson, V. L., eds. (1989). *Carl Rogers: Dialogues.* Boston: Houghton-Mifflin.

Laing, R. D. (1969). *Self and Others.* 2nd ed. Baltimore: Penguin.

Oakeshott, M. (1975). *On Human Conduct.* Oxford: Oxford University Press.

Pentony, P. (1987). "Some Thoughts About Carl Rogers." *Person-Centered Review* 2: 419–21.

Peterson, J. D. (1976). "Carl Rogers and His Ways of Being in Interpersonal Relationships." Masters thesis, Kansas School of Religion and University of Kansas.

Roffey, J. W. (1980). "A Hermeneutic Critique of Counseling Psychology: Ricoeur and Rogers." Doctoral dissertation, University of Kentucky.

Rogers, C. R. (1957) Dialogue with Martin Buber: Nature of Man as Revealed in Interpersonal Rel. Unpublished notes from The Carl R. Rogers Collection, Collections of the Manuscript Division, Library of Congress, Washington, D.C. (Box 46, Folder 6).

———. (1980). *A Way of Being.* Boston: Houghton-Mifflin.

———. with Russell, D. E. (1991). *The Quiet Revolutionary* (Draft 1/25/91). Santa Barbara: Library Oral History Program, University of California at Santa Barbara.

Seckinger, D. S. (1976). "The Buber-Rogers Dialogue: Theory Confirmed in Experience." *Journal of Thought* 11: 143–49.

Watzlawick, P., Beavin, J. H., and Jackson, D. D. (1967). *Pragmatics of Human Communication.* New York: Norton.

CHAPTER 13

DECEPTION AND THE RELATIONAL

Martin Buber and Sisela Bok—Against the Generation of the Lie

VIRGINIA SHABATAY

The presence of the lie is not new. Our time and our place are no different in this regard: the Word still goes astray. In the eighteenth century the Baal Shem Tov, the founder of Hasidism—the Eastern European mystical sect of Judaism—said: "What does it mean when people say that Truth goes over all the world? It means that Truth is driven out of one place after another, and must wander on and on" (*TH: Early*, 71).

And so it is in our days. When I asked myself which of the words of Martin Buber I wanted to draw on for this essay, the answer came easily for our times: his call for the absence of duplicity, without which no wholeness of the person or relationship or community is possible. Karl Wilker says of his contact with Buber: "The longer I knew him, not only through his works but also face to face, the more strongly I have felt that his whole personality tolerates no untruthfulness and no unclarity" (Friedman *LoD*, 5).

Dialogue is central to human affairs, but no genuine dialogue can take place where lying occurs, and no genuine peace can take place where mistrust is present. Mistrust is brought about by many conditions, but certainly lying is one source. Mistrust injures the personal, the social, and the political realm. "That peoples can no longer carry on authentic dialogue with one another," Buber writes, "is not only the most acute symptom of the pathology of our time, it is also that which most urgently makes a demand of us" (*PW*, 238).

Sisela Bok, an ethicist at Harvard and daughter of two Nobel Prize winners, Alva Myrdal and Gunnar Myrdal, is equally disturbed by both the prevalence and the spread of the lie. She recognizes that remaining faithful to the truth is not always easy, that "whether to lie, equivocate, be silent, or to tell the truth in any given situation is often a hard decision" (Bok 1979, xvi). For example, should we lie to protect peers and clients? Should leaders lie for the public good? Should social scientists use deception on subjects in the name of research? Are we justified in lying in a crisis, in lying to liars or enemies, in telling white lies?

Do we want to be lied to? What do we expect from our friends and loved ones? What do they expect from us? Lying always has a purpose: to protect, to gain advantage, to avoid confrontation, to injure. People vary in their desire for truth: some would rather *not* know certain facts. Some respect the privacy of others to withhold information. Some feel that lying protects their independence.

Most people would probably say they tell only "white lies" and those only occasionally. Bok set out to find a moral theory to aid in making choices between telling the truth and telling a lie in problematic situations; the result of the pursuit was her highly respected book *Lying: Moral Choice in Public and Private Life.* What surprised her was the scarcity of material available. She reports that "The index to the eight-volume *Encyclopedia of Philosophy* contains not one reference to lying or to deception, much less an entire article devoted to such questions" (xx).

Bok offers three instances where the lie might be permissable: first, in the defense of life—whether another's or one's own. The justification is that since we allow the use of force in self-defense, the lie can be equally permissible under such conditions (43). Second, lies might be permitted in a crisis and in what Bok calls drawing a line. For example, she tells of a woman who was "making a university-sponsored visit to a village of former head-hunters":

> She was well received and presented with the special delicacy of the tribe: baby mice, taken by the tail, dipped in melted butter, and swallowed alive. After a moment's thought, she announced regretfully that she wished she could taste the mice, but that to do so would be against her religion. (122)

Third, to determine which lies could be justified by reasonable people, Bok asks for the test of publicity. Open discussion should be held in classrooms, seminars, and public forums about the policy of secrecy and lying.

When Tzu Kung asked Confucius: "Is there any one word that can serve as a principle for the conduct of life?" Confucius answered,

"Perhaps . . . reciprocity: Do not do to others what you would not want others to do to you" (Bok, 98). But liars do not live by that code. The paradox about liars is that unless they are operating under a system of bargaining at a flea market or playing poker with other individuals who have entered into a contract of deception for certain purposes, they expect others to tell the truth.

Whereas Bok seeks a moral theory to help us in quandaries over deceitful practices, Buber, as a philosophical anthropologist, is concerned more with the nature of the lie and its impact on the human spirit and on human relations. Would Buber, who believes that "the end never sanctifies the means, but the means can certainly thwart the end" (PW, 218), concede that there might be a time for the lie? Might there be guidelines for telling the truth or telling a lie in problematic situations?

One incident in his life indicates that he would adhere to no absolutist position. When Buber was twelve years old he was involved in an incident at school where he was asked to report on the suspected improper behavior of some of his fellow classmates. Buber tells that during recess two boys began to behave in ways which took on a sexual character. These games were never discussed afterwards among the classmates. Later Buber was called to the director's office. There he was faced with a conflict from which he learned the problematic between "maxim and situation." The director was friendly, but he asked Buber what he knew about the behavior of the two classmates. Caught between two loyalties, the young Martin cried out, "I know nothing!" The director pressed on just as gently as before. "We know you well," he said, "you are a good child, you will help us." But Buber remembers that he wanted to cry out, "Help? Help whom?" He was so overcome that he had to remain home for several days, and when he returned to school the two classmates in question were no longer there (Meetings, 25–26).

This incident revealed to Buber that one cannot always follow maxims for the moral decisions one must make. Buber was a "good boy" and would tell what had happened. He would tell the truth, it was assumed, but the director failed to realize the bind in which he had placed the young boy. At that time Buber experienced "the nature of the true norm that commands not our obedience but ourselves" (26).

Was Buber dishonest? We can say that the boy gave an honest response—not to the director, but to the situation in which he was placed. This call of the situation, however, is far from the heart of Buber's assessment of the prevalence and problematic of the lie. He would not conclude "lie when you need to; tell the truth when you can." We might, however, classify Buber's response under Bok's category of drawing a line.

What do Buber and Bok say about the impact of the lie on the individual, the interpersonal, and the communal? First, both agree that lying damages liars themselves. Liars disturb their own being: A lie, Buber writes, results in the spirit practicing "treason against itself" (*G & E*, 7). The lie not only injures the liar but destroys the heart of relationship and community. Buber turns to Psalm 12, where the psalmist cries out to God for help against the faithless, those with "smooth tongues." The psalmist refers here to the deceptions the liars create for their listeners: "They spin illusions for them; in particular they spin a way of thinking for them which they themselves do not follow." Liars claim power for themselves by saying: "Our lips are with us, who is lord over us?" (*G & E*, 10–11). Tellers of lies weight the balance of power in their favor—they claim a control denied to the persons lied to. Now the deceived lack necessary information to make decisions, and they operate with a false premise.

To give the lie "the stamp of truth, the liar speaks 'with a double heart,' " and, Buber observes, "develops two hearts: one which knows the truth, the other which claims to know his or her lie as the truth (*G & E*, 10). The liar may no longer be able to discern his truth from his lie. He may convince himself that the lie is the truth—telling the lie so many times may make him claim it as truth, especially when self-interest is at stake. The liar brings the force of denial to work with the creation of fiction as truth. A person who "wishes to prevail in a dispute cannot possibly see the truth," the Bratslaver rebbe reminds his followers. "He will give no credence to that which he beholds with his own eyes" (Newman 1946, 88).

Second, what of the repercussions the lie has on relationships? The deceitful pay a stiff price for their lies. In Arthur Miller's provocative play *All My Sons*, the father, Joe Keller, appears at first to suffer little from his deceptions. He is a factory owner who makes airplane parts during the war. There are deadlines and pressures—one time a batch of cylinder heads comes out with cracks. The night foreman calls the partner, Herb Deever, and Herb phones Joe at home. Joe tells him to cover up the cracks and ship the parts out. He says he'll take responsibility for it. Many soldiers die as a result of Joe's choice, and when the defects are discovered, Herb is sent to jail and Joe is free. As Herb's son says, "On the telephone you can't *have* responsibility." Only years later does the truth come out. Joe's wife must hide the truth from herself and others, for the truth would have meant acknowledging that her husband was responsible for the death of their son (and many more of America's sons) because he refused to spend the necessary money to correct faulty airplane parts. By the end of the play, the lives of two families and of all the sons who died as a result have been damaged far beyond a loss of integrity. In order to go on living, the Kellers had to believe their lies.

In *Death of a Salesman*, Miller deals just as forcefully with lying, with why people succumb to lies, and with why deceits are so destructive. Miller's play is a vivid portrait of a family whose structure is such that each member lies to him or herself, to each other, and to friends. As a salesman, Willy Loman works as one who has to sell himself—and nowhere do we see more clearly the damage wrought by deception. By the age of sixty he is a tragic figure, a victim of the indifference of a company for which he has worked most of his life, of the forces which urge a person to try to achieve material and personal success at any cost, and of the indifference of society to the problems of aging. What Willy wants is to be a success, and the only way he can achieve the success he has defined for himself is to lie. This way of life he teaches to his boys. His wife, desperate to help Willy, joins in the deceptions, and the sons struggle to maintain his dream for them by creating illusions for themselves.

In *Hasidism and Modern Man*, Buber writes that "the origin of all conflict between me and my fellow men is that I do not say what I mean, and that I do not do what I say. For this confuses and poisons . . . in increasing measure, the situation between myself and the other." To prevent one from becoming a slave to his or her fabrications, there is, Buber tells us, only one way out: everything depends on oneself and on the crucial decision: "I will straighten myself out (158).

When one lives one's life essentially based on the impressions one wants to make on others, one becomes what Buber calls a "seeming" person. Willy Loman and Joe Keller take on a "seeming" existence because each pretends to be something he is not. The longer one dwells in seeming, the more difficult it is, Buber writes, "to penetrate the increasingly tough layer which has settled down on [a person's] being" (*KM*, 78). Willy is unable to understand why he fails because the images he spins are so real to him and he insists they be real to others.

Another way in which individuals separate themselves one from the other is by "unmasking." Here the teachings of Marx and Freud, Buber writes, have encouraged us. It is not enough to question whether someone is honest; now we want to know what the other's motives are. We question "the inner integrity of his existence itself" (*PW*, 224). We do this by analyzing the other: "Seeing-through and unmasking is now the great sport between men." The danger here is not that one understands the other more but that one knows the other less. Casting the other in a mold is substituted for relationship; control is substituted for openness. There is in this attitude a mistrust, an assumption that the other needs to be de-masked, and once we have crystallized that attitude within ourselves, then we are prevented from open exchange.

Finally we look at the impact of lying on the communal level, on society. Because our tendency is to limit our vision to ourselves and our own, we fail to recognize the greater community which we all shape. Such failure opens the way for manipulation and deception toward those we suppose are not a part our world. Nadine Gordimer, winner of the Nobel Prize for Literature, has as one theme of her novels and stories the folly of believing that whatever happens to others does not happen to ourselves. Need more be said than that Gordimer is a South African writing about the plight of the peoples of her country?

George Orwell's *1984* remains a classic model of what happens when fear and mistrust shape a country. Bok is apprehensive about those who maintain that lies can be justified when the lies are harmless, when they protect the secrets of others, and when they protect others from danger: "When these . . . mingle with another—a desire to advance the public good—they form the most dangerous body of deceit of all" (Bok, 175). Because such lies appear to be altruistic, they can be the most damaging. The danger is that rulers and public officials who use these as justification for their actions are claiming a moral superiority over those they govern. The way is clear for them to do as they please. Neither do they consider the perspective of those deceived. Bok suggests that accountability be made policy and that public debate be held over whether and when leaders should withhold information or release misinformation: "Deceiving the people for the sake of the people is a self-contradictory notion in a democracy, unless it can be shown that there has been genuine consent to deceit" (182).

Buber makes an important contribution by understanding community to be the shared world, that which is common to all of us. In his splendid book *The Knowledge of Man*, he quotes Heracleitus that one should follow the common—i.e., join with others in building a common world of speech and a common order of being. This one cosmos is common to all people (*KM*, 90–91). A person has experiences as an I and has experiences with others, "but it is as We, ever again as We" that we develop a world (107).

Historically, humankind has tied the political realm to deception, believing that such is necessary for one group to conquer another or one group to survive another's attacks. We cannot imagine a community where all members are honest. But what is needed is an open spirit, one which cares as much about the needs of others as it does about the needs of its own people. Within the people, Buber maintains, lives the spirit which desires that which truth represents: a willingness to be candid, a willingness to bring oneself to the meeting. But such is not possible if the individual or the state has not made peace within (*PW*, 189).

Here Buber is speaking not to the sphere of the intellect or the political but to the spirit.

There are real differences between peoples, justified differences. These cannot be dealt with in an atmosphere of mistrust, but they can be negotiated when the inward spirit is open. When will such occur? According to Buber, in a late phase when the crisis makes persons "despair of power and its autonomous decisions, when power for power's sake grows bewildered and longs for direction" (*PW*, 191).

Can we any longer afford to wait for that late phase? The "universal mistrust of our age" keeps us apart:

> What does it avail to induce the other to speak if basically one puts no faith in what he says? The meeting with him already takes place under the perspective of his untrustworthiness. And his perspective is not incorrect, for his meeting with me takes place under corresponding perspective. The basic mistrust, coming to light, produces ground for mistrust. (*PW*, 222–223)

The basis of the life we share is under continual threat from the lie. We must seek alternatives to deceitful practices in those social and professional situations where lying is prevalent and look for standards in moral philosophy to determine the impact of the lie on social relations. As Bok points out, we can let others know that we do not need to be told white lies. We can state, even in small matters, our "preference for honesty" (257). Trust and integrity "are precious resources, easily squandered, hard to regain. They can thrive only on a foundation of respect for veracity" (263).

Finally, the erosion of the trust of a people destroys society and leaves suspicion, isolation, and violence in its wake. "Those in government and other positions of trust," Bok writes, "should be held to the highest standards. Their lies are not ennobled by their positions; quite the contrary" (191). There needs to be open debate and public consent in advance as to when lies can be considered at all justifiable. Business should make it less lucrative for people to lie, and educational institutions should raise moral issues and seek guidelines for those in business, law, medicine, and education.

We use words freely and often casually. We learn early that we can shape words to get what we want, that we can form them to protect us from harm, that we can use them to evade, to distance, to invite, to probe. Maurice Friedman states that the importance of Buber's concept of the common world as built by the common speech-with-meaning can hardly be overestimated: "Speech . . . is the stuff of reality, able to create or destroy it. . . . Speech may be falsehood and conventionality, but it is also the great pledge of truth" (Friedman in *KM*, 40). It is speech which brings forth nothing less than ourselves: shall it be false and thereby estranging, or shall it be that which allows us courage to bring ourselves forth to meet the other?

"One cannot strive for immediacy, but one can hold oneself free and open for it. One cannot produce genuine dialogue, but one can be at its disposal. Existential mistrust cannot be replaced by trust, but it can be replaced by a reborn candor" (*PW*, 206).

REFERENCES

Bok, Sisela. (1979). *Lying: Moral Choice in Public and Private Life*. New York: Vintage.
Buber, Martin. *G & E; KM; PW; TH: Early;* "Meetings."
Friedman, Maurice. (1960). *Martin Buber: The Life of Dialogue*. New York: Harper.
Miller, Arthur. (1977). *The Portable Arthur Miller*. New York: Penguin.
Newman, Louis. (1946). *The Hasidic Anthology: Tales and Teachings of the Hasidim*. New York: Bloch.

CHAPTER 14

THE INTERHUMAN DIMENSION OF TEACHING

Some Ethical Aspects

ASLAUG KRISTIANSEN

This essay discusses some elements related to the life between student and teacher; in particular it is concerned with the element of trust and the relationship between ethics and trust. Martin Buber's contributions to this subject cannot be overestimated; his focus on trust as a necessary element to a genuine teacher/student relationship is invaluable in the field of moral education.

Up to now the main research in moral education has in large scale been dominated by a rule-oriented way of thinking. In short, this is an approach to the moral field where the focus has been on the moral development of the individual and how the student, with the help of ethical principles, can solve ethical dilemmas. I believe that Buber's way of thinking represents an alternative. For Buber the ethical is rooted in the interhuman and must be fulfilled in the concrete situation insofar as each partner moves beyond the mere observance of ethical norms as they have been taught and authenticates such in real relationship.

In addition to Buber, the work of the Danish philosopher and theologian Knud E. Løgstrup (1905–1981) is important. His work in the field of ethical research has a growing influence in Scandinavia and Germany, and I see his way of facing the ethical challenge as having much in common with Buber's thinking. Each is concerned with the life between person and person.

Løgstrup's approach is phenomenological; his own experiences and others inform his thinking. He believes that there are phenomena in human existence with an ethical character which so far have received little attention in the study of morality. These include openness, forgiveness, compassion, love, and trust (Løgstrup 1982, 108). He gives the following reason for this lack of attention: "It is a common observation that the most elementary phenomena of our existence are the ones we are least aware of" (Løgstrup 1971, 16).

Those phenomena are linked to life between people. They can be described as facts, but this in itself is insufficient. There is a demand as well in the phenomena. Løgstrup argues that since both descriptive and normative elements are inherent in the interhuman phenomena, a sufficient description must also include the phenomena's inherent demand (Løgstrup 1976, 48). His concern here is to point out that there is an intimate connection between the fact and the demand, that to a great extent the demand grows out of the fact. "In other words," he writes, "the fact forces upon us the alternative: either we take care of the other person's life or we ruin it. Given man's creatureliness, there is no third alternative. To accept the fact without listening to the demand is to be indifferent to the question whether life is to be promoted or ruined" (Løgstrup 1971, 19).

One basic fact is that human beings are delivered to each other: "We are each other's world," and "each other's destiny" (Løgstrup 1975, 25). The notion that human beings live in relationships of mutual dependence represents a characteristic of human existence which Løgstrup calls "interdependence" (Løgstrup 1966, 24). Interdependence implies that no person is anything merely in him- or herself. Because of the interdependence of existence, every human being bears some responsibility for the quality of life of another. That is, we carry in our hands part of each other's opportunities in life. Løgstrup characterizes it as an ethical challenge to take care of other people's quality of life regardless of how much or how little of his or her life a person, by trusting, gives into the hands of another (Løgstrup 1975, 25). By linking ethics to interhuman phenomena, Løgstrup makes ethics a part of the basic conditions of human existence. Ethics are "interwoven" into our existence; they are an integrated part of our daily life.

There are interesting similarities here to Buber's thought. "One basic fact of interhuman life itself," Buber writes, "is men's dependence upon one another" (KM, 68). "Man exists anthropologically not in isolation," Buber believes, "but in completeness of the relation between man and man" (74). This understanding about life between person and person is a presumption for the interhuman.

Buber speaks of the "sphere of the interhuman" which are "solely actual happenings between men, whether wholly mutual or tending to grow into mutual relations" (KM, 65). The unfolding of this sphere Buber calls dialogical. True human life is entering into mutuality, according to Buber. Mutuality arises when we answer the address—the reaching out to us—from the other. Buber describes human life as continuous challenges of addressing and responding:

> In our life and experience we are addressed; by thought and speech and action, by producing and by influencing we are able to answer. For the most part we do not listen to the address, or we break into it with chatter. But if the word comes to us and the answer proceeds from us then human life exists, though brokenly, in the world. (BMM, 92)

Both Buber and Løgstrup show that certain demands or challenges grounded in our existence are to be fulfilled if human life shall come to existence. Buber describes life as being address, a word is demanding an answer (BMM, 10). In the same way Løgstrup says "our existence demands of us that we protect the life of the person who has placed his trust in us" (1971, 18).

Løgstrup starts his analysis of the phenomenon of trust by saying, "It is a characteristic of human life that we naturally trust one another" (1971, 8). This is true, he feels, not only with persons that we know but also has to do with strangers. For example, when we ask a stranger, a woman, say, whom we have never before met, where to find a certain street or house, we trust that her response will be the truth as far as she knows or does not know the answer to our query. Under normal circumstances we accept the word of the stranger. "Initially we believe one another's word," Løgstrup writes; "initially we trust one another. This may indeed seem strange, but it is part of what it means to be human. Human life could hardly exist if it were otherwise" (1971, 8).

I think Buber would not disagree with this, but more than Løgstrup I think he is aware of the difficulties and challenges in creating trusting relations. The question of trust, according to Buber, concerns not only life between people but existence itself. Trust has to do with being at home in the world. According to Maurice Friedman, "Our age is seen as the most homeless of all because of the loss of both an image of the world . . . and a sense of community" (in his introduction to BMM [1978], xix and xx). In many ways I think that a good many modern persons have turned themselves into onlookers without having a sense of belonging to the world. Their relation to the world has in large part been turned into an "It." Modern human beings have lost "the unconscious humanity of being part of participation and partaking" (*BMM*, 87).

In spite of much of Buber's own life experiences wherein loss of trust was prevalent, his philosophical starting point is not mistrust, mismeeting, or lack of belonging to the world. To the contrary, his starting point is genuine human life—the life of dialogue. For such a life, trust is the basic element.

Løgstrup has defined trust as "to deliver oneself over to the hands of another" (1971, 9). He argues that in the very act of addressing a person we make a certain demand on him or her. This demand is not merely for a response—something more fundamental is involved. "In addressing the other," he says, "we step out of ourselves in order to exist in the speech relation with him" (15). If our address is turned down, we as whole persons are turned down. We have dared to extend ourselves in the hope of being accepted, but our unarticulated demand has not been answered or accepted. In this Løgstrup finds the essence of communication and the fundamental basis for ethical life. "Regardless of how varied the communication between persons may be, it always involves the risk of one person approaching the other in the hope of response" (18).

There are many reasons why our addresses are not always answered. Buber distinguishes between two categories of existence. The first is the life of monologue, which is characterized by one person lacking awareness of the other, the failure of the one to really see the otherness of the other. The second category is the life of dialogue, and this is characterized by "real outgoing to the other" (*BMM*, 20). This "turning towards the other" (22) also involves responding to "the reaching out," whether this is spoken or tacit. This implies that a person is given to me in trust and responsibility. "He addresses me," Buber says, "about something that he has entrusted to me and that I am bound to take care of loyally. He addresses me from his trust and I respond in my loyalty or refuse to respond in my disloyalty" (45).

Both Buber and Løgstrup argue that trust implies that something is given to the other, a challenge one has to take care of or refuse to do. The attentive person will enter into the situation with his or her whole being and respond to what is reaching out to him or her. Neither Buber nor Løgstrup believe that genuine responding is found in the merely habitual act or in the moral act, though Løgstrup would agree with Buber's idea that no responsible person is a stranger to norms (*BMM*, 114). Løgstrup argues that even if the demand is to take care of the other person, nothing is thereby said about how this caring is to be done. The demand is a silent one, and "the individual to whom the demand is directed must himself in each concrete relationship decide what the content of the demand is." The person must figure out for him- or herself what the demand requires (Løgstrup 1971, 23).

Buber is critical of an ethical tradition that has lost its contact with life itself. "The idea of responsibility," he writes, "is to be brought back from the province of specialized ethics, of an 'ought' that swings free in the air, into that of lived life." "Genuine responsibility," according to Buber, "exists only where there is real responding. Responding to what? To what happens to one, to what is to be seen and heard and felt" (BMM, 16).

In his own life Buber early on became aware of the problematic relation between maxim and situation. According to Friedman, Buber came to realize the choice "between finding security in the once-for-all general moral norms—to be a good child, obeying authority—and living with the insecurity of being open and responding to the unique and irreducible situation to which no general categories could ever do justice." Buber learned from his own experience that "the true norms command not our obedience but ourselves" (Friedman, MBLW: Early, 152). Buber wrote:

> . . . every living situation has, like a newborn child, a new face, that has never been before and will never come again. It demands of you a reaction which cannot be prepared beforehand. It demands nothing of what is past. It demands presence, responsibility: it demands you. (BMM, 114)

The first characteristic of trust in the context of education, according to both Løgstrup and Buber, is that trust involves the whole person. How well does the teacher really educate the character of his or her charge if the teacher is not giving all of his or herself to the pupil. Before the teacher can begin to influence the student, Buber says, the student must first accept the educator as a person:

> . . . the only way to affect the whole being of the student is when the teacher acts in his whole being, in all his spontaneity: For education of character, you do not need a moral genius, but you do need a man who is wholly alive and is able to communicate himself directly to his fellow being. (BMM, 105)

The teacher who acts out of his or her whole being does not cling to a presentation of rules and ethical instructions. Instead the teacher is a person, and as a person takes part in the student's life. He or she is one who tries to "see the seen with all the strength of his [my] life, hear the heard with all the strength of his [my] life, and taste the tasted with all the strength of his [my] life" (PW, 28).

What does it mean to *really* face the student? Let me illustrate this with an example. In the little town where I live—Kristiansand—I have for some time been talking with teachers about the question of trust between them and their students. One group I have been seeing regularly consists of language teachers who teach the Norwegian language to refugees. The students are all adults who have come from different parts of the world. In our first meeting I asked the teachers if they could give me examples from their daily life of situations where trust was involved. Instead, they gave me different examples of situations characterized by mistrust. Most of the situations they related had to do with not telling the truth. Karen, one of the teachers, told a rather typical story:

> One of my students started to come late in the morning. In the beginning I said nothing. But it happened again and again. Then I asked him, "Why are you always coming so late?" He gave me a rather ridiculous explanation. He did not catch the bus. He still continued to come late. When some days later I asked him again, he gave me another unbelievable explanation. So I stopped trusting him. It was clear that he was lying to me, and that hurt me.

One month later I met again with the same group of teachers. Before we started talking, Karen wanted to tell me something. "One day last week," she said, "I happened to sit near this particular student during lunch. He started to tell me about his background and some of the difficulties he had faced during his life in Norway. We had a nice talk. Suddenly I saw the student in a different light!" Her attitude toward the student was changed. This does not mean that the problem was solved, but certainly she would face the problem in a different way. Whereas she had played the role of policewoman in her relationship to this student, she was now able to concern herself with his life. Having turned to the other human being, as Buber has taught us, she was able to "open herself to him" and receive "the world in him" (*BMM*, 30).

In a teaching situation each participant must bring him- or herself to the situation. The teacher is in the teaching situation with his or her feelings of homelessness in the world, his or her disappointments, fears, and mistrust. But the situation also represents a possibility of mutuality. "Trust, trust in the world," Buber exhorts us, "because this human being exists—that is the most inward achievement of relation in education" (*BMM*, 98).

Trust involves a movement towards the other, an access to the other person's world. It represents a possibility or potentiality for mutuality. "Confidence implies a breakthrough from reserve," Buber tells us, "the bursting of bonds which imprison an unquiet heart" (BMM, 107). Each student who confronts her teacher with a reason for not being properly prepared for class puts part of her life into the hands of the teacher. To move toward another, whether it be the student toward the teacher or the teacher toward the student, always involves risk.

To take part in the life of another involves responsibility. The teacher in the schoolyard can bring all of herself to the story the pupil is telling her or she can only partially attend to his words. Will she take care of what is given her? Is she prepared to do all she can in order to find the best solution to the problem of the pupil? Will it be possible for the teacher in this particular situation, as Løgstrup puts it, "to contribute to tearing down the walls around the other person and make him see a wider horizon" (1975, 37)? The teacher can do this only if she really hears the voice of the student and responds with as much resources as are granted her in that situation.

There are many ways in which a teacher can erode the trust of his student. He can make the pupil feel stupid or give the child the impression that he doesn't believe what the pupil is telling him. Each of us recognizes those moments when the teacher is not really hearing what is being said to him by the pupil. Trust is so easily destroyed when one is not taken seriously by the other. And even when the teacher responds to the pupil, does he attempt to impose his own will? Or will he allow the pupil to be independent of the teacher? Løgstrup believes that "The will to determine what is best for the other person . . . must be coupled with a willingness to let him remain sovereign in his own world" (1971, 27). Any speaking, silence, or action must never rob the other person of his or her independence.

Buber's concept of inclusion is helpful in illuminating this particular aspect of responding. Inclusion means genuinely going out to the partner, trying to grasp her in her actual presence but at the same time being aware of the other as something different from oneself. It is the act of experiencing from "over there" (BMM, 100).

Each human being represents a unique reality, according to Buber. Løgstrup agrees, saying:

> The fact that we are one another's world does not mean that we hold another person's will in our hands. We cannot intrude upon his individuality and will, upon his personhood, in the same way that we can affect his emotions and in the same way even his destiny. (1971, 29)

When it comes to education the teacher must not take his influence as an excuse to invade the realm of other lives. Buber makes an important distinction between propaganda and education. While the propagandist imposes himself, his opinion, and attitude on the other, the educator is a helper who believes that in every person what is right is established in a single and uniquely personal way (*KM*, 72–73).

It would be a wrong interpretation of Buber's view to say that the best thing for the pupil would be to leave the pupil to him- or herself. Then he or she would grow like an untended plant. Even if Buber strongly recognizes the value of freedom, a more basic achievement in education is creating communion—"it means being opened up and drawn in" (*BMM*, 91).

Both Buber and Løgstrup have in common a strong ethical concern that touches on the question of being human. If teaching in its best sense is dialogical, then trust is the core of entering into genuine dialogue in education. If dialogue is an act of mutual creation, then trust must be the access to this mutuality. A most fitting conclusion to the ideas presented in this essay is the insight of Maurice Friedman, who once said that if he had to choose one sentence to summarize the whole message of Buber's life and his thought it would be the words Buber spoke at the end of his acceptance speech on the occasion of being awarded the Peace Prize of the German Book Trade in 1953: "Let us dare, despite all, to trust!"

REFERENCES

Buber, M. *BMM; KM; PW.*
Friedman, M. (1978). Introduction to *BMM* (Buber).
―――. (1988). *Martin Buber's Life and Work: The Early Years, 1878–1923.* Detroit: Wayne State University Press
Løgstrup, K. (1966). *Kunst og Etik.* Gyldendal, København.
―――. (1975). *Den etiske fordring.* Gyldendal, København.
―――. (1971). *The Ethical Demand.* Forward by J. G. Gustavson. Philadelphia (Translation of *Den etiske fordring.*).
―――. (1976). *Norm og Spontanitet. Etik og Politik mellom teknokrati og dilettantokrati.* Gyldendal, København.
―――. (1982). *System og Symbol.* Essays. Gyldendal, København.

CHAPTER 15

MARTIN BUBER'S CONCEPT OF ART
AS DIALOGUE

GOUTAM BISWAS

PHILOSOPHY OF ART AND PHILOSOPHICAL ANTHROPOLOGY

Martin Buber's aesthetics is an extension of his philosophy of dialogue. Dialogue for Buber is essentially a reality and a method in and through which a person is known by another person. It forms the perspective of *I-Thou*. Dialogue signifies *relationship* between human and human, a live communication rather than a sheer exchange of meaningful words. It is a communication based upon communion from where words may follow, but words do not constitute it. Or one can say words become identical with the specific mode of existence. "I-Thou," according to Buber, is a "primary word" which is "spoken from the being."

Both methodologically and ontologically, "dialogue" is a very important concept in our philosophico-anthropological enterprises. No monologue can yield a concept of the human person in a comprehensive manner. The moment we raise the question "How is knowledge of man by man possible?" we have to set ourselves in relation to each other and consequently to the entire world lived by us.

But what kind of relation is this? Is it a kind of relation that we have with objects? Are we related to one another as pure subjectivity? Since a person is always more than what he or she is at a certain spatio-temporal point, he or she, as a knowable, cannot be reduced to an object as a "spoken fact" with a fixed meaning. Nor can one be treated as a pure subjectivity away from the purview of knowledge. The concept of the human being as a pure subjectivity results in unknowability of the human as such. The person-in-oneself cannot be known. But can there ever be a person-in-oneself? Is he or she not always in a communicative state—in relation to someone real or imagined?

We always strive to establish the meaning of our existence by discovering our relations with the universe. Yet such discoveries cannot remain isolated within the precincts of an individual life. Their verity must be tested and ensured in a human social perspective where each individual is in relation with the other.

Buber bifurcated this relational reality into two ways of existence—*I-Thou* (reciprocal) and *I-It* (subject-object). But the most primitive mode of existence for human creatures is I-Thou. The primitive function of knowledge contains no analysis or reflection which is separation. It knows the *relation* and not the *object* as an independent being having its very own structure. Here neither the subject nor the object but the relation itself is the "category of being, readiness, grasping from, mould for the soul" (*I and Thou*, 27). An anthropological investigation puts it this way:

> For modern, scientific man the phenomenal world is primarily an "It," for ancient and also for primitive man it is a "Thou." . . . The world appears to primitive man neither inanimate nor empty but redundant with life.[1]

The child's self, too, for Buber, is enabled through his personal relation with other human beings; it comes to the knowledge of external reality as "It" when it is enabled to *differentiate* between that which is a Thou to him or her and that which does not speak to him or her but acquires a meaning in terms of the child's particular use of it. Buber's statement in this regard is quite revealing: "The development of the soul in the child is inextricably bound up with that of the longing for the *Thou*, with the satisfaction and the disappointment of this longing, with the game of his experiments and the tragic seriousness of his perplexity" (*I and Thou*, 28).

But which of these two ways should we follow in knowing the human who is capable of both ways of living? Stated differently: "How is knowledge of human by human possible?" The question is both methodological and ontological. We have already seen that it is not possible to view the human being either as an "It" (object) or as a pure subjectivity (a lone "I") in a Buberian perspective. So, methodologically, Thou-orientation (i.e., dialogue) is the only alternative for us. Ontologically, too, Buber thinks that there is an "inborn thou" within us which unfolds in our relationship with the other. This "inborn thou" obliges us to know the other in his or her essentiality as a Thou and not as an It or a he or a she. In our act of addressing the other as Thou we address the whole being of that person. But when we *refer* to the other in the third person, we reduce that one to an "It," treating him or her as an object with some definite aspects. Whereas in the "I-Thou" form of relationship the whole being of the human is addressed, "I-It" form reveals only aspects of him or her. The whole being of the person includes the inexhaustible competence of the human *to be* in both modes of existence, viz. I-Thou and I-It. Being dialogical, the I-Thou mode of existence brings us to the knowledge of the human being in his or her entirety which takes into account also person as forming meaning even in the world of It.

As Buber contended, even the world of It owes its meaning to Thou. "Only *I-Thou*," Maurice Friedman tells us, "gives meaning to the world of It, for I-Thou is an end which is not reached in time but is there from the start, originating and carrying-through" (*LoD*, 67). Meaning, which we can talk of or assign to objects, facts, or events that may be physical or psychical, is in the course of time hardened into an It and estranged from any direct human participation. To carry on in a human world, "again and again that which has the status of object must blaze up into presentness and enter the elemental state from which it came, to be looked on and lived in the present by man" (*I and Thou*, 40). The human being has a personal existence which is not identified by any of one's manifest aspects but from the core of which one offers oneself to the world in newer relations and thereby changes the meaning of the fact-ridden world. The personal existence of the human being creates a demand within one to relate oneself to the world in ever new ways and not always with reference to a given meaning-structure. If the world of It is not renewed time and again by a Thou-orientation, it ceases to be in the human world.

Unlike animals, human beings do not remain satisfied simply by using things. We desire also to enter into personal relationships with things and to imprint on them our relation to them. Here lies the origin of art. According to Buber, art transcends the thingly nature of the thing. "It ceases to be accessory to a tool and becomes an independent structure" (*KM*, 66). But this independent structure is not to be dissociated from the purview of relation; it beams only in the light of relation. Artistic creation and awareness proceeds from our dissatisfaction with the stringent meaning-contents of the world of It and our urge to elevate it to a level of intimacy with our own being. Buber says:

The form indicated by even the clumsiest ornament is now fulfilled, in an autonomous region as the sediment of man's relation to things. Art is neither the impression of natural objectivity nor the expression of spiritual subjectivity, but it is the work and witness of the relation between the *Substantia humana* and the *Substantia rerum*" (*KM*, 66).

The aesthetics of Buber consists primarily in an investigation into the origin and raison d'être of art wherein he draws heavily upon his philosophical anthropology. As Louis Z. Hammer points out: "The fact that some men are artists is to be grasped, within the framework of Buber's thought, not as a mere accident, but rather as an outcome of what man essentially is."[2] That Buber's question concerning art is a philosophico-anthropological one is also clear from its very formulation: "What can be said about art as about a being that springs from the being of man?" (*KM*, 149). He starts his essay "Man and His Image-Work" by hitting upon this relation:

The question of the connection between the essence of man and the essence of art must be posed anew. That means that art must be regarded as the image-work of man, the peculiar image-work of his peculiarity. We ask about the connection between what is essentially peculiar to man and what is essentially characteristic of art. (*KM*, 149)

The connection can be articulated within the framework of Buber's philosophical anthropology. The centrality of human existence, Buber says, is sought in man's relation to all existing beings:

What appears here as the *humanum*, as the great superiority of man before all other living beings known to us, is his capacity "of his own accord," hence not like the animals out of the compulsion of his needs and wants but out of the overflow of his existence, to come into direct contact with everything that he bodily or spiritually meets—to address it with lips and heart or even with heart alone. In distinction from the animal, man can grasp all that encounters him on his life's way as a being existing in itself beyond his own interest. He can enter into relationship with this independently existing other. By knowing and acknowledging the other at times as a whole, he can at times himself relate to it as a whole. (*ABH*, 119–20)

The essential characteristic of art, for Buber, also consists in this meeting—the relationship of a dialogical kind. One cannot come into direct contact with things as long as they remain under the purview of knowledge—the I-It or nondialogical mode of being: "one misses the basic nature of art . . . if one moves it so close to knowledge, indeed directly subsumes it under the latter" (KM, 152). Here "knowledge" means "knowledge of"—a discursive mode of awareness where there is no meeting or encounter. "The overflow of man's existence" does not find any outlet in the world of It because here one cannot overpass the border of necessity. In conformity with what Buber depicted as "the great superiority of man before all other living beings known to us" in a nonutilitarian urge to "meet" and "address" all beings as "independently existing others," he said about art activity: "Perception draws out of the being the world that we need: only vision and, in its wake, art transcends need and makes the superfluous into the necessary" (KM, 160). Here, to transcend is to transcend through relation of a dialogical kind which consists in a personal meeting between I and Thou.

For Buber, both anthropological knowledge and aesthetic cognition require a Thou-orientation. The knowledge which is generated in dialogue is not discursive—it is immediate. It is not a property of the agent or the object; its verity is established within the perspective of relation alone, through a continuous self-giving, by discharging one's being to give shape to the "object" and thereby accruing a so far unknown identification from the "object" which is really no-object but a "partner" in the process. It happens so not only in the case of our knowledge of the human being but also in our art experiences. One enters into a dialogical relation with one's image-work; the created form is taken up into the meeting of I and Thou and not left out as a detached object of observation, use, and analysis. In Buber's words, "all art is from its origin essentially of the nature of dialogue" (BMM, 25).

In a Buberian perspective the complementarity between philosophical anthropology and philosophy of art can be understood in the following terms: (1) The method of philosophical anthropology is incorporated into that of our understanding of art-experiences and art-objects. About the phenomenon of art, Buber says: "It is, indeed, neither the mystery of the things nor that of the spirit that is represented in art, but the relation between the two" (KM, 165). (2) Our art activities point back to the peculiarity of human nature which consists in a relational reality between "I" and "Thou." Buber's aesthetics endorses the view that man is essentially dialogical. It is interesting to note what Buber says regarding man's art activity:

The artist is the man who instead of objectifying what is over against him forms it into an image. Here the nature of the action in which perception takes place no longer suffices: the working must play a substantial part if that which stands over against him is to become image. That which stands over against, I say; that does not mean this or that phenomenon, this or that piece of the external world, some complex of appearances given to the sight or hearing in the actual experience, but whatever in the whole possible world-sphere enters into that sense with which this particular art is associated, the whole possible world-sphere of sight, the whole possible world-sphere of hearing. (KM, 160)

Since the image-work (i.e., the art object) is encompassed by "the whole possible world-sphere" of sight or hearing, depending on the sense with which it is associated, the scope of hermeneutical understanding remains open with the art appreciator. The meaning of the particular art-object does not remain fixed as the whole possible world-sphere percolates through it, generating new meanings in it for the spectator or audience. It happens so because we are in an unending dialogue with the image-work under perception. This bringing forth of oneself in one's creative move to the world through art and art through world triggers us back to man's beginning in relation, his trust in it, and finally, his mission to *be* in it.

(3) The ontology of the human being is equated by Buber with the ontology of the *between*. For him, the real is relational: "In the beginning is relation," and "the aim of relation is relation's own being, that is, contact with the *Thou*." This relational realm is the realm of the between. The person with his or her inexhaustible spirit is real only in this realm. In the world of "I-It," we "extract knowledge" from things about their constitution, use, etc. We thereby "win experiences" from them—the experiences that belong to things. The things may be physical or psychical: "Inner things or outer things, what are they but things and things?" (*I and Thou*, 5). The concept of the human being becomes the concept of the human as a collector or manipulator of experiences from things: the logos of the human is lost in the logos of things—man/woman appears before man/woman with a camouflage. One gets oneself reified to a thing. Only in an I-Thou perspective does one's being find its own locus which is "the relation's own being."

Methodologically, Thou-orientation to the human being suspends all of his or her third-person aspects (It-aspects)—such as, toolmaker, engineer, homemaker, office-bearer, rational animal, member of a social class, etc.—and focuses on the fundamental phenomenon of his or her being in relation, i.e., human being as a *phainomenon* who can simply be faced and addressed. Our knowledge of the human person then follows:

his or her specificities are then linked with this humanum and assessed on its basis. Ontologically, Thou-orientation places the reality of man/woman in the reality of relation and its manifestations.

This phenomenological ontology of Buber does not suffer any profanation in his treatment of art. For him the ontology of art is to be sought in terms of one's relation to it, i.e., in the ontology of the between. "The common principle that we find effectively present in sufficient concreteness in each of the arts" is envisaged by taking this relational dimension into account, one's relation to the image-work accomplished or unaccomplished so far (*KM*, 150). In *I and Thou* Buber says: "a man is faced by a form which desires to be made through him into a work (of art)" (9). Like a Thou, an art-form encompassed by the whole possible world-sphere (of sight or hearing) has a reality character:

> This form is no offspring of his [man's] world, but is an appearance which steps up to it and demands of it the effective power ... if he speaks the primary word out of his being to the form which appears, then the effective power streams out, and the work [of art] arises. (9)

With regard to our anthropological knowledge-situation, Buber holds that the situation is relational and the relation consists in mutuality: "Relation is mutual. My Thou affects me, as I affect it" (*I and Thou*, 15). But does the image-work or form which is yet to be transformed into an image reciprocate our feelings as does the other human being in an anthropological knowledge-situation? Is there any mutuality in our relationship with the being of art?

On the one hand, Buber maintains that the being of art springs from the being of the human; on the other hand, he holds that art (which includes works of art within the purview of human perception) has a "reality character" and it needs to be addressed as "Thou." But if the being of art is parasitic upon the being of the human, can it be said to have a life of its own? In what sense is art real and its reality manifested in sufficient concreteness in each of the arts and works of art? These are some of the problems which must arise as far as the co-implication between philosophical anthropology and philosophy of art goes in a Buberian perspective.

I think these problems center mainly around the concept of the being of art in the context of aesthetic experience. Buber's contention that the being of art cannot be isolated from its experiential dimension is quite in consonance with the spirit of the contemporary phenomenology of art (e.g., that of Mikel Dufrenne) and should draw attention of researchers in this field. At the same time, we must bear in mind that his concept of the being of art as springing from that of man/woman is

proposed primarily in the context of anthropology of art in its philosophical sense, and it must not be isolated from art's being and its "reality-character" manifested in the sphere of human cognition. To take the
analogy of a child—a child is given birth by his or her parents and that
child's growth is dependent on them in many ways, but the child cannot
be denied his or her own being.

I make this distinction between two senses of being in order to understand Buber with more clarity and to dispel the confusion, but neither of
these senses can really be isolated from one another. In fact, these two
senses of being are knitted together in Buber's writings. Art is real only in
the context of its relation with us—its ontology of this relation. Buber holds
that the question concerning the being of art as springing from the being of
man "is an anthropological one in the philosophical sense of the word," and
"every anthropology of a subject touches on its ontology, hence . . . every
investigation of a subject in its conditioning by the manner, the nature, the
attitude of man leads us toward this subject's place in being and its function
in meaning" (KM, 149–50). At the same time he says that the question concerning the relation between being of the human and being of art

> must begin in the sphere in which the life of human senses
> dwells; it is that in which the dependence of man on the exis-
> tent properly constitutes itself and that which determines the
> reality-character of all art so that no mental and no emotional
> element may enter into art otherwise than through becoming a
> thing of senses. (KM, 150–51)

What Buber may mean is that human consciousness in art-activity is
first directed to something which the consciousness is not, and then gradually the being of art becomes manifest in view of its relation to consciousness—within human experiential dimension. As one is bound to put faith
in this reality-character, and one's whole being is involved in meeting with
the art-form encompassed by the whole possible world-sphere, so is the
particular art which could never be conceived without being in relation to
a person. The independence of the two poles, however, is not of primary
importance; what matters is that there be a relation between the two. Is
this independence not a necessary condition for there being a relation?
From Buber's point of view independence is asserted in relation. The co-
implication between philosophical anthropology and philosophy of art is
rather a follow-up of the relational ontology of Buber. The being of art cannot be placed beyond it. Hence questions or doubts concerning the reality-
character of a work of art ("image-work") arise in the context of I-Thou
relational framework where a "lively" role of the work is a natural expectation. This problem is discussed in the following section.

THE BEING OF ART AND AESTHETIC EXPERIENCE

Buber's inquiry into our art experiences has a clear phenomenological footing as he does away with psychologism on the one hand and objectivism on the other (i.e., the concept of art as representing the mystery of the spirit or that of things). Art, for him, as has been said, represents relation's own being. Hence he says:

> Our behaviour rests upon innumerable unifications of movements to something and perceptions of something. There is no movement that is not directly or indirectly connected with a perception, and no perception that is not more or less consciously connected with a movement. There is nothing in and of us that is fully removed from this base; even the images of fantasy, dreams, madness draw their material from it. (*KM*, 156)

In art this movement figures in "meeting" or "dialogue." By "experience" we cannot any more mean "experience *of*" so far as our experiencing something in a relational realm is concerned. In Buber's dialogical framework "experience" would mean *living the life of that which is being experienced*. The eternal source of art is, he said, "a man faced by a form which desires to be made through him into a work," and in the sustaining source of an I-Thou relationship aesthetic cognition must yield to the need for exclusiveness, for sacrifice, so that the work appears in its wholeness and concrete uniqueness:

> The work does not suffer me . . . to turn aside and relax in the world of It; but it commands. If I do not serve it aright it is broken, or it breaks me.
> I can neither experience[3] nor describe the form which meets me, but only body it forth. And yet I behold it, splendid in the radiance of what confronts me, clearer than all the clearness of the world which is experienced. I do not behold it as a thing among the "inner" things nor as an image of my "fancy," but as that which exists in the present. . . . And the relation in which I stand to it is real, for it affects me, as I affect it. (*I and Thou*, 10)

Meeting makes the form in its presence. The transition from the level of the experience of something to experiencing something wherein the intentional acts of consciousness are submerged is shown here. It is a landmark of Buber's contribution to contemporary phenomenology. Friedman, in his introduction to Buber's *The Knowledge of Man*, says, "To Kant's statement that we can only know of the 'thing in itself' that it is, Buber adds for modern man the assertion 'and that the existent meets

us'" (55). This mode of intentionality is such that it does not simply
allow one to speak of the exclusive importance of subject or object.
Cartesian dualism has always instigated us to ask whether aesthetic
awareness is subjective or objective, and then led the way either to sub-
jectivism or objectivism. A work of art is not objectively set afar from the
human being. Nor is the human agency inclined against the world which
is its canvas or the work which awaits a meeting with man/woman. The
recent distinction between work of art and aesthetic object does not
occur in Buber's writings, but it is implied when he says, "The work produced is a thing among things, able to be experienced and described as a
sum of qualities. But from time to time it can face the receptive beholder
in its whole embodied form" (*I and Thou*, 10). Obviously, Buber's concern is with the work in an experiential dimension. It does not have any
aesthetic value as a thing among other things—"inner" or "outer."
Hence Buber would agree with Dufrenne's statement: "The work must
offer itself to perception: it must be performed in order to pass, as it were,
from a potential to an actual existence."[4] For Dufrenne, the being of the
work of art is not dependent on being experienced, while the aesthetic
object exists only as experienced by the spectator. The work of art is the
perduring structural foundation for the aesthetic object. As an unaccomplished, unfulfilled form it is within the domain of aesthetic experience;
after creation it sinks back into an It but awaits a Thou (i.e., the artist or
the beholder), to become an "image-work"—an aesthetic object.

Now the sphere of aesthetic intentionality is such that it has to be
dialogic in character because the aesthetic object which is really *no*
object defies any other description, use, or analysis than being confronted
as a Thou. The phenomenological symbiosis of I (Man-Woman) and
Thou (the aesthetic object) determines the being of art. This symbiosis
cannot take place until the intentional mode in our "experience *of* something" passes on to a dialogical level where that something demands a
Thou-orientation from us. In fact, it is this communion between the
human as an artist and/or spectator and the art object which forms the
central problematic of Buber's phenomenology of aesthetic experience.
Its relevance becomes obvious when one hears Dufrenne saying:

> The aesthetic object bears its own signification within it, and
> by entering more profoundly into communion with the object,
> one discovers its signification, just as one understands the
> being of others only by virtue of friendship. This communion is
> indispensable. Without it, the aesthetic object is inert and
> meaningless, just as without performance (when it requires
> one) it is still only imperfectly existent. (228)

The aesthetic object does not signify anything beyond itself. This is the function of any *signifying object* which, according to Dufrenne, is different from aesthetic object. An aesthetic object is *expressive*. It is the artist's gesture towards us. Dufrenne says it is an "originary speech which, instead of bringing forth a conceptual meaning, simultaneously awakens a feeling and conjures up a presence" (135).

In spite of Dufrenne's insistence on the communion, he holds that this communion becomes apparent through feeling which reveals *subjectivity*. Aesthetic expression reveals this subjectivity. Buber's aesthetic philosophy does not admit of any such priority to any subjective or psychological element such as feeling. His stand is exceptional because he sees communion (I-Thou) as the most fundamental phenomenon, which cannot be subsumed under the category of subjectivity or feeling or objectivity. Communion precedes feelings. It is not the feeling which conjures up the aesthetic present but the other way around: communion in simultaneity with the presence conjures up the feeling. Aesthetic experience without this relation is inconceivable. It is the "relation's own being" which becomes manifest as the being of art. And the being of art can be conceived concretely in relation (i.e., the experience *in* art).

From Buber's standpoint, I. A. Richard's concession to the phenomena of art as merely emotionally significant is intolerable. Also, Croce's conception of a true creative work as the inner intuition and formulation of the work of art as emotionally charged image, the embodiment of which in any external material being purely an affair of technical skill and not an essential part either of the creative act of inner expression or of the finished work of art, resplendent in the inner light of the creator-mind, is not acceptable in the relationalistic framework of Buber. On the same ground, Buber's view can be contrasted with Collingwood's expressionist theory of art according to which the essence of art is in the expression of emotions, or Suzanne Langer's concept of the work of art as a virtual image reflecting a pattern of feeling.

There may be different modes of aesthetic presence depending upon the interplay between the perceiver and the perceived. Accordingly there may be innumerable interpretations and ways of reception and presentation of an art object. But, from Buber's dialogical standpoint, the Thou-orientation is the fundamental condition for hermeneutics in art. The condition is not formal logical —it is existential. It *is there* like an unshakable ground on which the community of taste grows. Art-object, when it becomes an art-object under the dialogical mode of intentionality, does not remain a mere object of our free acceptance or rejection. In Buber's words: "it commands." In the words of Gadamer: "We must admit that the world of artistic tradition—the splendid contemporaneous-

ness that we gain through art with so many human worlds—is more
than a mere object of our free acceptance and rejection."[5] According to
him, an immediate truth-claim proceeds from the art-object itself and
an alienation into aesthetic judgement takes place on our part when we
withdraw ourselves and "are no longer open to the immediate claim of
that which grasps us." For Gadamer, "our sensitive-spiritual existence is
an aesthetic resonance chamber that resonates with the voices that are
constantly reaching us, preceding all explicit aesthetic judgement" (132).
This resonance shows a primordial, common accord between human
and human, human and world.

A concretization, renewal, and interpretation of this accord takes
place through our aesthetic experiences. Buber's aesthetic philosophy suggests that the hermeneutics in art has its legitimacy on this ground—the
ground of our saying "Thou" to the form, the image-work. This act of
addressing involves the whole of our being as well as the being of art.
They together form "relation's own being." Once this symbiosis is accomplished, the question whether the art-object in its own identity or reality-
character can be addressed or not becomes meaningful. It *can* be addressed
and through the act of addressing the modality of its existence in its own
right is established. It becomes real, but, unlike the reality of an object,
our knowledge of the reality of an art-object remains unfinished. It is so
because it, as an indefinite *x* and without any definite meaning-content or
even the possibility of such, *meets* us in our art experience. So its reality-
character is to be talked about in the context of one's perception from
one's contact with being. As Friedman elaborated on this point:

> The sense world is a preliminary stage on the way to artistic
> vision and "vision is figurating faithfulness to the unknown
> and does its work in cooperation with it." The meeting of the
> artist and world is not an encounter between perception and
> sense-object, but between the being of the artist and the being
> of the *x*. . . . The artist fashions the sense world anew through
> his figuration in vision and in work—not through trying to
> penetrate behind the world of the senses, but through complet-
> ing its form to the perfect work of figuration. (*KM*, 55–56)

In this experiential dimension (of the dialogical kind) the being of art is
established concretely. The anthropological significance of art can be sought
in the channelization of the creative competence of the human being into
this experiential dimension (i.e., the dialogical form of intentionality and
the recognition of the reality-character of the form or image-work).

But, unlike Gadamer, Buber would maintain that the speakability
of this experience—i.e., the experience *in* art—does not yield any alien-

ation. This speakability itself involves a creativity, as ordinary language does not suffice to depict the experience. Thus, for Buber the hermeneutics in art proceeds from our grasp of the immediate truth-claim of the work within the spell of a dialogical mode of intentionality; it matures through newer and newer modes of presence of the object to one's presence. These modes become transparent to us for the interpretive element in our understanding of it. To take the example of Hindustani classical music, the same raga is executed in different styles by different *gharanas* (schools), though the notes remain identical. Each way of presenting the raga has a unique impact on the audience. Perhaps there is no end of interpreting the specified notations of ragas in the available texts of Hindustani classical music. Interpretation always involves an otherness to which the person has to set him or herself in a relation. Each relation means a unique kind of communion which changes the context of a literary text, a mural, a sculpture, or, for that matter, any work of art. To put it differently, every context of the interpretive understanding of a work of art involves a suggestion making its decontextualization possible. An image to be embodied or a work to be appreciated is, from this stance, a Thou which is not bound by the precincts of strict meaning. It cannot be known through or inferred from anything which is already meant or formulated.

The creator and beholder must have a direct access to the art-object. The possibility of different interpretations of one and the same object is there even in cases of our understanding of objects belonging to the ordinary world of common sense and the statements made with regard to them. But this possibility is mostly in terms of changes of space and time, practical interests and biases, contexts and pretexts, and above all, a given meaning-structure. An artistic creation, on the other hand, unfolds itself in terms of its own space and time transcending the ordinary day-to-day world. Even the entire world, from the point of view of this single creation, is seen in a different way, in an intimate perspective of the creator and/or the beholder.[6] No observed facts are interpreted here which can be adjusted to a general scientific outlook or a common sense structure of meaning.

Despite an essential difference from Buberian approach, we can recall on this point Suzanne Langer's distinction between "symbols which express facts for discursive thinking" and "artistic symbols":

> Artists' symbols . . . are untranslatable. Their sense is bound to the particular form which it has taken . . . though the *material* of poetry is verbal, its import is not the literal assertion made in the words, but *the way the assertion is made.*[7]

Interpretation of an art form requires an entry into this way, and thereby a transcendence of the natural attitude. The aim of such interpretation is not to *explicate* the art-form (as we do in cases of geometric symbols), but to *describe* it as it exists *in relation* to the human being. This relation is important for interpretation because the object (in this case) has to be *in the presence* of the observer and the observer, too, has to be *in the presence* of the object. *Being in the presence of* is a necessary requisite for interpreting an art-object.

We can outline a phenomenology of aesthetic experience keeping this dialogical mode of intentionality as our focal point and thereby picture all other dimensions of phenomenon of art in the light of it and in a well-fabricated manner. According to Buber, art is one of the forms of I-Thou relationship. It responds to human onlookers in an unspoken language, the translation of which is the task of contemporary philosophy of art. The task can be accomplished if we delve into this mode of intentionality.

NOTES

1. H. and H. A. Frankfort, John A. Wilson and Thorkild Jacobson, *Before Philosophy* (Hammondsworth, Eng.: Penguin Books, 1968), 13–14.
2. Louis Z. Hammer, "The Relevance of Buber's Thought to Aesthetics" in Paul A. Schilpp and Maurice Friedman, *PMB.*
3. By "experience" Buber here refers to the usual concept of experience *of something.*
4. Mikel Dufrenne, *The Phenomenology of Aesthetic Experience,* trans. by Edward S. Casey (Evanston: Northwestern University Press, 1973), 79.
5. Hans-Georg Gadamer, "The Universality of Hermeneutical Problems," in *Contemporary Hermeneutics,* ed. Joseph Bleicher, (London: Routledge & Kegan Paul, 1980), 129.
6. Cf.: "Each painting, each book, is a rediscovery of the totality of being," (Jean-Paul Sartre, *What is Literature?* [New York: Harper & Row, 1965], 51).
7. Suzanne Langer, *Philosophy in a New Key,* (Cambridge: Harvard University Press, 1983), 260.

REFERENCES CITED IN TEXT BUT NOT IN NOTES

Buber, Martin. *BMM; I and Thou* (Smith); *KM.*
Friedman, Maurice. *LoD;* introductory essay in *KM.*

CHAPTER 16

MARTIN BUBER AND *KING LEAR*

PAT BONI

For Martin Buber, the question asked by the Psalmist (cf. Psalms 5 and 8), by Job, and by all who wish to authenticate their existence—"What is man?"—can be answered only by beginning with man/woman. In discussing this essential question, Buber says that only the person who feels him- or herself solitary is best disposed and fitted for self-reflection. Only the one "who by nature or destiny or both is alone with himself and his problematic," who in blank solitude succeeds in meeting herself, succeeds also in discovering woman/man in her/his own self, and the human condition in her/his own:

> In the ice of solitude man becomes most inexorably a question to himself, and just because the question pitilessly summons and draws into play his most secret life he becomes an experience to himself. (*BMM*, 126)

Shakespeare's Lear, having first entered in Act I a berobed, besceptered, and crowned King, now stands, halfway through the play, in solitude in the midst of a relentless storm on an uncharted heath "unbonneted," having given his crown away, and naked, having stripped himself of his "sophisticated lendings." Close to the end of his life, almost fifty years beyond the halfway point, he is midway through his journey and the flames of his particular inferno as well as its ice. He has toppled from the heights of kingship to the nadir of "unaccomodated man." He has given away a kingdom whose geography had been measured and mapped;

now this man who we are told "ever-so-slenderly knew himself" finds himself in *terra incognita* with three men who are other than they seem: a fool who mouths wisdom, a peasant who is a nobleman, and a sane man feigning madness. We cannot fail to see the irony, for in their deliberate "seeming," these three really "be." And ironic, too, is that out on the heath contending with the "to and fro of conflicting elements," Lear, who has hidden and been hidden from undue tempests, is coming out of hiding and discovering himself to be the "thing itself," that "poor bare forked animal" which he has taken Edgar (disguised as Mad Tom) to be. In so doing he has stripped off the trappings of eighty-plus years of doctrines, verities, speculations, identities, personae, etc. Lear *has* asked the question "Who is it who can tell Lear who he is?" and in the tempest of his solitude on the heath, he has stood before the void and has been called to himself.

But Buber's Single One cannot be established by opting out of this world; like Hillel's being-for-himself, he must also become-for-others, and this must be done now. He must face the hour which moves toward him—his own biographical and historical moment in all its entire world content and senseless contradiction:

> and he must hear the message, stark and untransfigured, which is delivered to him out of this hour, presented by this situation as it arrives . . . he must recognize that the question put to him, with which the speech of the situation is fraught—whether it sounds with angels' or with devils' tongues—remains God's question to him. (*BMM*, 65–66)

One of the ways we can avoid the message which calls us into genuine existence is to remain with the collective. Buber refers to "the tyranny of the exuberantly growing *It*, under which the I, less and less able to master, dreams on that it is the ruler" (*I and Thou*, 48). This tyranny is seen in the very first act of the play *King Lear*.

Lear enters this play with the intention to "shake all cares and business from [his] age and confer them on younger strengths" (noble, indeed). To the daughter who loves him the most shall go the greatest portion of his kingdom. And so the love-auction begins. It is difficult for us to understand how a king who has retained his rule, his lands, his kingdom for so long can now demand the verbal display of affection from his daughters which sets into motion the tragedy of *King Lear*.

Buber says that three of the things which impede the growth of genuine relationship between persons are the invasion of seeming, the inadequacy of perception, and imposition (*KM*, 82–83). All three of these modes are witnessed in the first act of the play. From the outset Lear has attempted to master the situation rather than face creation as it is happening, and when Cordelia, authentic enough to be unable to "heave [her] heart into [her] mouth" since she is sure that her "love's/More ponderous than her tongue," fails to give her father what he wants, she is banished. Here is a good example of what Buber calls "reflexion" (*Ruckbiegung*)—the basic movement of the life of monologue. Lear is concerned with his *my*—*my* kingdom, *my* daughters, *my* terms. What is that of the other has no actuality for the king. Bending back on himself, withdrawing from accepting with his essential being Cordelia in her particularity, Lear can allow his daughter to exist only as his own experience, only as a part of himself. In banishing her, withdrawing from her, "the essence of all reality," as Buber would say, "begins to disintegrate" (*BMM*, 22–24).

Regan will say of her father, "to wilful men, The injuries that they themselves procure/Must be their schoolmasters," and though said by a wilful woman, the insight is true of Lear. He would will what Buber repeatedly tells us cannot be willed:

> Man's will to profit and to be powerful have their natural and proper effect so long as they are linked with, and upheld by, his will to enter into relation. There is no evil impulse till the impulse has been separated from the being; the impulse which is bound up with, and defined by, the being is the living stuff of communal life, that which is detached is its disintegration. (*I and Thou*, 48)

I see the heath on which Lear contends as symbolic of the "between" as Dover (in Act IV) represents another "between." If, as the Maggid of Mezritch believed, nothing in the world can change from one reality to another unless it first turns into nothing (*TH: Early*, 104), then Lear (whom Fool has called "Nothing") must confront what is over against him as possibility, and this must, perhaps, take place within himself—though this cannot be relation or presence of "streaming interaction" according to Buber. But I do not believe that what Lear experiences on the heath is merely self-contradiction. Buber may be correct when he speaks of confrontation of one's self within one's self—whether one explains it as relation, even religious relation—as self-deception, and this may be "the verge of life, flight of an unfulfilled life to the senseless semblance of fulfilment, and its groping in a maze and losing itself ever more profoundly" (*I and Thou*, 69–70), but, though Lear has undoubtedly lost himself through not knowing the other as Thou, for focusing unnaturally on an "I" that is in reality a mere "me," I do not believe he loses himself ever more profoundly on the heath—losing the old Lear yes, but coming to the real Lear.

Buber says:

> I call a great character one who by his actions and attitudes sat-
> isfies the claim of situations out of deep readiness to respond
> with his whole life, and in such a way that the sum of his
> actions and attitudes expresses at the same time the unity of
> his being in its willingness to accept responsibility. (*BMM*, 114)

In the fourth act of the play in the French camp at Dover, Lear will
respond from the depths of his being as he goes forward to meet Cordelia.
Reconciliation, according to Buber, cannot take place in the type of guilt
which can be rationalized away or which one holds on to in ever-deepen-
ing self-preoccupation. We have witnessed in the previous scenes Lear's
preoccupation with his daughters' "ingratitude" ("how sharper than a
serpent's tooth it is . . ."); he has rationalized away his own guilt and held
on to the voice of the crowd, but we have never seen him beat his breast
inauthentically or rake the muck to the left or the right as he wallowed
in his "guilt feelings." He had momentarily condemned his "organs of
increase"—a foolish and bad-faith attempt at guilt—but his genuine guilt
has not ultimately been rationalized away, and reconciliation takes place.
     When Lear awakens and his initial fears dissipate, we can say that he
has moved from the lower realm of conscience, what Buber calls the
"vulgar conscience," to its heights. As such he has "independently mastered the material delivered to him" by his conscience. He had, first, to
illuminate the darkness that obscured his guilt; second, he had to hold on
to the "newly-won humble knowledge" of who he is now in relationship
to what he has been; and third, in his place and according to his capacity,
"he can restore the order of being injured by him through the relation of
an active devotion to the world—for the wounds of the order-of-being can
be healed in infinitely many other places than those at which they were
inflicted" (*KM*, 136). The restoration of the injured order takes place not
in the kingdom Lear has relinquished but in a tent in the French camp at
Dover—foreign, yet not so foreign territory for Lear.
     The words Lear speaks to Cordelia in this scene are simple, the
poetry plain. "I am a very foolish fond old man," he tells his daughter.
"Fourscore and upward, not an hour more or less." And "to deal
plainly," he adds, "I fear I am not in my perfect mind." He thinks he
should know Cordelia and Kent (whom he had banished in Act I, but
who had returned to serve Lear as the peasant Caius)[1] but he is not sure
how he has come to the place in which he now finds himself. His desire
that Cordelia's presence be real overrides his fear of being shamed, and
he says, "Do not laugh at me/For as I am a man . . ." He is indeed a man
and no longer *seeming* to be. Buber believes that the essence of man,

that which is his uniqueness, can be directly known only in living relation. All real living *is* meeting, and Lear becomes *Real* (royal and
authentic) through the meeting. And as he is a man, he thinks "this
lady/To be my child Cordelia." And so she is; she is. She weeps, and her
father, for whom tears—his own, certainly—had been a cause for dis-
grace, a sign of weakness, is deeply moved by this genuine act of love on
the part of Cordelia. No words of love, no quantification of affection verbally expressed, are necessary this time. Buber said, "Love meets us
through grace . . . it is not found by seeking" (*I and Thou*, 41, 44).

In conscience Lear needs to attain to his own self; only then can the
good thrive through him and only then will the reparation of his guilt take
place. Verbal confession is always possible, Buber said, but is not authentic without "the small light of humility that alone can illuminate the
abyss of the guilty self in broad waves" (*I and Thou*, 143). If the refusal to
take on guilt is an escape from self-illumination, then Lear's acknowledgement of his guilt marks him as one who has gone from "ever so slenderly
knowing himself" to self-recognition. By resolutely intending to make
reparation in the present for that which he deeply regrets having done in
the past, he moves toward wholeness. He has responded to that which
summoned him to his guilt and, resolving to heal the wounds for which
he is responsible, tells Cordelia she has cause to do with him as she will,
for he has wronged her. She tells him he has "no cause, no cause."

Lear asks, "Am I in France," and the response from Kent intends
more than its literal meaning: "In your own kingdom, Sir." The French
camp at Dover, a coastal region connecting France and England, is the
setting, and Shakespeare, we can be sure, did not arbitrarily choose his
locations. Lear is back to himself, but it is not a land-locked self, and
though his position is still precarious, drifting toward the sea as his mind
begins to recall the torment, the tempest, the chaos, he cannot appropriate artificially the grounding he needs. He does not yet walk, but he
rests—on the narrow ridge of insecurity, perhaps?—in his own kingdom.

In the course of becoming human, Buber said, two constituent factors of the human person appear. One is dissatisfaction with "being limited to needs," and the other is the "longing for perfected relation" (*I
and Thou*, 163). We do not know the hidden structure that enables Lear
to become *for others* rather than solely for himself,[2] but Buber tells us
that with the awakening of personhood awakens the dissatisfaction
with using and getting. Lear, having been that which accoutrements of
office and title had deceived him as being ("They told me I was everything . . ."), desires more than this. He chooses humanity in place of
kingship. "You must bear with me," he tells Cordelia. "Pray you now,
forget and forgive; I am old and foolish." He fulfills himself as man in

his confession. The two exit, too late having come together, he to rest at last on her kind nursery.

The capacity to love presupposes self-awareness, for it carries with it the ability to know ourselves as well as to know the other. To be able to love we need to be independent, since we cannot love another if we *need* the other for our own ends (or if, conversely, we believe that the other needs *us* in order to be). Lear's desire, voiced in the beginning of the play, that Cordelia's "kind nursery" would be the balm of his last years was the "need" of one who had never stood alone against the elements, who had not yet come to the man himself. To love, he now comes to know, he had to "cut the cord" and stand, unbound, alone in the universe. He has come to recognize that the platitudinous prattle, the verbal protestations of love as mouthed by Regan and Goneril, have nothing to do with love. He has learned that the love of his daughters cannot be bought ("I gave you all . . .").

Real love is not *dependence* on an other, but *interdependence*. Like Auden's young man in "The Age of Anxiety," it can be said here of Lear: "So, learning to love, at length he is taught/To know he does not." And like Adam, who must discover he has hidden himself *before* he can begin on his way, and yet whose acknowledgement of such hiding *is* the beginning of the true way, so we, too, must learn before we can love how more often than not we fail to *really* love. Feelings dwell in each of us, Buber says in *I and Thou*, but the human being "dwells in his [or her] love . . . love does not cling to the *I* in such a way as to have the *Thou* only for its "content,' its object; but love is *between I* and *Thou* (14).

When we next see Lear and Cordelia they are on their way to prison. The father seeks to allay the fears of his daughter:

> We two alone will sing like birds i' th' cage.
> When thou dost ask me blessing, I'll kneel down,
> And ask of thee forgiveness.

Buber writes:

> Only he who himself turns to the other human being and opens himself to him receives the world in him. Only the being whose otherness, accepted by my being, lives and faces me in the whole compression of existence, brings the radiance of eternity to me. Only when two say to one another with all that they are, "It is *Thou*," is the indwelling of the Present Being between them. (*BMM*, 30)

Lear would have an eternity with Cordelia even in a walled prison. "We'll live," he tells her, "And pray and sing, and tell old tales, and laugh . . ." And there will be more; there will be time to ponder what Lear in his fourscore years and upward has never considered: "And take upon's the mystery of things/As if we were Gods' spies . . ." Too late—a major theme of this play—for she will be hanged and Lear will enter in the final scene with his beloved daughter in his arms, crying: "Howl, howl, howl, howl . . ."

We suffer dreadfully with the King in his penultimate moments, but his ultimate act is his death. We suspect, when the academic reawakens in us, when we have, as Buber would say, distanced ourselves from and related to the event, that the old King has earned his death and that Shakespeare intended that we see this. If the final lines that Shakespeare gives to the protagonists of his plays are characteristic of that which he wants the audience to understand in terms of the entire play, then Edgar's last lines are particularly telling with regard to authenticity and inauthenticity, dialogue and monologue.

> The weight of this sad time we must obey;
> Speak what we feel, not what we ought to say . . .

Bidden to speak as the King commanded, the inauthentic ones mouthing the words they felt they *ought* to say, the dialogical one remaining silent, the tragedy of *King Lear* began. The tragedy of King Lear was that he had such slender knowledge of himself, that he lived at least two scores too many before he thought the thought or voiced the question, "Who is it that can tell me who I am?" Indeed he ought not to have been old before he was wise.

Whether salvation, retribution, poetic justice have occurred at the end of the play is not the theme of this study. That the deaths of Lear and Cordelia assault us with almost every missile the gods can send down is undeniable. No *deus ex machina* has descended; God has not appeared from out of the whirlwind, and whether rewards and punishments have been meted out to satisfy our sense of justice is debatable. At the end of the play, we still do not know why "a dog, a horse, a rat have life" and Cordelia no breath at all. What we do know is that when an old man who barely knew himself finally came to know himself and could begin to live a genuine life of dialogue, to know and love others, he died.

We may be horrified that Lear's penance was not rewarded with an extended and happy life in Cordelia's loving care, but we may not see Lear's struggle as anything less than his having become what he had been created to be. Turning, Buber has told us, is always possible, but we do not turn with *kavanah*[3] if we hope to tempt the gods to send incense down upon our heads. To repent for something other than to be what it is our human vocation to be is to hold on to the sin against humanity, and all the suffering in the world will not wash it away. It is not the fear that penance is impossible that is evoked in this play, it is that penance will not guarantee any bounty in this world.

The confession of one's sin against existence—genuine repentance made in sorrow and with intention to repair the injured order—is always possible. As Buber has taught us, every single one of us can turn, can recognize the Center and turn again to it. And Lear had done so. In his act of turning, all the power of entering into relation that he had buried rose again to give new life to his world. He turned to the other human being and he opened himself to her, thus he received the world in her. Her otherness, accepted by his being, brought "the radiance of eternity" to him. With all that they were the two did say to one another: "It is *thou*," and the indwelling of the Present Being was between them. The tragedy is not that a penitential man brutally died, but that his turning had come so late.

The fear shared by the play's audience is what Paul Tillich speaks of as the "anxiety of guilt and condemnation." Our being is not only given to us, it is demanded of us. We are required to answer for what we have made of ourselves, and when we take on the question we take on the anxiety of guilt relatively, condemnation absolutely. We are supposed to fulfill our destiny. "In every act of moral self-affirmation man contributes to the fulfillment of his destiny, to the actualization" of what he or she potentially is (Tillich, 52). Similarly, Buber has written:

> Each one who knows himself . . . as called to a work which he has not done, each one who has not fulfilled a task which he knows to be his own, each who did not remain faithful to his vocation which he had become certain of—each such person knows what it means to say that "his conscience smites him." (*EG*, 87)

What we fear in *King Lear* is not that we inhabit an imbecile universe (as one critic suggests) but that we may open ourselves to the voice of conscience only as we stand on an unknown heath in a tempest-tossed world at an unripe old age; that though we know time cannot be halted we will cling to the hope that it can; that there will be for us, as there was for Lear, "tomorrow and tomorrow and tomorrow" until that time comes when our freedom to choose to go out to meet our destiny can no longer be authenticated. The fear the play touches us with is that we too may be old before we are wise, that we may be "fools of Fortune," inauthentic, irresolute, buffeted about by whatever comes our way, ending our life by ultimately coming to no decision. That we may try to flee in the face of death and, like the old King, be pursued by it as we try to evade it.

The fear elicited by *King Lear* is that we may never come to realize that there may be more to life that this, that we will always be content with being limited to needs and never long for perfected relation—that the "higher wish" may never appear and thus the genuineness of our person not be manifest (*KM*, 163). That like Lear, we may, not knowing ourselves, lack the ability to know the other, hence lack the ability to love; and like Lear, needing others for our own ends, we may end losing that one precious love that we have come so late to recognize. That by the time we become *I* our *Thou* will be taken from us. The fear that we encounter in our dialogue with this play is that we may never experience the fear of God—the dread which is the beginning of wisdom, the gateway to the love of God.

Whether the "pagan" Lear has been denied entrance through that portal or not I cannot say, but I believe redemption—not in the theological sense, perhaps, but in the sense of recovery of that which had been lost—has taken place. Lear, having turned away from his ownmost authentic self, returned to that which was most essentially himself and went forward to the meeting.

We tremble at his death, then, not because penance is impossible but because we may come to turn too late to be in this world, too late to restore the community, to live that "life of dialogue" in which we *really* "have to do with those with whom" we have to do; too late to go out to meet the world and thus encounter God, and to make holy that which is given us each day. "Man's loving speech," Buber said, is one of the portals leading into the "presence of the Word" (*I and Thou*, 102). Lear learned too late the difference between dialogue and monologue, being and seeming, authentic and inauthentic speech, but he was not denied the vision of what it means to be, and he became. Lear had turned, and "the event that from the side of the world is called turning is called from God's side redemption" (120).

NOTES

1. I don't think I am stretching things by seeing Kent's name change to Caius (whether one pronounces Caius with a hard "g" or hard "c") as reflecting the change in Lear's *erKENnTnis* (knowledge) to chaos. (Cf. again, Dov Baer's understanding that in order to go from one thing to another one needs the "between"—the period of "chaos" when the seed is no longer a seed but has not yet come into being what it has been created to be [*TH: Early*]). When Kent is banished and no longer attendant on Lear as such (only disguised as Caius),

his place is taken by Fool. The folly that attends the King when reason is banished is concretized. But let's hold the paradox: how "foolish" is Lear's Fool, really?

2. The first indication in the play that Lear is concerned with someone other than himself is seen in Act III when he says to Fool as they are about to enter the hovel: "Come on, my boy. How dost, my boy? Art cold?" (III, ii, 68). He adds "Poor Fool and knave, I have one part in my heart/That's sorry yet for thee" (72–73). In Scene iv, standing outside of the hovel in the storm, he addresses the "Poor naked wretches . . . That bide the pelting of this pitiless storm" and comes to the awareness that he has taken "Too little care of this!" He then says:

> Take physic, Pomp;
> Expose thyself to feel what wretches feel,
> That thou mayst shake the superflux to them
> And show the heavens more just. (III, iv, 33–36)

He is beginning to "experience the other side" here. Earlier he had cried out to Regan in an attempt to halt the diminishing of half his train of men: "O, reason not the need! Our basest beggars/Are in the poorest thing superfluous" (II, iv, 161–62). Now he would equalize the extremes: "Here's a remedy for those in power, you pompous ones, you 'haves': 'Imagine the real,' and experience the side of those who have not!" He prays, not to the gods but to the poor, that heaven treat the wretches more equitably than has been the case.

3. *Kavanah* is "intention," or "dedication." It is "the mystery of a soul directed to a goal," as Buber describes it in *Hasidism and Modern Man* (1958). Its meaning and mission is that it is given each and everyone of us the capacity to "lift up the fallen and to free the imprisoned." We do not wait for a messiah to come; we work toward redemption in our own sphere of being. *Kavanah* is the bringing of all that we are into our prayer. A profound example of Shakespeare's understanding of this is found in *Hamlet* when King Claudius, unwilling to turn with his whole being, acknowledge his guilt in the murder of his brother, and give up throne and Gertrude, prays his prayer without *kavanah*: "My words fly up, my thoughts remain below./Words without thoughts never to heaven go".

REFERENCES

Buber, Martin. *BMM; EG; HMM; I and Thou* (Smith); *KM; TH: Early.*
Tillich, Paul. (1952). *The Courage to Be.* New Haven: Yale University Press.

PART IV

ECONOMICS, POLITICS, AND HISTORY

INTRODUCTION

LAWRENCE BARON

Martin Buber's philosophy compelled him to respond to contemporary economic and political developments, particularly when they affected the Jews in his native Germany and his adopted homeland of Israel. The hierarchic and instrumental nature of modern economic and political systems epitomized Buber's concept of the "I-It" relationship in which people were exploited as a means to aggrandize individual or governmental wealth and power. Conversely, his idea of the "I-Thou" relationship implicitly criticized the dehumanizing forces operating in the twentieth century and explicitly pointed to attitudinal and institutional changes for creating conditions that would nurture more meaningful personal and social interactions.

In this regard, Robert Hoover posits Buber's vision of decentralized federations of voluntary producer and consumer collectives as a viable alternative to capitalist and communist economies. The latter foster oligarchic management styles for large-scale enterprises and depend on maximizing growth. The limits to sustaining such growth have become increasingly apparent with the approaching exhaustion of nonrenewable resources, the disappearance of vital ecosystems, and global warming. According to Hoover, Buber's communitarian socialism possesses a "moral sustainability" derived from the commitment of its advocates to subordinate purely economic considerations to the quality of their relations with each other and their natural environment.

Mark Lutz pursues this theme further by arguing that Buber's philosophy provides an alternative to the current prevailing view of human

249

nature held by most economists—namely, that of the "rational eco-nomic man" whose behavior is guided by objective decisions to enhance material self-interest. Buber attacked both capitalist individualism and bureaucratic state socialism. The first sacrifices human solidarity to the cultivation of egoism, and the second individual freedom to the power of the state. Neither system pays sufficient attention to the spiritual need of human beings to sanctify their daily encounters with the "Thous" who comprise their communities. Lutz concludes that the revival of interest in Buber's *Paths in Utopia* among many economists may indicate their recognition that the dominant economic paradigms of this century have neglected the ethical concerns which Buber placed at the center of his feasible "utopianism."

In the realm of politics, Buber was actively involved in debates over Israeli policies after Israel became a state in 1948. In contrast to the pop-ular assessment of Buber as a "marginal figure" on the Israeli political scene, Michael Keren contends that Buber served as a significant role model for how Israeli intellectuals conceived of their relationship to the state. Buber believed that intellectuals should be social critics of the injustices committed by the states in which they are citizens. He per-ceived this position as a continuation of the tradition of the Hebrew prophets who acted as the moral conscience of the Biblical Jewish states. Keren supports his thesis by citing Buber's success in provoking public inquiries into the ethical issues raised by Israel's relations with postwar Germany, the Eichmann Trial, the massacre of Israeli Arabs at Kfar Kassim in 1956, and the espionage trial of Aharon Cohen. Thus, Keren asserts that Buber made an important contribution to preserving Israel's young democracy at a time when the Israeli government easily could have invoked security concerns to silence its critics.

In the last article of this section, Jerry Lawritson defends Buber against the charge leveled by Emil Fackenheim and others that Buber neither recognized the extent of evil manifested by the Holocaust nor provided a satisfactory philosophical response to its horrors. Lawritson reminds us of Buber's personal courage in the face of Nazi persecution and of his tireless educational efforts on behalf of German Jewry between 1933 and 1938. After he emigrated to Palestine, Buber, like most of his contemporaries who lived beyond the control of the Third Reich and its allies, did not fully fathom the unprecedented magnitude of the Nazi slaughter of the Jews until the end of the war. Buber subse-quently condemned the Holocaust "as the greatest crime that was ever initiated by a state organization," but also realized that it was humanly impossible for someone who was not a survivor of it to comprehend totally what it had been like. Lawritson also places Buber's admission that he found the Arab-Israeli War of 1948 more "grievous" than World War II in its proper context. Buber felt a greater personal sense of guilt over the former because it was conducted by a Jewish state whose creation he had long supported; whereas the Holocaust was "ultimately a problem of the German people." Finally, Lawritson enjoins Buber's readers to discern the depth of despair expressed in Buber's notion of the "eclipse of God" during the Holocaust, as well as the theological meaning of "staying with God" in the wake of such a cataclysm.

CHAPTER 17

BUBER'S WAY TOWARD SUSTAINABLE COMMUNITARIAN SOCIALISM

Essential Relationship Between the Political and Bio-Economy

ROBERT C. HOOVER

The Event Situation: Diminishing Returns of Economic Growth

Economic growth is approaching the point where each incremental input produces increased costs and diminished benefits. This is manifest in events of historically decisive nature: the expanding holes in the earth's protective ozone layer, warming of the planet from increased levels of CO_2 in the atmosphere; loss of essential life species from destruction of habitats, particularly in the tropical rain forest; mounting risk to life from industrial catastrophes such as Chernobyl, Three-Mile Island, and Bhopal; and so on. Further costs of economic growth include 31 million hectares of forest cover lost annually to pollution/acid rain in industrialized nations; annual loss of 26 million tons of the world's topsoil; bio-death of lakes in the Northern Hemisphere; groundwater demand in excess of recharge capacities in Africa, China, and North America; rising world climatic temperature with corresponding rise in ocean levels; and 6 million hectares of new desert forming each year (equal in area to the state of Maine) (Brown 1988, 3–21; Daly and Cobb 1989, introduction; Barney 1982).

Concurrently, the world economy has already begun to slow from an annual growth rate of 4.6 percent in 1950–60 to 3.4 percent in

1970–80 (Brown 1981, 126). This is fundamentally a function of restraints
upon the economy from the diminishing yield of the earth's natural
resource systems. *Global 2000* (Barney 1982, 16) projects this diminishing rate to 1.5 percent for 1985–2000. Moreover, the burgeoning population increase combined with demands for expanding per capita economic
growth portends ecological catastrophe. For example, by the year 2000,
the oil inventory will be half its 1975 level (no allowance for the Kuwait
oil burn, 1990–91); fresh water will have declined c. 35 percent; the growing stock of wood, 47 percent; forest cover, more than 40 percent (39–41).

The Tragedy of the Commons

A radically individualistic model would hold that, given the prospect of
visibly diminishing resources, pure short-range self-interest will drive
individuals to secure a larger personal share of the dwindling resources
while they are yet to be had. Thus, competition for the remainder before
it is exhausted would further cause the declining base to deteriorate at
an accelerated rate, as panic added to pride-cum-greed runs amok
(Hardin 1968). Before the point of absolute exhaustion is reached, this
acceleration will be aggravated by unfriendly corporate takeovers,
monopolization, and, no doubt, wars and insurrections (e.g., the Gulf
War, 1990–91). This exposes the end of the downward spiral toward
which present economic drift is leading, and which Heilbroner dis-
cerned in 1974:

> We cannot reconcile the requirements for a lengthy continuation
> of the present rate of industrialization of the globe with the
> capacity of existing resources of the fragile biosphere to permit or
> to tolerate the effects of that industrialization. . . . is there hope
> for man . . . without payment of a fearful price . . . [T]he answer
> must be: No, there is no such hope. (Heilbroner 1974, 136)

An Unlikely Alternative

Heilbroner modified his Spenglerian mood somewhat in 1975, suggesting that an alternative is possible, though highly improbable given that
the operational theology of biology continues to be survival-through-
competition; of economics, growth through individualistic self-seeking
and greed. Were these tenets of Social Darwinism to be exorcised, he
saw an improved outlook for the now ill-starred twenty-first century. He

was justifiably skeptical that rational individual self-interest could be translated into a sense of altruism toward society and its future unborn generations. Adam Smith could not convince him that the rigors of an amoral market could be effectively countered by a presumed innate sense of "sympathy" in every human breast (Smith 1759 as explained in Schweitzer 1960, ch.12). And he did not see how, by mere wishing, tooth-and-claw survival instincts could be translated into an ethics of community responsibility.

The Onus on Faith(s)

Heilbroner hoped that, seeing ourselves as the "executioners of mankind," we might ask the question, "If mankind *should* survive." This is a religious question, he contended, while remaining quizzical about discovering a religious affirmation "naturally" welling up within us as we "careen toward Armageddon" (1975, 173–76). Moreover, the question then arises: which faith, which religion, or what combination of them will generate this deep concern for long-term sustainability of the planet? In this context of honest doubt, he nevertheless held forth a modicum of hope. Not bad for a"dismal scientist"!

THE SUMMONS: THEREFORE, CHOOSE SUSTAINABILITY

The industrial economy is a voracious consumer of material resources of hard, durable, "low entropy" nature. At present rates of depletion, transference of these materials into manufactured "goods" requires *heat*— enough to deplete the ozone layer, warm the oceans, and, in general, hasten the day of ecocatastrophe. This is obviously the world of *It*, poor in spirit and rich in things. Carried to its logical end, this way of It, by itself, leads to increasing shortages of essential materials, overheating the planet, and on the social side, to war, famine, pestilence, and death (Sivard 1979–89). It involves mining of replaceable resources such as agricultural land and fishes, and depletion of basic metals and mineral aggregates through planned obsolescence and status-oriented consumption. It depends on endless reserves of energy and fossil fuels. All this is characterized, in turn, by excessively large-scale, hypercentralized, overspecialized facility construction, organization, and operation. This fortifies vertical, oligopolistic management control; concentrates risk; discourages innovation; and entrenches bureaucracy while creating "system losses" from elegance of design and extended lines of supply, distribution, and communication (Lovins 1977, Solomon 1980, Schumacher 1975, Theobald 1978, Galbraith 1967). Allegedly aimed toward efficiency, this central-ized behemoth eventually shows the weaknesses of the dinosaur, the Armada, and the great empires—Babylon, Persia, Rome, Spain, Great Britain, Soviet Russia, and the United States of America. Yet, Buber insists over and over that bigness is not intrinsically evil except when arbitrary control through centralization becomes an end-in-itself, obscuring the essential relationship among peoples, and between them and their planet home (PU, 134).

Centralization and the Political Principle vs. Decentralization and the Communal Principal

Buber testifies to the need for power, politics, centralization, and the world of It. Yet, he gives them no more than their due as useful ends of survival in a world of cruel necessity (PW, 213). Since mere survival ends are placed in strongest focus by war, the State generally tries to reduce all life to the political by demonstrating, or fabricating, the threat of war or some equivalent threat to survival (173ff.). An essential aspect of the It-based Political Principle, then, is centralization, which left unchecked, will exceed in magnitude and intensity any alleged neces-sity for true security, survival or reasoned efficiency (216–17; PU, 132). One can only guess how Buber redivivus would speak to our tempus in our topos, but the sting of his prophecy rankles within us (cf. IW, 111–12). He maintains that there is no rule by which to gauge the proper augmentation of the political principle or its offspring, centralization. Each historical situation must be confronted in all its concreteness and limitations. Then, over against the political principle of centralization is the living process of building mutual and reciprocal relationships among persons, "groups, circles, unions, cooperative bodies, and communities varying widely in type, form, scope, and dynamics" (PW, 174–75). However, as noted, the current challenge is from political authoritarian-ism undergirded with technological necessities which breed oligopoly, concentration of risk, discouragement of innovation, entrenchment of bureaucracy, erosion of human rights, and related abominations. All these things Buber said must defer to the demand for human freedom, autonomy, self-reliance, spontaneity, and creativity (134ff.). But, how and when? The answer is to set out the fitting line of judgment, drawn ever anew, between the sphere of centralized necessity and the sphere of local initiative and self-reliance. And the mark of our humanity is that when the two are in conflict, the social or communal principle will receive the benefit of the doubt over the merely political principle. For to the It of the State is owed what is of survival necessity; but to the Thou of community relationship grounded in the interpersonal reality is owed all that is possible in the given existential circumstances (219). It has been argued here that more than justice is at stake in our present situation. It is our relationship with our home, our habitat, that is simultaneously at issue. But, it now becomes apparent that the connection between our physical survival and the achievement of genuine community is unbreakable. If we are to relate to each other, we must relate to our planet home, and vice versa. The criterion of judgment, then, is simply Community itself: the relation between persons and peoples, and between peoples and the earth, in all of their shared life together.

A sustainable communal relationship which works toward a fitting and becoming round of life and work for present and future generations will incorporate (1) moral sustainability, (2) material sustainability, (3) sustainable technology, and (4) economic sustainability. Buber's communitarian socialism embodies all of these essentials of sustainable community.

BUBER'S GUIDANCE TOWARD A SUSTAINABLE SOCIALISM

Undifferentiated economic growth as an idolatry diminishes the biophysical resource base of the market society. But it also draws down the social and moral underpinnings of the market system itself (Daly and Cobb, 50–51).

A GENUINE DIALOGICAL SOCIALISM VS. A MERELY POLITICAL SOCIALISM

Daly and Cobb emphasize the superior efficiency of the market to centralized bureaucratic planning, and favor private operation of the means of production through worker-ownership and cooperative types of economic organization. For them, socialism is distinguished by its capability to nurture and enable the interpersonal and intergroup relationships which "wage" community (Daly and Cobb, 8–14). Not precisely Buber's socialism, but one in essentials congenial to his. For Buber envisions the Full Cooperative (incorporating both producer and consumer functions) in wide territorial association, yet existing, side-by-side without dogmatic rigidity, in the most diverse social and organizational forms (PU, 78–79).

Buber insists that this federation of diverse forms be articulated horizontally, through relationships of openness in which it is always

possible that useful workaday contacts can grow into relationships of I
and Thou, and on the wider scale, of "Essential We" (BMM, 175–77) and
further into "Communities of Communities" (PU). It would be ever
alert to ward off excessive centralization or the subordination of economic production to the convenience or aggrandizement of a nonrelational, vertically focused power-elite or its bureaucracy.

Moral Sustainability, Key to Any Sustainability

Either the market or the Full Cooperative tends to undermine its own
moral foundation, left to itself (BMM, 176; Daly and Cobb, 50). A communal infrastructure of such values as "honesty, freedom, initiative,
thrift" is essential to the moral operation of the market. But, such moral
capital is soon depleted in the operation of an amoral market responsive
in the main to mere radical self-seeking. Indeed, Buber would emphasize
that these values are not copy-book abstractions—they grow out of real
everyday experience of real persons with each other. Likewise, the
attempt to build vertical, centralized bureaucratic structures is the negation of the relationship of the "Essential We." Indeed, this moral capital
is more valuable, more fundamental than fiscal or physical capital, and
it is the form of capital most easily eroded. In fact, the present poverty
of these moral resources is what leads Heilbroner to doubt that the
world can yet be saved from social and ecological catastrophe.

Dialogical Social Education vs. The Economist-Ecologist King

Heilbroner tends to see the only answer in an over-arching despotism of
ecologist-economist kings (Heilbroner 1975, 160–61). By contrast, Buber
would commence the slower process of teaching by example so as to
produce a generation "with a truly social outlook and a truly social
will" (PW, 176). Buber says this of social education:

> there is a way for Society—meaning at the moment the men
> who appreciate the incomparable value of the social principle—
> to prepare the ground for improving the relations between itself
> and the political principle. That way is Education, the educa-
> tion of a generation with a truly social outlook and a truly
> social will. . . . Social Education is the exact reverse of political
> propaganda . . . [which] seeks to "suggest" ready-made will to
> the members of a society, i.e., to implant in their minds the

notion that such a will derives from their own, their innermost being. Social Education, on the other hand, seeks to arouse and develop in the minds of its pupils the spontaneity of fellowship which is innate to all unravaged human souls and which harmonizes very well with the development of personal existence and personal thought. (*PW*, 176)

COMPARATIVE EMPHASES:
CONVENTIONAL INDUSTRIAL IT VS. COMMUNITARIAN THOU

The necessities of It inherent in the conventional industrial society are countered by the summons to confront the world relationally—i.e., as a Thou. Buber, supra, guides us to give the necessary Its their due deference, but to devote to the relational world of Thou whenever it is possible. It must be ever placed on the defensive and made accountable; the relational realm of Thou is always to be given the benefit of the doubt.

It-economics is "billiard ball" economics: high-tech, atomistic, individualistic, hierarchical, centralized, mechanical, chance-determined, inorganic, capital-intensive, focused on short-term gain in a value-free market (Breton and Largent, 9–20). Thou-economics is whole—seeking relational economics: holistic, low-tech, interpersonal, networking, noncentralized, biotic, labour-intensive, spontaneous, anarchic, communitarian. It is motivated by long-term common interest through a market conditioned by the communitarian values of compassion, justice, and care for the whole earth and all of its life forms.

Ecologically, It-economics holds the costs of environmental stewardship to constitute "overhead" which must be reduced or eliminated if it impedes industrial production throughput. Per contra, Thou-economics pays these costs (waste treatment, pollution control, organic cropping) in full in order to save the ecological goose which lays the golden eggs of environmental sustainability both in the present and over the long pull. While It is environmentally prodigal in the interest of immediate satiety, Thou is environmentally sustainable because it has a communitarian relationship with generations still unborn. It respects non-human life forms only grudgingly, by reducing "harvests" of plants and/or animals only to that level which just maintains the "stock" [*sic*] and only preserves the gene pools of life-forms currently considered essential to human existence. However, Thou distrusts the idea of "harvesting," especially that of animals, for it sees all of life possessing some measure of intrinsic value (read "holiness") to be sustained and nurtured as much as possible (Livingston).

Geosophically, It considers the planet Earth to be a bundle of resources which needs only to be exploited for the maintenance of high throughput in a high-consumption society. Thou, however, regards the earth and its resources as a living system in the aggregate, requiring relational care if it is to continue as a home for biotic life and for people. This is expressed rudimentarily by Buber when he says, "In considering the tree, I become bound up in relation to it" (*I and Thou*, 7–8). It is consistent with Lovelock's concept of earth itself as a life form which demands a new order of people-and-earth relationship (Lovelock 1991).

Socially, It affirms the significance of persons as having usefulness as a factor of economic production, but carefully affirming that services to enhance human well-being are to be held to that low minimum essential to insure such utility. A "social safety network," grudgingly accepted in principle, is deemed an overhead cost which undercuts the growth of economic production. On the other hand, Thou affirms that persons, families, neighborhoods, and communities are to be valued intrinsically for their own sake, and that their well-being is to be supported inasmuch as possible by the whole community. So, social well-being, along with environmental sustainability, has become a nuisance overhead charge for It-economics rather than an investment in the present and future well-being of the community. The big news for Buber's type of communitarian socialism is that the ecological and social order alike are more likely to generate investment costs than overhead charges.

Technologically, It affirms that technology is relatively inexhaustible in its potential since there are presumed to be no practical limits to terrestrial resource exploitation. Research and development, it is maintained, can increase resource availability parabolically almost forever. But, Thou counters that there are indeed unevadable *limits* to earth's life and natural resources, that these limits cannot be endlessly expanded even by the most daring and brilliant R-and-D. Limits to growth exist, and they follow the geometry of the *S*-curve, not the *J*-curve or parabola. Thou further summons us to shift community development emphases away from exploitation of nonrenewable resources—notably fossil fuels—and toward renewable resources such as prudently managed silvaculture, horticulture, permacultures of field crops, fishes, and solar energy sources.

OTHER COMPARATIVE EMPHASES

A random selection of the aspects of any biopolitical economy follows: Time, Measurement of Economic Benefit, Life Style, Urbanism, Capital-

Labour Relations, Risk Factors, Energy, and Comparative Risk will be examined from the viewpoints of It and Thou .

Time: It regards time as the measurement of events by external repetitive rhythms of the cosmos, what Buber calls "cosmological" time. In this there is no room for the problematic of life or of human decision. All is determined and measured in uniform repetitive units of physical duration. Thou time (i.e., human or *anthropological* time) elapses between the occurrence of historically critical events in which both God and his people participate decisively, in which nothing is predetermined, and life and humanity are problematic and unpredictable (*BMM*, 126–45; Friedman 1960, 116).

State socialism sets deadlines and schedules and performance standards in terms of cosmological time. Spontaneity is discouraged as the political economy is propelled toward politically determined ends without any real connection between the people-community and the state. Friedman reminds us that Buber sees this as the enemy of community because it wipes out those "remnants of true community which exist in the capitalist state" (*LoD*, 46–48). State socialism expects the realization of Utopia in cosmological time; the mark of the It-political economy and a give-away indicator of the Political Surplus.

Long-term projects which bind the present by the dead hand of the future, megaproduction based on creation of extended-term markets, while at times necessary, are predominant in the late Industrial Age, and they are inimical to communitarian socialism. They cramp all of life and the environment into a procrustean schedule of cosmological time, must be maintained by propaganda and hype, and build structures of dependency from which neither labor nor management dare withdraw, for to do so incurs massive job cutbacks and ruined public or private investments.

Measurement of Economic Benefit

It-economics presumes that most all exchange decisions are made "rationally," i.e., to maximize Benthamite gratification in the immediate present. Thus, the convenient measure of benefit becomes the uncriticized volume of goods and services exchanged over a given year as expressed in base-year dollars—in short, the gross national product. This calculus assigns the same number of brownie points to dollars spent on accident prevention and hospitalization for accidents occurring, for soil-saving practices as for soil-mining, for family expenditures as for divorce court lawyers, for neighborhood development as for slum clearance. If the positive life-enhancing expenditures are displaced by the (usually much more expensive) negative remedial activities, the GNP could climb even while well-being of the community is declining. When GNP is slavishly applied as a measure of overall community benefit, then dental health can be made a function of the number of extractions performed; scholarship, the number of articles published and papers delivered, the dollar amount of research a scholar brings to an institution, etc. These are all measures of input expenditures which are supposed to be surrogates of community (Daly and Cobb, 139–51). But genuine community is not bought or sold in market exchanges, nor is it obtained without them. The measure of community is in the relationships which build the everyday tissues of common concern, mutual assistance, and meaningful living. These occur in the sphere of social interaction which justifies and validates what goes on in the political economy. These relationships are incommensurable. They are the result of people who live community in their minds and hearts day by day (Friedman, *LoD*, 46).

There are serious attempts to apply measures to the promotion of the community factors of positive sustainable health and human welfare. Notable among such efforts is that of Cobb and Daly in their "Index of Sustainable Economic Welfare." Their index would devalue the negatively directed costs as offsets to the positive—e.g., expenditure for TB cases hospitalized would be a negative offset to base-year dollars spent for TB prevention and positive promotion of pulmonary hygiene. This, however, is not quite communitarian Thou-economics. Only when economic activity is underpinned by the practical shared commitment of a people to *become* and to *be* community, as the mother of all other objectives, can there be a genuine and sustainable Thou-economy of communitarian socialism (see Daly and Cobb, 401–55). As this occurs by grace and will, in plural societies such as those of North America, the economic measuring devices of the late modern age will, perhaps, become as dead as the post-Thomian scholasticisms of the declining Middle Ages.

OTHER COMPARATIVE EMPHASES

Lovins (1977), Illich (1972, 1977), and Schumacher (1973) set forth a number of helpful comparisons between what are here considered "Communitarian-Thou" societies and the "Conventional Industrial It" cultures. The following is drawn from their works on the responsibility of this author.

Life-Style: It–lifestyle is currently characterized by a high and ever-heightening standard of consumption of goods and services; *Thou*–life-style, on the other hand, by "elegant frugality" with increasing emphasis on thrift, simplicity, diversity, neighborliness, and craftsmanlike production.

Urbanism: In the It kind of urbanism, cities are large megalopitan masses of dwellings and production facilities connected by superhighways and dominated by centralized economic and social service institutions, dispensing their benefits across widespread service areas from a few city-center locations with little or no service delivery at the community or neighborhood levels. However, Thou-urbanism encourages strong, self-reliant communities of neighborhoods, and neighborhoods of families. Identity with one's own street, block, and neighbors takes precedence over impersonal metropolitan mass consciousness.

Capital-Labour: It-production tends to be *capital intensive*, with more and more emphasis on megaprojects (public and private)—e.g., supermarkets, discount houses and mass-production factories. High investment costs for each increment of capital-creation are paid off by reductions in labor employment. Thou-production tends toward *labor-intensity* within the network of small firms hiring, say, one hundred or fewer workers each. The community's employment is enhanced as managers replace capital intensive operations with labor-intensive activities due to the high and increasing costs of capital.

Risks: It-system risks are relatively high due to the high concentration of fiscal and physical pitfalls in capital-intensive megadevelopments. As Mayor LaGuardia once said: "If you make a mistake, it's a beaut!" Thou-risks are of a lower magnitude and far less traumatic because they are scattered across a wide array of smaller service and production units. Moreover, experimentation and innovation risks can be undertaken without imperiling the larger economic enterprise of the total culture. Reduction of risk, in this way, allows Thou-economics to consider lower interest charges.

Energy: It-energy is commonly called the "hard" energy emphasis. The integuments of hard energy are facilities which create a high degree of monopoly, hence dependency, on a single energy source across a wide geographic area and/or a large dependent population. The epitome of hard energy is the nuclear reactor, but also included are liquid natural gas terminals, offshore petroleum wells, tar shale and sand digs, concentration of solar power towers, and other facilities which, because of their scale, prevent the development of alternative energy sources. Hard-energy development sinks heavy costs in advance planning, concentrates risks as we have seen, and often creates a professionally elite group of operators who speak only to each other in a strange and elegant language. These hard-energy, high-tech projects breed conservatism because innovation is considered a death threat to the professional control of the group. Hard energy must define and create its own market because operational downtime reduces throughput and threatens the revenue flow on which its survival relies. For example, state-of-the-art incinerators for hazardous wastes are notorious for importing PCBs, dioxins, etc., from far-distant locations in order to keep the plant running at highest efficiency. Once planned, hard-energy facility plans are almost impossible to replan because they will have incurred such enormous sunk-in planning costs. Once constructed, they are almost impossible to rebuild because of the overwhelming sunk-in construction costs (see Hohenemser 1978, 12; Solomon 1980, 228–29). In this perspective, Lovins (148) says high-tech, hard-energy megaprojects maximize the displacement of service goals by instrumental goals; in short, they are breeder reactors for what Buber long ago called "the political surplus." They

> concentrate political and economic power . . . distort political and social priorities, increase bureaucratization and alienation, compromise professional ethics . . . enhance the . . . paramilitarization of civilian life . . . reinforce . . . centrifugal politics . . . and nurture—even require—the elitist technocracy whose exercise erodes the legitimacy of democratic government.

Thou-energy is generally called "soft energy." Soft energy employs a wide diversity of alternative power sources under local control but interacting in mutual support. As much as possible, it maximizes renewable sources such as sun, wind, vegetation, and falling water, using small-scale facilities—e.g., mini-hydro, small solar collectors, wind rotors. They are of intermediate sophistication, minimizing high-tech elite skills of nuclear physicists and thermal engineers. They reduce the need for electricity transmission in which up to 50 percent of energy generated turns into entropic waste heat (Wade 1978).

Soft energy is especially helpful for developing countries where great gobs of capital are not available (Schumacher 1973, 161–79). Soft energy is Thou-energy because it is compatible with an open, pluralistic, democratic, decentralized society. It distributes risks of energy shortages across a wide geographical area, maximizes local energy decision-making. It requires little in the way of policing, and its exports of technology do not proliferate war-making capabilities. It enables a decentralized socialism through which "communities of communities" may become "peoples of peoples," and the earth itself a nation of mutually self-supporting nations. Soft technology is a basic weapon for waging Buber's kind of peace. Thou-energy is essential to any serious effort to actualize a communitarian socialism in our time.

CONCLUSION

In this hour, industrially developed cultures are dragging the world toward an eroding social, moral, and environmental future. The "tragedy of the commons" (Hardin) will take place around the year 2025 or sooner. The operational aspects of sustainability—material, technological, economic—are mere spin-offs of moral sustainability or genuine community. Moral sustainability—community—is, Buber and Heilbroner say in their different ways, a matter of faith. However, Buber, ever practical, searches out this faith in the universal language of humanity, i.e., in the elemental relationships between person and person and community and community, in the everyday living situation. Only *as* people mean community with all their hearts and all their souls and all their minds can community go forward in that everyday toward a Thou-type of sustainable communitarian socialism. The goal will never by won decisively, once and for all. But it can be won ever and again by each generation as it, in its own time and situation, transforms by will and grace the It principle of the political surplus into the Thou expression of the truly interhuman and the social.

RECOMMENDATION

Thou and *It* are good philosopher terms. They do not grab the people who need to relate to them quite often. Accordingly, it is proposed that we start speaking of Thou-technologies and biopolitical economies as *gentle*, and of It-technologies and biopolitical economies as *harsh*.

REFERENCES

Barney, G. (1982). *The Global 2000 Report to the President, Entering the Twenty-First Century*. New York: Penguin.
Brown, E. (1981). *Building a Sustainable Society*. New York: W. W. Norton.
———. (1988). *State of the World 1988*. New York: W. W. Norton.
Buber, M. *BMM*; *I and Thou* (Smith); *IW*; *PU*; *PW*.
Daly, H., and Cobb, J. (1989). *In the Common Good: Redirecting the Economy Toward Community, the Environment, and a Sustainable Future*. Boston: Beacon.
Friedman, M. (1960). *Martin Buber: Life of Dialogue*. New York: Harper.
Galbraith, J. (1967). *The New Industrial State*. Boston: Houghton-Mifflin.
Hardin, G. (1968). *Science 1968*: 1243–8.

Heilbroner, R. (1974). *An Inquiry into the Human Prospect*. New York: W. W. Norton.

———. (1975). *An Inquiry into the Human Prospect With Second Thoughts*. New York: W. W. Norton.

Hohenemser, K. H. (1978). "Energy—Can High Technology Solve our Energy Problem?" *Environment* 20 (November): 9.

Illich, I. (1972). *Deschooling Society*. New York: Harrow.

———. (1977). *Disabling Professions*. London: Boyars Burns & McEachen.

Livingston, J. (1981). *The Fallacy of Wildlife Conservation*. Toronto: McClelland Stewart.

Lovelock, H. (1991). *Healing Gaya, Practical Medicine for the Planet*. New York: Harmony.

Lovins, A. (1977). *Soft Energy Paths: Toward a Durable Peace*. New York: W. W. Norton.

Power, T. (1988). *The Economic Pursuit of Quality*. London: M. E. Sharpe.

Sivard, R. (1979–1989). *World Military and Social Expenditures 1979–89*. Leesburg, Va.: World Portfolios.

Schweitzer, A. (1960). *The Philosophy of Civilization*. New York: Macmillan.

Schumacher, E. (1973). *Small is Beautiful*. New York: Harper Torchbooks.

———. (1975). "Intermediate Technology." *Centre Magazine*, Jan-Feb.

Smith, A. (1759). *The Theory of Moral Sentiments*. New York: Garland, 1971.

Solomon, L. (1980). *Energy Shock: After the Oil Runs Out*. Toronto: Doubleday.

Suzuki, D. (1991). "Why Conventional Economics Spells Doom." *Toronto Globe and Mail* (Mar. 2).

Theobald, R. (1961). *The Challenge of Abundance*. New York: Chas. Potter.

Wade, N. (1978). "Soft & Hard Energy." *New Republic* (Feb. 25).

CHAPTER 18

THE RELEVANCE OF MARTIN BUBER'S PHILOSOPHICAL ANTHROPOLOGY FOR ECONOMIC THOUGHT

MARK A. LUTZ

Economics has long prided itself on being the queen of the social sciences, its special scientific status and credentials being demonstrated by the annual awarding of the Nobel Prize. It deliberately tries to model itself as a natural science with a strongly positivistic orientation.

Of course, there have always been dissenters, inspired in part by the growth of knowledge school (Ward 1972) and more recently by postmodernism (McCloskey 1985; Samuels 1990). At the same time, there is a growing sentiment that the discipline's conventional toolkit fails to offer much in overcoming such pervasive problems as mass poverty, alienation at the workplace, consumerism, and environmental decay. Clearly, there must be some relationship between the growth of social problems and the growing dissent among its practitioners. It points to the need to reconsider basic foundational issues, particularly the philosophical anthropology implicit to contemporary economic thought.

The purpose of this chapter will therefore be to examine some of these methodological and philosophical issues currently under debate in the light of Martin Buber's philosophy of dialogue. More specifically, we will attempt to apply his philosophical anthropology in three ways: first with respect to the methodology of social science, second to a critical examination of Rational Economic Man (REM), and third to explore the timely relevance of his concept of the "interhuman" in socioeconomic organization.

I. THE LIMITS OF POSITIVE ECONOMIC SCIENCE

First and foremost, it must be stressed that Buber harbored a great respect for pure or "objective" science, as the following quotation readily shows:

> I have often indicated how much I prize science, so called "objective knowledge." Without it there is no orientation in the world of "things" or of "phenomena," hence no orienting connection with the space-time sphere in which we have to pass our individualized life on earth. Without the splendid condensations, reductions, generalizations, symbolizations that science turns out, the handing down of a "given" order from generation to generation would be impossible. On it, on its current "position," man's current world-images are built. (PI, 48)

Yet, he adds immediately that its value in terms of application to "the work of a man who executes faithfully his office in the service of life" is quite a different story. In the hands of a man "without true vocation," science becomes deceptive and misleading. In particular, Buber denies that any meaningful normative generalizations can be derived from these objective studies.[1]

In his 1938 inaugural lecture at the Hebrew University in Jerusalem, Buber focused on the normative/positive distinction within sociology. There he deplored the modern tendency to restrict the discipline to an "objective" science, aiming "to present and to explain facts and connections without expressing any value-judgment in so doing" (PW, 180). He argued that sociology needs to be also a "philosophical discipline" seeking to understand the meaning and purpose of social existence and of social events. The genuine social philosopher acts as a representative of the spirit, he must educate and act to *change* the world. To simply resign to a value-free sociology implies condoning the status quo.

It seems reasonable to assume that what Buber said about sociology also applies to economics: we need *also* an economic philosophy. Such necessity of explicitly recognizing the normative nature of social science also involves the kind of social questions that have been phrased in quantitative rather than qualitative terms. Buber offers the following example: "What is, with the greatest productivity of the total economy, the maximum share of the working man in the fruits of his labor, and what measures shall be taken to let him have this maximum?" In the process we have tended to neglect the questions of eminently qualitative character, such as: "How does the worker work at present in a factory highly developed in the technique of work? As a man or as an external part of a machine? And how in the future can technique be set the task of including man as man in its calculations?" (ABH, 93).

Clearly, Buber would not limit himself to putting maximum consumption as the sole end of economics, but also those aspects of economic activity and organization that allow for meaningful work, greater quality of life enabling us to live more fully as genuine persons. Similarly, he would have seriously questioned the continuing movement towards ever-increasing formalism and technical modelling as well as the climate of philosophical impoverishment and cynicism prevailing among the student bodies of most leading graduate schools in the discipline.[2]

II. THE ANTHROPOLOGICAL POVERTY OF RATIONAL ECONOMIC MAN

Ever since J. S. Mill, "Homo oeconomicus" was never meant to be a "whole man," but only an agent engaging in a particular subset of all possible human actions. Some saw him as a "Partial Man," an "Imaginary Man," and, in his modern dress, he hides under such aliases as "behavior equation" or "objective function" (Machlup 1972, 99). But virtually all economists agree that "homo oeconomicus is not supposed to be a real man, but rather a man-made man, an artificial device for use in economic theorizing" (114). In other words, a homunculus, a useful abstraction helpful in analyzing economic activity. In Buber's terms, he would certainly qualify as one of those "splendid reductions that science turns out" in its vital quest for accumulating objective knowledge. There would be nothing wrong per se with the use of REM, as long as the concept would be confined to analytic *description* of observed phenomena *only*. A major problem, however, does arise when REM also provides the basis for normative generalizations made in the name of science. And such intrusion into the normative is readily admitted by economists (Green 1971, 25). Instead of a Buber-type demand for a genuine economic philosophy, economists choose to employ a dispirited pseudophilosophy disguised as normative science when addressing questions of social and human welfare. Accordingly, an inquiry into the essential limitation of Economic Man imposes itself.

At the heart of REM and economics we find the a priori principle of maximizing.[3] It is now generally agreed that this is a metaphysical postulate (Boland 1981; Caldwell 1983). But whatever its epistemological

status, maximizing behavior is to economists the very essence of rational action. So, for example, Hahn and Hollis (1979) define rational
choice as follows: "Given the set of available actions, the agent chooses
rationally if there is no other action available to him, the consequences
of which he prefers to that of the chosen action" (4). In other words, we
always strive for the most preferable consequences. In the days of
Edgeworth and Marshall this was simply expressed as "utility maximization." Later, as the above definition suggests, it was generalized to
an "index of preferability," or some vague notion of a desire-based "feel-
ing-good index." As such, economics is not confined to sole acts of a
purely selfish nature, but can be readily expanded to also include action
based on benevolent sympathy. And it is this very fact that makes economics *appear* general and all-encompassing, and luringly relevant to
represent some of our very highest and most human aspirations.[4] Even
such a foremost scholar as the late Kenneth Boulding has been led to
believe that "there is nothing in the theory of preference or decision
which says that an individual cannot exhibit love, benevolence, a sense
of community, an identification with a larger group, and so on"
(Boulding 1979, 10). All we need to do is to allow preference functions to
be more inclusive; more specifically: "If we can identify the welfare of
another as our own, we can take care of this informal theory by simply
supposing that the preference function that governs our behavior has
goods possessed by others in its domain as well as goods that we possess
ourselves" (Boulding 1968, 69). In short, maximizing REM is portrayed
as capable of overcoming selfishness by "identifying with others,"
implying an "extension of the self," and Boulding assures us that it is
"precisely this extension of self which is implied in the concept of love"
(1968, 213). But, as we will attempt to show, all these claims for incor-
poration of human qualities such as love, sympathy, etc., may be exaggerated. REM, even Boulding's noble version, remains totally confined
to the infrahuman world of I-It. Everything, whether phenomena of
nature, other human beings, or even a conception of a divine being, is
ultimately reduced to an ingredient, argument, or object, in some kind
of "objective function" to be maximized. Everything and everybody is
nothing but "bundles of experienceable, influenceable, manageable,
usable properties," mere objects to be experienced and used for the ultimate purpose of gratifying one's desires. According to the economic way
of thinking, the recipient of a gift is viewed entirely instrumentally by
the donor, so that an individual will behave "altruistically" only to the
point where *his or her own* incremental utility is equal to *his or her
own* incremental cost. "The recipient's utility is simply a consumption
good like any other seen from the point of the donor" (Hamlin 1986, 35).

The life of maximizing REM is clearly that of Buber's "self-withholding man" asserting himself against the world. Similarly, maximization by its very essence implies action that is mediated, reflective, and oriented to expected consequences to one's own self. It sharply contrasts with spontaneous action in response to something one meets and which is other than oneself. Similarly, the "other" that the maximizer confronts is not a genuine Thou, a "neighborless, seamless whole filling the firmament," but rather merely a "thing among things" to be taken into account when maximizing.

In dialogue, there are no posited ends for a utility or objective function. The very ends/means distinction melts away, and all that is left is one's self-transcending will to "let it happen," to let go of one's preconceived "ends" and perceptions, one's "little will" (the desire for individual gain and power), and to enter into relation or communion with one's destiny or "grand will."[5]

Interestingly enough, one economist, Philip Wicksteed, recognized one exception to the notion of altruism as including other people's interests in one's objective function: As agents, we are not allowed to be concerned with the interests of our immediate trading partner. He called that "tuism" and held that when tuism actuates one's conduct, it ceases to be wholly economic (Wicksteed 1910, 180–81). Here we have some sort of admission that maximization and dialogue do not mix.

Finally, it is easy to see that any "other" that can be included in one's (lovingly stretched) self is intrinsically incompatible with Buber's idea of the whole self being unique. The very concept of "unique" defies categorization, intellectual comprehension, and in the process also the enclosing of an other in an expanded self. Almost by definition, the unique as unique can never be fitted into a mathematical equation or an objective function, thereby suggesting that economics only *pretends* to be compatible with genuine love. The love that it does incorporate is at best a confined love, a mere feeling of love.[6]

The economic doctrine of "all is maximization" also corresponds to the prevailing notion that all is self-interest, a practice that has been widely honored since Adam Smith and Edgeworth's assertion that the "first principle of economics is that every agent is *only* actuated by self-interest" (Edgeworth 1881, 16, emphasis added).[7]

Martin Buber would have been highly critical of any discipline built on "a first principle" of self-interest only. He makes clear that without ego—directed passion, "man would woo no woman and beget no children, build no houses and engage in *no economic activity*, for it is true that all travail and all skill in work is the rivalry of man with his neighbor" (*G&E*, 94, emphasis added). Yet, to reduce all passions underlying human action and all vital energy simply to a Freudian type libido is what makes for an animalization of human reality (126). In deep contrast to animals, "man can grasp all that encounters him in his life as being existing in itself *beyond his own interests*" (*ABH*, 119, emphasis added). The modern attempt of social scientists to "go back to a 'natural' foundation, to unconcealed instincts," and their assumption that the life of the individual as well as that of every people must be grounded in simple self-assertion, may be understandable but also deplorable. It is understandable as a disillusioned reaction to the pretension of special interests claiming to have a monopoly on the interpreting spirit and truth. At the same time, Buber deplores this tendency as misguided naturalism. We, as subjects, are capable of engaging in actions for the sake of truth, as manifested in genuine dialogue and in action responding to our innermost apprehensions and conscience. It is an issue of morality and conscience: self-interested REM is a human being without conscience and restraint. He holds no image of what he ought to be. Like the evil identity of the "wicked" individual, "one is what one wants and one wants what one is" (*G&E*, 137).

In contrast, the kind of total human action implied in dialogue is one where one acts with one's whole being—meaning one acts without inner conflict or against conscience. In a sense, one could argue that Buber replaces conventional economic rationality implying noncontradictory or "consistent" gratification of impulses and preferences with what may be termed "integral rationality" where there is no contradiction between actual behavior and morally preferable behavior.

To conclude, REM, whether "enlightened" or not, is unable to overcome maximization and thereby always prisoner of the I-It world, unable to respond and driven by the unholy spirit of use-directed self-assertion. Grounding normative generalizations in this observed pathological attitude may very well lead to misguided policy conclusions and to the promotion of social institutions and types of economic organization that tend to be in contradiction to the demands of the true spirit.

Similarly, by teaching students that this "economic way of thinking" is the correct way to interpret our actions, our "rational" self, the economist may be actually helping to make or remake students in that very manner (Marwell and Ames 1981, 18).

The real problem of an REM-based economics relates to the fact that the same picture of "Man" underlies both descriptive and normative economics. Now, while it is certainly true that, particularly in the sphere of commerce, most of us tend to behave as REMs most of the time, it constitutes a giant and most dangerous leap to advocate institutions that would best accommodate such distinctly inhuman behavior.

An example would be the proposals that we approach politics through "public choice theory" considerations; that we encourage, in the name of allocative efficiency, the domain of explicit contracts and commercialization; and, worst of all, that judges interpret common law in order to enable wealth maximization. This phenomenon, called "economics imperialism," seeking to export the notion of economic (instrumental) rationality into all human sciences, is no doubt the ultimate and most dangerous application of atomistic REM.[8] Similarly, the economist's ideal of unrestrained individualistic competition through an appropriate institutional framework may indeed foster a climate where moral evaluations, self-restraint, and human dialogue become increasingly rare and difficult.

In short, an exploration into a type of economics that is more responsive to the distinctly human features of its agents is certainly indicated. As a first step, we need to start building real persons into economics, a task long pursued by the smaller subdiscipline of "social economics" and more recently by a group of scholars pursuing "socioeconomics."[9] Quite obviously, once we center economic discourse around the whole or authentic person, there is much to be gained in turning to Martin Buber's work.

III. CAPITALISM, SOCIALISM, AND COMMUNITY

Although Martin Buber did not directly address matters of economic theory, he did repeatedly focus on some of the most basic questions of socioeconomic organization. It is perhaps fair to say that his opposition to Marxism on idealistic grounds helped more than anything else to make him popular with many economists. But, unlike most social theorists caught in the net of existing ideological polarity, he was a critic of both individualism and collectivism, seeing in each fertile soil for the It-world to proliferate relentlessly "like weeds."

To Buber, the conflict between free-market capitalism and a bureaucratic state socialism reflected on a deeper level the struggle between two principles: the economic, expressed as the *will for profit* (*Nutzwillen*), and the political, representing the *will for power* (*Machtwillen*). The problem, according to Buber, is not so much which principle dominates: "whether it is the state that regulates the economy or the economy that directs the states is unimportant as long as both are unchanged" (*I and Thou*, 99).

1. Buber on Individualism, Collectivism, and Communal Socialism

In the present age, the spirit is not obeyed but abused, severing there-
with the I from the It. Direct meetings between persons have become
increasingly mediated by institutions that take on an independent status. The world is seen as divided into an "It district" and an "I district,"
between the worldly institutions "out there" where one works and
competes and the homey world of inner feelings. As the life in the
dispirited external world becomes more and more exploitive, painful,
and threatening, individuals seek shelter by withdrawing into their
world of feelings. The stage is set for psychologism and individualism.

There is nothing wrong with individualism, free markets, and the
underlying economic principle as long as all is embedded in a framework of human community rich in personal relations or social fabric.
On the other hand, community can never be subordinated to economy.
Subordination of the social-economy to the economic principle enslaves
us to the imperatives of technology, a "bottom-line" mentality, and the
underlying force of self-interest. Even though the spokesmen of the
industrial establishment instruct us "that the economy is taking over
the heritage of the state; you know that there is nothing to be inherited
but the *despotism of the proliferating It* under which the I, more and
more impotent, is still dreaming that it is in command" (*I and Thou*, 97;
emphasis added). It is with such a poetic but merciless observation that
Buber ends up equating the free reign of Adam Smith's "invisible hand"
with a dangerous and destructive despotism of an *impersonal force* that
snuffs the true spirit. Unadulterated and disembedded capitalism is
incompatible with human wholeness, social responsibility and genuine
spirituality. The essential defect of capitalist society is its social structure or social fabric, which is not only weak but "growing visibly poorer
every day" (*PU*, 13–14). What individualism fails to see is that society is
naturally composed *not* of disparate individuals but of relations and
associations between them.

As a grand alternative to individualism based on the dominance of
the economic principle, modern humans have increasingly opted for an
escape to an authoritarian society grounded in the dominance of the
political principle, or the state. Here the *true* nature of Human is no
longer the mere "bourgeois" abstraction of an individual but the "species
human." All "true" values are defined and articulated by the political
representatives and their leaders. What counts is not individual utility
and individual freedom, but social power and material security. Private
property and free exchange are replaced by state property and bureaucratic management: "life between man and man gets lost in the process;

the autonomous relationships become meaningless, personal relationships wither and the very spirit of man hires itself out as a functionary"
(PU, 132).
The consequences of a centralist collectivism are equally dehumanizing:

> . . . if individualism understands only a part of man, collec-
> tivism understands man only as a part. . . . Individualism sees
> man only in relation to himself, but collectivism does not see
> man at all, it sees only "society." With the former, man's face
> is distorted, with the latter, it is masked." (BMM, 200)

Under collectivism, the individual is joined to the reliably functioning
"whole." The person's isolation is not overcome but "overpowered."
Individual responsibility is submerged to the collective responsibility of
the centralized state which acts as spokesman for truth and justice. And
this very sacrifice of personal responsibility and response amounts to
nothing less than a sacrifice of the spirit. The It, no longer proliferating
as it did in free-market–type capitalism, now overshadows everything
and casts society into the gloomy darkness of a burial chamber.
Accordingly, Buber saw the choice between capitalism and centralized
socialism as a choice between Scylla and Charybdis. What is needed is to
go forward in constructing a genuine alternative which cannot be reduced
to either of the other two. In the process of reforming economic institutions and structures, special attention needs to be devoted to the question
of the interhuman and the social fabric. In terms of the three principles of
the French Revolution (liberty, equality, fraternity), we need to successfully
unite freedom and equality by regenerating brotherhood and sisterhood, by
managing our lives more in common. And convinced that "common management is only possible as socialistic management," Buber asks what
kind of socialism is it to be? It is here where Buber carefully studied the
history of non-Marxian socialism, in particular the ideas of Proudhon,
Kropotkin, Hess, and his own slain friend Gustav Landauer, in search for
the idealistic and spiritual element in socialism. Those very elements had
been purged by the Marxists and labeled "utopian" and futilitarian.[10]
Buber distinguished two kinds of utopian elements; (1) quasi-
mechanical schematic fictions exemplified by Fourier, and (2) the more
process-oriented type of "organic planning" which he associated first with
Proudhon and others preoccupied with regenerating the social fabric of
atomistic capitalism. He wholeheartedly identified with the latter alternative. It expresses a deep longing of the suffering soul for a more just and
meaningful social order, and its wish-pictures or visions need to be demol-
ished as "bound up with something supra-personal that communes with

the soul but is not governed by it" (PU, 7). Such meliorist socialism aims at realization of community and like the realization of any idea, can never be more than "the moment's answer to the moment's question" (134).

2. Buber and the Reconstruction of the Social Fabric

For a socialism that proceeds "not from the needs of the stomach but from the needs of the heart," Buber looked to the cooperative movement. Here he distinguishes three levels of co-ops: At the base are *consumer cooperatives* initiated by the Rochdale pioneers in the 1840s. Consumer cooperatives can be established relatively easily, yet their significance for social reconstruction he saw as relatively limited. Individual participation is, except in times of crisis, relatively limited. In normal times, responsibility for purchasing passes to its staff and the cooperative, particularly if successful, resembles increasingly a capitalist enterprise with a specialized, impersonal orientation centered around the goal of economic efficiency.

On a higher level, we find *producer co-ops* or worker–self-managed enterprises. The "common production of goods implicates people more profoundly than a common acquisition of goods for individual consumption; it embraces much more of their powers and their lifetime" (PU, 78). Yet, the historical record of such co-ops has, in contrast to consumer-oriented kin, been disappointing. The greatest danger here tends to come from within, from their capitalization, which tends to transform the more successful ones back into regular capitalist undertakings. It seems that neither consumer co-ops nor producer co-ops can be counted on to function sufficiently as cells for the type of social renewal Buber has in mind.

This brings us to the *full cooperative* as the ideal socioeconomic unit. Here consumer and worker, consumption and production, industry and agriculture are all integrated in a larger whole. But, it is a union whose vitality for socialism can only be harnessed if it does not remain in isolation. Yet, that is precisely what has in the past characterized their history and sealed their fate.[11] The only way that full cooperatives or village communes can be expected to transform society lies in their federation, that is, "their union under the same principle that operates on their internal structure" (PU, 141). But, as Buber was forced to admit, "hardly anywhere" has it come to this; the exception being the early Jewish settlements in Palestine and later the Kibbutz movement.

Yet, a structure of federated full cooperatives constitutes the fundamental structural task of a truly progressive humanity. Whether or not it can emerge in a competitive capitalist environment is a question that remains. It is a battle between the "despotism of the proliferating It" of the market and the wholeness of real community. Already in 1929, Buber, after advocating the existential need for creative work and the humanization of technology, realized that world market competition is one of the greatest obstacles for creating a more human economy. We cannot really solve the problem of meaningful work without first overcoming the problem of global competitiveness imposing everywhere a monotone, uncreative working routine (Buber 1985, 388–89). It was for this reason, too, that Buber recognized the need for some social control over what he saw as the "prevailing anarchical relationship among nations." In 1951 he mentioned "cooperation in control of raw materials, agreements on methods of manufacture of such materials, and regulation of the world market" (PW, 174).

In short, Buber's vision of a better world definitely can be seen to imply a maximum possible reliance on local and regional autonomy that would be wherever necessary supplemented by national and global regulation of socioeconomic conduct. Its ideal was neither capitalism nor state socialism, nor a mixture of the two, the so-called mixed economic system. Instead, he must be seen as a pioneer pointing in the direction of a new organizational alternative whose most essential principles cannot be found in either. He pointed to a market economy without laissez-faire, and a minimal state ensuring as one of its prime tastes a full employment economy where work is meaningful and consistent with the demands of human dignity (Friedman 1983, ch. 20). In addition, his vision would seem to entail an economy with group or community ownership of the means of production rather than the type of absentee ownership implied by investor-owned corporations.

Although Buber's sociology, as I have here presented it, was by and large conceived by him in the interwar period, it has been gaining additional power with the current events in Eastern Europe. In an almost prophetic insight, when concluding his critical discourse on Marxian socialism, Buber wrote in the mid-1940s:

> The picture I have hastily sketched will doubtless be laid to the documents of "Utopian Socialism" until the storm turns them up again. Just as I do not believe in Marx's "gestation" of the new form, so I do not believe either in Bakunin's virgin-birth from the womb of Revolution. But I do believe in the meeting of idea and fate in the creative hour. (PU, 138)

No doubt, the stormy events since 1989 have reopened the old questions surrounding the ideal of real socialism.

The current disillusionment with Marxism does clear the way for the alternative type of socialism advocated by Martin Buber. As long as there is a human spirit there will always be the craving for a better world, a world of true liberty and equality, a world of brotherhood and sisterhood. By this view, corporate capitalism and atomistic individualism, too, are bound to end up as museum pieces in the archives of a communitarian New Humanity.

Buber, in negating capitalism, pointed to cooperatives, particularly worker cooperatives within a framework of community enterprise. Of course, he was no economist, and therefore unable to prescribe adequately organizational details of these new forms. But history has since started to fill this gap. Most important, in this respect, is the recent evolution of the Basque Mondragon cooperatives which during the last three decades have emerged as one of the most important firms in Spain, employing over 20,000 worker members.[12] Similarly, the reformers in Eastern Europe (especially Slovenia) and elsewhere have started to show an increasing interest in replacing state enterprises by worker ownership.[13] Ironically, the challenge for a more humane and morally sound social economy is now just as likely to come from the transforming East, instead of merely from within the West itself.

CONCLUSION: MARTIN BUBER'S IMPACT ON ECONOMICS

Modern analytical economics was conceived in the 1870s, the very decade that also witnessed the birth of Martin Buber. Today, more than a century later, it becomes painfully obvious that his influence among pure economic theorists has been essentially nil. And this should not surprise us since economics, more than any other social science, relentlessly pursued a kind of abstract and positivist knowledge which for Buber held no fascination and very little promise.

In short, neoclassical economics and Buber's thought mix no better than water and oil. But we should immediately add that such a general and negative assessment slurs over the important point that in the more applied domain of economics, especially the question of alternative economic systems, he has had considerable impact. In the economics of socialism, for example, scores of economics students have been reading his *Paths in Utopia*. It remains one of the very few books making the case for a kind of socialism that is fundamentally and radically different from the Marxist variety now under attack all over the world. I have very little doubt that it helped legitimate a growing interest in the economies of cooperation and, in the process, stimulated research in this new direction. Today, the picture painted by Buber some fifty years ago provides perhaps one of the few alternatives to a world dominated by globally based capitalist corporate institutions. For this reason alone, the final story on Buber's influence may yet be told. But there is another reason to dwell as an economist on Buber's work. He offers a philosophical anthropology that rejects positivism, and he does so on grounds that seem to avoid the treacherous terrain of contemporary relativistic postmodernism. Buber, when discussing the "human sciences," did, of course, strongly reject mindless empiricism and dangerous abstractions, but he nevertheless held onto a universal human image, and always stressed the qualitative difference between the animal kingdom and the distinctly human capacity to overcome both self-"interest and cultural pressures in the pursuit of one Truth relating to one Reality. In short, Buber was no nominalist. Similarly, for him there was also such a thing as genuine progress and social development, although these terms have little in common with their traditional (nineteenth century) and prevailing contemporary interpretation (see Lutz 1990a).

As modern economics falls deeper into a state of crisis, there have been growing attempts to reexamine its philosophical foundations. In particular, we have been witnessing more and more economists following in the footsteps of Amartya Sen, questioning the utilitarian and reductionist conception of human action underlying economic theory and policy. More recently, it has led to the establishment of the new discipline of socioeconomics brought about by the eminent sociologist Amitai Etzioni, who got the ball rolling with his book *The Moral Dimension: Toward a New Economics*. There he states that "its social philosophical foundation may be characterized as the responsive community, *or in deference to my Master-teacher, Martin Buber*, the 'I and We' view" (Etzioni 1988, 8, emphasis added). Etzioni now also edits a new journal called *The Responsive Community*, which may be seen as an initial opening for the injection of Buber's thought into the field of economics. Time will tell. Whatever happens, economists, perhaps more than any other social scientists, would do well to familiarize themselves with the work of Martin Buber. Only by starting to recognize a Dialogical Person side-by-side with Logical Man can the discipline be expected to appreciate the increasingly scarce value of genuine community and help its construction out of the recalcitrant material of the present moment.

NOTES

1. Buber flatly asserts: "normative generalizations that are made in the name of science have no real meaning for me" (*PI*, 49).
2. For a recent picture of graduate education in economics, see Klamer and Colander 1990.

3. According to several scholars, the maximizing principle is the dis- tinguished and only common denominator of *all* schools of eco- nomic thought. See Ruth 1975 (chs. 1–2).

4. At least one eminent economist, Harvard's Amartya Sen, disagrees, claiming that maximization cannot account for human conduct motivated by commitment (Sen 1979, 95–102).

5. More specifically, the "willful" or capricious man posits ends and devises means all in the name of "freedom": "His world is devoid of sacrifice and grace, encounter and present, but shut through with ends and means" (*PU*, 110). He lives in a world of aimless freedom, "entangled in unreality" and pervaded by doom.

6. But such feelings, according to Buber, merely "accompany the meta- physical fact of love, but they do not constitute it. . . . Feelings one 'has,' love occurs. Feelings dwell in man, but man dwells in love" (*I and Thou*, 66).

7. For more on the assumption of self-interest in economic theory, see Sen 1979, Hamlin 1986 (ch. 2), and Lutz and Lux 1988 (chs. 3–5). Most textbooks in the field deny that self-interest is the prevailing behavioral assumption. Yet, the very same texts end up conceding that to pay for public goods (roads, defense, etc.), it is rational to be a "free rider" (i.e., to take advantage of others). It should be noted that in economics, "rationality" is defined in a purely instrumental sense pertaining to means only.

8. For a sketch of "economics imperialism," see Lutz and Lux 1988, ch. 9.

9. It is noteworthy that Martin Buber has made an entry into both. See Lutz 1990b.

10. See Buber, *PU*, chapters 1–4.

11. Wherever dogma reigns supreme, isolation is the natural result: "the exclusiveness of 'the only right form' precludes union with like minded establishments, for in every single one of them the 'faithful' are completely obsessed with the absolute character of their unique achievement" (*PU*, 73). Even without dogma, the same isolation tends to result from the economic and spiritual seclusion of the set- tlement. In place of individual egoism we have a collective egoism.

12. See, for example, the recent books by White and White or Lutz and Lux (1988, chs. 8 and 13). Of particular interest is the idea of individ- ualized internal capital accounts that, at least in theory, allows worker cooperatives to finally overcome the fatal flaw that has tra- ditionally handicapped their performance and institutional survival. There is now reason to believe that these new co-ops are at least as competitive as their capitalist rivals.

13. For a recent analysis on this important issue, see Ellerman 1990, 1992.

REFERENCES

Boland, L. (1981). "On the Futility of Criticizing the Neoclassical Maximization Hypothesis," *American Economic Review* 71 (December): 1031–36.

Boulding, K. (1968). *Beyond Economics*. Ann Arbor: University of Michigan Press.

———. (1979). "Ethics of the Critique of Preferences." In W. N. Finnin and J. A. Smith, eds., *The Morality of Scarcity*. Baton Rouge: Louisiana State University Press, 9–23.

Buber, M. *ABH; BMM; G & E; I and Thou* (Kaufmann); *PU* (5th ed.); *PW*.

———. (1964). "Interrogation of Martin Buber." Edited by M. Friedman, in S. Rome and B. Rome, eds., *Philosophical Interrogations*. New York: Rinehart and Winston, 13–117.

———. (1985). *Pfade in Utopia: Ueber Gemeinschaft und deren Verwirklichung*. Expanded new edition. Heidelberg: Lambert Schneider.

Caldwell, B. (1983). "The Neoclassical Maximization Hypothesis: Comment." *American Economic Review* 73 (September): 824–27.

Edgeworth, F. Y. (1881). *Mathematical Psychics: An Essay on the Application of Mathematics to the Moral Sciences*. London.

Ellerman, D. (1992). *Property and Contracts*. New York: Basil Blackwell.

———. (1990). *The Democratic Worker-Owned Firm: A New Model for the East and West*. Boston: Unwin Hyman.

Etzioni, A. (1988). *The Moral Dimension: Towards a New Economics*. New York: Free Press.

Friedman, M. (1983). *The Confirmation of Otherness*. New York: Pilgrim Press.

Green, H. A. J. (1971). *Consumer Theory*. Baltimore: Penguin.

Hahn, F., and M. Hollis, eds. 1979. *Philosophy and Economic Theory*. New York: Oxford University Press.

Hamlin, A. (1986). *Ethics, Economics and the State*. New York: St. Martin's.

Klamer, A., and Colander, D. (1990). *The Making of an Economist*. Boulder: Westview.

Lutz, M. (1990a). "Socio-Economic Development: An Alternative View." *Humanomics* 6(3), 20–59.

———. (1990b). "Emphasizing the Social: Social Economics and Socio-Economics." *Review of Social Economy* 48(3): 303–20.

Lutz, M., and Lux, K. (1988). *Humanistic Economics: The New Challenge*. New York: Bootstrap Press.

Machlup, F. (1972). "The Universal Bogey." In M. Peston and B. Corry, eds., *Essays in Honour of Lord Robbins*. London: Weidenfeld and Nicolson.

Marwell, G., and Ames, R. (1981). "Economists Free Ride, Does Anyone Else?" *Journal of Public Economics* 15: 295–310.

McCloskey, D. N. (1985). *The Rhetoric of Economics*. Madison: University of Wisconsin Press.

Rome, S., and Rome, B., eds. *PI*.

Ruth, G. (1975). *The Origin of Economic Ideas*. London: Macmillan.

Samuels, W., ed. (1990). *Economics as Discourse: An Analysis of the Language of Economists*. Boston: Kluwer Academic Publishers.

Sen, A. (1979). "Rational Fools: A Critique of the Behavioral Foundations of Economic Theory." Reprinted in F. Hahn and M. Hollis, eds., *Philosophy and Economic Theory*. New York: Oxford University Press.

Ward, B. (1972). *What's Wrong with Economics*. New York: Basic Books.

White, K., and White, K. (1988). *The Making of Mondragon*. New York: ILR Press.

Wicksteed, P. (1910). *The Common Sense of Political Economy*. London: Routledge and Sons.

CHAPTER 19

MARTIN BUBER'S IMPACT ON POLITICAL DIALOGUE IN ISRAEL

MICHAEL KEREN

INTRODUCTION

In this chapter, I would like to cast doubt on one of the most widely held "truisms" about Martin Buber, namely, that he had no impact upon Israeli thought and life—that his intellectual and political influence in Israel was minimal and did not match his influence worldwide. This belief has affected Buber's reputation in Israel too. The press, by which he was often interviewed, made it a custom to portray him as a prophet without followers. During the Buber centenary conference held in 1978, philosopher Walter Kaufmann sparked a heated debate over Buber's failures, but nobody in the audience objected to Kaufmann's statement that "in Palestine he was, and in Israel he remained, a marginal figure" (Kaufmann 1984, 6).

Such a statement calls for scrutiny. What does "marginality" mean? Considering Kaufmann's contention in the same speech that Buber's writings "still confront us" (6), what are the criteria by which his impact ought to be measured? These questions touch upon the essence of the intellectual's role in society and should not be easily dismissed. For one, the question of Buber's impact cannot be answered simply by distinguishing between Buber's impact in the "long run" and in the "short run" or between some "indirect" vs. "direct" influence—if only because such typologies fail to account for Buber's role as a political figure. Buber never

settled for the role of the saint whose influence is acknowledged in the
long run, but was operating, to use his own words: "through politics
itself" (PW, 133).

In what follows I elaborate on Buber's conception of the intellectual's role as expressed in his inaugural lecture, which he delivered at
the Hebrew University in Jerusalem in 1938, and claim that this conception strongly influenced the tradition of Israeli intellectuals. By "tradition" I refer to the set of beliefs by which intellectuals define the codes
of behavior concerning their productive work and their relation to political authorities (see Shils 1973). No one lecture or individual may be
seen as sole founder of any intellectual tradition, but Buber's inaugural
lecture contributed a great deal to the way many of his colleagues at the
Hebrew University and elsewhere viewed themselves and their relation
to the polity in the early years of statehood.

I then discuss the impact of the intellectual tradition inspired by
Buber on Israeli politics. Buber not only had an impact on the formation
of the tradition but became its main propounder and implementor.
There was hardly an activity by the intellectual community—publication, petition, public meeting, etc.—in which he did not take part or
which did not relate to him. I argue that his and his colleagues' frequent
involvement as critics of the political process in the early years of statehood, and the pragmatic nature of their critique, has had a constraining
effect on political behavior in Israel. I argue, too, that the charismatic
overtones given that involvement by the intellectuals had a constraining effect on their own ability to bring about institutional change.

BUBER'S CONCEPTION OF THE INTELLECTUAL'S ROLE

Buber's inaugural lecture reveals three conceptions which not only
guided him in his relationship with political authorities but had an enormous impact on the self-perception of Israeli intellectuals in the years to
come. These conceptions were: (a) the view of the intellectual as participant in the process of social transformation; (b) the consideration of political dialogue as empirical rather than historicist; and (c) the definition of
the relationship between intellectuals and the state as charismatic.

The Intellectual and Social Transformation

Buber began his presentation by reference to Henri Saint Simon and
Lorenz von Stein, whom he considered the founders of modern sociology

in the sense in which he considered that endeavor—part of man's attempt to overcome the crisis of the human race. The science of society for Buber was part of the attempt to come up with a new spiritual attitude that would precede the formation of new social institutions. To Buber, modern sociology originated in the meeting of the spirit with the crisis of human society, which the spirit accepts as its own crisis and which it undertakes to overcome through a spiritual turning and transformation.

Buber's conception of the social thinker stands in contrast to the view of the Hebrew University as an ivory tower and of its professors as taking no part in the life of the community. This image, prevailing in the thirties, did not change for many years, but eventually Buber's view altered it. While many professors were educated in institutions stressing the development of knowledge for its own sake, Buber's conception of sociology as insight into the nature of the crisis of humanity developed roots among scholars, many of whom subsequently preoccupied themselves with the nature of Israeli society and its practical tasks (Keren 1983). They defined the thinker not as one who merely learns about social crisis but one who, in Buber's words, "stands with the world in the crisis" (PW, 178).

The social involvement of the scholar implies changes in traditional scholarly behavior. For instance, it calls for a rejection of Max Weber's conception of a value-free sociology, and for a shift in the scholar's attention towards questions of societal importance. Buber added an important element: the social thinker must become reality's partner, not its spokesman. In other words, his or her role is that of critic, not of ideologue who rationalizes the status quo. At a time in which the socially involved thinker in Palestine was asked to legitimate the prevailing values of the community (see Keren 1989), Buber put forth the model of the intellectual who speaks to a world that must be changed.

The Pragmatic Nature of the Dialogue

In the second part of his lecture Buber discussed the effectiveness of the social thinker; the strong antihistoricist views he expressed became the building blocks of Israeli political philosophy (see especially Rotenstreich 1957; Talmon 1957 and 1960). He strongly rejected the historicist idea according to which "The spirit is still effective indeed, but only in so far as it places itself under the sway of powerful groups, under the dictates of what rules in history, that is, of power" (PW, 182).

Although not clear enough on this point, Buber referred to Plato's conception of the "truth," which unfolds a preconceived idea of the historical process rather than develops it as part of an open, empirical investigation (see Popper 1945). When Buber talks about the "spirit's call to the assumption of power" (PW, 184), he has in mind Plato's theory of the soul that recollects that which it had formerly beheld. Plato, said Buber, "is the most sublime instance of that spirit whose intercourse with reality proceeds from its own possession of truth" (PW, 185–86).

This Platonic model is contrasted to the Hebrew prophets, who criticized society as it existed in empirical reality and aimed at its improvement. To Buber, the prophetic spirit does not believe, as does the Platonic, that it possesses a universal and eternal ideal truth. The Hebrew prophet invariably receives only a message for a particular situation. He sets no universally valid image of perfection, no pantopia or utopia, he wrote. The prophetic task is one of criticism and demand within the present situation. This adherence by the critic to the pragmatic situation, rather than to an absolute model of society to be achieved in the end of days, is exactly what makes his critique, in Buber's eyes, effective and timely in manifold situations in human history.

The Charismatic Nature of the Relationship

By defining the role of the intellectual as active participant in the process of social transformation, and by limiting that participation to the critique of empirical situations rather than to outbursts of Platonic visions, Buber introduced a demand for a pragmatic and civilized dialogue between intellectuals and those in power. However, in the same lecture we also find the seeds of a tradition which is partly inconsistent with such pragmatism—one conceiving the relationship between intellectuals and political authorities in charismatic rather than political terms. This stems from Buber's use of the prophet as role model: "wherever a living historical dialogue of divine and human actions breaks through," he declared in 1954, "there persists, visible or invisible, a bond with the prophecy of Israel" (PW, 203). Buber never defined the role of intellectuals in political terms (i.e., in terms of their location in the power structure). He rather endowed them with charisma—a Godly gift.

Edward Shils' portrayal of the intellectual as having a charismatic relationship with the political authorities holds true for Buber. "The man of spirit," wrote Buber,

> is one whom the spirit invades and seizes, whom the spirit uses
> as its garment, not one who contains the spirit. Spirit is an event,
> something which happens to man. The storm of the spirit sweeps
> man where it will, then storms on into the world. (PW, 187)

Buber hesitated to explicitly attribute a prophetic message to the modern intellectual. The social thinker is not a prophet but a philosopher, he admitted in apparent confusion at the end of his lecture. The thinker cannot be seen as having a prophetic message, he added, he has a teaching. At the same time, the social thinker was all but endowed with prophetic qualities. His is the prophetic task of criticism and demand within the present situation, Buber said. "Where an urgent question impinges, he cannot, of course, express criticism and demand as a message, but he can certainly express them on the basis of his knowledge" (PW, 190).

BUBER AND ISRAELI POLITICS

Buber and his disciples who followed the above tradition in the early years of statehood had, in my opinion, a greater impact on Israeli politics than has previously been acknowledged. Let me now demonstrate that impact by reference to three main issue areas: (a) Israel's relations with Germany, (b) the treatment of the Arab minority, and (c) the Aharon Cohen case.

Israel's Relations with Germany

Buber's position on the complex question of Israel's relations with Germany after the Holocaust was rather hard for most Israelis to identify with. His conciliatory statements as well as his willingness to accept prizes and other honors by German institutions, especially the peace prize granted him by the German Book Trade in Frankfurt in 1953, sparked angry response in Israel and throughout the Jewish world. He could hardly expect understanding of his statements in praise of a "German authenticity that had overcome the German self-betrayal" (quoted in Friedman MBLW-Later, 121) or of the Holocaust as a "historical fact" which is "ultimately a problem of the German People" (127). Neither had Buber's involvement in this matter been too helpful to those, such as Prime Minister Ben-Gurion, who supported German-Israeli relations in the economic and diplomatic spheres for reasons of realpolitik. Their cause was not enhanced by demands for reconciliation in an ethical or theological sense.

However, the dialogue over relations with Germany, which lasted in an intense form for two decades, had also been part of Israel's attempt to define its raison d'être as well as its position in the world—and here

Buber played a decisive role. Ben-Gurion utilized the question of relations with Germany in order to ideologically justify placing the sovereign state of Israel at center stage of Jewish life. The Eichmann trial in
particular had been an opportunity for the prime minister to redefine
Israeli sovereignty in a way that would elevate the new state to be the
champion of Jewish destiny (Keren 1991). In Ben-Gurion's words, "The
Jewish state (which is called Israel) is the heir of the six million who
were murdered, the only heir" (Ben-Gurion 1960). Ben-Gurion considered Israeli sovereignty as the only plausible response to the persecution
of Jews in history, and the Israeli government the only legitimate
authority to put Eichmann on trial.

The way a new nation-state defines its sovereignty, especially the
boundaries of its sovereignty, is by no means a trivial matter from a practical point of view. How different things could have been in Israel may be
seen by recalling statements by those who considered the German question, and other questions concerning Israel's relations with the world-
community, in tribal terms. To the right-wing ideologue Israel Eldad, for
instance, the trial of Eichmann did not even require involvement of the
state's system of justice: "There is a law of the Torah regarding Amalek,
which is both a law of justice and a law of vengeance, since vengeance is
also justice" (Eldad 1961). As the experience of many new nations
reveals, tribalist norms could easily have turned into government policies were it not for the intellectuals who had balanced them. In the
Eichmann trial, as in other matters, Martin Buber led the camp demanding that the new state behave in accordance with universalist norms.
True, his objection to the trial was rather incomprehensible, and his call
to not execute the Nazi murderer raised more furor than sympathy. But
the very debate over universal norms—the call for an international tribunal, the claim that there is no retribution for crimes of such magnitude, the need to prevent expiating the guilt felt by young Germans,
etc.—did not allow vengeance to become the sole criterion for evaluating
Israel's position vis-à-vis Germany or vis-à-vis other societies.

Treatment of the Arab Minority

In the early years of statehood, Buber's activities in the sphere of Jewish-
Arab relations were conducted mainly as part of the tiny Ihud (Union)
group formed within the League for Jewish-Arab Rapprochement in
1942. The group included only a handful of intellectuals, and its publication Balavot (Problems), replaced after independence by the biweekly
Ner (Light), had no large audience. As Maurice Friedman has noted, Ihud

"remained a limited circle without strong impact on public life, making its appeal to the people more by the written than the spoken word" (*MBLW:Later*, 10). And yet the words written in *Ner* played an important historical role in a limited but crucial number of instances—notably in the Kfar Kassim massacre.

On October 29, 1956, the day the Sinai campaign began, forty-seven Arab civilians were murdered by an Israeli border patrol zealously enforcing curfew in the Arab village of Kfar Kassim, which lived under Israeli military rule. The cold-blooded execution of villagers returning from work in the fields, who were not even aware of the curfew, shocked Israeli society and became a sad landmark in its history. The trials of those responsible for the massacre did not diminish the pain inflicted by the incident as well as the realization that the Jewish state failed in avoiding injustices which some defined as the inevitable cost of statehood (Steiner 1985).

The important role of public opinion in this matter must be recalled. Governments are always reluctant to admit to crimes, especially at times of war, and have many means with which to whitewash incidents of that nature. True, immediately after being notified of the massacre, David Ben-Gurion called for an investigation. The investigation had been completed within a week and charges were filed without delay. Yet the government's first announcement of the incident on November 6 reveals how reluctant it was to open up the matter. Only on December 12, as a result of growing pressure by public opinion, did Ben-Gurion make a formal announcement to the Knesset providing a detailed account of the events.

Buber's Ihud group played an important role in the mobilization of public opinion in this incident. Its council held an emergency meeting on November 15, condemning the actions and demanding the trial of the offenders in public and not in camera. Ihud demanded that the accusation not be limited to some local officers but rather include all those responsible, notwithstanding rank and position. A letter in that spirit was sent to the Prime Minister (see *Ner* 1956). *Ner* had put the Kfar Kassim incident in perspective, hinting at the analogy to pogroms suffered by Jews in their history. This way the events could not easily be interpreted as an outgrowth of the tension created by the Sinai campaign. It was a police action conducted within the boundaries of the state against peaceable and unarmed citizens, Ihud charged. Buber and his associates placed the full responsibility on the government and called for mass protests, wondering why other thinkers, religious figures, professors, judges, and doctors remained silent.

Ner also played an important role through its interpretation of the Prime Minister's address to the Knesset on December 12. Ben-Gurion's address defined the massacre as an act that strikes at the most sacred foundations of human morality, drawn from Israel's Torah, and went on to talk about the pride the Jewish people can take in their respect for human life. He recalled the Torah's demand for one law for the stranger and the citizen, quoting at length the appropriate verses from the Hebrew Scriptures. As recently claimed by historian Yigal Elam, this was part of a process whereby the tragic incident was turned into a purifying ritual of a whole society priding itself on its system of justice (Elam 1991). But *Ner* stood firm against it. An article by Rabbi Benyamin exposed ingenuine elements in Ben-Gurion's speech, stressing the need to analyze the motives and reasons which led to the Kfar Kassim massacre rather than engage in quoting biblical commandments. He referred to the militaristic mood which made the murders possible and demanded of the country's leadership that they ask for forgiveness as an indication of change in that mood (Benyamin 1956).

This was one of several cases in which the high, prophetic language of politics of the Ben-Gurion era was challenged by the topical, empirical tradition of the intellectuals. Ben-Gurion had been known for frequently drawing connections between deeds by the state of Israel and prophetic morality. The intellectuals, however, refused to associate the earthly state with heavenly ideals, realizing that such an association sanctifies every act of the state. To Ben-Gurion, present reality in the state of Israel represented the unfolding of messianic vision. Buber realized the danger implied by such historicist notions which subordinate the human spirit to the political principle. Buber not only engaged in theoretical discussions over this matter (see Syrkin 1957), but constantly pointed at those instances in which the state's behavior was inconsistent with the principles professed by Ben-Gurion. This was particularly apparent as regards the issue of military rule over the Arab population in Israel until the mid-sixties.

As in other matters, it is hard to measure the effect Buber had in the question of military rule. His diverse activities in this area—writing letters and articles, participating in public meetings, setting up study missions, calling press conferences, etc.—obviously did not persuade Ben-Gurion himself. But it set the stage for the abolition of military rule shortly after Ben-Gurion's resignation.

Moreover, Buber's activities and those of other intellectuals had a constraining function all along, preventing the well-known phenomenon whereby minorities are suppressed for decades without anyone paying attention. The intellectuals served as spokesmen for people who had difficulty forming pressure groups of their own. They monitored the conditions among Israel's Arabs and did not allow politicians to rely on the public's short memory as far as their past statements and promises were concerned. They provided important legitimacy to political groups committed to the nonpartisan public movement against military rule. Intellectuals analyzed contradictions in policies, nullified misleading concepts, specified the normative questions involved, and stated universal norms—such as equal rights—which ought to be adhered to. They confronted religious figures allegedly devoted to such norms and exposed inconsistencies between politicians' declarations and their voting record. Above all, they kept the issue on the public agenda.

The Aharon Cohen Case

Nothing is more crucial to the workings of an open society than keeping issues on the agenda. For example, in 1958 Aharon Cohen, a kibbutz member and scholar, was arrested for unlawful contacts with a Soviet agent. The protocol of Cohen's investigation, published recently (Cohen 1991), reveals once again how important it is to conduct the affairs of state in the open. The investigation brings to light how difficult it is for an individual, however powerful, to prove his innocent motives to government officials determined to incriminate him. It also reveals how crucial the involvement by Buber had been in this case. Buber appeared as the defense's first witness in an open session of Cohen's trial, which was otherwise conducted behind closed doors, and contributed a great deal to putting the trial in perspective. Defendants in espionage trials cannot usually expect fair treatment by public opinion, especially when their trial is not conducted openly. However, Buber's portrayal of Cohen's sincerity helped provide a balanced picture of the person and his deed.

This minor incident in Israeli history is rather indicative of the political importance of Buber's presence and activities in those years. Israel lived under severe security threats and faced massive espionage efforts by the Soviet Union. The Soviet espionage network relied heavily on local supporters, and Aharon Cohen, a scholar associated with the Marxist Mapam movement, secretly exchanged information with a member of the "Soviet Scientific Mission" in Jerusalem. No wonder the security services were furious and a heavy sentence was demanded. At the same time, several intellectuals felt uncomfortable, suspecting a government plot to prevent publication of an unfavorable book by Cohen on Arab-Israeli relations. In perspective, both sides were probably wrong; Cohen was no spy, and the government did not conspire to ban publication of his book. What is significant, however, is that Cohen's trial was conducted under

the watchful eye of the intellectuals. The Israeli public became quite perplexed but was spared the ugly phenomena associated with espionage trials (e.g., the development of unjustified purges).

CONCLUSION

Intellectual dialogue plays a decisive role in open societies, determining
their capacity to remain open or fall prey to authoritarianism. During
the Ben-Gurion era, the conditions were ripe for an authoritarian regime
to evolve, given the great external threat, deep social and political cleav-
ages, many economic hardships, the presence of a charismatic leader,
and the lack of political experience. Yet Israel remained democratic.
This may be partly attributed to the intellectual tradition discussed
here, one encouraging critical dialogue between society and the state
and endowing intellectuals with the role of watchdogs over the government. The willingness of Israeli intellectuals to play this role and their
focus on concrete issues, especially those concerning the Arab minority,
were crucial to the maintenance of an open society.

However, the tradition endowing the intellectual with prophetic
spirit and the definition of the relationship between intellectuals and the
state in charismatic terms, rather than in terms of their location in the
institutional structure and the power game, prevented them from taking
a greater part in both. The important involvement by intellectuals in the
political process did not lead to a serious attempt on their behalf to
reform the political system itself. After all, one could not rely on occasional intervention by the intellectuals. Their contribution must be institutionalized, not necessarily through their own political groups but
through their role in fashioning well-functioning democratic institutions.

The intellectuals' lack of attention to political reform was particularly apparent during the Lavon Affair—a political scandal over a security
mishap—which dominated Israeli politics in the 1960s. Ben-Gurion
demanded the establishment of a judicial committee to investigate the
mishap, while the intellectuals sided with the political forces objecting
to that demand. The intellectuals' stand, stemming from their perception
of the Lavon affair as a prophetic struggle against "political messianism"
(Avinery 1965), contributed to Ben-Gurion's resignation in 1963. In perspective, however, they were on the wrong side, missing a historic opportunity to support the principles Ben-Gurion stood for in that affair:
division of powers and adherence to appropriate judicial and political procedures in the life of the state. For such procedures are the main guarantee against the abuse of government power in democratic societies.

REFERENCES

Avinery, Shlomo. (1965). "Israel in the Post Ben-Gurion Era: The Nemesis of Messianism." *Midstream* 11 (February): 16–32.

Ben-Gurion, David. (1960). Letter to Joseph M. Proskauer, July 7. Ben-Gurion Archives, Tel Aviv.

Benyamin, Rabbi. (1956). "Kfar Kassim Be'sha'arei Haknesset." *Ner: Monthly for Political and Social Problems and for Jewish-Arab Rapprochement* 8 (November–December).

Buber, Martin. "The Demand of the Spirit and Historical Reality" and "Prophecy, Apocalyptic, and the Historical Hour," in *PW*.

Cohen, Aharon. (1991). *Guf Rishon, Guf Shlishi*. Tel Aviv: Sifriat Hapoalim. (Hebrew)

Elam, Yigal. (1991). *The Executors*. Jerusalem: Keter. (Hebrew)

Eldad, Israel. (1961). "The Nazi Argument . . ." *Haboker* (August 18). (Hebrew)

Friedman, Maurice. (1983). *Martin Buber's Life and Works: The Later Years, 1945–1965*. New York: Dutton.

Kaufmann, Walter. (1984). "Buber's Failures and Triumph." In Haim Gordon and Jochanan Block, eds., *Martin Buber: A Centenary Volume*. New York: KTAV.

Keren, Michael. (1983). *Ben-Gurion and the Intellectuals: Power, Knowledge and Charisma*. DeKalb: Northern Illinois University Press.

———. (1991). "Ben-Gurion's Theory of Sovereignty: The Trial of Adolph Eichmann." In *David Ben-Gurion: Politics and Leadership in Israel*. London: Frank Case.

———. (1989). *The Pen and the Sword: Israeli Intellectuals and the Making of the Nation State*. Boulder, CO: Westview.

Ner: Monthly for Political and Social Problems and for Jewish-Arab Rapprochement. (1956). Vol. 8 (November–December).

Popper, Karl. (1945). *The Open Society and its Enemies*. London: Routledge.

Rotenstreich, Nathan. (1957). "Israel and Zionism: A Discussion" (Correspondence with Ben-Gurion). *Jewish Frontier* 24 (December).

Shils, Edward. (1973). "Intellectuals, Traditions and the Traditions of Intellectuals: Some Preliminary Considerations." In *Intellectuals and Tradition*, S. N. Eisenstadt and S. R. Graubard, eds. New York: Humanities Press.

Steiner, George. (1985). "Our Homeland, the Text." *Salmagundi* 66 (Winter-Spring): 4–25.

Syrkin, Marie. (1957). "Out of Zion: A Report of the Ideological Conference." *Midstream* 3 (Autumn):

Talmon, Jacob L. (1957). *Utopianism and Politics.* London: Conservative Political Centre.

———. (1960). *Political Messianism: The Romantic Phase.* New York: Prager.

CHAPTER 20

MARTIN BUBER AND THE SHOAH

JERRY D. LAWRITSON

Did Martin Buber respond to the Shoah? If so, in what way? When a person addresses these questions, he or she might well be reminded of the words written by Carl Kerenyi: "The men of fire also have to do with great darknesses" (*PMB*, 637).

It was to be Buber's role as the leader of Jewish Education in Germany between 1933 and 1938 (when he finally left Germany for Jerusalem) that was to make him, along with Rabbi Leo Baeck, the leader of Jewish spiritual resistance against the Nazis in Germany. As one assesses Buber's response to the radical evil of the Nazis and to the Shoah, this five year period of his life cannot be allowed to remain out of account. Abraham Heschel once remarked: "This was the period of Buber's true greatness" (Friedman, *MBLW:Middle*, 177).

Events in Buber's life between 1933 and 1938 tell us something singularly important. Today scholars and students may discuss radical evil as present in the Nazis, but Buber faced it in the midst of the lived concrete. The measure of the man's stance in relationship to the Nazis and the Shoah must be placed within the historical and sociological context of the time and not simply removed to the level of an abstract debate. In the lived situation Buber showed himself to be partially blind, but still able to penetrate to the truthful reality more quickly than many, and to be a man of great courage.

Perhaps one of the most remarkable exchanges that Buber had at this time was with Mahatma Gandhi. On November 26, 1938—only

seven days after *Kristallnacht*—Gandhi published a statement in his
paper *Harijan* suggesting that the Jews in Germany use soul-force and
nonviolent resistance against the Nazis. Buber wrote a public reply inasmuch as the effect of Gandhi's statement was the demoralization of
much of the Jewish community in Germany. He refused Gandhi's parallel between the Indians in South Africa in 1905 and the Jews in
Germany in the 1930s. He proclaimed that he had seen, during the last
five years in Germany, many instances of Jews exhibiting soul-force and
nonviolent resistance, "instances showing a strength of spirit wherein
there was no question of bartering their rights or of being bowed down,
and where neither force nor cunning was used to escape the consequences of their behavior." Yet, these actions had not the slightest effect
upon their opponents. Buber's words to Gandhi did not shrink back in
the face of the evil of the hour:

> Now do you know or *do you not* know, Mahatma, what a con-
> centration camp is like and what goes on there? Do you know
> of the torments in the concentration camp, of its methods of
> slow and quick slaughter? . . . Testimony without acknowledg-
> ment, ineffective, unobserved martyrdom, a martyrdom cast to
> the winds—that is the fate of innumerable Jews in Germany.
> God alone accepts their testimony, and God "seals" it, as is
> said in our prayers. . . . Such martyrdom is a deed—but who
> would venture to demand it? (*MBLW:Middle*, 173)

Yet, it seems clear from the record that Buber, like so many others
who had lived in Germany, had, as a member of the Jewish community,
become accustomed to a certain level of anti-Jewishness in the culture
surrounding him and in which, up until 1933, he had deep communal
affiliation. While Buber was quick to reach the insight that the German-
Jewish symbiotic relationship had come to an end and recognized the
full threat of the Nazis' neopagan and totalitarian state to Germany, its
culture, and its history, he still could not fathom the actual threat to the
German Jewish community. Like most of his contemporaries he had no
way of anticipating the extermination of the Jewish people; the actual
threat remained, even to him, hidden. It was as though even he, with his
tremendous power to penetrate into the depths of life, could only penetrate so far and no further. What inhibited further penetration to deeper
insight was a long life lived with some level of anti-Jewishness.
Persecution in the Diaspora was partly what defined its historical character. What made the Nazi threat and persecution any different? What
indeed! But, as soon as we say that, we have uttered our words from the
position of hindsight. In that time and in that place, few anticipated,

understood, or—when reports began to flow—even believed it possible. In the midst of the monster's maw, Buber saw the teeth, but did not think they would close so tightly. Still, in Germany during the Nazi years of 1933–1938, he did everything he could to resist the Nazi order, define its true nature, help the people of the Jewish community retain their identity as Jews, hold their heads high, gather courage in their lives, and refuse the forces of dehumanization. He also taught a whole generation spiritual rootedness before they went to Palestine, to other parts of the world, or to the death camps. He did his best to accept and fulfill the responsibility of being a teacher.

The distinguished contemporary Jewish philosopher Emil Fackenheim wrote in his book *To Mend the World*:

> How was it with Buber? . . . did he—could he—confront the Holocaust? That the prospects in this regard are unpromising is recognized by any student of Buber's thought. Buber had a life-long difficulty with the recognition of evil. (1982, 195)

Inasmuch as Maurice Friedman has shown that Buber was preoccupied with the problem of evil during the course of his life's work, this seems a strange statement from Fackenheim.[1] Be that as it may, we must now, after understanding something about Buber's life in Germany under the Nazi regime, seek the answer to the question of whether Martin Buber confronted the Shoah.

Fackenheim, again in *To Mend the World*, wrote: "Remarkably enough, Buber's *thought* was, despite all, shaken by the Holocaust, and this not at its political periphery but rather at what may be called its religious center" (196, italics mine). However, we must understand that it was not just Buber's *thought* that was so shaken but his living, that is, his living the lived concrete. Buber's *life* was shaken. Anyone who understands Buber perceives that his thought served to express what he had first come to know, i.e., in the original Hebrew sense of to touch or be connected, through event and meeting. This is a crucial understanding when anyone comes to assess or critique Buber's response to the Shoah. To this understanding we shall return. First let us look at what is known about Buber's initial response to the Shoah.

By the early 1940s reports of the mass murder of Polish Jews reached Jerusalem. Even though Buber had known of the camps, and even though his friend Otto Hirsch had been murdered in Mauthausen in 1941, he could not fully credit these reports of mass murder. He thought that if only 10 to 15 percent of what was being reported was true this would be frightful enough. He saw this as a consequence of war and as something that should not be exploited for political purposes.

This was a stance common not only in Jerusalem but in the United States (Lipstadt 1986).

Walter Goldstein, Buber's friend, commented concerning him: "For a long while afterward he did not perceive the cruel reality. . . . His whole being resisted 'accepting' what exceeded his imagination and was incompatible with any of his basic views" (MBLW:Middle, 306). It is fair to say that Buber held a high view of human beings. This was derived from his own lived life, from roots sunk deep in the Bible and Hasidism and in much of the European Enlightenment. His basic views would not have been compatible with ready acceptance of Auschwitz. To what degree this constitutes a real critique of him is an open question. What may be more incisive is that he "resisted 'accepting' what exceeded his imagination," as Walter Goldstein put it. I would argue that it was not a case of "'accepting' what exceeded his imagination" at all. Rather it was Buber's inability to know the "cruel reality" from his own life stance of "inclusion," the capacity to feel the other's side of the event. A primary example is when Buber lay in bed for a week feeling in his own body the kicks and blows that struck and killed his close friend Landauer. Even at the end of his own life Buber could not speak of Landauer's death without great difficulty. Another example is what he wrote in 1914 in his short essay "To the Contemporary" (TTF, 59–60). Here the pain of those suffering the brutalities of World War I comes to him as the "invading power of the contemporary" and "hurl[s] the earth-space of this moment like a firebrand" upon his breast. He wondered how he could withstand the infinity of that moment. In my judgment, it was not that the Shoah presented Buber with views incompatible with his own that prevented him from "perceiving the cruel reality." It was, rather, that the "cruel reality" presented him with an "other" that was incapable of "inclusion." And this shook Buber's life and caused him the rest of his days to be preoccupied with the Shoah. So, when a lifelong adjustment to anti-Jewishness that dimmed sight was finally broken for Buber, the way passed into a "cruel reality" with which in the final grasp no "inclusion" could form an adequate relationship. Dimmed sight passed into darkness—the darkness of the eclipse of God.

Thus, any discussion of Buber and the Shoah must include the acknowledgement of four further elements. First, when the credibility of reports regarding the Shoah became clear in Jerusalem in 1945–1946, Buber finally believed them, even though he still could not fathom the unimaginable horror. He once said that for the rest of his life not an hour passed in which he did not think of the Holocaust (MBLW:Middle, 306). Second, in 1944 in his article "Silence and Outcry," Buber took to task those who saw the unprecedented catastrophe only in terms of individual relatives or friends and thus hid the true dimensions of the horrible event from view. In addition, he could not understand why the Jewish Settlement knew what was happening months before and kept it a secret from the rest of the community. When the community heard what was going on, it kept silent, and Buber found this incomprehensible. He challenged his contemporaries, but also himself, with words of existential importance and courage:

> [It is] our duty to display a sufficient amount of imagination . . . to weave whatever happens into the fabric of our lives—not in order to emit the customary roar of revenge in which there is mere relief of tension, but rather in order to be effective, to cooperate where it is possible to do something. (308)

Buber went on to say that the outcry that came after the silence of the community was that the reports were used by various factions within Palestine for their own political purposes at the direct expense of harming the rescue effort itself! Buber's own outcry opposed and resisted this turn of events. What was needed at this late hour he concluded was "to save as many Jews as possible by treating realistically the various practical questions with all means at our disposal, wherever and whenever there is still someone to be saved" (309).

Third, Buber, because of the Shoah, knew the concrete world to be unredeemed. In 1943 he stated this in a letter to the Jewish disciple of Leonhard Ragaz, Lina Lewy:

> I may not believe in a Messiah who has already come . . . because I sense the unredeemedness of the world all too deeply to be able to agree with the conception of a completed redemption—even if it be only of the "soul" (I will not live with a "redeemed" soul in an unredeemed world). (MBLW:Later, 46–47)

Again, in his memorial address for Leonhard Ragaz, who died in December of 1945, Buber spoke of the profound unredeemedness of the world reflecting the terror of the Shoah. "In our view redemption occurs forever," he said, "and none has yet occurred. Standing, bound and shackled, in the pillory of mankind, we demonstrate with the bloody body of our people the unredeemedness of the world" (47).

Fourth, Buber judged the Shoah to be an event of unprecedented cruelty, the greatest crime ever undertaken by a state organization. This must be underscored because of something Buber himself wrote in 1948 in his foreword to his book Two Types of Faith: "The work involved has helped me endure in faith this war, for me the most grievous of the three" (15).

Emil Fackenheim, along with others, views this statement as "a lapse in judgment." This conclusion is drawn by Fackenheim and others because Buber here is referring to the first Arab/Israeli war and the so-called seige of Jerusalem during which time he wrote *Two Types of Faith*. But, since the other two wars indicated in Buber's words are World Wars I and II and World War II includes the Shoah, Buber's "lapse in judgment" seems apparent (Fackenheim 1982, 195–96). It must be noted, however, that a distinction must be drawn between guilt and responsibility. In this statement Buber is acknowledging his own sense of guilt in relationship to the first Arab/Israeli war. After all, he had been a long time leader in the Zionist movement and had undertaken much work toward educating German and European Jews so that they might fulfill their tasks in Palestine as Jews. He accepted his own sense of guilt for what now had taken place in Palestine, in Jerusalem.[2] The simple fact is that Buber did not acknowledge guilt for the Shoah even though he knew himself to be responsible for responding to those directly involved in it as victims, onlookers, or executioners. This response he made very clear in his address given at Frankfurt-am-Main in Paulskirche on September 27, 1953, upon the occasion of receiving the Peace Prize of the German Book Trade. His second paragraph began:

> About a decade ago a considerable number of Germans—there must have been many thousands of them—under the indirect command of the German government and the direct command of its representatives, killed millions of my people in a system-atically prepared and executed procedure whose organized cru-elty cannot be compared with any previous event. (*PW*, 232)

Referring to those who took part in this procedure, Buber concluded his second paragraph by saying:

> They have so radically removed themselves from the human sphere—so transposed themselves into a sphere of monstrous inhumanity inaccessible to my conception, that not even hatred, much less over-coming hatred, was able to arise in me. And what am I that I could here presume to "forgive"! (232)

We find here that Buber was able to alter his basic views when con-fronted by an "other" that really demanded it of him. We find also here that very important concession on his part that this "other" still remained "inaccessible" to his "conception." Buber faced the radical evil of "monstrous inhumanity," named it, and condemned it.

In 1959 Buber was interviewed in Jerusalem for a German televi-sion station by Thilo Koch. In response to a question asked about the

Shoah, Buber said that "although millions of Jews were murdered," for him "the historical fact is ultimately a problem of the German people." He went on to state:

> I do not forget for a moment and cannot forget what has happened. But I ask myself ever again from where and how did it happen, and then I do not arrive at any general motive of hatred of the Jews but at a particular historical crisis of the German people that I hardly understand, something that has taken place only once in history: that such a people has succumbed to the subhuman, and by such a people I mean precisely the people of Bach and Hölderlin. (MBLW:Later, 127)

Thus Buber saw the Shoah as an unprecedented act of subhuman or antihuman proportions, the kind of which history had never before known. Again, in 1963, Buber said of the Shoah that it "remains inscribed in world history as the greatest crime that was ever initiated by a state organization as such" (MBLW:Middle, 176). Clearly, Buber understood the gravity of the Shoah and responded to it. He suffered no lapse in judgment along these lines. He spoke, and his speaking was, as his friend Werner Kraft said, "like a belated shudder" (221).

Earlier it was said that for Buber dimmed sight passed into darkness. It is to the darkness of the eclipse of God that we must turn. We must do so because Buber's conception of the eclipse of God is his profound response to the Shoah.

That the conception of the eclipse of God (already alluded to in 1928 in "Dialogue") occupied Buber from 1939 until his death in 1965 is well documented. It must be stated from the outset that a thorough explication of Buber's conception of the eclipse of God, to my knowledge, has still to be written. Be that as it may, we may still indicate some important aspects of this concept as they relate to Buber's response to the Shoah. This, I think, may be done in a very brief and limited fashion.

If we ask concerning the roots for Buber of the conception of the eclipse of God we would have to name Biblical roots, Kabbalistic roots, Hasidic roots. To students of these various strands of tradition, this would come as no surprise. Nor would it come as a surprise to students of Buber. What may also be noted is that this conception also has roots in Buber's work in sociology, specifically his preoccupation with the formation of genuine community. Pivotal in this regard is his encounter with A. D. Gordon in 1921. Gordon was a Russian labor philosopher and pioneer who came to Palestine at the age of fifty and worked on a kibbutz for sixteen years until his death. Above all it was Gordon's witness from the depths that seized Buber. Gordon had said: "We lack religious faith in everything we do" (OZ, 158). This carried, for him, concrete sociological consequences in terms of community. This situation is destructive of that very relationship upon which community rests. Earlier Buber had written that one suffers "a radical forlornness," or "what the religious individual would call distance from God, a void of God." He wrote this in 1919 and stipulated that the way out of such a situation rested in "turning," by which he meant the bold assertion that the renewal of community was possible (Mendes-Flohr 1989, 113–14). I underscore the sociological roots of Buber's conception of the eclipse of God for a simple reason. The conception had a reference for him that was anything but abstract or spiritualized (i.e., removed from the mundane). Even as Buber undertook his interpretive study of the hiding God in the prophetic witness of ancient Israel, he was mindful that for the prophet this meant a concrete event and was not simply a theologism. In 1963 he wrote in "Replies to My Critics":

> But when does God hide Himself? That Isaiah had already clearly expressed once (8:8,17.20): if a people "scorns" the "slow water" of the true historical happening, then God hides His face from before it until it turns "to instruction and to witness." (PMB, 730)

True historical happening for Buber was event, concrete event, paradoxical as that event might be. Unless we come to understand that for Buber the eclipse of God carried concrete reference, we miss the clear profundity of his utterance concerning this event during the last twenty-six years of his life. It is as though he had taken the scroll of the prophet Isaiah and read 45:15—"Truly, thou art a God who hidest thyself, O God of Israel, the Savior"—then putting down the scroll, looked at those around him and said, "Today this reading has been fulfilled in your midst!" For Buber, the eclipse of God was no lapse simply into tradition or metaphor. What then was it?

André Neher has indicated that for Buber the Biblical metaphor of "God hiding His Face" is understood primarily at the metaphysical level. That is: "It is a wager on the unknown and on silence." There is hope here in the face of disaster. There is liberty here in the face of death. But nothing concerning the future is assured beforehand (Neher 1981, 53). Neher also makes the salient point that both Martin Buber and Elie Wiesel have this Biblical understanding as a source of their philosophic ideas. It is a point that should not be lost to us.

Buber first used the phrase "eclipse of God" to interpret his own contemporary understanding of the hiding of God's face in his Hasidic-Chronicle novel Gog and Magog (For the Sake of Heaven), written in

1941 (116). Much has been said and could be said about this classic book, a work that Buber wrote in direct response to World War II. Apart from what explicit language is used or not used (the phrase "eclipse of God" is not used often in the book), the obscuring of the light of heaven by something that steps in between God and humanity forms a core element in the novel. It is a book about evil, trust, and turning. But, the darkness of the light of heaven covers its pages and its *niggun* (melody). Yet, Buber's most stark utterances concerning the eclipse of God came later in other addresses, a book, and letters. It is not my purpose here to cover all of this material. I wish only to bring to the fore three major aspects of Buber's conception of the eclipse of God as his response to the Shoah.

First, there is a profound *ontological* aspect to Buber's conception of the eclipse of God. As we have already heard, André Neher understands Buber's conception as one resting on the level of metaphysics. At the end of his lecture on "God and the Spirit of Man," Buber states: "In our age the I-It, gigantically swollen, has usurped, practically uncontested, the mastery and the rule. . . . It steps in between and shuts off from us the light of heaven" (*EG*, 129). As Buber later made clear to Fackenheim in "Replies to My Critics," this is not the I-It relationship itself, but its hubris, our own selves are meant.[3] And to this issue Buber devoted an entire book titled *The Eclipse of God*. Something ontological has here occurred. Relationship itself has been overpowered and altered. We may not hear or know God because we think there is no God to hear. We may hear God but only as the God within ourselves, a product of our subjectivist reductionism in extremis. At any rate, we have altered the ontology of the between. This has been much discussed not only by Buber himself but by Fackenheim and others. But, to complete the ontological aspect of the eclipse of God one must understand the other side of the dialectic. In his reply, Buber continued:

> That is the side of the event known to us. The other, the divine side, is called in the holy books of Israel the hiding of God, the veiling of the divine countenance. Nothing more than such an anthropomorphic image seems to be granted us. (*PMB*, 716)

Here, Buber truly means the hiding of God, the turning of God's face away from the human. This is no abstraction for Buber. It is a presentiment, a knowing, a seeing. An alteration to the ontology of the between has occurred. Humanity is not the same. God is not the same in the sense that the Absolute Person has concealed the Divine Face. The "between" of the relationship has been changed. In speaking of the Kingdom of Night, Elie Wiesel has said that something ontological happened. Because he is a survivor of Auschwitz, we take Wiesel with great seriousness when he gives such considered testimony. And we should. But what we have to understand is that Martin Buber had pointed to the alteration of the ontology of the between in his conception of the eclipse of God from at least 1941 to the time of his death. Both sides of the ontological aspect of the eclipse of God must be seen or the profundity and gravity of Buber's insight shall be lost to view. When Wiesel stated that "With the advent of the Nazi regime in Germany, humanity became witness to what Martin Buber would call an eclipse of God" (*MBLW:Later*, 146), he was pointing to this ontological alteration manifest in the Shoah. Neither he nor Buber would disagree in this understanding.

This brings us to the second major aspect of the eclipse of God as Buber understood it. In his reply to Fackenheim, Buber continued in a most disturbing manner:

> One may also call what is meant here a silence of God's or rather, since I cannot conceive of any interruption of divine revelation, a condition that works on us as a silence of God. One is right to see here a "most troubling question." These last years in a great searching and questioning, seized ever anew by the shudder of the now, I have arrived no further than I now distinguish a revelation through the hiding of the face, a speaking through the silence. The eclipse of God can be seen with one's eyes, it will be seen.[4]

As can clearly be understood, Buber points us to the dimension of *silence* and to silence as communication, indeed, revelation through silence. Considering that his reply to Fackenheim appears to be his last written statement on the eclipse of God, this is no small matter. We are reminded of the famine of God's Word as described by the prophet Amos (*Amos* 8:11–12). We are also reminded of the "thin silence" that was the Voice speaking to Elijah (*I Kings* 19:12–13). It is crucial to note that Buber is silent on the *content* of this revelation. The reason for this is that Buber consistently denied objective content as a primary aspect of revelation. What works on Buber here is no content—it is the silence itself. A silence, thin or thick, that is so manifestly real for him that he says it can and will be seen! Further than this he cannot go; therefore, he cannot say. Silence, for Buber, is the second major aspect of the eclipse of God, and a most disturbing one at that. What we must note and note well is that Wiesel himself is the primary witness for the silence issuing from the Kingdom of Night. He explores throughout his work the various levels and meanings of silence. This is most significant coming from a survivor of the death camps. Of course, Buber did not explicate the dimensions of silence. But, he did emphatically point to silence as a major aspect of the eclipse of God in our own historical hour (Neher 1981, 210–26). Again, this is a most disturbing insight and an even more disturbing reality, but neither Buber nor Wiesel will let us evade it.

The third major aspect of Buber's conception of the eclipse of God may be spoken of as *staying with God*. The degree to which Buber took seriously the dimension of silence and yet stayed with God is set forth in a remarkable letter he wrote on July 2, 1950, to Ernst Szilagyi. This letter ends as follows:

> How is a Jewish life possible after Auschwitz? Today I no longer know what this is—a Jewish life. Nor do I expect ever again to experience it. But this I know: what it is to stay with Him. Those who in our time stay with Him lead over to that which one day may be called a Jewish life. (Fackenheim 1982, 197n.)

This is a troubling statement from one who readily accepted the Nazi epithet of being an "arch"-Jew." We must also note that Buber's last lectures on Judaism were given following the writing of this letter. May we surmise that Buber renewed his efforts to understand and live a specifically Jewish-humanistic existence precisely because of the Shoah? Be this as it may, we have here Buber's contention that he will "stay" with God. That he does not use the word "speak" with God is, as Fackenheim has underscored, hardly insignificant. Buber had long held that a person could not speak about God, but could speak to God. Here, he enters the dimension of silence and, while not speaking, stays. That this, for Buber, might also constitute a form of speech should not be lost to us. But it is a speaking, if at all, that is permeated by silence. Most important, it seems to be a staying in the face of silence—his own and God's—where what may be said is not yet known, and speaking itself is not assured ahead of time. I do not think this is an unfair rendering of Buber's intent as explicated in this letter.

During the remaining fifteen years of his life he continually warned against the gigantically swollen It, called upon human beings to turn and become once again human, and to stay with God though this latter may be most difficult.[5] Again, it must be noted that Wiesel also takes the life stance of staying with God. But he warns that the real agony, the real problems begin when a person chooses to stay with God instead of letting go. The real agony is that of the believer. "When one accepts God's presence, if not participation in history," he tells us, "his real agony begins" (Wiesel 1985, 250). That this "staying" with God is a struggle for Wiesel is well known to any who have heard him speak or read his work. It was, to be sure, also a struggle for Buber. Both the Jew Wiesel and the Jew Buber have struggled with God to stay with God—and this in spite of the Shoah.

That Buber explicitly linked his conception of the eclipse of God and the Shoah is a matter of record. In one of his most astounding addresses that comprised one of his three new speeches on Judaism given in 1951, he made this link publicly. "The Dialogue Between Heaven and Earth" deserves to be studied in its entirety, but for our purpose we quote only from its conclusion.

> In this our own time, one asks again and again: how is a Jewish life still possible after Auschwitz? I would like to frame this question more correctly: how is a life with God still possible in a time in which there is an Auschwitz? The estrangement has become too cruel, the hiddenness too deep. One can still "believe" in the God who allowed those things to happen, but can one still speak to Him? Can one still hear His word? Can one still, as an individual and as a people, enter at all into a dialogic relationship with Him? Can one still call to Him? Dare we recommend to the survivors of Auschwitz, the Job of the gas chambers: "Give thanks unto the Lord, for He is good; for His mercy endureth forever" (Psalm 106:1)? . . .
>
> And we?
>
> We—by that is meant all those who have not got over what happened and will not get over it. How is it with us? Do we stand overcome before the hidden face of God like the tragic hero of the Greeks before faceless fate? No, rather, even now we contend, we too, with God, even with Him, the Lord of Being, whom we once, we here, chose for our Lord. We do not put up with earthly being; we struggle for its redemption, and struggling we appeal to the help of our Lord, who is again and still a hiding one. In such a state we await His voice, whether it comes out of the storm or out of the stillness that follows it. Though His coming appearance resemble no earlier one, we shall recognize again our cruel and merciful Lord. (*OJ*, 224–25)

In this truly stark and profound statement, Buber inexorably links the Shoah and his response, the felt vision of the eclipse of God. He also steps forth as one who chooses to stay with the hiding God, contending with this God in the lived concrete and walking the narrow ridge of the holy insecurity of existential trust in this God. This is no bland assurance. Buber knows neither how nor where this God will reappear. Indeed, he does not even know *whether* this God will reappear. But Buber stays and contends with this God, trusting that it will be so. The human face turns toward God and waits for God's hiding to end. If we then ask what was Buber's response to the Shoah we are led into the depths of existence—our own existence—and to Buber's felt vision of the eclipse of God.

In closing it must be emphasized that Buber understood that he had not lived the Shoah. He understood that he stood outside of it, that he was never, like his friend Rabbi Leo Baeck, in Theresienstadt (*MBLW: Middle*, 221). Further, as we have discovered, though he thought of the Shoah hourly, Buber never could perceive it or understand it. When he did directly refer to it, he did so in the most measured and responsible terms. Finally, Buber never completely comprehended the eclipse of God. He felt it. He saw it. He went to the window and pointed to it for the rest of us. But, it remained for him an enigma sealed in a mystery. He struggled to plumb the depths of the human side of this eclipse, our own human responsibility for it. But God's side of the eclipse—Buber would never presume to know or speak about.

It is my contention that Buber, more than any other person of his generation, responded to the Shoah in fully human and responsible terms, terms that led him into the desert night to point to an event the likes of which no other of his contemporaries spoke, if they spoke of the Shoah at all.

Today we ourselves must wrestle in our own existence with the haunting question Buber left with us. And we? Do we perceive the eclipse of God? Before we answer, Buber's own words stand as warning:

> No way can be pointed to in this desert night, even though we can help men of today to stand fast, with their soul in readiness, until the dawn breaks and a path becomes visible where none suspected it. (*MBLW:Middle*, 325)

> But, He, however, who today knows nothing other to say than, "See there, it grows lighter!" he leads into error. (Schilpp and Friedman 1987, 716)

NOTES

1. Friedman 1955. Cf. especially part 4 on the nature and redemption of evil. On p. 101 of the 3rd edition, Friedman points out that Buber himself wrote that he had "been preoccupied with the problem of evil since his youth." Also, I must add that while a student in a graduate course on the life and work of Martin Buber at San Diego State University in 1989, Dr. Friedman remarked how he once tried to engage Dr. Fackenheim in personal conversation about *To Mend the World*—an attempt which the latter refused.

2. I owe this insight to Maurice Friedman, who commented along these lines at the Martin Buber Conference at SDSU in San Diego in the fall of 1991.
3. Schilpp and Friedman 1957, 715–16. But cf. also 738. Clearly in the latter statement Buber is concerned with the human turning toward God, the overcoming of the gigantically swollen I-It through the Hasidic teaching he brought into the world against its own will.
4. Schilpp and Friedman, 716. Buber here is referring to Fackenheim's statement on p. 289 of this same volume which has prompted this reply that may well be Buber's last written statement on the eclipse of God. It must also be noted that, in response to Fackenheim's question of whether a divine silence might persist "no matter how devoutly we listen," Buber's response was human turning toward God by saying "Thou" once again to the known human being; but, this *did not* mean for him a then automatic turning or non-hiding of God's face. It remains, as Neher wrote, "a wager on the unknown and on silence."
5. *The Later Years.*, esp. p. 166. The full range of Buber's believing humanism is set forth in this volume. Cf. also Grete Schaeder, *The Hebrew Humanism of Martin Buber.*

REFERENCES

Buber, Martin. *EG; FTSH; OJ; OZ; PW; TTF.*
Brown, Robert McAfee. (1983). *Elie Wiesel: Messenger to All Humanity.* Notre Dame: University of Notre Dame Press.
Fackenheim, Emil L. (1968). *Quest for Past and Future: Essays in Jewish Theology.* Boston: Beacon Press.
———. (1970). *God's Presence in History: Jewish Affirmations and Philosophical Reflections.* San Francisco: Harper & Row.
———. (1982). *To Mend the World: Foundations of Future Jewish Thought.* New York: Schocken.
Friedman, Maurice. *MBLW: Middle; MBLW: Later.*
Gilbert, Martin. (1985). *The Holocaust: A History of the Jews of Europe during the Second World War.* New York: Holt, Rinehart and Winston.
Gordon, Haim, and Bloch, Jochanan, eds. (1984). *Martin Buber: A Centenary Volume.* New York: KTAV.
Levin, Nora. (1968, 1973). *The Holocaust: The Destruction of European Jewry 1933–1945.* New York: Schocken.
Lipstadt, Deborah E. (1986). *Beyond Belief: The American Press and the Coming of the Holocaust 1933–1945.* New York: The Free Press.

Mendes-Flohr, Paul. (1989). *From Mysticism to Dialogue: Martin Buber's Transformation of German Social Thought*. Detroit: Wayne State University Press.

Neher, André. (5741, 1981). *The Exile of the Word: From the Silence of the Bible to the Silence of Auschwitz*. Trans. D. Maisel. Philadelphia: The Jewish Publication Society of America.

Schaeder, Grete. (1973). *The Hebrew Humanism of Martin Buber*. Trans. N. J. Jacobs. Detroit: Wayne State University Press.

Schilpp, Paul Arthur, and Friedman, Maurice, eds. *PMB*.

Wiesel, Elie. (1985). "The Fiery Shadow—Jewish Existence Out of the Holocaust." *Against Silence*. Vol. 1. Ed. I. Abrahamson. New York: Holocaust Library, 249–52.

PART V

DIALOGICAL PSYCHOTHERAPY AND CONTEXTUAL (INTERGENERATIONAL FAMILY) THERAPY

INTRODUCTION

VIRGINIA SHABATAY

I-Thou, I-It, presentness, imagining the real, wrestling with the polarities, confirmation—all part of Martin Buber's philosophy of dialogue—are central to psychotherapy. A dialogical psychotherapist creates an openness that encourages a meeting to take place between the one who has come for nurturing or healing and the one who aids in that healing. Such a setting allows for the I-Thou to enter.

The opposite of this climate is expressed well by T. S. Eliot in his poem "The Love Song of J. Alfred Prufrock":

> And I have known the eyes already, known them all—
> The eyes that fix you in a formulated phrase,
> And when I am formulated, sprawling on a pin,
> When I am pinned and wriggled on the wall,
> Then how should I begin
> To spit out all the butt-ends of my days and ways?
> And how should I presume?

Physicians and therapists can bring a patient to utter silence by retreating into a label—a label which may seem to the one in charge (and sometimes to the patient as well) as a place of security. This can prevent a setting out on the high seas to discover what one may find; one thinks one knows in advance. Thus does the I-It enter.

This is not to say that there is no place for the I-It, that realm where information and systems of "shared meanings" are present. However, as

313

James DeLeo notes in his essay "What is—Psychotherapy?" only in "the dynamic of relation" can we reach the client. The therapist who sees the client as a scientific object to analyze and dissect fails to enter into relationship. The "between" of which Buber writes only evolves out of relationship and can take place only through dialogue. Only then can "the atrophied personal center of the client" be healed through the meeting of therapist and client.

Rose Graf-Taylor's chapter, "Philosophy of Dialogue and Feminist Psychology," brings forth Buber's contribution to the women's movement by highlighting what it means to be in relation. A central issue for women has been the conflict between self and other. Feminists have pointed out that a woman's experience has not followed "the prescribed notions of the ideal self as autonomous, self-sufficient, and independent but that a different set of values and developmental imperatives exists." Instead, being in relationship, connecting with others, has been the way in which women live and develop. This being with others has been both women's danger and their strength. When a woman has banished her self and chosen to be a caretaker, she has succumbed to the pressure to negate her self. She buys into the notion that self-assertion is selfish and "contradictory to care for others," and thus she becomes servant and not partner. A woman cannot be an I to a Thou without the recognition that distance from others is central to relationship, a concept Buber discusses at length in *The Knowledge of Man*. Feminists have helped eliminate this choice between self and other.

In "Problems of Confirmation in Psychotherapy," Tamar Kron and Maurice Friedman define confirmation as both acceptance of and challenge to the client. Kron and Friedman examine five areas of potential conflict and illustrate some with several interesting case studies: (1) Can the first interview balance diagnosis with the personal? (2) Can the therapist push beyond the symptoms the client brings to other areas which appear problematic? (3) How does the arrangement of the therapy setting (fees, time constraints) affect the therapist-client relationship? (4) Does silence have a part to play in therapy? (5) What are the ramifications of confrontation and acceptance?

Rich Hycner's chapter, "The Wisdom of Resistance: A Dialogical Psychotherapy Approach," deserves special mention not only because for more than ten years Dr. Hycner has been the leading spirit of the Institute for Dialogical Psychotherapy and Co-Director with Maurice Friedman and James DeLeo of that institute, but also because he adds a special dimension to this section on Dialogical Psychotherapy—namely, that which comes from his years of immersion in and practice of Gestalt therapy. I can do no better here than quote what Maurice Friedman wrote of the closely similar chapter in his Preface to Hycner's *Between Person and Person: Toward a Dialogical Psychotherapy:* "In his brilliant conclusion on 'The Wisdom of Resistance' Hycner carries forward Gestalt therapy's valuation of the creativity of resistance into a deeper and more concrete understanding of the relation of resistance to the 'between' than any of his psychotherapeutic forbears has ever done." In his essay Hycner holds that "resistance," so far from being an impediment to therapy that must be broken through, is an important stage in the dialogue between therapist and client that must be honored in itself.

In "Reflections on the Buber-Rogers Dialogue Thirty-five Years After," Maurice Friedman highlights the subtle difference between Buber's and Rogers' understanding of mutuality, and confirmation and acceptance in therapy. He points to two areas of disagreement. First, because the patient can have an impact on the therapist and can change the therapist, Rogers believes there is mutuality between patient and therapist. But for Buber, the focus is on the patient who has come for help; thus, the relationship is not mutual. The second issue of disagreement concerns acceptance and confirmation. While both agree that acceptance of the client allows the client freedom to trust and explore, Buber adds another dimension. Confirmation means wrestling with the client, opposing him or her if necessary, yet accepting the person as she or he is. Only then does the therapist acknowledge the polarities that exist within the client and allow the client an opportunity for new direction. Friedman supports Buber's position and says that the therapist enters into the client's wrestling: "It is only insofar as you share with me and struggle together that I can glimpse the person you are called to become."

In "Relational Ethics in Contextual Therapy: Commitment to Our Common Future," Ivan Boszormenyi-Nagy notes that not only are individual family members in need of justice but so are those generations who have gone before. Families (1) are influenced by the patterns that have been established in preceding generations, (2) are influenced by behaviors that occur in the family that exist today, (3) currently affect the communities in which they live, and (4) will influence and leave a legacy to generations yet unborn. Thus, each member of the family is bound by loyalties and positive and negative entitlements. For Boszormenyi-Nagy, "concern about the quality of human relationships is to be included among other aspects of concern about global survival." Our task is to work toward a caring and just community.

"Ethical Imagination: Repairing the Breach," by Barbara R. Krasner and Austin J. Joyce, stresses the importance of "direct address." Family members must be able to share their truths, face conflict, hear differences. Each member must resist what Buber calls the "seeming" stance and act out of his or her being. Each must feel secure enough, or dare to risk enough, to be forthright. The authors state that "knowing one's own truths and embracing them, and then testing them in circumstances loaded with possibilities of many-sided injuries and potential retribution" earn the person his or her freedom. Only then can real justice be brought forth for the family. Furthermore, imagination, dialogue, unfair blame, intergenerational relations are central to therapy. Crucial to this process of family growth is the recognition of justice and connectedness. Ethical imagination can enable us to know that "merit never lies in one person alone but is always intrinsic to each relating partner."

CHAPTER 21

WHAT IS—PSYCHOTHERAPY?

JAMES V. DELEO

Paul and I had spent the last four months talking weekly about his restlessness, fatigability, tachycardia, sleep disturbances, and irritability. Despite his professional success and close circle of family and friends, the symptoms of anxiety would not go away. As a forty-eight-year-old man with two years of previous psychotherapy, he had remarkable insight, good judgment, and a warm, mature interpersonal style. On this particular morning, Paul began the session by telling me about a recent argument with his son. Spitting the words out, he told me of his twenty-two-year-old son's insensitivity, ungratefulness, and selfishness. He was desperately trying to control himself but, to no avail, as the coffee he was sipping spilled onto his lap. He jumped up, cursed, and hurled the coffee cup at the wall. Taken by surprise, I glanced back and forth from him to the black liquid spilling down the white wall before I cried out, "What the hell is *this* all about?"

Standing two inches from me and hovering over me, he pointed his finger at my face and shouted, "I'll tell you what its all about. It's about spoiled rotten young kids who don't give a damn about anything but themselves. It's about twenty-two years of busting my ass to pay for dentists, doctors, shrinks, and college. It's about staying up nights consoling his mother while I'm scared to death myself that he would be killed on that damn motorcycle. That's what the hell this is all about, and I'll pay for the cleaning of your goddamn wall."

Getting up suddenly and staring straight at him, I shook my hand and said, "And do you know what else this is about? Sure, it's about

Kevin and your anger and pain about him but it's also about you and your father. It's about your embarrassment over his lack of education, his dirty, grubby hands, his accent, and your guilt about not visiting him last year. That's what this is also about. And the coffee didn't stain the wall, so don't worry about it."

We stared at each other. He looked away. I looked away. When he looked at me again, his eyes were filled with tears. He walked to my desk, sat down, put his head on the desk and sobbed. I sighed and sat down in my chair. For a moment, I thought about my father, and for another moment I missed him. Paul got up from the desk, sat in the chair across from me, wiped his tears, and loosened his tie. We sat in silence for the remaining minutes of the session. Then he said: "See you next week."

Walking him to the door, I said: "Take care."

What is psychotherapy? Formulated within the tradition of depth psychology, psychotherapy is, to borrow Bakhtin's phrase describing Dostoevsky's creative method, a "dialogic penetration" of the client's personality. Viewed in this way, the unit of psychological study is the personality of the client, and the task of the therapist is to assess, diagnose, and treat the client's disorder as rooted in his/her personality. In planning treatment, the therapist proposes interventions based upon a systematic scientific explanation of the client's symptoms, syndrome, and disorder. This explanation which guides therapeutic technique generally makes use of some fundamental metapsychological points of view—genetic, economic, adaptive, dynamic, topographical, or structural. This formulation of psychotherapy, borrowed as it is from the physical sciences, has the consequence of turning the client into an object in contrast to the therapist as subject.

The criticism of this naturalistic-positivistic-mechanistic concept of the person as adopted by Freud and many psychological theorists since then is, by now, an old one. C. G. Jung was one of the first of Freud's followers to object to such a formulation. Jung was primarily concerned with questions of personality and the roots of human existence and secondarily with questions of psychopathology. In attempting to answer these questions, he incorporated a philosophical and religio-mystical perspective into his analytical psychology. He supported this perspective by drawing on mythological and alchemical teachings. As a result of this integration, Jung was led to the position that self-knowledge and individuation come from introversive experience. One observation of this formulation in made by Sborowitz, in his postscript to Hans Trüb's *Heilung aus der Begegnung*:

If Jung's path of healing and path of salvation achieves its fulfillment in individuation, then, Trüb asks, is there a path leading
back from individuation to the world? Trüb states that Jung's
answer to this question was in the negative. (Trüb 1949, 123)

Jung's answer is in accord with the great traditions of Theravada Buddhism and the introversive mysticism of the Greeks. His answer suggests
that the journey to wholeness is an inward path. This path of introversive
mysticism moves the individual further and further away from the world
of others. These great traditions did, however, suggest another path
expressed in the form of Mahayana Buddhism and extraversive mysticism. It is, however, Jung's emphasis on the introversive path in his analytical psychology that delimits therapy to assisting the client encounter
the various strata of his/her unconscious.

As valuable and fruitful as these formulations of therapy may be,
they are, nevertheless, constrained by the Cartesian lesion and tend to
treat psychological abstractions as concrete material events. The consequence of this reification when applied to therapeutic practice is three-
fold. First, it can remove the client from the everyday world of others in
which he or she exists. Second, it can objectify the client, making him
or her a thing to be taken apart and reconstituted. Third, it can engender
in the therapist a naturalistic attitude and mechanomorphic approach to
therapy.

These consequences grow out of the theoretical foundation that
most therapists receive during the course of their training. Many practicing psychotherapists accept the foundation without question. Others
note that, despite the careful integration of theory and technique, anomalies—in the form of some people getting better and others not—occur.
These anomalies may be indicators of the uniqueness of each person
and, therefore, the uniqueness of each relationship. This issue of individual uniqueness, as contrasted with individual differences, may point
to what Kuhn calls the "counter-pattern." Kuhn makes the point in his
renowned book *The Structure of Scientific Revolutions* (1978) that it is
this counter-pattern that contradicts the normal pattern of scientific
self-understanding.

The attempt to understand the meaning of individual uniqueness
challenges not only the foundation upon which these theories of personality and psychotherapy rest, but also the very ground of a scientific psychology that attempts to find universal laws behind human change and
behavior. This essay is an initial effort to pursue the meaning of human
uniqueness by drawing upon some of the insights contained in Martin
Buber's ontology and applying them to the practice of psychotherapy.

What is before psychotherapy is one whole being and another whole being. What is required then of the therapist is a knowledge of being. An ontology, when formulated as a specific philosophical anthropology, offers the therapist a way to go beyond approaches that treat the person simply as a scientific object. In addition, a philosophical anthropology helps organize and explain the wealth of information provided by the knowledge base of psychology. This knowledge, understanding, and appreciation of the person as a whole being is central to the practice of psychotherapy. A philosophical anthropology, by providing the psychotherapist with an understanding of what a person is, allows the therapist to properly view and treat psychopathology, which is, after all, what a person is not.

Martin Buber's philosophical anthropology, as expanded upon by Maurice Friedman, suggests an approach to the practice of psychotherapy. Buber is most commonly looked upon as philosopher who devoted most of his attention to the way in which the person relates to the world, to others, and to God. His interest in psychotherapy is well documented in Friedman's study of Buber's thought in *Martin Buber: The Life of Dialogue.*

The application of Martin Buber's philosophy of dialogue to the practice of psychotherapy has been extensively written about by Maurice Friedman. The Friedman oeuvre in this respect is quite large—a bibliography of over twenty books with a contribution to fifty others and more than a hundred and fifty articles. In most of his work, he has tried to present Buber's theme of dialogue and its implications for psychotherapy. Friedman's amplification of Buber's philosophy of dialogue, further clarifying the distinction between the dialogical and psychological, has made it possible for us to formulate and practice a psychotherapy of dialogue.

Psychotherapy begins as a meeting between two whole beings, Buber writes in *Between Man and Man*:

> The fundamental fact of human existence is man with man. What is peculiarly characteristic of the human world is above all that something takes place between one being and another the like of which can be found nowhere in nature. Language is only a sign and a means for it, all achievement of the spirit has been incited by it. Man is made man by it; but on its way it does not merely unfold, it also decays and withers away. It is rooted in one being turning to another as another, as this particular other being, in order to communicate with it in a sphere which is common to them but which reaches out beyond the special sphere of each. I call this sphere, which is established with the existence of man as man but which is conceptually

still uncomprehended, the sphere of "between." Though being realized in very different degrees, it is a primal category of human reality. This is where the genuine third alternative must begin. (203)

This is the fundamental fact of psychotherapy: person with person. And as the therapist turns to the client and the client turns to the therapist, the sphere of the between is established. This is, as Buber expresses it, "the primal category of human reality" and where psychotherapy begins. The between that occurs through the act of entering-in-relation by therapist and client is the dynamic of relation. It is not static but always becoming. The session between Paul and me occurred within this dynamic of relation, not only within the context of space and time. If we attempt to analyze it only within the temporal and spatial context we make it static and tear it from its very ground of the meeting between the two of us. This purely static-analytic approach contributes to the mistake of methodology which in its attempt to understand through analysis ends up murdering through dissection.

The conversation that unfolds as the therapist listens to and examines the life history of the client must not be confused with dialogue. Dialogue means speech between two actual beings. As an example, the conversation about the client's life history can be monological—that is, the therapist can speak to a conceived other. The questions that the therapist asks, which are designed to determine the etiological pattern of the client's symptom cluster in order to arrive at a dynamic diagnosis upon which to base a treatment plan, are examples of this talking to a conceived other. The conception is, in this example, based upon theoretical abstractions about personality development and psychopathology. Paul was more than an individual who was suppressing his feelings of guilt for the manner in which he treated his father. He needed more from me than insight and catharsis. He needed a direct, immediate experience of relation which would allow for real knowledge and understanding.

The client may also speak to a conceived other. Many clients enter psychotherapy with a preconceived notion of therapy and therapists. They, therefore, speak to this preconceived notion; some even provide information about the precipitating, predisposing, and reinforcing factors involved in their distress without being asked. Paul, because of his previous experience in psychotherapy, was extremely articulate in clarifying for me the dynamics of his childhood and the resultant effects upon his self-esteem, self-concept, and interpersonal relationships. There were times when our sessions sounded much like a television talk show. I was the affable host and he the celebrity guest. The paradox here is that though the rhyme and rhythm of the session may have *sounded* like a dialogue, it was really what the developmental psychologists call a collective monologue. This form of communication is characterized by the therapist and client interacting within a system of shared meanings and psychological stimulus and response. This is Buber's realm of the "I-It," and this realm is as integral to the process of therapy as is the realm of the "I-Thou," for they are both integral to the person.

In turning to the client as person, the therapist is challenged to adopt, in Husserl's phrase, a "personalistic attitude." The adoption of this personalistic attitude is in accordance with the principle of science which dictates that the method of study must correlate with the manner in which the phenomenon being studied presents itself. This attitude is the one we adopt in our everyday life with family and friends. It is the attitude that prompts us to ask: how was your day, how are you feeling, what do you think about this or that? It is an attitude of care, concern, curiosity, and interest. It is our natural attitude but not a naturalistic one. It is contained in our being present for the client and not necessarily vocalized. For Buber it meant "accepting with his [our] essential being another person in his particularity . . . (*BMM*, 23).

The relevance of this attitude to psychotherapy is expressed by Friedman in his chapter on confirmation in therapy:

> This problematic includes the fact that the therapist values the other enough to treat him or her as a human being, and not just as a sick person. This care means helping the other to reach the place where he or she can enter into dialogue, first with the therapist and then with the other persons in his or her life. (*HDP*, 139–40)

This "personalistic attitude" challenges the therapist to intimately participate in the therapeutic meeting. Upon accepting this challenge, true healing can occur. Friedman writes:

> At some point, therefore, the therapist must enter a second stage in which he helps the client resume the interrupted dialogue with the community. He does this by placing on the client the demand of the community—not from above, but rather by really standing his ground as the person he or she is *and* by representing and bearing the community values that he or she embodies. Without that second stage—not replacing, but combined with the first stage—there can be no real healing. (139)

When Paul jumped up and hurled his coffee cup at the wall we reached the stage that Friedman is talking about. Taken by surprise, I spoke directly, personally: "What the hell is this all about?" This personal address to Paul evoked in turn a personal response when he shouted back: "I'll tell you what it's all about . . . "I demanded an account of what was behind throwing the cup at my wall. He gave it to me.

It must be noted that this "personalistic attitude" allows for the intuition of the therapist. It suggests that the therapist's intuition may provide a direct insight of the client. Intuition as a valid way of knowing is not, in the history of ideas, a new or radical notion. Spinoza (1632–1677) described intuitive knowledge as characteristic of the person who had risen to the third level of existence and hence had incorporated the empirical and rational knowledge of the previous stages. Bergson (1859–1941) argued that intuition in contrast to discursive reasoning can understand the world in its essential fluidity. But Buber's understanding of intuition differs from Bergson's in one important respect. Bergson viewed intuition as overcoming the duality of the subject observing and the object observed. Buber, on the other hand, acknowledged the duality of subject and object as ontic and, therefore, incapable of being overcome by intuition. Intuition, then, is not a special ability, a trait, but rather a state of relation in which "our whole being becomes one in the act of knowing." There is not, for Buber, the fusion of the knower with the known as Bergson would have it.

It is to the traditions of depth and behavioral psychology with their emphasis on empiricism and rationalism that intuition appears as a radical and even regressive tendency. To many practicing psychotherapists, intuition is one of the cornerstones of the therapeutic process. In my encounter with Paul I knew that his anger and pain were about Kevin, but I also knew they were about his relationship to his father. This, however, was not intuition, for I had this information rationally presented to me by Paul in our previous sessions. But in that moment of Paul's shouting and pointing his finger at me, I knew with my whole being what was behind his hurling the coffee cup.

What is psychotherapy? Formulated within the philosophical anthropology of Martin Buber, psychotherapy is the healing of the "atrophied personal center" of the client through the meeting of the therapist and client. Paul's problems did not originate in his symptoms of anxiety. They had their origins in the events that occurred *between* him and his father and *between* him and his son. His psychological symptoms were merely announcements of his broken "interhuman" relationships. His need for psychotherapy arose from the sickness in his relationships. Because of this, the goal of psychotherapy was to provide a container whereby Paul could encounter this reality. The therapeutic meeting is the medium through which the person comes to understand, express, and discern the meaning of his/her symptoms. One task of the therapist is to use his/her skills of assessment and diagnosis to understand the psychological, that which is happening within the person. The other task is to see the psychological as ancillary to the dialogical and approach therapy and the client in partnership. This is the point that Richard Hycner makes in his book *Between Person and Person*:

> the understanding of the unconscious never becomes the exclusive focus of the therapist. The understanding of the unconscious is not something that is separate from a relationship, rather it is *only* in a "partnership" relationship that the full range of the unconscious can be explored. (1991, 59)

In planning treatment, the therapist proposes interventions based upon the inability or unwillingness of the client to respond to the call of the world. The understanding of this inability or unwillingness to respond and the particular manner in which it is manifested within the therapeutic relationship and experienced by the therapist and client is what guides therapeutic technique.

The practice of dialogical psychotherapy rests upon the assertion that a person can only be understood in relation to an other whose reactions and responses shape the person's definition and sense of self. If a person wants to know the I that addresses the world, he/she must come to realize that the I that is spoken is not a singular word connoting a single one. The I, as Buber means it, is either of the I-Thou or I-It. These word-pairs are expressive of different relationships. The I-Thou is expressed in one's full being arising from encounters with the spheres of nature, other people, or art. There is nothing between the I and Thou. The I-It is mediated by desire, anticipation, purpose, foreknowledge, and is, therefore, incomplete. It is this mediation upon which the dialogical therapist focuses during the course of psychotherapy.

In attempting to further understand these mediations, the therapist can make use of certain metapsychological constructs and the results of empirical psychological research. For example, in the case of Paul a genetic point of view concerning his symptoms of a generalized anxiety disorder was extremely helpful in understanding the wounds he incurred during the intimacy versus isolation phase of his personality development. The manner in which he attempted to adapt to these wounds further explained the nature of his defensiveness and provided me with an indication of the manner in which he would respond to certain therapeutic interventions. Empirical research concerning the correlation of anxiety to cognition suggested the use of other therapeutic interventions.

I was aware, however, of Paul's uniqueness—a uniqueness that transcended these constructs and research about people. My awareness of his uniqueness came not as a result of observing him but through stepping into an elemental relation with him. When I cried out, "What the hell is *this* all about?" it was a question addressed to his personal wholeness. When he shot back with, "I'll tell you what it's all about," this was an unmediated response to me as a Thou. we had entered into relation as individual selves, and I had to meet with him in true dialogue. What happened happened between us as partners in dialogue and through existential grace. If any healing occurred during our session together, it occurred in the relationship between us and proceeded back to our individual selves.

REFERENCES

Buber, Martin. *BMM; I and Thou* (Smith).

Friedman, Maurice, *HDP; LoD*.

Hycner, Richard. (1991). *Between Person and Person: Toward a Dialogical Psychotherapy*. New York: The Gestalt Journal.

Kuhn, T. (1970). *The Structure of Scientific Revolutions*. Chicago: University of Chicago Press.

Trüb, Hans. (1949). *Heilung aus der Begegnung*. Stuttgart: Ernst Klett Verlag.

CHAPTER 22

PHILOSOPHY OF DIALOGUE AND FEMINIST PSYCHOLOGY

ROSE GRAF-TAYLOR

Feminist psychology, particularly the research and theory construction which is associated with the Stone Center, is shifting the perspective of psychology from the individual and intrapsychic focus to an understanding of "self-in-relation" (Jordan et al. 1991, 51). The self-in-relation theory is primarily grounded in feminist research and experience. The philosophy of dialogue as it was formulated by Martin Buber has to do with an image of the human that is "at one and the same time concern for what is authentic *human* existence and concern for what is authentic for us in particular" (Friedman 1991, 11). Buber's basic ontological premise that "all real living is meeting" claims validity for human existence beyond the gender gap and at the same time acknowledges the uniqueness of each meeting.

Human existence is seen as always being existence in relation, in terms of the actual present and in terms of the personal history. We become who we are in relation with others. There is no isolated entity called a human being, "no *I* taken in itself" (*I and Thou*, 4). There are only persons-in-relation. Psychology has focused on individuals and, following the subject-object split, treated their relatedness as an *external* factor influencing their development. The feminist approach goes a decisive step further in its attempt to understand the connectedness of human life. It does so by investigating female development and experience. However, so

far it lacks the philosophical grounding which can illuminate its significance beyond the realms of female experience.

Buber responded as a philosopher to the imbalance of human existence
brought about by the propagation of an image of the human as an
autonomous individual who fulfills his destiny when he makes the world
do his bidding. The self-in-relation theorists respond to the same imbalance
when they claim that at least female experience does not follow the prescribed notions of the ideal self as autonomous, self-sufficient, and independent but that a different set of values and developmental imperatives exists.

The similarities between Buber's philosophical statements and the
conclusions from feminist research regarding the development of self in
women is often astounding. However, the philosophy of dialogue and its
application in form of dialogical therapy point beyond current theory in
several important ways and, in my opinion, can expand and deepen the
theoretical framework and practice of feminist psychology. At the same
time, dialogical therapy can be enriched by the self-in-relation theory
through its in-depth studies of development in relation and its analysis
of many of the same issues that are a focal point in dialogical therapy.

I AND THOU

Connectedness of human life has evolved as a basic principle in feminist
psychology. It also is the primary touchstone in the philosophy of dialogue. Buber suggests that this connectedness exists in a two-fold attitude which cuts across all formal distinctions of relationships. It is
presented to us in its two-fold way of personal connectedness and ser-
vice-oriented connectedness—I-Thou and I-It. The importance of this
differentiation becomes immediately visible when we understand that
the growth of a person in her wholeness takes place only in *personal*
relation, while I-It is the attitude which takes care of physical survival
and comfort. The acquisition of knowledge and skills can take place in
I-It relationships. Human knowing and integrity are not possible without I-Thou.

Both have their place in human life. We are, however, often confronted with an invasion of I-It into the personal realm, which makes
the return to the Thou impossible. Depersonalized skill and knowledge
become dehumanized technology and procedure. Personal relationships
become eroded by a dominance of I-It. The between atrophies, and the
partners find themselves isolated, empty, used, and abused.

Apart from this general orientation toward "it" in our society,
women and men have been and still are subjected to a process of It-ing

which is clearly gender-specific and which violates our integrity. For women some examples of this are the promotion as sex objects, physical and sexual violence and abuse, the continuous attempt to reappropriate women as wombs, and the exploitation of women through unpaid and underpaid labor.

In a world where women were "It," we were likely to give up "I" in the attempt to say "Thou," thus losing both. Women's insistence on realizing themselves as persons and being treated as persons is a presupposition to establishing genuine and mutual relationship—that is, to shift from I-It to I-Thou. Feminist emancipation empowered many women to say "I." The direction toward the Thou in women's lives is just now being acknowledged.

The world of I-Thou "teaches you to meet others, and to hold your ground when you meet them" (*I and Thou*, 33). This is and has been a main struggle for women to remain in relationships as whole persons. To meet the other while holding our ground is crucial for women whose values and experiences differ significantly from those of mainstream patriarchal culture and society. To hold her ground means to bring her female knowing and experience to the dialogue and to trust it. Grounded in this trust we can be open to the other.

Feminist psychology teaches us that women clearly experience the necessity of personal and mutual relationships and its connection with personal growth. Janet Surrey states:

> The basic elements of the core-self in women can be summarized as (1) an interest in and attention to the other person(s) which form the base for the emotional connection and the ability to empathize with the other(s); (2) the expectation of a mutual empathic process where the sharing of experience leads to a heightened development of self and other; and (3) the expectation of interaction and relationship as a process of mutual sensitivity and mutual responsibility that provides the stimulus for the growth of empowerment and self-knowledge. (Jordan et al., 58ff.)

When I-Thou is realized it is a moment of genuine meeting between persons. It is characterized by directness, presence, and mutuality. There is sharing in each other and responding to each other; there is acceptance and confirmation. I-Thou does not have a goal outside of itself—not even that of personal growth—and thus does not constitute people as means to goals. Instead it makes them present in their personhood as partners in this relationship. Jordan states the same point when she speaks of mutuality: "Crucial to a mature sense of mutuality is an

appreciation of the wholeness of the other person, with a special awareness to the other's subjective experience. Thus the person is not there
merely to take care of one's needs, to become a vessel for one's projec-
tions or transference, or to be the object of discharge of instinctual
impulses" (Jordan et al., 82).

Mutuality must be understood in the context of dialogical relation.
It is not merely a reciprocal exchange or equity between two people. It is
a quality of the *relationship* maintained through a commitment of the
partners to be present, responsive, and responsible to each other and to
the relationship.

Living congruently, women experience the necessity not only for
changes in personal relationships but for changes in the structure of
social life as well. Genuine dialogue is the way toward those changes
which is congruent with the core-self in women, as Surrey stated it.

DIALOGUE

Genuine dialogue is I-Thou in action. It requires that the partners bring
themselves to it and at the same time are turned to one another "with
the intention of establishing a living mutual relationship between himself and them" (*BMM*, 19). What Surrey calls "relationship authenticity," "the ongoing challenge to feel emotionally 'real,' connected, vital,
clear, purposeful in relationship" (Jordan et al., 60), certainly applies to
genuine dialogue. Buber speaks of the necessity to overcome semblance
and the willingness "to say what is really in his mind about the subject
of conversation" (*KM*, 85).

> It is in this kind of dialogue that personal growth and empow-
> erment can take place. The innermost growth of the self is not
> accomplished . . . in man's relation to himself, but in the rela-
> tion between the one and the other . . . that is pre-eminently in
> the mutuality of making present . . . together with the mutual-
> ity of acceptance, of affirmation and confirmation. (71)

Research with women supports the notion of inseparability of personal development and relationship. "Relationship *and* identity develop
in *synchrony*" (Jordan et al., 63). For women, genuine dialogue is often
realized in relationships with other women (Gilligan et al., 1989).
Developmentally these relationships are crucial in gaining a clear sense
of self and personal power *and* allowing women to stay connected. The
notion which links individuation with separation is not valid here. Those
relationships allow the space *within* the relationship to be oneself and

confirm the person in her uniqueness. Thus they foster the ability to be in genuine dialogue.

For women, genuine dialogue presupposes awareness of how the world addresses us as women and how this has an impact in our personal lives as well as in our standing in society: "What occurs to me addresses me. In what occurs to me the world-happening addresses me" (*KM*, 11). Much of the emerging values and experiences of women illuminate what patriarchal culture has pushed aside, to the detriment not only of women but all of us. Our genuine response is the contribution women can make to shift our relationships toward mutuality and to change the injustice inherent in a dominator system.

DISTANCE AND RELATION

Dialogical relation is governed by a twofold movement which Buber called the "primal setting at a distance" and "entering into relation" (*KM*, 60). Setting at a distance means to recognize an other as a separate being, as unique, as otherness. This is the presupposition to entering into relation with her, with her not in an *aspect* of her existence which meets my need, goal, or purpose, but with her as the unique person she is. Entering into relation means being "present in my whole person" (*KM*, 63) and making the other present as a whole and a unity.

This is the context for responsibility grounded in a "guiding principle of connection" (Gilligan 1982, 57). Responsibility is not understood here as a list of duties which come with rights we claim. This is asked from us: to exercise our ability to respond genuinely and fully to what addresses us: "The idea of responsibility is to be brought back from the province of specialized ethics, of an 'ought' that swings free in the air, into that of lived life. Genuine responsibility exists only where there is genuine responding" (*BMM*, 16).

Carol Gilligan (1982) comes to a somewhat similar notion of "response/ability" in her investigation into the moral development of women. Surrey points out that "inherent in this model is the vision of women's development from a relationship of caretaking to one of consideration, caring, and empowering" (Jordan et al., 63). Response/ability in this sense is based on the twofold movement of distance and relation as it is responding to an other whom I have made present to myself and to whom I make myself present.

Surrey states that "for girls, 'being present with' psychologically is experienced as self-enhancing . . . 'Being with' means 'being seen' and 'feeling seen' by the other and 'seeing the other' and sensing the other 'feeling seen,' which is the experience of mutual empathy" (Jordan et al., 55). She then points to the dark side of empathy when a lack of differentiation between self and other leads to confusion about "whose feelings belong to whom."

It reflects the confusion in our understanding of empathy with regard to the extent that empathy requires a bracketing of oneself or "temporarily and partially to give up one's own identity" (Greenson 1977, 105). Buber's terms "inclusion" and "imagining the real" stress that presence with one another does not mean losing one's own ground. The balance of the movements of distance and relation remains intact. It is I in my uniqueness who is opening myself to you and your life to "concretely imagine what the other person is thinking, willing, and feeling" (Friedman 1985, 198).

Without the first movement of setting at a distance the second is not possible. Without the recognition of separateness and otherness there is confusion. Any attempt to relate is bound to be reflexion and reaction. Looking at the other, one sees oneself superimposed over the other; every interaction with the other is primarily a reaction to one's own images, desires, hopes, and fears. There is only monologue.

Carrying out the first movement does not mean the second will necessarily be carried out too. A person can set an other at a distance without making her present and being present to her. "The first movement . . . puts men into mutual existence . . . the second movement puts them into mutual relation" (KM, 71). Entering into relation requires a mutual turning toward each other. Personal making present and confirmation happen only here. They are, however, crucial to becoming a person. What is not seen and confirmed by an other becomes a mere shadow.

The understanding of distance and relation has profound implications for development. The younger a child, the more she depends upon the parent to provide the distance and relation in their relationship. Only if the parent allows the space for the child's otherness to unfold can she experience herself as a separate being. Only if the parent makes the child present and confirms her in her uniqueness can she gain the sense of who she is in this relationship and that she is valued for the person she is.

Scheu (1977) reviewed studies that targeted parent-child interactions with newborns and toddlers. She observed that the emphasis of stimulations and training parents provide for baby girls frequently runs contrary to their needs at a given moment, while it conforms to the boys' particular needs. Already in the first weeks of life the girls in these studies were not allowed the psychological and relational space to unfold their individuality to the same degree as boys but were more bent to the needs of their caretakers. The resulting disconfirmation acts on a deep level of self because the physical-emotional aspects of existence which are predominant at this stage are not yet differentiated from other mental and spiritual aspects. Gender-specific socialization at later stages tends to repeat this process on different levels of development when the girls' need to care is exploited in a context which coerces them to disregard themselves, punishes self-assertion as selfishness, and marks it as contradictory to caring for others.

This process possibly lies at the root of women's difficulty to maintain their sense of separateness in relations and to value themselves for who they genuinely are. Not having experienced distance in relationships as the mutual recognition of the otherness of the other leaves women vulnerable to codependency. The disregard of her self by others leaves her with the impossible choice between self and relationship. The twofold movement of distance and relation is torn apart into two isolated modes of existence. There seems to be only lonely integrity or relationship at the price of personhood. In a situation where this seems to be the choice, women for many reasons tend to choose the second.

In reconstructing distance and relation as the twofold movement governing mutual relationships, women regain their sense of self, their personal power, and their ability for genuine dialogue. "The difference between an empowered woman and a 'co-dependent' woman is not that empowered women love less," writes O'Hara (1991), "but that they love more mutually." Holding their ground they do not lose themselves in the other; being open to the other they respond to the reality of her/his being and the concrete between of their relationship.

REFERENCES

Buber, M. *BMM; I and Thou* (Smith); *KM*.
Friedman, M. (1985). *The Healing Dialogue in Psychotherapy*. New York: Jason Aronson.
——. (1991) *Dialogue and the Human Image: Beyond Humanistic Psychology*.
Gilligan, C. (1982). *In a Different Voice*. Cambridge: Harvard University Press.
Gilligan et al. (1989). *Making Connections*. Cambridge: Harvard University Press
Greenson, R. R. (1977). "That 'Impossible' Profession." *The Human Dimension of Psychoanalytic Practice*. Ed. K. A. Frank. New York: Grune and Stratton.

Jordan et al. (1991). *Women's Growth in Connection.* New York: The Guilford Press

O'Hara, Maureen, videotape—"Conviction, Passion, Community: Women's Reality in a Gendered World." Available from Encinitas Center for Family and Personal Development.

Scheu, Ursula. (1977). *Wir Werden Nichts als Mädchen Geboren. Wir Werden Dazu Gemacht.*" Frankfurt: Fischer Verlag.

CHAPTER 23

PROBLEMS OF CONFIRMATION IN PSYCHOTHERAPY

TAMAR KRON AND MAURICE FRIEDMAN

Mutual confirmation is essential to becoming a self—one who realizes one's uniqueness precisely through one's relation to other selves whose distance from one is completed by one's distance from them. We do not exist as self-sufficient monads that only secondarily come into relationship with one another, any more than we are mere cells in a social organism. We exist as persons who need to be confirmed in our uniqueness by persons essentially other than ourselves:

> The basis of man's life with man is twofold, and it is one—the wish of every man to be confirmed as what he is, even as what he can become, by men: and the innate capacity in man to confirm his fellow men in this way. That this capacity lies so immeasurably fallow constitutes the real weakness and questionableness of the human race; actual humanity exists only where this capacity unfolds. (KM, 57–58)

> Sent forth from the natural domain of species into the hazard of the solitary category, surrounded by the air of a chaos which came into being with him, secretly and bashfully he watches for a Yes which allows him to be and which can come to him only from one human person to another. (61)

"Confirmation" in Buber's sense of the term is a central concern of psychotherapy, particularly for that psychotherapy that Buber calls "healing through meeting" and Maurice Friedman calls "the healing dialogue" (HDP, 1985). According to Buber's philosophical anthropology we become selves through our relation to other selves that have been set at a distance from us. The inmost becoming of the person takes place when another person makes one present through active "inclusion," or "imagining the real," and that person knows that he or she is made present. "Making present" is an event that happens partially wherever persons come together, but in its essential structure only rarely.

In making the other present we imagine concretely what that person is thinking, feeling, willing—in Buber's words, we "imagine the real." We acknowledge all this, and we add something of our own will to what we imagine. This means that I not only perceive you but that I also want to strengthen you in your uniqueness and help you find your personal direction. In confirming you I do not have to choose between your uniqueness and mine; nor do I impose myself on you, but help you in your uniqueness to realize itself in relation to me.

While Carl Rogers' concept of "unconditional positive regard" is widely known by psychotherapists and used as a vehicle to growth and healing, Buber's confirmation fills in an empty space which, in our judgment, Rogers' acceptance of the client cannot fill.

To take seriously the central role that Buber's concept of confirmation may play in therapy is also to confront the problems that may arise in the very act of confirmation. Confirmation in therapy means holding the tension of opposites because we exist simultaneously as unique persons yet in relationship as persons in social roles, as professionals, and as partners in relationships, as guided by rule and structure and as responding spontaneously in situations.

In this essay we shall discuss five common problems in psychotherapy: (1) Can the first interview, which is often directed to diagnosis, also have elements of that relationship of mutuality, openness, immediacy, and presence which Buber calls "I-Thou"? Can the professional stance of this diagnostic interview allow for the evolution of a dialogue between therapist and client without the one interfering with the other? (2) Is it ethical for the therapist to deal with the whole person and not just the presenting problem? What right does the therapist have to respond to the client as a whole person when the client comes only to relieve specific symptoms? (3) How does the very structure of the therapeutic relationship—meeting at a set time and place, getting payment for the hours of therapy—affect the relationship between therapist and client? (4) What is the role of silence in therapy? Can the therapist and the client accept silence in comfort as an integral part of the process? (5) What are the practical implications of confirmation as confrontation as well as acceptance? How can therapist and client alike handle the tension that arises when we distinguish, as we must, between confirming the person and accepting his or her actions and achievements?

The Swiss psychotherapist Hans Trüb makes an important distinction between two stages of therapy. The first is that in which the therapist plays the part of confidante, big brother or sister who offers the client the understanding that the community has denied him or her. The second stage is one in which the therapist brings before the client the claim of the community. This claim may lead to rejection of the therapist by the client because of the lack of wisdom and poor timing of the therapist *or* because the client is too comfortable in Trüb's first stage of being accepted and understood and does not want to change it (Friedman, *TWE*, 497–99).

THE PROBLEM OF THE FIRST INTERVIEW

The first interview gives the therapist necessary information about the client, but it also sets the tone for the ongoing relationship between therapist and client. If that tone is too one-sidedly professional there may not be a second interview or the relationship may be set in a predominantly "I-It," or subject-object mode of knowing and using in which it becomes difficult or even impossible to break through to a genuine dialogue between therapist and client. On the other hand, a professional stance is needed in order to do justice to the client. The therapist has to evaluate the client's problems, personality make-up, strengths and weaknesses, even the client's ability to be in a relationship. In order to do this the therapist must, to some extent, remain a detached observer, even while remaining open to dialogue and meeting on another level.

We believe that even in the most professional and detached interview there can be elements of the "I-Thou" relationship of mutuality, openness, presence, and immediacy, though the therapist may not always recognize and acknowledge it. Therapists differ in the degree to which they will allow elements of I-Thou to enter into the evaluation process. Moreover, in the same moment when the therapist gets into the I-Thou relationship, he or she evaluates the client's ability to be in such relationship. There are, for example, clients who become panicky when the relationship threatens to become too intimate too quickly.

This applies to even small details in the handling of the therapeutic session, such as the distance between the chairs in which the therapist and client will sit. This threat is present whatever methods and techniques are used. For example, in hypnotherapeutic sessions, the therapist will come very close to the client and even touch him or her when the therapist thinks it is needed. The question arises whether the therapist pays attention to the problem mentioned above concerning the client's ability to be close. Those therapists who preserve the same distance at all times may miss the opportunity of helping to establish a relationship *and* while so doing evaluating the client's ability to be in relationship.

The first interview with a nineteen-year-old Arab woman student in a crisis intervention center on an Israeli university campus began as an evaluative session but then changed midway to an attempt on the part of Dr. Kron to help "Alia" with the mourning for her mother which she had delayed in favor of her studies. In the second half of the session Dr. Kron suggested to Alia that she lean back in the armchair and think about her mother. Alia's whole body relaxed, and she talked and wept without inhibition. She let herself be touched both physically and mentally, and she let herself go into herself and into her pain with sincerity and with trust. Dr. Kron sat very close to Alia this whole time, caressing her hand and reassuring her. She even took over the mother's role and assured her that her mother was not angry at her for falling asleep when she died or for studying.

This case illustrates how, despite the possibility of mutual interference, in the first interview a dialogue can be started simultaneously with an evaluative process. Alia could get into her delayed mourning only because she could trust the therapist enough to risk exposing herself to the great pain of her mother's death which she had formerly worked so hard to push under.

The risk for the therapist lies in his or her becoming too much involved in the first stage, even to the point of being overwhelmed by the relationship. If this happens, the therapist will miss some of the data necessary for a good evaluation. On the other hand, if the concern for acquiring data leads the therapist to adopt a role of pure detachment, putting all concern for dialogue on the back burner, the therapist runs the risk of failing to establish the foundation for an ongoing relationship.

THE PRESENTING PROBLEM VERSUS THE WHOLE PERSON

Every client comes to the therapist seeking help for what she or he conceives to be the problem that is blocking her or his life—the presenting problem. No one consciously enters therapy in order to find a relationship. Yet the therapist is confronted not only with the client's statement of his or her problem, which could have been put in a letter, but the whole person, including the history of the client that is revealed in the first and succeeding interviews *as well as* the client's entire manner of being-with-the-therapist—verbally and nonverbally, consciously and unconsciously. With the exception of the radically behaviorally oriented therapist, most therapists are trained to listen and look for underlying problems that have to do with the whole life course of the client and not just the symptom of the moment. Indeed, the behavioral therapist underlines this problem by his or her insistence on dealing only with symptom relief, justifying this attitude by the claim that it is unethical to respond to anything other than the client's verbal complaint. Most therapists have, explicitly or implicitly, a different ethic, for they hold that it is precisely their expertise as therapists that entitles them to help the client to see the deeper dimensions of his or her presenting problems—problems the client may not have hitherto seen.

Alia is a case in point. Her presenting problem was that she could not study successfully. Yet the whole context in which she presented this problem—the history of her forced study during her mother's final illness—compelled Dr. Kron not only to discuss and deal with Alia's delayed mourning but to take the risk of urging Alia in that opening interview to go deeply into her pain over her mother's death.

Another example that is equally dramatic in a negative way is a client who came to see Dr. Friedman when he was a counselor at a university. The patient complained of depression, and Dr. Friedman asked the young man to tell him something of his total situation. The young man described a home in which his unemployed father wasted his life sitting in front of the television screen, and so moved was the young man as he related this that he cried throughout the telling. Dr. Friedman was astonished that the patient's deep feelings had come into the open so quickly and in the first session. He concluded that the patient's depression was connected with his deep tie to his father and imagined that they would continue on this line in future sessions. But the client complained at the end of the hour that Dr. Friedman had not relieved him of the symptom that he presented, and he never returned!

One more example, both negative and positive, is that of a student of Dr. Kron's who was working in an adolescent ward in a psychiatric hospital. One of the clients told this student that he preferred to have her as counselor more than any of the others because she was a psychology student and by that token a true professional. The student felt compelled by the patient's choice to comply with his wishes and maintain her appearance as a professional. In Buber's terminology, she was pushed into being a "seeming" person in order that the client would confirm her. The patient was clearly using her as an "It" and blocking any possibility of an I-Thou relationship, and so was she in complying with his stated wishes.

This attitude on both sides continued until one day when the counselor accompanied the client on a visit downtown. The client forgot something at the cinema and wanted to go back for it, but the counselor sternly refused because it would make them late for the bus. "You don't have any pity for me," the client shouted at the counselor. The counselor, to her own surprise, burst out laughing. At first the client looked at her in dismay; then he too joined in the laughing. From that moment on the relationship changed into one of dialogue with his plaint, "You have no pity for me," as a theme song that they would laughingly repeat in their meetings.

What we can conclude from the above examples is that while clearly the therapist would be unwise to press too deeply and quickly into areas hidden from the client's own view, the therapist must live with the paradox that he or she *does* see more than the client sees. In Buber's terms, whatever mutuality of contact and trust and of concern for a common problem, for the relationship to be a truly healing one there cannot be mutuality of "inclusion." The therapist can and must experience the client's side of the relationship—imagine quite concretely what that person is thinking, feeling, and willing. But the client cannot practice inclusion with the therapist. That means that even if the client comes to see the therapist with a medical model of symptom and treatment in mind, it still behooves the therapist not only to be open to dialogue with the client but to sense what lies behind his or her stated complaint. At the same time the therapist must continually hold the tension of being at both poles of the relationship and be careful not simply to impose his or her own insights on the client. As Rollo May says, the client cannot really have an insight until he or she is ready to act on it.

SPONTANEOUS DIALOGUE WITHIN FIXED STRUCTURE

It would be hypocritical and naive to believe that even the most radical of therapists have no fixed structure of psychotherapy. By structure we mean the rules of the game: the length of the therapeutic hour, the fee, the place of the session, the ethical norms for the therapist's behavior, etc. Yet within that very structure the therapist longs for the spontaneity of genuine dialogue—the meeting that comes about only when neither therapist nor client are focusing on the structure even though they both know that it is there. This is a variant of the interaction that holds in general between I-It and I-Thou. We cannot meet at all unless we set a time and place for our meeting. Yet if a genuine meeting occurs, in a very real sense the time and place are within our meeting as well as the other way around.

An example of the paradox of spontaneity in structure has to do with the problematics of the fee. Almost every therapist has had the experience of being reproached by the client for taking a fee. The client cannot believe that the therapist feels something genuine for him or her if the therapist takes money for the session. One of Dr. Kron's patients compared therapists to whores. Both of them are being paid for "friendship by the hour." There are clients who get into very long discussions about the place of the fee in the therapeutic relationship. It is as if the client confronts the therapist with the paradoxical nature of intimate interchange being set within a professional structure. Even though most therapists act as if this paradox does not exist for them, and their answers to their clients' reproaches come easily to them, it is still a fact that they too are caught in this tension.

Once Dr. Friedman was having a final session with a woman client whom he had seen for almost a year within the university counseling center setting. He informed her that though his year of internship was over, he could continue to see her privately for a small fee. The client, an exceptionally good-looking woman who had expressed surprise in earlier sessions that Dr. Friedman had not responded to her as such, now told the well-known story of the man who asked a woman if she would sleep with him for a million dollars. When she agreed, he said, "How about $2.00?" The woman responded indignantly, "What do you think I am?" to which the man retorted, "We have already settled what you are. Now we are just quibbling about the fee!" Needless to say, that was the last time Dr. Friedman saw this client.

One of Dr. Kron's most painful cases illustrates how difficult it is in practice to maintain the right tension between structure and spontaneous dialogue. This case so pushed the limits of structure to an extreme that it might well be regarded as the proverbial exception that proves the rule. A young woman asked for Dr. Kron's help in her distress over her separation from her husband. Her decision to separate from him came after he had been depressed for a long period, his depression seriously injuring their family life. Though she realized his psychopathology, she was all the same enraged by his seeming to lack any will to get better and break out of his pattern of illness. After much hesitation she decided to ask him to move out.

She was in therapy with Dr. Kron for about three months before she decided to ask for a divorce. At about the same time, her husband sank into an even deeper depression. Worried about his state, she tried unsuccessfully to contact his therapist. One day she burst in unannounced in Dr. Kron's home, shouting and weeping. "My husband killed himself!" she cried. "I knew it would happen." Dr. Kron hugged her and offered what comfort she could. The client told Dr. Kron how she went in fear to her husband's place and found him hanging on the wall. As the client was in no state to do anything of what was needed, Dr. Kron took it on herself to call the medical first-aid organization and the police. The client stayed at Dr. Kron's home for about five hours, during which time the police officers came and interrogated her. Later that week Dr. Kron visited the patient during her week of mourning (the traditional *shiva*).

The client continued therapy for about four sessions in which she talked mainly about her children's distress over their father's death and asked for Dr. Kron's advice on how to deal with them. At the fifth session, she unexpectedly announced that she had decided to terminate therapy. Her reasons for this were her feelings that at this period of her life she did not need therapy since her main reason for beginning it was her ambivalence about separating from her husband. "Now I have to deal with practical things and not with inner feelings," she said. She resisted going into other possible reasons for her decision to terminate therapy.

Dr. Kron was quite perplexed by this decision. After she had helped the client in her most painful hour in a way that went far beyond what was ordinarily expected of a therapist, the client responded by cutting her off. Only later did Dr. Kron fully comprehend the problematics of her own overstepping of the limits and breaking the rules that she herself had set as the structure within which therapy took place. The paradox lies in the fact that even while comprehending these problematics, Dr. Kron realizes that if the same thing should happen again, she would probably act in the same way.

As Martin Buber writes in his essay "Healing Through Meeting":

In a decisive hour, together with the patient entrusted to and trusting in him, he [the therapist] has left the closed room of psychological treatment in which the analyst rules by means of his systematic and methodological superiority and has stepped forth with him into the air of the world where self is exposed to self. (*ABH*, 142)

The psychotherapist . . . will return to [his method] . . . as one to whom the necessity of genuine personal meetings . . .

between the one in need of help and the helper has been
revealed . . . a modified method in which . . . the unexpected,
which contradicts the prevailing theories and demands his
ever-renewed personal involvement, also finds its place. (140)

This was exactly the situation in which Dr. Kron found herself when her
client came to her home shouting that her husband had hanged himself.

THE PROBLEM OF SILENCE

The issue of silence in the therapy hour and the problem of confirming
the silent client can only be satisfactorily answered, in our opinion, in a
dialogical way, by moving from empathy to inclusion. Dr. Friedman
focuses on distancing (and by implication silence) as a part of speech:
"Living speech presupposes the distancing which gives man the possibility of a world. It also presupposes the synthetic apperception whereby
the world becomes one. But above all it presupposes that men become
selves in relation to each other" (Friedman, "Introductory Essay" in *KM*,
4). Silence is a part of dialogue as much as speech. They both are poles of
a relationship. There is a dynamic of silence and speech as there is a
dynamic of distance and relation. In inclusion the therapist can be at
both poles at the same time, thus keeping the therapeutic relation open
to that dynamic. For that she or he must forgo the conventions of the
therapeutic conversation and her or his own vulnerability as a human
being. Only then will the therapist be able to confirm the client in his or
her silence with all possible meanings. Laying himself or herself bare to
silence evokes anxiety and feelings of incompetence. But by letting him
or herself sink into these feelings without reserve, the therapist becomes
open to the possibility of meeting the silent client in the place where he
or she is.   •

A meaningful experience of meeting in silence came for Dr. Kron
when one of her clients who started the hour with resentment and anger
fell silent after some minutes. The therapist waited for her to speak
again, then considered reflecting on her silence, then decided not to,
waited some more, considered interpreting the silence as resentment,
then decided not to and fell into her own feelings of doubt, resentment
toward the silent client, anxiety, and guilt. Going through all this, while
the client continued to keep silent, her head sunk, the therapist found
herself, to her surprise, breathing deeper and feeling calm and relaxed.
Though silence continued as before, the atmosphere changed into intimacy and warmth. The hour came to an end, and the client raised her

head, looked into the therapist's eyes and said, "To my surprise this was the most meaningful hour for me in this whole therapy." With these words she got up and left the room. In the next session the client told the therapist that not having to reveal all the different emotions that welled up inside her while she was silent made her feel respected by the therapist even more than when the therapist expressed verbally her interest and concern.

CONFIRMATION AS ACCEPTANCE AND CONFRONTATION

Affirmation, accepting the other as he or she currently is, ought not be identified with confirmation. Because confirmation is a reality of the "between," no one can offer another blanket confirmation, regardless of what that other says, does, or is. Such a blanket confirmation would be valueless, for we need to be confirmed in our uniqueness as what we are, what we *can* become, and what we are called to become, and this can only be known in the give and take of living dialogue. Therefore, that affirmation which accepts the other as he or she is, is only the beginning of dialogue and must be distinguished from that confirmation which has to do with the development of the person over time. As Buber put it in his dialogue with Carl Rogers in 1957, "Just by my accepting love, I discover in you what you are meant to become" (*KM*, 172). I help the other with and against his or herself by taking part in that person's own struggle to find direction and to bring the aimless whirl which does not want to find direction into his or her dialogue with life.

True relationship begins with acceptance but must go on from there to a dialogue in which the psychotherapist may wrestle and contend with the client to help the client find his or her personal direction. In other words, confirmation is not synonymous with acceptance or affirmation. Human beings are neither good nor bad but polar. The acceptance of one pole only leaves the other pole and the struggles between the poles unacknowledged. Rogers assumes that by my accepting you, you will become yourself. This is because of his notion of an organic process of growth.

Martin Buber, in contrast, says that until I evoke from you that movement toward finding and taking your personal direction, you will not become that unique person that you are called (by your created uniqueness and what comes to meet you) to become. Thus it is not enough to reflect back to you what you are and affirm it. I have to confront you with your unacknowledged polarity in order that you will be ready to take responsibility for it.

Kenneth Cissna and Rob Anderson narrow the difference between Rogers' acceptance and Buber's confirmation by pointing out that in some cases Rogers too struggled with the client (Cissna and Anderson 1990). They do not, however, touch on the difference between Rogers' assumption of organic growth and Buber's understanding of the polarity in the person that makes it necessary for the therapist to help in the struggle to convert the "no" of the aimless whirl into the "yes" of personal direction.

An example of confirmation in therapy as confronting as well as accepting is a young doctoral student who came for therapy with the aim of working on his low self-esteem and his lack of confidence in his mental abilities. The client is one of seven children of a North African, low socioeconomic, multiproblem family who grew up in a nonencouraging environment. Overcoming all his hardships, the talented youngster succeeded in his studies and is now a doctoral student in a highly valued natural sciences program.

Listening carefully to the client's way of describing himself, the therapist sensed a tone of arrogance concealed within his self-deprecation. During the next few sessions she verified her impression. When the client repeated his feelings of inferiority and despair at his inability to continue with his somewhat pretentious project, she stopped him and said, "But you know, actually you are arrogant and presumptuous." The client was taken aback and responded with surprise, "Arrogant? I never thought of myself as arrogant, for I usually feel so inferior."

The therapist told the client that side by side with his feelings of inadequacy he does feel proud of his high achievements in the face of his low background and his hardships. "You can be justly proud of yourself for all your achievements," she added, "but you are still arrogant for being the only child in your family who made it and climbed up into the academic world."

The client became quiet and reflective. In the next session he said, "Last time I felt hit as though you had sent a missile at me. I was confused and bewildered the whole week. I feel as if my whole self-image is being turned upside-down." He then told of a dream he had in which he sees himself standing precariously on a hill of stones. He looks down the hill and feels afraid that the stone will start rolling down and he will fall and get himself hit hard. He then starts to descend the hill very slowly and cautiously, holding on to the more solid-looking stones with his hands and feet until he succeeds in going down all the way and standing on firm ground.

Both the client and the therapist understood the dream to be about the patient's ego-inflation, his fear of failure, and the acknowledged need to go slower and adapt his work to his present abilities.

In this vignette the therapist confirmed the client in all his polarities—inferiority-feeling and arrogance, high abilities and feelings of incompetence. While accepting his self-criticism and feelings of inferiority, she confronted him with his arrogance, of which he was unaware. The client could then see that he was in danger of ego-inflation and in his dream worked out the way to bring himself to a more integrated and balanced state.

THE "DIALOGUE OF TOUCHSTONES"

Looking at these problems of confirmation in therapy, we can understand more fully and deeply why the psychotherapist must walk what Buber calls the "narrow ridge." The therapist must hold the ever-present tension of a necessary polarity. The aim of the therapist, in the final analysis, is not just removal of this or that symptom or presenting problem but the confirmation of a person who has been disconfirmed by family and community. As Maurice Friedman puts it, in the deepest and most meaningful therapy there is a "dialogue of touchstones," in which the therapist helps the client who is confronted by the impossible choice between community and his or her own uniqueness to bring his or her touchstones of reality into the dialogue with others. Friedman speaks of this, in the language of a Hasidic tale, as "the secret of the bond between spirit and spirit" (HDP, 205–218).

This bond can never be reached in therapy through full mutuality but only through what Buber calls a "normative limitation of mutuality." Some important aspects of this limitation are those we have discussed in exploring the five problems of the tension between clinical detachment and intimate dialogue during the first interview, the ethical problem of responding to the presenting problem and to the client as a whole person, the tension that must be held between the structure of the therapy session and the spontaneous dialogue that it is hoped will arise within that session, the therapist's dilemma in responding to silence, and the tension between acceptance and confrontation in confirming the client.

REFERENCES

Buber, Martin. ABH (1990); KM (1988).
Cissna, K. N., and Anderson, R. (1990). "The Contributions of Carl Rogers to a Philosophical Praxis of Dialogue." Western Journal of Speech Communication 54 (Spring): 125–47.
Friedman, Maurice S. HDP; TWE (1991).

CHAPTER 24

THE WISDOM OF RESISTANCE

A Dialogical Psychotherapy Approach

RICH HYCNER

Each of us is encased in an armour whose task is to ward off signs. Signs happen to us without respite, living means being addressed, we would need only to present ourselves and to perceive. But the risk is too dangerous for us, the soundless thunderings seem to threaten us with annihilation, and from generation to generation we perfect the defence apparatus (*BMM*, 10).

As human beings, complete openness is not required of us, nor is that even possible. Our human challenge is to establish a creative balance of our hiddenness and our openness. Martin Buber, perhaps more profoundly than anyone in this century, has "pointed the way" toward this deeper understanding of human existence—particularly in helping us to understand the "resistant" parts of our being. My purpose here[1] is to provide a dialogical psychotherapy[2] perspective on the phenomenon of resistance in psychotherapy. Primarily, this means we need to understand resistance within the context of the "between." My main premise is that resistance is the *residue of an attempted dialogue cut short in mid-sentence*. The roots of resistance are interpersonal and ontological—not only intrapsychic. One of the implications of this is that the manner in which the resistant dimension manifests itself in the therapy is a product of the interaction of the therapist and the client, not merely a function of the client alone.

RESISTANCE AS SELF-PROTECTIVENESS

Resistance is an *essential* form of self-protectiveness. Whereas, tradition-ally, resistance has been viewed in a unilateral manner—that is, the client unconsciously placing barriers in the path of the therapy—it is that and more. All so-called resistance is a manifestation of just how vulnera-ble the "resisting" person feels. It is an "announcement" of the fear of taking risks that the prior experience of this person doesn't support.

Resistance is always a two-sided "wall." From the "external" view-point the person appears to be closed off, whereas from the subjective viewpoint he or she is simply trying to avoid injury to his or her vulnera-ble self. Resistance is the wall that encloses early, deeply felt wounds. It is a wall that is at best semipermeable. The daunting endeavor of the thera-pist is to assist the client in making this wall more permeable, to help the person become open to more-alive possibilities. This is never an easy task.

We can speak of there being a "wisdom" to the resistance if we con-ceptualize resistance as emerging at that point where the individual does not feel he or she has the internal support to deal with a threaten-ing situation. At that point, it is extremely wise to protect oneself; to throw up a wall to fend off what one is experiencing as a threat. It is wise to garner one's resources to use at a later date. The problem with resistance is that it is often anachronistic—not truly responding to the present situation. We forget the "decision" we made a long time ago and consequently fail to use our current resources in an appropriate manner. We fall into inertia—fear inhibits growth.

The resistance can be a *deep* expression of something the person des-perately needs, and it is the only way he or she knows how to take care of him- or herself. Resistance protects yet concurrently keeps the person from growing—it cuts off a dialogue with the world. This is what Buber poetically refers to as "the seven iron bands about our heart" (*BMM*, 4).

The intrapsychic roots of resistance are interpersonal. Their origins lie in the openness and vulnerability inherent in childhood. That pristine openness to others in our early years assures the inevitable pain that comes from, at best, "mismeetings," and at worst, the residual malice of the parents' own hurts and painful experiences. It comes from the shat-tering of the illusion of childhood perfection; the shocking awareness that I am not always accepted. Merely "being" is not sufficient; I also have to "do." Doing always entails risk and the fear of being found unac-ceptable and unlovable.

If, as dialogical psychotherapists, we take seriously the need to enter the experiential world of the client, then it is essential to under-stand the resistant aspects of a client's personality. Until the therapist can appreciate someone's resistance, his or her self-protectiveness, the therapist cannot fully enter into the client's experiential world. The resistance is *not* an epiphenomenon—it is this person's way of being-in-the-world-with-others. In fact, it is likely to be one of the more solidified parts of the self. That is, the client is used to being resistant in this particular manner, used to expecting someone to attack or to be invasive. Consequently, there is a security in predictably responding to others—a precarious security, but a security nonetheless. It may be "pathological," it may be self-destructive, but we should not underestimate how important it is for us to feel that at least we know that part of ourselves.

Often, we choose pathology over the unknown. Pathological predictability is safer than being present to *what is*. In many cases such predictability is like a piece of flotsam in the ocean; in a world experienced as precarious, it gives us something to hold on to. It saves us initially, but when saturated ultimately threatens to drown us. In such situations, a current vital defense becomes an anachronistic residue.

Clearly, when the client comes into therapy, he or she is not valuing his or her resistance. More likely this person consciously has disowned, often dissociated, that part of him- or herself. The initial task of the dialogical therapist is to appreciate the wisdom of this resistance.[3] This is a shift in attitude from the traditional perspective. It is a radical recognition of the betweenness of existence. Along with this appreciation, the therapist also must recognize how limiting resistance can be. This is obvious, yet the therapist needs to focus on this later in the process of the therapy. To make it the focus too early is to make the therapy a battleground, with a winner and a loser, rather than a healing endeavor. This is a difficult "dance" that the therapist is called upon to engage in. It is a dance with the client and with his or her resistance. It has a rhythm all its own—one often difficult to move with. It is a dance participated in gingerly, for there are many potential missteps.

It is necessary to teach the client that to impose external goals on him- or herself to overcome his or her resistance *paradoxically* guarantees increased resistance. The first step in this process is for the therapist to help the client to *experience* his or her resistance. Frieda Fromm Reichmann once said that the patient needs an experience, not an explanation. Once the client has an experiential sense of his or her resistance, it is then necessary to help the client to begin to acknowledge, to appreciate, to accept the resistance as an *integral* part of one's self. This is no small task given the history of the client in disparaging and dissociating from his or her resistance. However, this truly is starting with the phenomenological experience of the client.

THE CREATIVE VALUE OF THE RESISTANCE

The therapist needs to see in the resistance its creative value. This is often a fig-ure-ground reversal for the thinking of the client and even that of the therapist. It defies our normal logic. Though many therapists certainly have discussed the dual nature of resistance, none that I am aware of has put the central emphasis on the inherent phenomenological wisdom of the resistance. This approach can't be a "trick" or merely a technique on the therapist's part. Rather, it has to be a genuine appreciation of the resistant dimension of this person. By this attitude, this modeling, the therapist invites the client to begin to appreciate this previously disowned part of him- or herself.

Part of this task is to find out what the resistance is "saying." What is the message? When the client is able to understand and incorporate this message, then genuine change will occur. This message often comes from the deepest part of one's self. The client will not make real progress in therapy until first of all she or he is willing to acknowledge and then appreciate the wisdom of her or his resistance—that there is something *invaluable* about the resistant behavior.

Resistance is *not* to be castigated, but rather to be *embraced*. Resistance is not to be broken through, but rather to be incorporated. The message to the client is: *The only way to get to where you want to be is to accept where you are, even if where you are is not where you want to be.* What healthy growth requires is an integration of seemingly opposed polarities. It is the paradoxical valuing of *all* of one's self—including those parts perceived as undesirable—that begins the road to recovery.

A fundamental question that the therapist needs to ask of the client is: *"How* is this resistant behavior supportive to you?" An example of this might be a fifty-year-old woman who has been overweight all her life, has said that she wants to lose that weight, yet can't, and therefore beats herself up emotionally to no avail. In fact, that is what she has done all her life. Her weight is one way in which she has learned to interact with the world with a margin of safety. It is *a monologue desirous of a dialogue.* There is a psychological strength to her weight and that manner of being in the world that she should not dismiss eas-ily. For example, for many women with whom I have worked, being overweight has been a way of protecting themselves from men and from sexual feelings. By putting the weight between them and others, they reduce the threat of vulnerability. It may even be a way of trying to love one's self. When you can't get the love from others, getting the "nurtu-rance" from food may be a substitute, though obviously a poor one.

With another client, the presenting symptom of being depressed seemed to me to have more of the quality of being resistant, rather than being a true clinical depression. Her depression was primarily a stubbornness. It was a protection against taking risks with others—especially in the therapy with me. She often felt lost, as if there were no options for her. Her stubbornness kept the threat of others out, while maintaining a tenuous sense of self. This was someone who had very little trust in herself, much less in the good will of others. Her wall of stubbornness protected her. Here she had staked her claim to herself and because of her history with her parents was not going to let anyone in or let anyone tell her what to do. The more perspicacious my advice, the more she resisted. She viewed any attempt by me to get beyond her wall and establish a more intimate relationship with her as an affront. The more I tried to reach her directly, the more I failed—as had others before me. I began to lose hope of ever establishing the kind of relationship I thought necessary to provide a healing environment. As I started feeling hopeless, she became acutely sensitive to this, and it fed into her experience of people giving up on her. Resistant and frightened as we might be, each of us is terrified that others will give up trying to reach us. Each of us desperately wants someone to reach out to us, yet correspondingly we are also terrified of losing our self or our protectiveness. This is the ontological ambivalence inherent in all resistance.

Finally, I realized that I needed to appreciate the sagaciousness of her resistance. It had been her companion long before I had entered into a relationship with her and would be there for her long after our therapy ended. That is not to say that I could not be of help to her, but rather it was necessary for us first to acknowledge this as an *essential* aspect of her being— which in its anachronistic manner had given the semblance of some protectiveness. Only by learning to *trust that part of herself* would she tentatively learn to trust me. Therefore, I told her that she needed to learn to value, and even enjoy, her stubbornness, given how integral her stubbornness was to her sense of self. In response to this surprising suggestion, she said that she felt "found out." In a sense this had been her secret— even a secret to herself. Later she stated that she could let herself appreciate the value of her stubbornness for only a few seconds at a time. The image she used at this point was that of being on one side of a dam, where the water was building up behind it, and she was putting sandbags on top of the dam. The internal pressure to overflow the container, the resistance, was continuously building up through our developing dialogue, and her first impulse was to shore up her resistance. In doing so, she would not allow me or anyone else to help her. This was another level of resistance, once removed from her earlier, more primitive defense.

This was progress. She was a "psychological Joan of Arc," singularly alone and stoic. From one perspective, her refusal to allow much assistance from others may have looked foolish and at best quixotic, yet when I genuinely was appreciative of her fears, what was most striking to me was her heroism. Psychologically alone and feeling embattled, she had been able to survive. It was survival at a cost, the Faustian pact with the devil that perhaps we all make—and the devil is our own fears.

She embodied *both* the grandeur and tragedy of a human life. Consequently, I told her to acknowledge, at least to herself, her heroism in this struggle. This was quite disconcerting to her since she always mercilessly had criticized herself for this "go-it-alone" attitude; even though for years she seemed incapable of letting anyone be helpful to her (and therefore experiencing the vulnerability that comes with that). This was the first tenuous beginning of her learning to re-own that previously disowned aspect of herself. She was beginning to recognize that she was more than merely her conscious goals and awareness. It was the first step toward recognition and integration of her *whole* being.

THE RESISTANCE BETWEEN

A client's resistance is often an aspect of what therapists traditionally refer to as transference. The client relates to the therapeutic situation with many of the same fears and expectations he or she has in other interpersonal situations. However, this does not mean, as was sometimes thought, that the client superimposes previous experiences on the therapeutic situation, irrespective of who the therapist is or how he or she responds. Transference resistance is very much a function of the between—the meeting of therapist and client. There is no resistance without another person to be resistant to—either present or imagined to be present.

One of the soul-searching questions that every psychotherapist must ask is: "Who is being resistant, the client or me?" Often it is both. A natural, human tendency for therapists, as self-protective beings, is to get defensive with the resistant client. The main defense for the therapist is to view resistance only as the client's defense—here, defense meets defense, resistance meets resistance. The therapist's resistance exacerbates the client's own resistance; this resistance doesn't allow the therapist to encompass fully the client's behavior. The forward movement of the therapy becomes stymied. This has led some therapists to propose that there are no resistant clients, only resistant therapists. That swings the pendulum in the opposite direction, and once again violates a dialogical understanding of the between, as does the more traditional viewpoint that the client is the only one being resistant.

The therapist's own resistance is the most potent force for contributing to a therapeutic impasse. Therapists are human beings, well-trained professionals, but ultimately subject to all the vagaries of human vulnerability that our clients exhibit. In fact, it is this *very humanness* that contributes to the healing in the therapy. Clients can see the human shortcomings of the therapist—as well as the therapist's courage in struggling to deal with these existential limitations. This is important modeling for the client. Our human limitations are *not* a stopping point but rather a *meeting point.*

The therapist will certainly become aware of some of his or her resistances in the therapy, though that is not the focus in the therapy. There certainly is wisdom also in the therapist's resistance. This informs the therapist as to the limits of his or her openness and acceptance of others and the need to expand those limits. However, more is, of course, asked of the therapist than of the client. If there are significant resistances on the therapist's part, and these are more a function of the therapist's personality, then he or she needs to explore them outside of the therapy in supervision or even in the therapist's own therapy.

The therapist needs to keep focusing on the therapeutic meeting and not derail the therapy by repeating the "mismeetings" that have plagued the client in his life. Mismeetings will always occur; one cannot avoid this. However, if there are significant and serious resistances on the therapist's part, then this calls for the therapist to look at her or his part in the mismeeting, and this should not serve as an indictment of the client.

The relationship is central in all of therapy, but perhaps especially so in dealing with resistance. A solid working alliance is necessary for success in dealing with resistance. It is here that the therapist needs to call upon all the credits built up in the relationship. Ultimately it is the trust in the therapist and the relationship that establishes a bridge across the seeming chasm of resistance. The trust in the relationship is what gets both through the moments of mismeeting.

RESISTANCE AS CONTACT

It is the creative task of the therapist to be able to meet the client *at the point of* his or her resistance. All resistance is, on the one hand, avoidance of some behavior; yet, on the other hand, it is intrapsychic contact with oneself. It is contact with earlier defensive needs while concurrently being *inter*personal contact—circuitous as it might be. Circuitous, because it is contact through conflict. Resistance is contact *with,* not merely contact against. It is not a direct "meeting," but rather a defensive and markedly delimited contact. However, it may be all that there is.

Its importance is underlined by the reality that it is precisely at this point that others have abandoned this person because of this seemingly insoluble conflict. It may not be the contact that the therapist desires, but it is contact nonetheless. Resistance on the client's part is always a challenge to the therapist as to how to establish contact with this unique person at this unique point of resistance. Perhaps it is the greatest challenge the therapist faces, the challenge of genuinely "being-with" someone whom the therapist experiences as oppositional. Buber once said: "The limits of the possibility of dialogue are the limits of awareness" (*BMM*, 10). The therapist's creative challenge is to find the means to establish a dialogue with this person and his resistance. The resistance is part of the *whole* person, *not* an anomaly. The challenge to the therapist is to meet the client at this point of contact, in a manner that *encompasses* that resistance rather than threatens it. It is to see the resistance genuinely as a point of contact *between*, rather than as merely an oppositional force against.

It is a task that may become a shared endeavor of therapist and client. It is a mutual struggle to get beyond missed understanding. It is a Promethean struggle for mutual understanding. It points out the basic humanness of both therapist and client. This struggle is not only an increased point of contact, but in fact provides the possibility for being an *essential* medium for healing. This is so because it is exactly at this point that the client is most wounded. This marks a new level of meeting between client and therapist. It is a level beyond false selves for both client and therapist. It is beyond artifice. It is the true descent into the labyrinthine struggle for realness. Seeing resistance as legitimate and essential—even as a wisdom—means the therapist must meet the client at the point of resistance, as well as join with the resistance.

Joining with is the next movement beyond contact at the point of resistance. However, to join only as a technique is not the same as genuinely and deeply *appreciating* the wisdom of the resistance. Only after making contact at the point of the resistance can a therapist genuinely join with the resistance. To join with means to stand in the client's shoes. Perhaps it would be better to say that one needs to stand in the shoes of the client's resistant side, because the client himself or herself might not be fully conscious of his or her resistance.

Only when the therapist joins the resistance can genuine healing—a making whole—occur. To join with means not setting oneself up as an opposing force, not creating a threat or a defensive reaction against which the client needs to resist. In fact, the dynamic of resistance requires an opposing force to reinforce it in order to give it energy. In joining with the resistance, the therapist is standing on the side of the client's fearful self. The resistance, though real in itself, is often an expression of what Winnicott called the "false self?" Often behind this is a very diminished, yet more central dimension, of one's overall self, the "real" hidden self. In many ways, we can say that the real self has been hiding all this time in a very small psychological "cubby hole" The layers of defenses and resistance have encased it. Joining with the resistance signals to the client the desire of another to enter gently that small "space" wherein the real self resides—it is to request an invitation not force one's self in. It is asking the client's real self, almost like asking a frightened child, whether it is okay to enter into the sacred privacy of this hiding place. It is enormously creative, yet trying at times, to discover the client's hideouts—to enter those spaces, and to feel what it must be like for the client to be so fearful. This communicates to the client: "There is someone here with me who cares." It is a deep existential recognition of the hiddenness of us all. It is a recognition that we are all scared. It is the shattering of the client's illusion that she or he is the only one who is so fearful. This affords the client the opportunity to recognize that being hidden is an existential reality, not a pathological state. It is a recognition of our common humanity. It is this deep shared existential recognition that allows healing to occur. We need not so much to fight against, as to appreciate our common fearfulness.

However, there is also the reality that sometimes resistance is *just* resistance. This initial effort of meeting at the point of the resistance, and joining it, does not exclude later efforts to challenge the resistance. In fact, such a challenging—perhaps a "supportive nudging"—occurs only after the therapist has thoroughly understood the client's meanings, empathized with them, and has established a bond with this person that provides the context for such nudging. The necessity and timing of when to challenge resistance is sometimes difficult to discern. Once again, this is part of the *art* of psychotherapy. The client needs someone there who is interested, cares, works to join with—yet also *in a loving manner* is willing to challenge him or her. Very often, not only is this a new experience for the client, but it is also a very profound one. It is a way of "pointing to" the possibility of genuinely meeting.

NOTES

1. The presentation at the Martin Buber and the Human Sciences Conference was based on the chapter "The Wisdom of Resistance" in *Between Person and Person: Toward a Dialogical Psychotherapy* (Hycner, 1991). This abridged and edited version of the chapter is reprinted here with permission of Rich Hycner and The Gestalt Journal Press.

356   RICH HYCNER

2. Dialogical psychotherapy is a therapeutic application of the philosophy of dialogue put forth by Martin Buber and further explicated by Maurice Friedman. The term "dialogical psychotherapy" was, I believe, first used formally to refer to a distinct psychotherapeutic approach in either late 1983 or early 1984. It was incorporated into the name of The Institute for Existential-Dialogical Psychotherapy in 1984 in San Diego, California. To focus more on this distinct approach, the name was later changed to The Institute for Dialogical Psychotherapy.

Clearly there were many antecedents to this more explicit approach. Hans Trüb referred to his approach as "healing through meeting" (1964). He also spoke of a "dialogical attitude" on the part of the psychotherapist and of a "dialogical-anthropological" procedure for psychotherapy. Martin Buber, in his introduction to Trüb's book, concurred with the description of the application of his philosophy of dialogue to psychotherapy as "healing through meeting." Maurice Friedman, furthermore, in an article in 1975, referred to a "dialogical approach to psychotherapy." Also, Section II of Friedman's *The Healing Dialogue in Psychotherapy* was originally titled "Toward a Dialogical Psychotherapy."

As a further note, "Contextual Therapy" seems to emerge from the same philosophical premises as dialogical psychotherapy. However, as far as I am aware, it primarily has been applied to family therapy.

3. This corresponds to Trüb's (1952/in *TWE*) two-stage understanding of therapy. The "first" stage is focused primarily on the patient's subjective world. The "second" stage brings in the actual existential reality of the world—the therapist as a *real* person sitting with another *real* person.

REFERENCES

Buber, M. *BMM*.
Friedman, M. S. *HDP; TWE*.
Hycner, R. (1991). *Between Person and Person: Toward a Dialogical Psychotherapy*. Highland, NY: The Gestalt Journal Press [Published in German as *Zwischen menschen: Ansätze zu einer dialogishen psychotherapie* (1989). Koln: Edition Humanistishche Psychologie. Portugese translation 1994]
Trüb, H. (1991). "Healing Through Meeting." W. Hallo, Trans. In Friedman, *TWE*.

CHAPTER 25

REFLECTIONS ON THE BUBER-ROGERS DIALOGUE

Thirty-Five Years After

MAURICE FRIEDMAN

In April 1957 a conference centered on Martin Buber was held at the University of Michigan at Ann Arbor. The high point of the conference was a dialogue between Martin Buber and Carl Rogers, which I moderated. There were four hundred people present in Rackham Auditorium, but they were not allowed to ask any questions. Only I as moderator ventured to raise what I hoped would serve as clarifying questions. When Martin Buber and I went into an anteroom after the dialogue, he said to me, "I was gentle with Rogers. I could have been much harder." But he also said, "Because of the way he brought himself, it was a real dialogue." Later, in fact, Buber made me delete the last paragraph of his essay "Elements of the Interhuman" (*KM*, ch. 3) in which he had written that it is impossible to have a genuine dialogue in front of a public audience.

When Carl Rogers asked Buber at the beginning of their dialogue, "How have you lived so deeply in interpersonal relationships and gained such an understanding of the human individual without being a psychotherapist?" Buber replied by telling Rogers, first of all, of his early interest in psychiatry and his study with Wundt, Mendel, Bleuler, and Flechsig. But Buber added:

About what mainly constituted what you ask, it was something other. It was just a certain inclination to meet people.
And as far as possible to change something in the *other*, but
also to let *me* be changed by *him*. I, in 1918 . . . felt that I had
been strongly influenced by . . . the First World War. . . . I was
compelled to . . . live it. . . . You may call this *imagining the
real* . . . it finished by a certain episode in May 1919, when a
friend of mine, a great friend, a great man, was killed by the
anti-revolutionary soldiers in a very barbaric way, and now
again once more—and this was the last time—I was compelled
to imagine just this killing, but not in an optical way alone, but
may I say so, just with my body. . . . From now on, I had to give
something more than just my inclination to exchange thoughts
and feelings. (*KM*, 157ff.)

Later on in this same dialogue Buber said of himself that he met
with problematic persons for whom life has become baseless, persons
who need to know that the world is not condemned to deprivation,
degeneration, destruction. A year later Buber said that he had founded
his entire philosophical thinking on a study of actual human beings
from the time of his youth (Friedman, *MBLW: Later*, 344).

As early as 1952 Rogers defined the person as a fluid process and
potential, in rather sharp contrast to the relatively fixed, measurable,
diagnosable, predictable concept of the person that is accepted by psychologists and other social scientists (to judge by their writing and
working operations). The person as process is most deeply revealed,
Rogers wrote, in a relationship of the most ultimate and complete
acceptance, a relationship Rogers described in Martin Buber's terms as a
real I-Thou relationship, not an I-It relationship. The person moves in a
positive direction toward unique goals that the person can but dimly
define. Rogers told how he changed his approach to therapy from the
intellectual question of how he could treat the patient to the recognition
that changes come about through experience in a relationship. He found
that the more genuine he was in relationship, the more aware he was of
his own feelings, the more willing he was to express his own feelings
and attitudes, the more he gave the relationship a *reality* the person
could use for his own personal growth. He also found that the more he
could respect and like the client, showing a warm regard for the client
as a person of unconditional self-worth while accepting each fluctuating
aspect of the other, the more he was creating a relationship the client
could use. This acceptance necessarily includes a continuing desire to
understand the other's feelings and thoughts, which leaves the other

really free to explore all the hidden nooks and frightening crannies of his or her inner and often buried experience. This includes, as well, complete freedom from any type of moral or diagnostic evaluation (Rogers 1961).

As a therapist, Rogers wrote,

> I enter the relationship not as a scientist, not as a physician who can accurately diagnose and cure, but as a person entering into a personal relationship. Insofar as I see him only as an object, the client will tend to become only an object. I risk myself, because if, as the relationship deepens, what develops is a failure, a regression, a repudiation of me and the relationship by the client, then I . . . will lose . . . a part of myself.

The therapist conducts the therapy without conscious plan and responds to the other person with his or her whole being, that is, total "organismic sensitivity":

> When there is this complete unity, singleness, fullness of experiencing in the relationship, then it acquires the "out-of-this-world" quality which therapists have remarked upon, a sort of trance-like feeling in the relationship from which both the client and I emerge at the end of the hour, as if from a deep well or tunnel. In these moments there is, to borrow Buber's phrase, a real "I-Thou" relationship, a timeless living in the experience which is *between* the client and me. It is at the opposite pole from seeing the client, or myself, as an object. It is the height of personal subjectivity. (Rogers 1961, 201–2)

Through the therapist's willingness to risk, and his or her confidence in the client, the therapist makes it easier for the client to take the plunge into the stream of experiencing. This process of becoming opens up a new way of living in which the client feels "more unique and hence more alone" but at the same time is able to enter into relations with others that are deeper and more satisfying and that "draw more of the realness of the other person into the relationship" (203).

In 1967 Rogers published a brief statement that can well serve as a summation of his view on healing through meeting:

> I find that when I am able to let myself be congruent and genuine, it often helps the other person. When the other person is transparently real and congruent, it often helps me. In those rare moments when a deep realness in one meets a deep realness in the other, it is a memorable I-Thou relationship, as Buber would call it. Such a deep and mutual personal encounter is experienced

by me as very growth enhancing. A person who is loved appre-
ciatively, not possessively, blooms and develops his own unique
self. The person who loves non-possessively is himself enriched.
(Rogers, 1967, 18–19)

In "Healing through Meeting," Buber suggested that there are times
when the therapist must put aside his professional superiority and his
method and meet the patient as self to self (*ABH*, 138–43). Yet in his dialogue with Rogers, Buber would not accept Rogers' insistence that the
relationship between therapist and patient should be seen, within the
relationship itself, as fully mutual. To understand Buber's stance on this
issue, we must look at his concept of "inclusion" and of the "normative
limitation" of inclusion in the therapy situation. In friendship and love,
"inclusion," which Buber also called "imagining the real" and "experiencing the other side," is mutual. In the healing relationship, however,
it is necessarily one-sided. The patient cannot equally well experience
the relationship from the side of the therapist or the pupil from the side
of the teacher without destroying or fundamentally altering the relationship. This does not mean that the therapist is reduced to treating his
patient as an object, an It. The one-sided inclusion of therapy is still an
I-Thou relationship, and it is only in this relation that real therapy can
take place. If "all real living is meeting," as Buber says in his classic *I
and Thou* (1958), all true healing also takes place through meeting.

If the psychotherapist is satisfied to "analyze" the patient, "i.e., to
bring to light unknown factors from his microcosm, and to set to some
conscious work in life the energies which have been transformed by
such an emergence," then, wrote Buber in his 1958 Postscript to *I and
Thou*, he may be successful in some repair work. At best he may help a
soul that is diffused and poor in structure to collect and order itself to
some extent, but the real matter, the regeneration of an atrophied personal center, will not be achieved. This can be done only by one who
grasps the buried latent unity of the suffering soul with the great glance
of the doctor, and this can only be attained in the person-to-person attitude of a partner, not by the consideration and examination of an object.

A common situation, however, does not mean one that each enters
from the same or even a similar position. In psychotherapy, the difference
in position is not only that of personal stance, but also of role and function,
a difference determined by the very difference of purpose that led each to
enter the relationship. If the goal is a common one—the healing of the
patient—the relationship to that goal differs radically as between therapist
and patient, and the healing that takes place depends as much upon the
recognition of that difference as upon the mutuality of meeting and trust:

In order that he may coherently further the liberation and actualization of that unity in a new accord of the person with the
world, the psychotherapist, like the educator, must stand again
and again not merely at his own pole in the bipolar relation,
but also with the strength of present realization at the other
pole, and experience the effect of his own action. . . . the specific "healing" relation would come to an end the moment the
patient thought of, and succeeded in, practising "inclusion"
and experiencing the event from the doctor's pole as well.
Healing, like educating, is only possible to the one who lives
over against the other, and yet is detached. (I and Thou, 133)

The issue that arose between Buber and Rogers on the subject of
mutuality between therapist and client is a subtle one, to do justice to
which we must look at what each of the two said. Rogers began his side of
the dialogue with a description of his own approach to therapy and ventured that it was, as he himself had often written, an I-Thou relationship:

I feel that when I am being effective as a therapist I enter the relationship
as a subjective person, not as a scrutinizer and not as a scientist. I feel too
that when I am most effective that somehow I am relatively whole in
that relationship. . . . When in such a relationship I feel a real willingness
for the other person to be what he is, I call that acceptance. . . . I am willing for him to possess the feeling he possesses, to hold the attitudes he
holds, to be the person he is. . . . in those moments I am able to sense
with a good deal of clarity the way his experience seems to him, really
viewing it from within him, yet without losing my own personhood or
sacrificing in that. And then, if in addition to those things, on my part,
my client or the person with whom I am working is able to sense something of those attitudes in me, then it seems there is a real experiential
meeting of persons in which each of us is changed (KM, 159–60).

It is not surprising that Buber characterized what Rogers had said as
a very good example of a certain moment of dialogic existence. For there
are present here all the elements that Buber himself emphasizes: meeting the other as a partner and not an object, experiencing the client's
side of the relationship without losing one's own, bringing oneself as a
whole person, accepting the other as the person she is in her otherness.
It is important to note that in this description Rogers does not, in fact,
claim total mutuality. As a therapist, he sees the patient from within,
whereas the patient's inclusion is limited to sensing something of the
therapist's attitude toward him and does not touch on the therapist as a
person with problems of his own.

Buber suggested that in this situation, which the therapist and the patient have in common, it is, from the point of view of the therapist, a sick person coming to him and asking for a particular kind of help. Rogers objected that if he looked at the patient as a "sick person," he would not be able to be of real help to him. Buber discarded the word "sick," but retained the description of the situation as one in which the person comes to the therapist for help and insisted that this makes an essential difference in the role of therapist and patient.

> He comes for help to you. You don't come for help to him. And not only this, but you are able, more or less, to help him. . . . He is, may I say, entangled in your life, in your thoughts, in your being, your communication, and so on. But he is not interested in you as you. It cannot be. You are interested . . . in him as this person. This kind of detached presence he cannot have and give. (*KM*, 161)

In Buber's philosophical anthropology there are two movements—distancing and relating. Buber was saying that this person, because of his or her problems, has lost that capacity for distancing that enables one to appreciate the other from where he or she is. He was also saying that the structure and the demand placed on the great therapist to experience the relationship from both sides precludes complete mutuality. This does *not* mean that there is no mutuality. There is mutuality of contact, mutuality of trust, and mutuality of sharing a common problem, for every problem a patient or client brings is part of the whole communal reality with which both therapist and client must be concerned. But mutuality in the sense of inclusion, of experiencing the other side, cannot be demanded.

Years ago I sent Erich Fromm a copy of an article on Buber and psychotherapy entitled "Healing through Meeting." When I saw him some time later, Fromm said to me, "I like that title very much. In fact, my patients heal me." I'm sure that there is no therapist who is not in some way healed by his or her clients, and there is no good teacher who is not to some extent taught by his or her students. But you don't set it as a demand or as a goal.

Buber went on to say that in the common situation Rogers was able to observe, know, and help the patient from both his own side and that of the patient. The therapist can experience bodily the patient's side of the situation and feel himself touched by what he does to the patient, whereas the situation itself makes it impossible for the patient to experience the therapist's side of the relationship. "You are not equals and cannot be. You have the . . . great self-imposed task to supplement this need of his and to do rather more than in the normal situation. . . . I see you *mean* being on the same plane, but you cannot." These are the sometimes tragic limitations to simple humanity *(KM,* 162). Rogers agreed that if the client could really experience the therapist's side of the situation fully, the therapy would be about over, but he also insisted that the client's "way of looking at his experience, distorted though it might be, is something I can look upon as having equal authority, equal validity with the way I feel life and experience it. It seems to me that really is the basis of helping" (162). "Neither you nor he look on your experience," Buber said to Rogers. "The subject is exclusively him and his experience." In response, Rogers suggested that what Buber said applies to the situation looked at from the outside; this has nothing to do with the actual therapy relationship that is "something immediate, equal, a meeting of two persons on an equal basis even though in the world of I-It it could be seen as a very unequal relationship." Buber replied that effective human dialogue must be concerned with limits and that these limits transcend Rogers' method, especially in the case of the schizophrenic and the paranoid:

> I can talk to the schizophrenic, as far as he is willing to let me into his particular world that is his own. But in the moment when he shuts himself, I cannot go on. And the same, only in a terrible, terrifyingly strong manner, is the case with the paranoiac. He does not open himself, he does not shut himself, he *is* shut. And I feel this terrible fate very strongly. Because in the world of normal men there are just analogous cases. When a sane man behaves not to everyone but behaves to some people just so, being shut. And the problem is if he could be open, if he could open himself. This is a problem for the human in general. *(KM* 165–66)

Rogers replied that in the most real moments of therapy the desire to help is only a substratum. Although he would not say that the relationship is reciprocal in the sense that the client wants to understand and to help him, Rogers asserted that when real change takes place it is reciprocal in the sense that the therapist sees this individual as he or she is in that moment, and the client really senses this understanding and acceptance. To this Buber responded that Rogers gives the client something in order to make him equal for that moment. This is a situation of minutes, not of an hour, and these minutes are made *able* by Rogers, who out of a certain fullness gives the client what the client wants in order to be able to be, just for this moment, on the same plane with the therapist. In all of this interchange Rogers never once actually suggested that he turned to the client with his problems or that the client was in any way concerned with his (Rogers') problems.

The second major issue that arose in the dialogue between Buber and Rogers concerned the difference between accepting the client and confirming him or her. Confirmation is central to Buber's philosophical anthropology, but it rests in its turn on the fact that in human life together we set others at a distance and make them independent. It is this primal setting at a distance that enables us to enter into relation, as an individual self, with those like ourselves. Through this "interhuman" relation we confirm each other, becoming a self with the other. The inmost growth of the self is not accomplished by our relation to ourselves, "as people like to suppose today" (61), but by the confirmation in which one knows oneself to be "made present" in one's uniqueness by another. Self-realization and self-actualization from this stand-point are not the *goal* but the *by-product*. The goal is completing distance by relation, and relation here means mutual confirmation, cooperation, and genuine dialogue.

True confirmation means that I confirm my partner as this existing being even while I oppose her. I legitimize her over against me as the one with whom I have to do in real dialogue. This mutual confirmation is most fully realized in what Buber calls "making present." Making the other present means "to imagine the real," to imagine quite concretely what another person is wishing, feeling, perceiving, and thinking. This is no empathy which leaves one's own ground in order temporarily to enter into the other but a bold swinging into the other which demands the intensest action of one's being, even as does all genuine fantasy. Only here the realm of one's act is not the all-possible but the particular, real person who steps up to meet one, the person whom one seeks to make present as just so and not otherwise in all her wholeness, unity, and uniqueness. One can only do this as a partner, standing in a common situation with the other, and even then one's address to the other may remain unanswered and the dialogue may die in seed.

A few years after his dialogue with Buber, Rogers adopted Buber's term *confirmation* for his own use, and he sent me a copy of the article in which he did so. In Rogers' use, "confirming the other" meant accepting the person not as something fixed and finished, but as a process of becoming. Through this acceptance, Rogers wrote, "I am doing what I can to confirm or make real his potentialities." If, on the contrary, wrote Rogers, one sees the relationship as only an opportunity to reinforce certain types of words or opinions in the other, as Verplanck, Lindsley, and B. F. Skinner do in their therapy of operant conditioning, then one confirms him or her as a basically mechanical, manipulable object and then tends to act in ways that support this hypothesis. Only a relationship that "reinforces" *all* that one is, "the person that he is with all his existent potentialities,"

Rogers concluded, is one that, to use Buber's terms, *confirms* him "as a living person, capable of creative inner development" (Rogers 1961, 55–56).

Rogers, however, tended to equate acceptance and confirmation, while Buber said in effect, "No, I have to distinguish between the two." I begin with acceptance, but then sometimes to confirm this person I have to wrestle with, against, and for him or her. Although one part of you may have personal direction, the other part of you is an aimless whirl. I have to help you in taking a direction rather than just remaining with the aimless whirl.

In the course of his 1957 seminars at the Washington School of Psychiatry, Martin Buber threw out some hints concerning confirmation in therapy and its relation to healing through meeting that help us understand this more exactly. The therapist's openness and willingness to receive whatever comes is necessary in order that the patient may trust existentially, Buber said. A certain very important kind of healing—existential healing—takes place through meeting rather than through insight and analysis. This means the healing not just of a certain part of the patient, but also of the very roots of the patient's being. The existential trust of one whole person in another has a particular representation in the domain of healing. So long as it is not there, the patient will not be able to disclose what is repressed to the therapist. Without such trust, even masters of method cannot effect existential healing.

The existential trust between therapist and patient that makes the relationship a healing one in the fullest sense of that term implies confirmation, but of a very special sort. Everything is changed in real meeting. Confirmation can be misunderstood as *static*. I meet another—I accept and confirm the other as he or she now is. But confirming a person *as he or she is* is only the first step. Confirmation does not mean that I take the person's appearance at this moment as representative of the person I want to confirm. I must take the other person in his or her dynamic existence and specific potentiality. In the present lies hidden what can *become*.

This potentiality, this sense of the person's unique direction, can make itself felt to me within our relationship, and it is that which I most want to confirm, said Buber. In therapy, this personal direction becomes perceptible to the therapist in a very special way. In a person's worst illness, the highest potentiality of this person may be manifesting itself in negative form. The therapist can directly influence the development of those potentialities. Healing does not mean bringing up the old, but rather shaping the new: It is not confirming the negative, but rather counterbalancing with the positive (*ABH*, 169–73; Friedman 1988, 28ff. in *KM* [1988]).

The heart of the issue that arose in the Buber-Rogers dialogue between *accepting* and *confirming* is located in Rogers' stress on *potentialities* and Buber's stress on *potentiality*—what the person is called to become in his or her uniqueness. I suspect that it is for this reason that at the end of the dialogue Buber repeated the contrast between "individual" and "person" that he had made in *I and Thou*. True acceptance, Rogers held, means acceptance of this person's potentialities as well as what the person is at the moment. If we were not able to recognize the person's potentialities, said Rogers, it is a real question whether we could accept him or her. If I am accepted exactly as I am, he added, I cannot help but change. When there is no longer any need for defensive barriers, the forward-moving processes of life take over. Rogers held that we tend to be split between our "should" part in the mind and a feeling part in the stomach. We don't accept ourselves, so if the therapist accepts us we can somehow overcome that split. If we overcome it, we will become the person we are meant to be.

In his stress on an unqualified acceptance of the person being helped, Rogers said that if the therapist is willing for the other person to *be what he is*—to possess the feelings he possesses, to hold the attitudes he holds—it will help him to realize what is deepest in the individual, that is the very aspect that can most be trusted to be constructive or to tend toward socialization or toward the development of better interpersonal relationships. Human nature, for Rogers, is something that can be trusted because the motivation toward the positive or constructive already exists in the individual and will come forward if we can release what is most basic in the individual. What is deepest in the individual can be released and trusted to unfold in socially constructive ways (*KM*, 169–70).

Buber replied that he was not so sure; for what Rogers saw as most to be trusted Buber saw as least to be trusted. This does not mean that Buber saw human nature as evil while Rogers saw it as good, but that Buber saw it as polar. It is precisely Rogers' assumption that the processes of life will always be forward-moving that Buber questions:

> . . . what you say may be trusted; I would say this stands in polar relation to what can be least trusted in this man. . . . when I grasp him more broadly and more deeply than before, I see his whole polarity and then I see how the worst in him and the best in him are dependent on one another, attached to one another. (170)

This doctrine of polarity leads inevitably to Buber's distinction between acceptance and confirmation; for confirmation means wrestling with the other against his or her self in order to strengthen the pole of direction and diminish the power of the other pole—that of the aimless whirl:

> I may be able to help him just by helping him to change the relation between the poles. . . . and the poles are not good and evil, but rather yes and no, acceptance and refusal. . . . perhaps we can even strengthen the force of direction in him because this polarity is very often directionless. It is a chaotic state. We could bring a cosmic note into it. . . . the good, is always only direction. Not a substance. (170–71)

Rogers spoke of acceptance as a warm regard for the other and a respect for the other as a person of unconditional worth, and that means an acceptance of and regard for a person's attitudes of the moment, no matter how much they may contradict other attitudes he or she has held in the past. In response to my question as moderator as to whether he would not distinguish confirmation from acceptance of this sort, Buber said:

> Every true existential relationship between two persons begins with acceptance. . . . I take you just as you. . . . Confirming means, first of all, accepting the whole potentiality of the other and even making a decisive difference in his potentiality, and of course we can be mistaken again and again in this, but it's just a chance between human beings. . . . And now I not only accept the other as he is, but I confirm him, in myself, and then in him in relation to this potentiality that is meant by him and it can now be developed, it can evolve, it can answer the reality of life . . . . Let's take, for example, man and a woman, man and wife. He says, not expressly, but just by his whole relation to her, "I accept you as you are." But this does not mean, "I don't want you to change." Rather it says, "Just by my accepting love, I discover in you what you are meant to become." . . . it may be that it grows and grows with the years of common life. (171–72)

Rogers, in his reply, recognized that we could not accept the individual as is because often he or she is in pretty sad shape, if it were not for the fact that we also in some sense realize and recognize the individual's potentiality. But he went on to stress the acceptance as that which makes for the realization of potentiality: "Acceptance of the most complete sort, acceptance of the person as he is, is the strongest factor making for change that I know" (172). To this Buber replied, with unintentional irony, that perhaps because he was not a therapist and because he had to do [as presumably therapists do not?!] with the problematic type of person—the person divided in his polarity—he was not so sure of that as Rogers was:

> I have to do with the problematic in him. And there are cases when I must help him against himself. . . . life has become baseless for him. He cannot tread on firm soil. . . . What he wants is a being not only whom he can trust as a man trusts another, but a being that gives him now the certitude that there *is* a soil, there *is* an existence. The world is not condemned to deprivation, degeneration, destruction. The world *can* be redeemed. I can be redeemed because there is this trust. And if this is reached, now I can help this man even in his struggle against himself. And this I can do only if I distinguish between accepting and confirming. (173)

Rogers said in effect, "I will come to you and I will be concerned about you. I'll have unconditional positive regard for you, I'll have empathic understanding of you, but I can only do so if I do it authentically as the person I am." That is what Rogers called "congruence." But confirmation, as distinct from congruence, has to do with the other person, not with the therapist. People do not just naturally develop so that all I have to do is accept them—in this I agree with Buber. They are in a struggle themselves about their own direction. While I cannot impose on you what your direction should be, I can listen to you and respond to you and, thus walking that stretch of the way with you, I can help you in your struggle.

I don't confirm you by being a blank slate or blank check. I can confirm you only by being the person I am. You'll never be confirmed simply by my putting myself aside and being nothing but a mirror reflecting you—in this Rogers and Buber would agree. But I do not see in Rogers' statements here or elsewhere the recognition that confirming you may mean that I do *not* confirm you in some things, precisely because you are not taking a direction. It is not just that I am watching you wrestle with yourself; I am also entering into the wrestling. It is only insofar as you share with me and we struggle together that I can glimpse the person you are called to become.[1]

NOTE

1. For an expanded version of these reflections, see my article of the same title in *Journal of Humanistic Psychology*, Vol. 34, January,

1994. For a fuller treatment of Rogers and a discussion of such central issues as "Empathy and Inclusion" and "Congruence and Unconditional Positive Regard," I refer the reader to chapter 1 in Carl Rogers and Martin Buber, "Self-actualization and Dialogue," in my *Dialogue and the Human Image: Beyond Humanistic Psychology*.

REFERENCES

Buber, Martin. *ABH* (1990); *I and Thou* (1958); *KM* (1988).

Friedman, Maurice. *DHI* (1992); *HDP* (1985); *MBLW: Later* (1984).

Rogers, Carl R. (1961). *On Becoming a Person: A Therapist's View of Psychotherapy*. Boston: Houghton Mifflin.

———. (1967). Articles in *Voices: Journal of the American Academy of Psychotherapy* (summer).

CHAPTER 26

RELATIONAL ETHICS IN CONTEXTUAL THERAPY

Commitment to Our Common Future

IVAN BOSZORMENYI-NAGY

INTRODUCTION

Martin Buber's writings have been a welcome ally in my lifelong struggle to find a way to help psychotics. This struggle for extending help to unfairly disfranchised people started in my teenage years and dominated my choice of medicine and psychiatry as well as later my choice of family therapy in the late 1950s. Subsequently, it became crucial for me to strive for a definition of the substrata of both pathology and health concerning psychosis.

It is correct to say that the touchstone of early family therapists was systems theory. The analysts had their weapons in exploring the unconscious; our magic was the system. It seemed to explain multiple individual psychologies in a simultaneous perspective. However, the notion of a superordinate, impersonal systems entity never appealed to me, and from early on I alluded to a "multiperson" system dynamic existing between relationally definable individuals.

In my search for the explanation of therapeutic effects, I developed the framework of an ontology of both the relational definition of the person and a personal definition of the relationship system. Classical, turn-of-the-century psychology, Freud included, emphasized the cognitive criteria of both identity and boundaries of the self. In my exploration of self-other definition, I relied on Hegelian (also Feuerbachian and Fichtean) dialectic in which each "I" is in need of a "non-I."

My first multiperson systemic model was a "dialectic intergenerational therapy" (Boszormenyi-Nagy 1965, 1967), which included a dialogue prototype originating from the notion of need-complementarity (1962). Obviously there was a strong alliance with the writings of Martin Buber, Gabriel Marcel, and Maurice Friedman. Gradually, I became aware of the importance of defining an ethic of mutuality as a dimension of both relationships.

From here on the dialogue has meant an increasing appreciation of meeting as responsibility, in addition to meeting as experience and ontic self-definition. I don't believe that responsibility in responding is a less important stress in Buber's definition of genuine meeting and dialogue than the experiential fulfillment and self-definition aspects of meeting are.

A 1979 formulation of *Contextual Therapy* states: "An ethical redefinition of the relational context characterizes Contextual Therapy whose primary resource is mutually merited trustworthiness" (Boszormenyi-Nagy 1979). The empirical basis of this therapy is the experience that through attention to issues of merit and fairness in relationships, a deeply relevant dynamic leverage becomes available for the therapist.

In this paper, I explore some of the challenges posed by the discrepancies between individual and relational understanding of the underpinnings of therapy. Also, through a broader view of relationships, I propose that therapy should concern itself with not only the quality of human survival but with the survival of humanity itself. Probably no other thinker of our century has expanded our understanding of the basic nature of spiritual health and sickness more deeply than Buber. Beyond ordinary notions of mental health and pathology, he describes the positive prospects of the human condition and leads the isolated individual *and* the therapist to the foundation of all close relationships so that ultimately one can be a vital participant in a genuine community. His distinction between the modes of I-Thou and I-It have brought us to the realization that the realms of therapy, education, and social influence are not separate from the ethics of family relationships.

Buber's understanding of what constitutes the most genuine type of relationship between client and therapist confirmed what I had come to see as the most helpful kind of therapeutic intervention. By "helpful" I mean caring about the welfare of the client rather than simply inducing behavioral changes. For Buber, "All *real* living is meeting," and meeting encompasses more than a psychological need of partners or even an experience of an existential nature. Meeting becomes what I describe as transgenerational solidarity (Boszormenyi-Nagy 1987). Through caring about their benefits and needs I "meet" even my remote descendants, whom I will physically never have a chance to see. Meeting includes then not only posterity's vulnerability to the consequences of our actions but also its rights to consideration by the predecessors, whose acts will be burdened with accountability for the captive future generation's needs and rights. Thus, responding occurs through responsibility, not through direct experiential closeness in meeting.

If we look at the statistics of family life, the figures show an escalating disintegration of close relationships. Child care, family stability, lasting commitments to married and family life have been steadily declining, while child abuse and abandonment are on the rise. The social structuring of Western civilization seems to be moving towards "social entropy": disappearance of complex structures (e.g., community, extended or even nuclear families) and dissipation of the energies needed to maintain lastingly responsible relationships.

"For the typical man of today," Buber wrote, "flight from responsible personal existence has singularly polarized . . . he flees either into the general collective which takes from him his responsibility or into the attitude of a self who has to account to no one but himself" (*KM*, 108). Totalitarian collectivism appears to be disappearing in our time, but materialistic callousness towards masses of underprivileged and disfranchised people may be on the rise. I would add that many contemporary parents inadvertently seek emotional security through draining the trust offerings of their children and thereby parentifying them. The family appears as a secure haven to the anxiously driven adult, yet the child cannot provide the safe and reliable retreat the adult craves.

Blaming the family is a mistake committed by many classical family therapists. In Contextual Therapy it is assumed that it is the broad disintegration and the fragmentation of relationships in our culture rather than excessively rigid family rules that pose the main problem in today's families. In our opinion, it is this very disintegration and fragmentation of meaningful relationships that parentifies today's young child. The insecure, bereft parent understandably clings to the young offspring, who is often held captive through his or her own dependency and family loyalty and even through his or her own failure.

RELATIONAL ETHICS

The ethics of responsibility for relationships or relational ethics differs from moral codes of self-denial of disciplined productivity. The ethics of

Contextual Therapy is fairness-based rather than value-based. It is not a judgmental, objectifiable opinion or decision. It is a lived "balance in motion" oscillating between the parties' mutual debts and merits.

What is the basis of trust and loyalty in families? Trust is well anchored if it is engendered by the partner's trustworthy behavior. On the other hand, trustworthiness is based on proven and predictable fair behavior. Exploitative unfairness is, of course, the opposite of trustworthiness. Fairness and justice are closely related to relational ethics. Relational ethics and justice are described in my article of 1976 as "an intrinsic dynamic property of human relationships according to which each party to the relationship is inherently accountable to the other for the existential impact mutually exerted on one another" (139).

MEETING AND TRANSGENERATIONAL RELATIONSHIPS

A major problem arises: the relationship between Buber's existential concept of "meeting" and the "existential impact" and pressure of accountability people exert on each other. Accountability means to exist not only for experiential satisfaction but also for consequences for the other. If responsibility for consequences is an important part of the concept of meeting, then transgenerational relating is also a form of meeting. The current generation meets its posterity through having an impact on their lives whether or not through accepting responsibility for the consequences for their partner's side. Caring about the pollution of the water or the air, for example, establishes meeting through both causing consequences and the implicit responsibility for consequences flowing from one generation to the subsequent ones. On a smaller scale, through weighing the consequences for his or her child (as, for example, in transgressing sexual boundaries), the parent is the one who has to be accountable, regardless of whether or not the emotionally hungry child colludes with the adult sexual advances by welcoming sexual closeness.

Dialogue means responding but not necessarily in a behavioral transactional sense. In transgenerational relationships one gives to the comparatively vulnerable posterity by considering its vital interests, for example by environmental precautions. Instead of the partner responding actively and behaviorally, his or her interests are voiced and represented through the giver's active concerns for the recipient. Thus the chain of generations makes the dialogue a feed-forward rather than feedback reciprocity. For their giving the forebears are repaid through benefit extended to generations of posterity and through entitlement earned through responsible action.

ENTITLEMENT

One of the key concepts of Contextual Therapy is entitlement. Its original meaning is of a legal and ethical nature. In legal terms it means legitimate rights or justifications. In an ethical sense it means the opposite of guilt, accountability or owing. As its psychological concomitant one can talk about "sense of entitlement" or "claim to entitlement." According to psychoanalytical authors, an ego attitude of entitlement constitutes an aspect of a type of narcissism. In Contextual Therapy it is very crucial to distinguish between *claiming* and *sensing* entitlement, which is the converse of what Buber describes as guilt feeling, and *having* entitlement, which is the direct opposite of real or existential guilt (Buber 1957 *Psychiatry* 20 pp. 114–29).

Buber's well-quoted phrase is "All real living is meeting." Meeting or dialogue in an intransitive sense of becoming then constitutes the vitally needed interhuman relationships that are experienced as meaningful. As I am meaningfully related to you, I gain the opportunity also to define or delineate myself. As described earlier (Boszormenyi-Nagy and Krasner, 1986), self-validation (i.e., the accumulation of constructive entitlement), is the most effective way toward self-delineation. Mutual self-delineation leads to what Maurice Friedman describes as "community of otherness" (Friedman, 1983). The existence of the other enables me to find my real self. In an ethical sense, through its relational integrity, the self confirms himself or herself through meaningful relationships.

Transferring the exploration of relationship into a transitive mode of "having" someone, each partner needs and uses the other for self-definition that requires a meaningful relationship. It is correct to say then that it is legitimate to "use" the relational partner, provided the mutual use is equitable and fair (I-Thou relationship) and therefore not exploitative. "Abuse," then, is an unfair, illegitimate use of the other (I-It). Ethics is compatible with mutually equitable distribution of burdens and benefits. "Using" the relationship is synonymous with getting returns from it. The corresponding transitive view of relational dynamics first has to translate all relational statements into balances of giving, receiving, and acknowledging. "Whom do you have to rely on?" or "Does your child usually try to console you when you cry?" are standard questions of assessment in Contextual Therapy's dimension of ethics of fairness. Such questions not only reveal what a person has received from his or her relationships with the other but also how correctly and fairly he or she can acknowledge what was received. Acknowledgment is a direct return; increased merit or entitlement is an indirect return.

The newborn child's inherent justification for care is unquestionable. This inherent entitlement is based on her vulnerability and her being and becoming a living being. In society she is entitled to her gender, racial, ethnic, and religious belonging. She is also entitled to be given a name, to be reared and to belong to her community. In order to grow up as a healthy person, she deserves being given attention, affection, acknowledgment, a chance to receive and give somewhat equitably. There should be a giver to fulfill her needs for equitable receiving and a recipient to help realize her needs for and right to equitable giving. Having someone to give to opens for the child the option for due giving. Thus she can "practice" her right to give, leading to constructive entitlement, freedom, security, and meaningfulness in life. Since the child is a link on the transgenerational chain of humanity, she has the obligation and justification for transmitting these elements of dialogue to her children and thereby to ensuing generations. In doing so, she acknowledges and pays her dues to her legacy of transgenerational solidarity and thus contributes to the survival needs of humankind as a whole.

DESTRUCTIVE ENTITLEMENT

One of the most important and controversial concepts of Contextual Therapy is destructive entitlement. As the ledger of justice turns definitely negative from the victim's side, his or her trust reserves become depleted and a felt right and tendency for revenge increases. The ethical credit underlying destructive entitlement can be channeled into revenge, often injustice to new, innocent victims. Not only do we deal then with the psychology of defensive displacement but also with the existential guilt or real guilt (Buber 1957; Boszormenyi-Nagy 1976) of causing new destructive entitlement in the victim appointed to be the retroactive culprit. Tragically, from a motivational point of view, the destructively entitled person acts as if he or she were insensitive to remorse and to due consideration of others. Entitlement can accumulate in proportion to having been damaged without any hope left for requital. This destructive (over) entitlement then "justifies" revenge. The persistent consequence of the inherent ethical fiber of relationships becomes, if relied on substantially, a tragic contradiction between the past injustices and an injustice turned toward the target of the substitutive revenge.

MOTIVATIONS

Motivation theory is the most dynamic aspect of any psychology or psychotherapeutic knowledge. By definition, any psychological statement is individual-based. However the intertwining between individual benefits and the consideration of the partner's side with a resulting gain through earned entitlement makes the genuine dialogue into a combined, individual, and relational goal. The contextual concept of relational resources points at options for such coincidences of altruistic and selfish goals. Its healing capacity follows from its self-sustaining, mutually motivating spiral character. Self-delineation and self-validation are both components of mutual confirmation. Or in Friedman's words, the community of otherness is supported by way of the dialogue of touchstones. On a larger scale, individual motivations aimed at self-validation inherently become coupled with an investing in the justice of the human order and ultimately in survival of humankind. Since threat to this survival is becoming a real possibility, increasing with every new technical discovery of progress in overproduction, the "resource" potential of any option for coincidence of individual gain with "altruistic benefits" is enormous.

ETHICS OF MEETING AND QUANTIFICATION OF ENTITLEMENT

Meeting in terms of relational ethics always raises questions of intrinsic quantification. Ethics, like economics, has an implicit quantitative side. Fairness, justice, equitability, symmetry are all questions of relative or comparative degrees of merit. Rarely is the question between the meeting partners "Who has or who has not merits?" but rather "Whose claims are weightier or more deserved?

In cases of earning of and relying on destructive entitlement, the question has to do with how much was given, taken, or received in the past of the partners? How much room or chance can one give to the other to live out his or her rights to receive or give equitably? How much did the initiator get back in the form of direct returns, and how much as indirect returns through accumulation of entitlement, inner freedom, and security?

Other questions can be raised, such as how much the damaged one was victimized through inherent relative vulnerability, e.g., genetic or historical deprivation. In a way, the more richly endowed of the partners is ethically obliged to give more to the relatively shortchanged other. Aside from such distributive injustices, how much was each relating partner subject to retributive injustices, in which case can someone be blamed for causing the damage? Of course, no human being is free from some measure of destructive entitlement. The quantitative questions become, "How much damage was each partner subjected to?" and

"How much was each partner part of an unjustly injured human order which deserves compensation?" Then, if hope for requital is diminishing, is it justified to rely on revenge?

On the other hand, as object relations theory informs us, early injustices establish psychological reliance on bad introjects. The tenacity of early psychological reactions is difficult to undo. However, any psychological reaction to unjust injury is only secondary to the ethical and even preethical reality that something unjust was done to the subsequent projector of blame, mistrust, and hostility. Thus, the psychology of deviant character formation has different rules of derivation but may parallel the establishment of and reliance on the ethics of destructive entitlement.

Of course, healthy dialogue includes one's honest and essentially trusting openness in claiming one's own needs, rights, and entitlement. Yet how much of really merited claim is there which is then thickly covered by substituting the current partner as a general target who has to stand for the injustices of the partner's prior relationships? It is useful to remember that one of the clinical signs of one's reliance on destructive entitlement is exactly one's blindness and indifference towards one's own unjust impact in current relationships. As a result, it is difficult for one person to objectively monitor how fair and due his or her claims are. This is why openness to the other one's needs and rights by itself earns entitlement.

THE INTRINSIC TRANSGENERATIONAL TRIBUNAL

The pervasive significance of relational ethics for relating in general led to the concept of an intrinsic transgenerational tribunal (Boszormenyi-Nagy 1987). The tribunal stands for the outcome of consequences from posterity's vantage point and thus it represents the "integration" of the sum total of all vertical and horizontal merit ledgers (309). Yet this "implied tribunal" is not a transactional-behavioral system or a forum. It is not separate from the aggregate relational intentions of the participants as discrete and separate individuals (311).

In a way the tribunal represents a dialogue between each of us and humanity as a whole—the justice of the common order. Buber often voices a concern about humankind as a whole, our species. From our point of view, the tribunal is the aggregate jurisdictional realm of concerns about fair relating. Transgenerational solidarity is one manifestation of a built-in human concern flowing from each generation's regard for values inherited towards posterity's right to transmission of valuable heritage only.

The ethical expectation of this responsible stewardship for posterity's benefits is called "legacy." It is another example of a forward-flowing mutuality characteristic of the negentropic (Schroedinger1962) properties of living things. Sorting out the good heritage is the opposite of the entropic dissipation of the more differentiated form of energy and matter. Concern about the quality of human relationships is to be included among other aspects of concern about global survival.

CONCLUSIONS

At the conclusion we come to an integration of Buber's genius and the practice of Contextual Therapy—an integration in which my empirical clinical experience meets one of the greatest humanists, a wise man of our age. The key resource in Contextual Therapy lies in the finding of unutilized options for mutual benefits, for receiving through giving. This is a controversial message to a civilization suffocating in a belief in self-limited success as a guarantee of effective socioeconomic organization and neglecting communal responsibility.

Regarding therapy, the conclusion is that prevention is inseparable from therapy; so is prevention of large-scale community disintegration. All that damages the trustworthiness of parenting will not only damage the child through transmitting destructive patterns of parental behaviors but also through engendering new destructive entitlement and therefore increasing the ominous freedom to take revenge on anyone, even the innocent posterity. Here is an enormous task for therapeutic practice and for preventive education. Destructive entitlement has to be prevented from being established rather than challenged once it does exist. Therapy cannot actually invalidate earned destructive entitlement; it may only diminish the person's tendency to rely and act on it. Divorce, remarriage, casual living together, single parenthood, abandonment of children, child and spousal abuse, or destructive parentification are only the more direct signs of relational fragmentation. Juvenile alcoholism, drug abuse, early teen pregnancy, suicide, lack of interest in education or career advancement,and diminished commitment to community participation, voting, intergroup relationships, religion, or any other affiliation are additional signs.

In a Buberian sense, all these areas need a rejuvenation of the trustworthy dialogue both between individuals and units of community. According to Contextual Therapy, the accumulation of destructive entitlement feeds into the transgenerational escalation of relational disintegration and symptomatic deterioration. The ominous future of our economic state, consciously or unconsciously, tends to underlie the destruction of relationship ties in a broad sense. Meeting in a Contextual as well as Buberian sense implies mutual benefit for the partners. By expanding Buber's notion of the dialogue into Contextual Therapy's principles of self-rewarding "resources," we have an additional human dynamic that works towards a responsible community. Our educational task, therefore, is not to promote an altruistic self-denying concern but to address the innate reciprocity between the self-interests of each generation.

Education is a process of giving and receiving. Yet without minimizing the demanding job of the teacher, it is clear that the child's role is the greater one—to be able to give an open mind, trust, and credit to the grown-up world (Boszormenyi-Nagy 1973). The more deprived the background of the child, the more she or he needs support and acknowledgment as a generous advancer of trust.

The teaching of ethics of family life is not a matter of book learning. Yet experience shows that children can be interested in concerns about environmental damage. Many have been reached by dedicated teachers of ecology. Here is an area of special training of teachers in matters of environmental damage and relational health. Teaching of parental ethics, roles, and behavior, of course, is not enough. Affluent societies cannot be excused for not setting up a far more rewarding taxation system for family support, for example.

Democracy in its best sense means justice, not just political freedom for the strong ones. This reaches into the ethics of welfare and taking care of the handicapped. The progress of democracy on earth no doubt increases chances of human survival. Democracy extends into the foundation of the United Nations. One of its great shortcomings is the lack of an interethnic code of democracy. The United Nations is officially defined as legally incompetent to deal with disfranchised ethnic groups other than officially admitted member nations. This leads to chosen inaction when it comes to regulation or arbitration between governments and minorities or other interethnic loyalty conflicts. Frequently this inaction leads to bloodshed and even war, the most recent example being the freedom struggles of component ethnic groups of the former Soviet Union or of Bosnia. Destructive entitlement of entire oppressed groups is a major source of the passionate defense of ethnic freedom. Typically, what is viewed as sacrificial heroism by the insiders is regarded as ruthless terrorism by the outgroup. Renouncing of power advantages of a military-industrial type lies at the core of an ethically based world order, a democracy between ethnic entities whether in minority or majority role. Thus issues of survival hinge on the state of international justice and legality, too. Loyalty of any ethnic or racial group to its own entity should be respected. Inasmuch as the United Nations fails to do justice to the non-self-governing loyalty (ethnic) groups, its mandate should be expanded. Without that, the disfranchised and oppressed groups will soon start relying on nuclear arsenals of their own. The brutal truth is that they do not have any forum that would at least receive documentation of their claims and aspirations.

Just as the psychological experiential driving force of the Buberian dialogue becomes a therapeutic resource in healing close relationships, the force of transgenerational concerns constitutes a potential educational and political resource for reorienting community leadership towards the ethics of a spontaneous consideration of ecological requirements. The motivating force locked into self-validation (i.e., self-worth accumulation) may constitute humanity's only leverage to prevent the Armageddon of a *"Bellum omnium contra omnes,"* driven by greed on the one hand and hunger, heat, cold, and lack of drinkable water on the other. A democratic social order of our hard-pressed, over-populated humanity—if it can still be built—has to be based on a transgenerational solidarity that might prevent the development of a cold-hearted, brutal dictatorial authority of the strong over the weak.

The scope of these conclusions reaches far beyond the boundaries of health concerns. This is where my own indebtedness to Martin Buber calls for the acknowledgment of a uniquely respected confirmation. The meeting of human beings in what Buber called "genuine dialogue" no doubt can add to the store of interhuman responsibility and trustworthiness. Beyond actual meeting, fair and due concern about the rights of future generations—despite material sacrifice to the self—can become a teachable resource. Earning of entitlement yields the rejuvenating power of a new freedom, compatible with responsible attitudes towards family cohesion and global survival.

REFERENCES

Boszormenyi-Nagy, I. (1962). "The Concept of Schizophrenia from the Perspective of Family Treatment." In *Family Process* Vol. I, no. 1, 103–113.

———. (1965). "A Theory of Relationships: Experience and Transactions." In I. Boszormenyi-Nagy and J. Framo, eds., *Intensive Family Therapy: Theoretical and Practical Aspects.* New York: Harper and Row, 33–86. Reprint (1987), New York: Brunner/Mazel.

———. (1967). "Relational Modes and Meaning." In *Family Therapy and Disturbed Families.* Ed. by G. Zuk and I. Boszormenyi-Nagy. Palo Alto: Science and Behavior Books.

———. (1976). "Behavioral Changes Through Family Changes." Reprint (1987) in *Foundations of Contextual Therapy*. New York: Brunner/Mazel.

———. (1979). "Contextual Therapy: Therapeutic Leverages in Mobilizing Trust." Reprint (1987) in *Foundations of Contextual Therapy*. New York: Brunner/Mazel.

Boszormenyi-Nagy, I., and Krasner, B. R. (1986). *Between Give and Take: A Clinical Guide to Contextual Therapy*. New York: Brunner/Mazel.

Boszormenyi-Nagy, I., and Spark, G. (1973). *Invisible Loyalties: Reciprocity in Intergenerational Family Therapy*. New York: Harper & Row Medical Division. Reprint 1985. New York: Brunner/Mazel.

Buber, M. *KM*.

Friedman, M. (1983). *The Confirmation of Otherness, in Family, Community and Society*, New York: Pilgrim Press.

Schroedinger, E. (1962). *What is Life? The Physical Aspects of the Living Cell*. New York: Macmillan.

CHAPTER 27

ETHICAL IMAGINATION

Repairing the Breach

BARBARA R. KRASNER AND AUSTIN J. JOYCE

This work is a unique distillation of Martin Buber's philosophical anthropology and Contextual Therapy's fundamental conviction that justice in the human order is most fully catalyzed through facing into the elemental triad (father, mother, and child) of intergenerational connectedness. Contextual Therapy was founded by Ivan Boszormenyi-Nagy and initially developed and nuanced by Nagy, Geraldine Spark, Barbara Krasner, and Margaret Cotroneo.

This excerpt is part of a book born out of the authors' respective passion for direct address, that catalytic claim for connectedness and willingness to test the premise that in one's own voice is the voice of a partner's suppressed longing.

Premises

- When people chronically give without taking or take without giving, injustices occur. Reworking injury to the common order of existence depends on the use of direct address.

This essay is excerpted from Barbara R. Krasner and Austin J. Joyce, *Truth, Trust and Relationships: Healing Interventions in Contexztual Therapy.* Brunner/Mazel, 1995.

- Direct address—a word, a tear, a touch, a look, a gift, a tone, a question posed—is the cornerstone of dialogic possibilities. It is a tool through which to catalyze ethical imagination and to attempt to initiate the process of dialogue. It is a way and a stance whether or not dialogue is its end result.

- In the long run, direct address is a healing intervention whose form is secondary to its substance, its context, and its goal of moving beyond interhuman stagnation and the destructive consequences of vital dissociation.

- A chronic inability to surface one's truth and to elicit the truth of another results in vital dissociation, the sickness and decay of organic forms of life (family, community, workplace) which enable people to live in direct relation and security with one another.

- The intrinsic significance of direct address is rooted in an interhuman ethic whose dynamic reality is that people in relationship both owe and deserve, and require dialogue to right imbalances.

- Direct address between person and person is ordinarily a courageous and demanding choice. But direct address between person and person in the elemental triad is even more so, though latent resources and residual trust are likely to be greater between the generations than in accidental relations—terror notwithstanding.

- The absence of direct address results in "seeming," which can be viewed as a form of collusion that protects people from having to know or having to be known, even in the midst of genuinely offered care.

- Caretaking can be an embodiment of seeming, a diversion from dialogue, an expression that one caretakes because his/her partner cannot take care of him/herself.

- Seeming is an inevitable consequence of failed imagination. The dislocation that seeming produces in a person, and between person and person, usurps freedom and converts the balletic movements of truth and trust into clumsy attempts to climb on stage.

- Seeming is the inauthentic stance of the would-be authentic person who longs to connect but despairs of ever truly doing so.

- Succumbing to a mandate to please, constrained by unreworked split and conflicting loyalties, and blindsided by the demands of felt or real unrelenting obligation, people take on a façade of seeming. Far from offering a safe haven, however, seeming corrodes being and corrupts the vision of healing through meeting.

- In the first instance flight into seeming is rooted in one's family of origin where, bound-to-please at the expense of one's truth, children soon learn to avoid direct address.

- The choice for direct address, to surface one's truth and to elicit the truth of another, results in vital association between people who have a legacy of give and take in common.

- Movement toward vital association signals a willingness to own my contribution to injustice and estrangement—in desperate hope that you will be willing to own your part.

- The very move from seeming to being provides a counterpoint to the impulse to please. Turning to face into the sources of injuries can level fear, free energy, open fresh options, and hallow the quality of day-to-day existence.

- Healing through meeting is made real when truth encounters trust, when trust elicits truth, and when the handmaiden of both is direct address.

- The healing resources which lie dormant in the sphere of the interhuman are catalyzed by ethical imagination (the ability to conceive and dialogically test what one owes and what one deserves).

- Contrary to human longings, the freedom to be (in contrast to the constraint to seem) is an earned freedom, sometimes enlivened by grace, which comes of knowing one's truths and terms for relationship, embracing and disclosing them, and testing them in circumstances loaded with possibilities of many-sided injuries and potential retribution.

- Despite our distaste for the fray and our wish for an easier path, none exists. But what does exist is sufficient.

- It is only when we stand in the grace of sufficiency that ethical imagination can break loose and inspirit reality.

ETHICAL IMAGINATION

This "seeing the other" is not . . . a matter of "identification"
or "empathy" but concrete imagining of the other side which
does not at the same time lose sight of one's own. Friedman,
LoD, 188–89)

Ethical imagination is a creative process born of the *two-fold imperative to be just and to be free.* It is grounded in the particularity of a specific context; it does not give way to generalizations. Ethical imagination is catalyzed by the ongoing recognition that merit never lies in one person alone but is always intrinsic to each relating partner. If a child is taught that only one of his parents has merit, he or she loses the ability to imagine that everyone has a side that counts. Carrying this logic to its furthest extreme, if a child sees one parent discount another, the child lives in anxious anticipation that he or she too may be discounted. Psychosexual emphases in traditional modes of psychology often hinder rightful exploration of a child's entitlement to consider and be considered by mother and father alike. Children who are inextricably caught between their parents grow up with a number of deficits which they then replay in their world at large. Failing the option of establishing a discreet relationship with both their parents (dual loyalties), they may spend the rest of their lives being for or against any relating partner—parent, mate, child, employer, friend, or cause. As they enter adulthood such children are typically unable to recognize the legitimacy in each of two or more opposing sides. A pattern of embracing one parent while dismissing or cutting off the other deprives people of the knowledge that they themselves have a side that counts. It can also convert them into self-proclaimed victims or self-righteous know-it-alls who can tolerate no deviation from a one-sided stance (Murrow 1991). Unprepared to wrestle with the inevitable ambiguities and paradoxes of day-to-day life, people flee into the seeming certainties of absolutes, ideologies, and zealotry. Parenting is none of these, but failed parenting produces all of these.

Straining the Imagination

There is no life situation more in need of ethical imagination than parenting. Society, offering little structure for parents and making many demands of them, strains the resources of young adults who themselves are trying to survive and thrive. Competing with their children for time, energy, and money, overburdened adults prepare to raise their young with little instruction other than the parenting they themselves received. They are left to guide their children, sustain their marriage, and earn a living surrounded by little available support. Isolated, unaddressed, and often depleted, parents cannot give what they do not receive. For how does a person continue to protect, nurture, teach, and enjoy a child when his or her own life has been reduced to function? It is true that parenting requires competency. But competency is not to be reduced to function nor is it to be had at the cost of connection. Real competency includes a capacity to meet the ordinary demands of day-to-day life and retain an ability to imagine what is required for one's own nurture and joy. The parent who gives without grasping his or her own limits or without assessing what (s)he requires or deserves in return will unwittingly transmit the burdens of a monologic stance: one-sided giving, untested assumptions, unspoken claims, and acts of retribution are the factors that obstruct the impulse towards connection and corrode the foundation of ethical imagination.

Parenting: A Dialogic Stance

Parenthood is a dialogic enterprise that begins with personal ground and shared commitment. In the first instance it contains a clear embrace of an ethic of caring give-and-take. But justice between the generations is held by a fragile thread woven into the fabric of imaginative questions: "My parents never call me"; Have I conveyed that they're intrusive? "My mother feels I'm unstable"; Can she learn to address honest difference? "My sixteen-year-old hates me": Have I ignored him for my new girlfriend? "My mother and father are always fighting": Can I tell them what their fights do to me? Like any other significant commission, parenting ultimately requires moments of quiet and direction wrested out of the stuff of ordinary existence. It requires parallel growth for parent and child. And most of all, it involves the ability to meet a child with the fear and trembling of one who has no ready made answers to life (Friedman 1955, 136).

Parenting is a dialogic stance born of accessible authority and imagination, ethically engaged with latent trust and untested hope. At the time of an offspring's birth, parents and child enter into a covenantal relationship which obliges both, and cannot be dissolved by either party, their objections notwithstanding. Above all else, parenting involves imagination, which is a catalyst that delivers meaning and vision to parent and child alike. When meaning and vision fade into function, they are replaced by regimentation, rigidity, and inaccessibility, which snuff out sparks of real connection. Failure of parental imagination quickly gives way to parental structure which, unhindered, results in recourse to moralisms, maxims, and categories. Then human life and interhuman justice lose their force as subjects of creation and quickly plummet into objects of despair.

Failed Imagination

The heart of man is not evil; only its imagination is so; that is to say what it produces and devises arbitrarily, separating itself from the goodness of creation. (Friedman, *LoD*, 154)

Unless the imagination of the young is stimulated to recognize the legitimacy of opposing sides and views, particularly but not only in "one"-parent contexts, they are predisposed to a victimized stance that lends itself to social pathology with its manifold expression of behavioral problems in school, delinquency in adolescence, and criminal behavior in adulthood. People can hardly be expected to imagine the full sweep of another person's reality if they cannot give terms or voice to their own reality. The paradox here emerges from an unspoken premise that someone else knows my mind and is bound to respond to it. But only an infant is so entitled. Still, I withdraw disappointed and absolve myself of further need to respond if my partner fails to offer me unsolicited consideration. "Why does initiative have to lie with me?" is a defensive if ordinary lament itself untouched by any hint of imagination. "Is what you want in your own vested interests?" Yes. "Can you imagine your partner's lack of imagination?" Yes. "Do you presume that you are being rejected rather than bumping against your partner's limits?" Yes. Blame and lack of imagination go hand in hand.

Blame is commonplace in every relationship. People have conflicting expectations. If you don't do it my way and things don't work out, then you're to blame. The notion of blame implies personal fault. Implied fault is a factor that sometimes has merit. A subway train crashes in New York. The driver is faulted for drinking. His actions are blamed by all concerned. Here blame is a communal expression of disapproval and an act of reproach, and can be justified as a demand for personal accountability. On the other hand, the uses of blame can be unfair, especially in relationships in which assumptions remain unexamined by participating partners and therefore stay unclear.

Unfair Blame

Unfair blame results from your excluding my truth in order to reinforce your own truth. Here blame is a one-sided act, an objectification of my reality and an imposition of your reality, a failure to grasp my motives, my context, my terms, my side. Under these circumstances blame is an arbitrary act in which my partner unilaterally exonerates himself or herself from any degree of culpability, and decides that fault for what is wrong between us essentially belongs to me. Out of this posture blame becomes an aggressive act. Unfair blame is often used as a haven from responsible response. Here I can justify hurt feelings without having to assume responsibility for corrective action. Constantly repeated as a mode of day-to-day relating, the use of unfair blame predisposes its user to a paradoxical dilemma: (S)he sees the limitless permutations of her own victimization, but discounts the injurious consequences of her own victimizing ways. When the reliability of one's truth is chronically deemed invalid, breaches of trust occur. Left unaddressed, patterns of unfair blame rupture the imagination, puncture justice in the human order, and cripple human inclination toward fair give-and-take. Failed imagination is a proclamation of what I feel and what I want, with massive disregard for the terms of another person. Ethical imagination is conceiving what I owe and what I deserve in a given context, with equivalent regard for my terms *and* for the terms of a relating partner.

Triadic Inclusion

The inclusive process that takes place among members of the elemental triad is the cornerstone of ethical imagination and due consideration. To wit, to what degree can child, father and mother be present to each other, have access to each other, and be mutually accountable without one or more of them having to pay an undue or escalating cost? Can I credit my father's merit and ask him to recognize mine, without fearing my mother's competitive ire? Do I know how to guide my youngsters to address their dad when they feel safer talking to me? When I mourn their divorce, will my parents hear me without feeling hurt, and blame each other for my grief or, worse, blame me? As an adopted child who carries a double triad, can I search out my birth parents without estranging my adoptive mother and father? Can I embrace my biological father without offending and being punished by my newly found biological mother?

Vital Dissociation

At its base, triadic inclusion has to do with the willingness of three people, who are inextricably linked, to move beyond "vital dissociation" (Friedman, 1955, 123) to ethical reengagement. To Buber, vital dissociation is the sickness of organic forms of life (including family) which enable people to live in direct relation and security with each other. Despite the outward preservation of some of the old forms, he says, inward decay has resulted in an intensification of human loneliness. In consequence, "direct, open dialogue is becoming ever more difficult and more rare; the abyss between man and man threatens ever more piteously to become unbridgeable" (ibid.).

On the other hand, ethical reengagement is the outcome of two people's decision to honor the connection that is already there. It is often a timid and wavering movement past old and stagnant impasses toward "a coalescence of constructive vital forces" (Boszormenyi-Nagy and Krasner 1986, 217) which, latent in the triad, are waiting to be mined.

Ethical Reengagement

Ethical reengagement involves a choice to repair the breach between people who have given and taken in vital association with one another. It is a signal of willingness to own my contribution to estrangement in desperate hope that you will be willing to own yours. My choice to reengage with you is clearly a self-serving act. It is also an act of contrition which contains at least a hint that you deserved something better from me than I was able or willing to give. Ethical reengagement between person and person is ordinarily a demanding and courageous task. Ethical reengagement between person and person in the elemental triad is even more so, though latent resources and residual trust are likely to be greater between the generations than in accidental relations—terror notwithstanding

The move towards inclusion in the elemental triad provides the basic antidote to repeated patterns of unfair blame. It is also the action component of ethical imagination. Nowhere are the seeds of justice and injustice, freedom and bondage, truth and propaganda, and trustworthiness and deceit more powerfully created, developed, and experienced than in the primal matrix of the elemental triad.

The causes of cyclical intergenerational injuries are squarely rooted in the breakdown that takes place in this elemental triad. Therefore the success of efforts to heal cyclical intergenerational injuries without facing back into this triad are invariably limited. Breaking transgenerational cycles of destructive and depleting patterns, which are precursors of emotional and physical violence, requires members of each elemental triad to find the imagination to turn to address each other—*whatever their limits and regardless of outcome.* Failing to do so reproduces and reintroduces the corrosive dynamics which undermine future attempts to participate fully in family, in community, in the culture or in the workplace.

REPAIRING THE BREACH

The widespread tendency to live from the recurrent impression one makes instead of from the steadiness of one's being is not a "nature." It originates. . . in men's dependence upon one another. It is no light thing to be confirmed in one's being by others and seeming deceptively offers itself as a help in this. (Buber, *KM*, 78)

Being and Seeming

Buber distinguishes between two different types of human existence: "The one proceeds from what one really is, the other from what one wishes to seem." He describes the duality between being and seeming as the essential problem of the sphere of the interhuman. He notes that all of us are subject to seeming and points to the human longing to be credited and confirmed. He implies the seductive quality of seeming, and the difficulties attached to being faithful to who one really is. He is careful to suggest that everyone is subject to seeming, and so focuses on the essential attitudes which are more or less characterized by being or seeming. He also implies the difficulties involved in self-disclosure or self-delineation, but regards the sharing of one's self as a sine qua non of relationship. Whatever else the meaning of the word "truth" may be in other realms, Buber writes, in the interhuman realm it means that human beings communicate themselves to one another as what they are.

Buber cites the tension between being and seeming, and acknowledges the cost of the "courage" to be, as well as the intrinsic flight from self and other involved in the "cowardice" of seeming. However, he stops short of examining some of the root causes that drive human beings to use seeming as a hiding place whose recesses obscure the light and the redemptive possibility of being. A stance of unilateral pleasing, or displeasing for that matter, takes root in a pathology of the soul and is the eventual consequence of truth and trust which have been repeatedly breached.

Seeming is an individual dilemma and a singular choice. From this perspective it can be viewed as a dependency on, even an addiction to external referents as the basis for one's internal terms. It is an abandonment of oneself as an equivalent referent in relating. *Pleasing becomes seeming when it leaves out my claim to be and my willingness to disclose it.* Seeming is also a form of collusion that protects people from having to know and having to be known even in the midst of genuinely offered care.

Bound-to-Please?

Consider the case of Kristin Hillman, one of four adult children who are struggling with a dilemma posed by their elderly parents, Mr. and Mrs. Jordan. Mr. Jordan, now eighty, has lived an active, hard-driving life, and has been deeply involved and committed to his career, to his community, and to his family, and seemingly beholden to no one. In the face of deteriorating health, he is contemplating the possibility of discontinuing dialysis treatments which occur three times a week and tie him to the distance between home and hospital. Increasingly depressed by the limits of his life and burdened by the constant bickering between him and his wife, he has told two of his offspring that he may refuse further dialysis. But he has not told his older daughter Kristin.

Kristin, fifty, learned of her father's wishes through her older and younger siblings. She adores her father and is frightened by the possibility of what she describes as suicide. Her father-in-law committed suicide several years ago, and family members have borne the consequences of that act ever since in profound and painful ways. Whether Mr. Jordan's eventual decision to halt dialysis is suicide or not, Kristin opposes the option.

In her press to be a loyal daughter, Kristin faces a watershed. Is she free enough to disclose to her father his meaning in her life? To risk telling him that his being still has its independent merit and from her side, and that she is terrified at the threat of loss she anticipates should her father volitionally choose to bring his life to an end? Or, still blindly driven by encumbrances of implicit and explicit familial and communal expectations to please, will she yield to seeming once again?

Constituent Parts of Seeming

At the moment, seeming appears to be Kristin's only alternative. In this situation the constituent parts of seeming include: (1) her decision to remain silent and act as if she were ignorant of what is actually going on; (2) her decision to avoid the risk of addressing her father and act as if she were without influence in his life; (3) her decision to collude with her father's protectiveness of her and act as if she were indifferent to his pain as well as to hers; and (4) her decision to duck her mother's wrath and denial of the gravity of her father's illness and act as if she were irreversibly caught between her parents without an alternative choice.

In the first instance, seeming as a way is always shaped in one's family of origin. Kristin learned to please her father at the cost of not addressing him. They enjoyed each other but never spoke deeply nor disclosed themselves to each other substantively. They spent a lot of time sailing together, an interest that has an almost mystical quality for both of them. But they never risked sharing their joy with Kristin's mother, who might have felt jealous or excluded. Despite their mutual love and attachment, father and daughter have no paradigm with which to overcome the seeming that comes of suffering in silence, a seeming that inevitably forces a wedge between people who care for each other and even offer each other care.

Seeming is an inevitable consequence of failed imagination. The dislocation that seeming produces in a person, and between person and person, usurps freedom and converts the balletic movements of truth and trust into clumsy attempts to climb on stage. Seeming is the inauthentic stance of the would-be authentic person who longs to connect but despairs of ever truly doing so. Succumbing to a mandate to please, constrained by unreworked split and conflicting loyalties, and blind-sided by the demands of unrelenting obligation, people take on a façade of seeming which permeates their being and distorts their vision of interhuman justice.

Looking for Guarantees

What Kristin and perhaps most people would like as a prelude to addressing her father is a guarantee that he will welcome what she has to say, and that neither he nor she will be "hurt" in the exchange. What she discounts is the degree of injury which they are imposing on each other by dint of their silence. Like many of us, Kristin had become habituated to withholding her truth, and to operating out of untested premises of what other people really want. She had become anesthetized to the merit of her own authority, blinded to the trustworthiness that has built between her and her family members in the midst of conflict and even harsh estrangements, and numbed to the latent resources that exist between person and person in her immediate world. She is also increasingly free to be, to unfold, and to become resilient, resourceful, determined, intrinsically fair and ethically imaginative.

Testing Premises

What would it look like for Kristin to test her untested premises against her closely held relationships with her father and mother? What questions could she raise, and what answers might she hope to receive?

Q: Has Kristin told her dad how precious he is to her?

A: No, I've told him how much fun it is when we talk about matters relating to sailing.

Q: Can Kristin imagine the healing impact on her father if she tells him of her pain?

A: Nobody in my family talks to each other like that. Why worry him about me when he already has so much to worry about on his own?

Q: Are Kristin's siblings and mother currently resources for her?

A: My mother always gets in the way of this kind of thing. It scares her. She interrupted my father's attempt to describe his circumstances to my brother. My brother and sister are the ones who told me what dad is thinking about. They didn't challenge him. They are inclined to believe that he has a right to do what he has to do.

Q: Can Kristin challenge her siblings to consider her differing point of view?

A: Yes, they would hear me, but I don't know how they'd respond.

Other questions exist and have no seeds of an answer yet:

Q: Will it occur to Kristin that she offers her father respect and dignity when she tells him her hard truth?

Q: Has Kristin given credence to her father's right to graceful resignation, enhanced by the balm of their lifelong connection and by her embrace of who her dad is and has been?

Q: Can Kristin receive her father's decision when it finally comes without making it the basis for further seeming?

The Task Of the Interhuman

The task of the interhuman requires each of us to face towards the fullness of being, to share our truth from the depths of ambivalence and to imagine the resources that can emerge from efforts at dialogue, however hostile or volatile they may threaten to be, and then to act. This is the way that points to the living substance of healing through meeting. It is the way in which real being staves off the necessity for seeming. It is a way that prefers the realism of despair to the tension of hysteria (Friedman, *LoD*, 136). The human disposition towards seeming can be overcome time and again through discovering the freedom to be. Kristin *did* go home again, buoyed by the conviction that it was in everyone's vested interests for her to speak her truth.

Going Home

I looked forward to going home in a way that I had never done before. I didn't clutch when I got there. I was far more personally ready just to *be* with them, to *be* me, and to let them *be* them. I've always been afraid of what I had to do to make it okay, to make me okay there. I have always been afraid that I was going to get caught in their clutches and be torn and turned around. This time I wasn't worried about that happening. I was just able to go. They were delighted to see me. I seemed more relaxed, and they seemed more relaxed. We were there together. It was what I always hoped I could be with my parents.

Sailing for Dad

Dad couldn't sail with me that day because he had to have a dialysis treatment. I said I would sail a little bit for him. He smiled at that. I did sail and had a wonderful time. When I came back I was invited to a dinner planned to honor my father for his generosity to the local seaport. I had originally said no to going, unaware that he was to receive an award. I did go and the event went well.

Reconnecting

The next morning before anyone else was up my mother and I talked alone. *For the very first time* we talked about the choices she had made, her distress, her sadness, her concerns for Dad. Then I told her of the sadness I feel for her. It was very hard for me to say it but I told her I felt that she had thrown in the towel on her life, and I was worried about her drinking. "I'm not drinking as much as I used to," Mother replied. "I don't know about that," I said in return, "but I do know that I'm worried about your health and about your falling again."

She was able to hear what I was saying. I wasn't judging her and she wasn't feeling judged. I asked her if she would consider therapy. "Would they do my alcohol or do my mental state?" she asked. She didn't say she would or would not go. But she expressed frustration that she hadn't found a mission or a passion in her life. "Can you tell me what you think I ought to do?" she asked. "I can tell you to raise monkeys," I replied, "but it has to be what you want, not what I think is good for you."

Love Me Now While I'm Alive

Mom wanted me to see some pictures and papers that she had, and one of them fell to the ground. "How did this get in there?" my mother asked. I knew it was a prime but inquired about it anyhow. It was a poem from a mother to her children sent to Dear Abby in 1987. Its most poignant sentence went like this: "Love me now while I'm alive, not when I'm under a cold stone with warm words. Give me the hugs and kisses that you know I want." With tears in my eyes I told her I loved her and gave her hugs and kisses until *she* let go.

Up to this point Kristin had always been burdened by her mother's attempts at affection. Up to now she had reacted against her mother's unspoken claims. It felt like a one-sided obligation to give intimacy while getting nothing in return.

Mom was thrilled. Not only did I not feel caught in her clutches but she didn't seem to clutch. So we both got plenty of hugs and kisses.

Truth and Trust

The next day I woke up Dad and said, "I want you out of bed." We three went to the dock and had a wonderful time. I expected it to be just Dad but I hadn't asked for that. Dad was tired when we got home and went into his office. I went in after him. The two of us were able to talk about the joys of the things we share; how important and precious he is to me; how I can enjoy sailing in the seaport without him but it's not nearly as much pleasure as it is with him. I told him that I knew the stress he was feeling and the distress of whether or not to continue dialysis. I told Dad that from my side, I can't afford for him not to continue dialysis. I need you here, I said, and our kids need you here too. Please, though it's hard, hang in there. You remember my father-in-law's decision ten years ago (for suicide). That was devastating to me. For years I was a crazy woman and I can't handle that again. But if I have to, I will. It's not the choice I want. Please take the best care of yourself. I know the pain but please try to stay.

Guided . . . to Harbor" (Psalm 107)

He kind of grumbled a bit and gave that face. "You know," he said, "I get poked every time I go, and sometimes I bleed for half an hour after that." I didn't know that. "Tell me about it," I said. "It's nasty to get poked twice, three times a week. But if you didn't get poked, you wouldn't be here. And I haven't seen you as happy as you've been since I've been here this weekend and we've been going down to the sea and doing ships." That is his favorite psalm, the verse about men going down to the sea in ships that says "They shall see the Lord." I was floating on air. After the talks with my Mom and Dad I got blessings poured across, around and over me.

Kristin's capacity to speak her truth in the crucible of lived life has given birth to new meaning in her world. In her passion to be heard, she has managed to transform collusion into claim, stagnation into reengagement, and seeming into being.

Freedom To Be

Contrary to our human longings, the freedom to be is an earned freedom, sometimes enlivened by grace, which comes of knowing one's own truths and embracing them, and then testing them in circumstances loaded with possibilities of many-sided injuries and potential retribution. Despite our distaste for the fray and our wish for an easier path, none exists. But what does exist is sufficient. The healing resources which lie dormant in the sphere of the interhuman are catalyzed by ethical imagination and surge forth when truth encounters trust, when trust elicits truth and when the handmaiden of both is direct address.

REFERENCES

Boszormenyi-Nagy, I., and Krasner, B. R. (1986). *Between Give and Take: A Clinical Guide to Contextual Therapy*. New York: Brunner/Mazel.
Buber, Martin. *KM*.
Friedman, Maurice.(1955). *LoD*.

Contributors

ROB ANDERSON, Ph.D., Professor of Speech Communication at St. Louis University, is the coauthor with Kenneth Cissna of several articles on the Buber-Rogers dialogue.

GOUTAM BISWAS, Ph.D., is Professor of Philosophy at the University of North Bengal and author of *Art as Dialogue*.

PAT BONI, Ph.D., is a Lecturer in Religious Studies, San Diego State University; Faculty member of the Graduate Religion/Human Sciences Program at the California Institute for Human Sciences, Encinitas, California; and author of a dissertation on Shakespeare's *King Lear* in relation to the philosophies of Martin Heidegger and Martin Buber

IVAN BOSZORMENYI-NAGY, M.D., Director of Family Therapy Section, Hahnemann University, Philadelphia, is the coauthor of *Invisible Loyalties: Reciprocity in Intergenerational Family Therapy*; coauthor of *Between Give and Take: A Clinical Guide to Contextual Therapy*; and author of *Foundations of Contextual Therapy: The Papers of Ivan Boszormenyi-Nagy*.

S. DANIEL BRESLAUER, Ph.D., is Professor of Religion at the University of Kansas. He is the author of *The Ethics of Judaism, Covenant and Community in Modern Judaism*, and *Martin Buber On Myth: An Introduction*.

SEYMOUR CAIN, Ph.D., former Religion Editor of the *Encyclopaedia Britannica* and the *Great Books* series, is the author of books on the French Catholic relational existentialist Gabriel Marcel and of articles on Mircea Eliade and on Buber; he is the Past-President of Independent Scholars of San Diego.

KENNETH N. CISSNA, Ph.D., Professor of Speech Communication at the University of South Florida, has published several articles written with Rob Anderson on the Buber-Rogers dialogue.

JAMES V. DELEO, Ph.D., Clinical Psychologist, is a member of the Core Faculty, California School of Professional Psychology, San Diego, and the Co-Director of The Institute for Dialogical Psychotherapy.

RICHARD A. FREUND, Ph.D., is Professor of Philosophy and Religion at the University of Nebraska at Omaha; and author of *Understanding Jewish Ethics.*

MAURICE FRIEDMAN, Ph.D., Professor Emeritus of Religious Studies, Philosophy, and Comparative Literature, San Diego State University, is the author of *Martin Buber: The Life of Dialogue; Martin Buber's Life and Work* (3 vols.); *Martin Buber and the Eternal; Encounter on the Narrow Ridge: A Life of Martin Buber; The Healing Dialogue in Psychotherapy;* and the coeditor with Paul Arthur Schilpp of *The Philosophy of Martin Buber,* volume 12 of *The Library of Living Philosophers.* He is currently Co-Director of the Institute for Dialogical Psychotherapy in San Diego and Director of the Graduate Human Sciences Program at the California Institute for Human Sciences, Encinitas, California.

ROSE GRAF-TAYLOR, Ph.D. (Germany), is a Lecturer at the Training Academy, Berufsverband deutsche Psychologen.

JONATHAN R. HERMAN, Ph.D., Assistant Professor of Religion, Georgia State University, is the author of *I and Tao: Martin Buber's Encounter with Chuang Tzu* (Albany: SUNY Press, forthcoming).

ROBERT C. HOOVER, Ph.D. (Canada), is Emeritus Professor of Environmental Policy, Brock University, St. Catherines, Ontario.

RICHARD HYCNER, Ph.D., is the author of *Between Person and Person* and editor of *The Healing Relationship in Gestalt Therapy* (in press). He is Co-Director of The Institute for Dialogical Psychotherapy and Adjunct Faculty member of the California School of Professional Psychology.

G. RAY JORDAN, JR., Ph.D., is a Professor Emeritus of Religious Studies at San Diego State University; and founder of San Diego Zen sesshin.

AUSTIN J. JOYCE, D. Min., is the coauthor with Barbara R. Krasner of *Truth, Trust and Relationships: Healing Interventions in Contextual Therapy.*

STEVEN KEPNES, Ph.D., is Associate Professor of Philosophy and Religion, Colgate University, Hamilton, NY; and author of *The Text as Thou: Martin Buber's Dialogical Hermeneutics and Narrative Theology.*

MICHAEL KEREN, Ph.D. (Israel), is a Professor of Political Science at Tel Aviv University; and author of *Ben Gurion and the Intellectuals* and *The Pen and the Sword: Israeli Intellectuals and the Making of the Nation State.*

BARBARA R. KRASNER, Ph.D., is the Director of the Center for Contextual Therapy and Allied Studies, King of Prussia, PA; coauthor with Ivan Boszormenyi-Nagy of *Between Give and Take: A Clinical Guide to Contextual Therapy*; and coauthor with Austin Joyce of *Truth, Trust and Relationships: Healing Interventions in Contextual Therapy.*

ASLAUG KRISTIANSEN, M.A. (Norway), is a Lecturer at Kristiansand Teachers Training College; and is presently at work on a dissertation on ethics and education in Martin Buber and the Danish philosopher Knud E. Løgstrup.

TAMAR KRON, Ph.D. (Israel), Senior Lecturer in Psychology and former Director of Counseling at the Hebrew University of Jerusalem, is the author of numerous articles on Buber and psychotherapy; co-convener of Israeli meetings on Buber and psychotherapy; and author of prize-winning books: *Ladies in Pink* (a study of postpartum depression) and *For the Love of Daniel* (a novella), both in Hebrew.

JERRY D. LAWRITSON, M. Div., is the Senior Minister of the Community Congregational Church (UCC) of Pacific Beach, San Diego.

ARTHUR S. LOTHSTEIN, Ph.D., is Associate Professor of Philosophy, C. W. Post Campus of Long Island University, and author of "The Affective is the Effective: Politics as Environmental Sculpture," Dewey prize essay awarded in 1977.

MARK A. LUTZ, Ph.D., Professor of Economics at the University of Maine at Orono, is the author of several articles on economics and coauthor with K. Lux of *Humanistic Economics: The New Challenge.*

DONALD J. MOORE, S.J., Ph.D., is a Professor of Theology at Fordham University, the Bronx; and author of *Martin Buber: Prophet of Religious Secularism* and *Abraham Joshua Heschel: Hallowing the World.*

VIRGINIA SHABATAY, Ph.D., is a Professor of English at Grossmont and Palomar Community Colleges, and author of a dissertation on "The Stranger in Kafka, Camus, and Wiesel."

JOHN STEWART, Ph.D., Associate Professor of Speech Communication at the University of Washington, Seattle, is the author of *Bridges not Walls* and editor of the *Western Journal of Speech Communication*.

MANFRED VOGEL, Ph.D., is a Professor of Philosophy at Northwestern University; and author of *Quest for a Theology of Judaism: The Divine, The Human, and the Ethical Dimensions in the Structure of Faith of Judaism*.

Index

403

Dionysius the Areopagite, 31, 107–109,
113, 177
dissociation, 384
vital, 390
distance
and relation, 16, 82, 83, 84, 243, 331–33,
343, 362, 364
setting at a, 177
"divine ignorance," 108, 109
doceticism, 104
Doctrine of the Mean, 121
documentary hypothesis, 86–87, 182, 188
dogma, 280
Dostoevsky, Feodor, 318
Dov Baer, 245
dread, 245
dualism, 82, 83, 84, 118, 232, 323
Buberian, 82–88
classical, 82, 83
Dufrenne, Mikel, 152, 229, 232,, 233, 236
Dych, William, 106

Eber, Irene, 116, 131
Eclipse of God (Buber), 11, 60, 97, 109,
110, 244, 303
economic(s), 249, 250, 253–266, 267–282,
377
imperialism, 273, 280
It-, 259–266
socio-, 273, 277
Thou-, 259–266
ecstatic experience, 107, 108
ecstasy, 7, 8, 108
Edgeworth, F. Y., 270–71, 281
education, 379–81
Jewish, 295
moral, 215
social, 258–59
See also teaching
educator, 74, 361. *See also* teacher
egoism, 250
Egypt(ians), 139
Eichmann, Adolph, 12
trial of, 250, 288, 293
Elam, Yigal, 293
Eldad, Israel, 288, 293
Elijah, 304
Eliot, T. S., 17, 137, 313
Ellerman, D., 280–81
empathy, 24, 332, 364, 368–69

emunah, 5, 17, 106
Encounter on the Narrow Ridge
(Friedman), 3, 137, 145, 193, 198, 199
energy, 26
hard (It), 263–64, 266
soft (Thou), 264, 266
entitlement(s), 315, 376–78, 386
destructive, 376–80
epistemology, 165
Erasmus Prize (Netherlands), 94
Essential We, 12, 258
eternal Thou, 4, 60, 62, 87, 96, 100, 110,
126, 173
eternity, 244
ethics, 77, 78, 80, 83. 85, 88, 91, 151,
215–16, 218–19
biblical, 78, 82, 83, 84, 87
Greco-Roman, 79, 82,
Jewish, 30, 77–91
of responsibility, 143
relational, 371–82
ethnography, 156
etymon, 162
Etzioni, Amitai, 279, 281
evil, 388
impulse, 239
radical, 295
existential concern, 65
existentialism, 54, 116
Jewish, 66
experience, 168, 230, 231, 232, 235–36,
349, 359, 363, 372
experiencing the other side, 24, 246,
360–63

Fackenheim, Emil, 250, 297, 300, 303–05,
307–08
fairness, 374, 377, 381
faith, 17, 56, 93–95, 98–101, 104, 105, 255
biblical, 52, 53, 54
falsehood. *See* lie
family, 315–16, 372–74, 381–82, 385–97
fanaticism, 137
Farber, Leslie H., 204
feelings, 242, 280, 358
Felton, Helen Martin, 170
Feuerbach, Ludwig, 158
Fishbane, Michael, 79, 89, 184, 188
Flechsig, 357
forgiveness, 216, 300